James Fowler Rusling

Men and things I saw in civil war days

James Fowler Rusling
**Men and things I saw in civil war days**
ISBN/EAN: 9783337224844
Printed in Europe, USA, Canada, Australia, Japan
Cover: Foto ©ninafisch / pixelio.de

More available books at **www.hansebooks.com**

# MEN AND THINGS I SAW

IN

# CIVIL WAR DAYS

BY

JAMES F. RUSLING, A.M., LL.D.

BRIGADIER GENERAL (BY BREVET) UNITED STATES VOLUNTEERS

NEW YORK: EATON & MAINS
CINCINNATI: CURTS & JENNINGS
1899

# PREFACE

This volume embodies many of my observations and experiences in our great Civil War. My first thought was to put these into historic form and chronological order. But ultimately I concluded to give them rather as portraitures and pictures of our great commanders mainly—as here.

It was my good fortune to come into contact with nearly all of these, from McClellan to Grant; and hence these sketches. A part have appeared before, in *The Christian Advocate*, of New York, and elsewhere; but these chapters have all been revised, rewritten, enlarged, and otherwise improved, as I trust; and hence this volume as a whole may be considered new—much of it entirely new.

Chapter XV, I have hesitated about somewhat; but finally concluded to publish, as not without some historic value. This chapter consists of old Army letters, as written home in 1861 to 1865; and while of moderate interest to some, it is believed nevertheless they will give realistic and vivid pictures of Army life to many—especially to our younger Americans. The illustrations are from photographs picked up during the war, or selected with care since then. Sherman's photograph is of special value; as see page

The basis of the whole volume is, 1st, An excellent memory; 2d, A diary and journal kept during most of the war; 3d, The memoirs of Generals Grant, Sherman, Sheridan, McClellan, Joe Johnston, and others; 4th, *A History of the Civil War in America*, by Comte de Paris, *Swinton's Army of the Potomac*, Badeau's *Life of General Grant*, and like publications; and 5th, Our War Records, both Union and Confederate, published by authority of Congress.

Perhaps I should add just a word as to myself and my opportunities for such observations and experiences. Briefly, then, I was born April 14, 1834, at Washington, Warren County, N. J.; was graduated at Dickinson College, Carlisle, Pa., 1854; Professor at Dickinson Seminary, Williamsport, Pa., 1854-58; admitted to the bar of Pennsylvania and New Jersey, 1857-59.

My Army record as follows:

Aug. 24, 1861, 1st Lt. and R. Q. M., 5th N. J. Vols. Infantry.

Nov. 30, 1861, Act. Brigade Q. M., 2d N. J. Brigade.

June 11, 1862, Capt. and A. Q. M. U. S. Vols., same Brigade.

Oct. 15, 1862, Division Q. M., 2d Div. 3d Corps.

May 27, 1863, Lt. Col. and Corps Q. M., 3d Corps.

July 31, 1863, Inspector Q. M. Dept. Army of the Potomac.

Dec. 1, 1863, Chief Asst. Q. M. Department of the Cumberland.

April 29, 1865, Colonel and Inspector Q. M., Dept. United States.

Feb. 16, 1866, Brigadier General (Brevet) U. S. Vols.

Sept. 17, 1867, mustered out and resumed practice of Law.[1]

---
[1] See Appendix, p. 391.

## Preface

These various appointments were at Regimental, Brigade, Division, Corps, Army, Department, and General U. S. A. Headquarters, respectively, both in the East and in the West, at post and in the field; and (I beg pardon for saying) afforded facilities and opportunities that fell to the lot of but few officers, whether Regulars or Volunteers. How well (or ill) I profited by them appears in this volume, and is submitted with diffidence to the reader, as the observations and experiences of a Staff Officer of Volunteers, 1861-65. J. F. R.

TRENTON, N. J., 1899.

# CONTENTS.

### CHAPTER I.
Abraham Lincoln.................................... 9

### CHAPTER II.
Andrew Johnson..................................... 19

### CHAPTER III.
George B. McClellan ............................... 24

### CHAPTER IV.
Ambrose E. Burnside................................ 41

### CHAPTER V.
Joseph Hooker...................................... 52

### CHAPTER VI.
George G. Meade.................................... 67

### CHAPTER VII.
George H. Thomas................................... 80

### CHAPTER VIII.
William Tecumseh Sherman........................... 106

### CHAPTER IX.
Philip H. Sheridan................................. 123

### CHAPTER X.
Ulysses S. Grant................................... 135

### CHAPTER XI.
Robert E. Lee...................................... 149

### CHAPTER XII.
Campaigning and Soldiering......................... 159

### CHAPTER XIII.
A Great Quartermaster.............................. 174

### CHAPTER XIV.
The Angel of the Third Corps ...................... 190

### CHAPTER XV.
Some Army Letters ................................. 195

Appendix........................................... 355

Index.............................................. 397

Abraham Lincoln, 1863.

# MEN AND THINGS I SAW
IN CIVIL WAR DAYS

## CHAPTER I

### ABRAHAM LINCOLN

My first knowledge of Mr. Lincoln was in 1857, when he dawned upon the nation as "The Rail-splitter of Illinois." This was when he was nominated there for United States Senator, and conducted his great debate with Stephen A. Douglas, then widely known as "The Little Giant of Illinois." Mr. Lincoln struck me then, in the progress of that debate, as a really great American: sagacious, far-seeing, and with a broad grasp of principles. And I was still more impressed with this in 1860, when he became the Republican nominee for President, and won as "Honest Old Abe."

My first real sight of him was in February, 1861, when he came East, and halted at Trenton, N. J., *en route* to Washington, D. C., to be inaugurated. I was then residing in Trenton, a practicing lawyer, as now. I stood within a few feet of him, in our State House there, when he significantly said, in the course of his brief remarks, that while he meant peace and hoped for peace, "it might become necessary to put the foot down *firmly* [and he brought his great foot down with a stamp]; and if it *does*, you will stand by me, won't you?" And he was answered by the people with wild applause, that shook the very dome of the Capitol.

On March 4th following, I was in Washington, D. C., and stood directly in front of Mr. Lincoln, not fifty paces away, in the midst of fifty thousand people, when he delivered his first inaugural, from the east front of the Capitol; and declared it to be his duty and purpose to "repossess and occupy our captured arsenals and forts;" and, with the vast multitude assembled there, cheered him to the echo. It was reputed he had weakened, under the menace of Secession, and that in his inaugural he would go back on his platform and record; but as he read on, with his spectacles far down upon his nose and glancing out occasionally over them, the real nature and fiber of his mind and heart more and more appeared, and before he concluded nobody could doubt where he stood as President. Not Washington could have been more patriotic and sagacious, nor Andrew Jackson more unyielding.

As Mr. Lincoln read on, Stephen A. Douglas stood near by, leaning against a pillar of the Capitol, with his hat off and long hair thrown back, gazing out over the vast assemblage like a lion in repose, and smiling his approval as the crowd cheered. That night I attended the inauguration ball, and shook hands with both Lincoln and Douglas. With the change of administrations, soon the nation breathed freer—now that Buchanan at last was *out* and Lincoln was *in*.

Then came the firing on Fort Sumter, Mr. Lincoln's first call for troops, and the great uprising of the North (April, 1861); but I still lingered in my office. Then came Bull Run, and other calls for troops; and soon afterward I closed my office and found myself in camp at Washington, D. C. (August, 1861).

It was not long before Mr. Lincoln visited our camp (5th Regt. N. J. Vols., 2d N. J. Brigade), as he was in the habit of riding or driving daily among the camps; and I seldom rode into Washington that I did not see him about the White House, or the War or Treasury Departments. Here he was always unattended, and generally alone, and walked along with the serious air of a country lawyer intent on business. His face had become graver, and his look more determined. But he was still chatty and cheery, when meeting an acquaintance (a member of Congress or a brigadier general); and cracked many a joke or told "a little story," as best suited to the occasion.

In December, 1861, our brigade was ordered down the Potomac, on the Maryland side, opposite Cockpit Point, Va., to a place significantly called "Rum Point"— though we found no "rum" there. It was not a village even, but only a projecting point of land. Here we joined the other two brigades of General Joseph Hooker, and with them constituted the famous "Hooker's Division" of the Army of the Potomac, and subsequently (in the spring and summer of 1862) made the Peninsula and second Bull Run campaigns under "Fighting Joe."

I saw no more of President Lincoln, until after the bloody blunder of Fredericksburg (December, 1862). Then Hooker was given command of the Army of the Potomac, and soon afterward (I think along toward spring) Mr. Lincoln came down from Washington and attended one of our grand reviews. It was a great day for General Hooker—Major General commanding the Army—and he was equal to it. I suppose fully sixty thousand men were in line or more—infantry, cavalry, artillery, wagon trains, etc. But as the artillery saluted the President, the mule trains took fright, and in spite of quartermasters, wagonmasters, and teamsters, went thundering down upon our well-ordered lines pell-mell—almost as bad as a Confederate cavalry charge. How the panic-stricken mules did "whee-haw" and the army wagons "rattlety-bang" that day over the Stafford plains! It was like another battle of Fredericksburg, on a minor scale! Mr. Lincoln was on horseback, of course, by the side of General Hooker, with Hooker's brilliant staff trailing after them like the tail of a comet, and apparently enjoyed our comical discomfiture and skedaddle to the full.

On this occasion, as on all similar occasions, when visiting the Army, Mr. Lincoln was dressed in citizens' black, with tall silk hat, long frock coat, and high top boots with spurs, and, though not a bad rider,

> "With his gaunt, gnarled hands,
> His unkempt, bristling hair,
> His garb uncouth, his bearing ill at ease,
> And lack of all we prize as debonair,"

was yet anything but a handsome horseman in the midst of our brigadier generals, colonels, captains, lieutenants, etc., well mounted as a rule and resplendent in gold lace and brass buttons on review, however plainly attired on the march or in battle.

The next time I saw Mr. Lincoln was on Sunday, July 5, 1863—the Sunday after the battles of Gettysburg and Vicksburg—and it happened on this wise: Gettysburg was fought on July 1, 2, and 3, 1863. In the great conflict of Thursday, July 2—(held by many to have been the real battle of Gettysburg, because of the heavy fighting and tremendous Confederate losses, which sapped the life of Lee's army)—General Daniel E. Sickles, of N. Y., commanding the Third Corps, had lost his right leg, and on the Sunday following (July 5) arrived in Washington, D. C., with his leg amputated above the knee. He was taken to a private dwelling on F Street, nearly opposite the Ebbitt House; and here I found him in a front room on the first floor, resting on a hospital stretcher, when I called to see him, about 3 P. M. I was then a Lieutenant Colonel on his staff, and naturally anxious to see my chief.

## Abraham Lincoln

We had not been talking long, when his orderly announced his excellency the President; and immediately afterward Mr. Lincoln walked into the room, accompanied by his son "Tad," then a lad of perhaps ten or twelve years. He was staying out at the Soldiers' Home; but, having learned of General Sickles's arrival in Washington, rode in on horseback to call on him, with a squad of cavalry as escort. They shook hands cordially, but pathetically; and it was easy to see that they both held each other in high esteem. They were both born politicians. They both loved the Union sincerely and heartily. And Sickles had already shown such high qualities, both as statesman and soldier, that Lincoln had been quick to perceive his weight and value in the great struggle then shaking the nation. Besides, Sickles was a War Democrat, astute and able; and Mr. Lincoln was too shrewd a Republican to pass any of these by in those perilous war days.

Greetings over, Mr. Lincoln dropped into a chair, and, crossing his prodigious arms and legs, soon fell to questioning Sickles, as to all the phases of the combat at Gettysburg. He asked first, of course, as to General Sickles's own ghastly wound; when and how it happened, and how he was getting on, and encouraged him; then passed next to our great casualties there, and how the wounded were being cared for; and finally came to the magnitude and significance of the victory there, and what General Meade proposed to do with it.

Sickles, recumbent on his stretcher, with a cigar between his fingers, puffing it leisurely, answered Mr. Lincoln in detail, but warily, as became so astute a man and soldier; and discussed the great battle and its probable consequences with a lucidity and ability remarkable in his condition then—enfeebled and exhausted as he was by the shock and danger of such a wound and amputation.

Occasionally he would wince with pain, and call sharply to his orderly to wet his fevered stump with water. But he never dropped his cigar, nor lost the thread of his narrative, nor missed the point of their discussion. His intellect certainly seemed as strong and astute as ever; and in an acquaintance with him of now over thirty-five years I never saw it work more accurately and keenly. He certainly got his side of the story of Gettysburg well into the President's mind and heart that Sunday afternoon; and this doubtless stood him in good stead afterward, when Meade proposed to court-martial him for fighting so magnificently, if unskillfully (which remains to be proved), on that bloody and historic July 2d.

"No," replied Honest Old Abe; "no, we can't do that. General Sickles may have erred; we are all liable to! But at any rate he fought superbly! He gave his leg—his life almost—for the Union! And now there is glory enough to go around for all."

When Mr. Lincoln's inquiries seemed ended General Sickles, after a puff or two of his cigar in silence, resumed the conversation substantially as follows:

"Well, Mr. President, I beg pardon, but what did you think about Gettysburg? What was your opinion of things while we were campaigning and fighting up there?"

"O," replied Mr. Lincoln, "I didn't think much about it. I was not much concerned about you!"

"You were not?" rejoined Sickles, as if amazed. "Why, we heard that you Washington folks were a good deal excited, and you certainly had good cause to be. For it was 'nip and tuck' with us a good deal of the time!"

"Yes, I know that. And I suppose some of us were a little 'rattled.' Indeed, some of the Cabinet talked of Washington's being captured, and ordered a gunboat or two here, and even went so far as to send some government archives abroad, and wanted me to go, too, but I refused. Stanton and Welles, I believe, were both 'stampeded' somewhat, and Seward, I reckon, too. But I said: 'No, gentlemen, we are all right and we are going to win at Gettysburg;' and we did, right handsomely. No, General Sickles, I had no fears of Gettysburg!"

"Why not, Mr. President? How was that? Pretty much everybody down here, we heard, was more or less panicky."

"Yes, I expect, and a good many more than will own up now. But actually General Sickles, I had no fears of Gettysburg, and if you really want to know I will tell you why. Of course, I don't want you and Colonel Rusling here to say anything about this—at least not now. People might laugh if it got out, you know.. But the fact is, in the very pinch of the campaign there, I went to my room one day and got down on my knees, and prayed Almighty God for victory at Gettysburg. I told Him that this was His country, and the war was His war, but that we really couldn't stand another Fredericksburg or Chancellorsville. And then and there I made a solemn vow with my Maker, that if He would stand by you boys at Gettysburg, I would stand by Him.

"And after thus wrestling with the Almighty in prayer, I don't know how it was, and it is not for me to explain, but, somehow or other, a sweet comfort crept into my soul, that God Almighty had taken the whole business there into His own hands, and we were bound to win at Gettysburg! And He *did* stand by you boys at Gettysburg, and now I will *stand by Him*. No, General Sickles, I had no fears of Gettysburg, and that is the *why!*"

Mr. Lincoln said all this with great solemnity and impressiveness, almost as Moses might have spoken when he came down from Sinai. When he had concluded there was a pause in the conversation, that nobody seemed disposed to break. Mr. Lincoln especially seemed to be communing with the Infinite One again. The first to speak was General Sickles, who, between the puffs of his cigar, presently resumed, as follows:

"Well, Mr. President, what are you thinking about Vicksburg, nowadays? How are things getting along down there?"

"O," answered Mr. Lincoln, very gravely, "I don't quite know. Grant is still pegging away down there. As we used to say out in Illinois, I think he 'will make a spoon or spoil a horn' before he gets through. Some of our folks think him slow and want me to remove him. But, to tell the truth, I kind of like U. S. Grant. He doesn't worry and bother me. He isn't shrieking for reinforcements all the time. He takes what troops we can safely give him, considering our big job all around—and we have a pretty big job in this war—and does the best he can with what he has got, and doesn't grumble and scold all the while. Yes, I confess, I like General Grant—U. S. Grant—'Uncle Sam Grant!' [dwelling humorously on this last name.] There is a great deal to him, first and last. And, Heaven helping me, unless something happens more than I see now, I mean to stand by Grant a good while yet."

"So, then, you have no fears about Vicksburg either, Mr. President?" added General Sickles.

"Well, no; I can't say that I have," replied Mr. Lincoln, very soberly; "the fact is—but don't say anything about this either just now—I have been praying to Almighty God for Vicksburg also. I have wrestled with Him, and told Him how much we need the Mississippi, and how it ought to flow unvexed to the sea, and how that great valley ought to be forever free, and I reckon

## Abraham Lincoln

He understands the whole business down there, 'from A to Izzard.' I have done the very best I could to help General Grant along, and all the rest of our generals, though some of them don't think so, and now it is kind of borne in on me that somehow or other we are going to win at Vicksburg too. I can't tell how soon. But I believe we will. For this will save the Mississippi and bisect the Confederacy; and be in line with God's laws besides. And if Grant only does this thing down there —I don't care much how, so he does it *right*—why, Grant is my man and I am his the rest of this war!"

Of course, Mr. Lincoln did not then know that Vicksburg had already fallen, on July 4, and that a United States gunboat was then speeding its way up the Mississippi to Cairo with the glorious news that was soon to thrill the country and the civilized world through and through. Gettysburg and Vicksburg! Our great twin Union victories! What were they not to us in that fateful summer of 1863? And what would have happened to the American Republic had both gone the other way? Of course, I do not pretend to say that Abraham Lincoln's faith and prayers saved Gettysburg and Vicksburg. But they certainly did not do the Union any harm. And to him his serene confidence in victory there, because of these, was a comfort and a joy most beautiful to behold, on that memorable July 5, 1863.

I never saw Mr. Lincoln again. In November, 1863, while serving at General Meade's headquarters (Army of the Potomac), I was suddenly ordered West to Tennessee (Department of the Cumberland) by Secretary Stanton; and I was still there in 1865, when Mr. Lincoln was assassinated. But this conversation made a deep impression upon me, and seems worthy to be recorded here. Clearly it settles the *questio vexata* of his religious faith forever. Perhaps it should be added that I made notes of it shortly afterward, and have often told it since, and now give it here as literally as possible—much of it *ipsissima verba*.[1]

The talk afterward took a wide range, but Mr. Lincoln said nothing conflicting with the above, and left the profound impression upon both General Sickles and myself that in these two great national emergencies he walked and talked with Jehovah—or at least believed he did. Did he not take like counsel on other occasions, as before Antietam and Chattanooga and Appomattox? For whatever he may have been in earlier years and under narrower conditions, it seems certain that our great conflict as it proceeded—involving a whole continent and a vast people, with world-wide and time-long results—sobered and steadied him, and anchored him on God as the Supreme Ruler of nations (as a like experience sobered and anchored William of Orange and Cromwell and Washington); and in the end Abraham Lincoln became a ruler worthy to rank with even these.

Of all the great figures of our Civil War, Abraham Lincoln alone looms up loftier and grander as the years roll on; and his place in the pantheon of history is secure forever. As was well sung of a true knight of old:

> "His good sword is rust;
> His bones are dust;
> His soul is with the saints, we trust."

---

[1] See Appendix, p. 355.

Andrew Johnson, 1864.

## CHAPTER II

### ANDREW JOHNSON

My first chapter being on Abraham Lincoln, it seems fitting to follow it with one on Andrew Johnson.

I became interested in Andrew Johnson before the war, as a senator from Tennessee, and an advocate of the Homestead bill, when all other Southern senators, I believe, were hostile to it. This bill proposed to divide our Western Territories into small farms of one hundred and sixty acres each, and to give them to actual settlers there, and therefore was in the interests of free labor, and, of course, the South opposed it because it was hostile to slave labor. Johnson, nevertheless, courageously supported it, Congress after Congress; but it never became a law until the Southern statesmen seceded, and then the Republican majority placed it on the statute book, and under its wise and beneficent provisions the great West soon became an empire of small farmers.

I always thought Andrew Johnson deserved credit for his manly advocacy of this bill, antagonistic as it was to his own section. Therefore, I was not surprised to see him take his stand by the Union in the dark winter of 1860-61, when the whole South, as a rule, went drifting to treason and rebellion.

I saw him first in March, 1861, in the Senate Chamber at Washington, D. C. I think it was March 3. On the invitation of an old and valued friend from Trenton, N. J., now a millionaire several times over (Samuel K. Wilson, Esq., the best friend I ever had), I had gone down there to "see Lincoln inaugurated," in common with many Republicans from the North, and on March 3 found myself and friend in the Senate gallery listening to the Southern senators as they made their farewell speeches. Among the rest was Wigfall, of Texas. He said, in substance, in his most bitter and eloquent style: "The *Star of the West*, flying your flag, swaggered into Charleston Harbor with supplies for Fort Sumter. South Carolina struck her between the eyes, and she staggered back; and now, what do you propose to do about it?" He sat down, and for a time nobody responded. It was a bitter taunt and defiance to the Union, and yet Seward and Sumner and Cameron and Chandler and Crittenden and all the rest sat silent, until the silence grew painful.

Then suddenly up rose Andrew Johnson, and in the midst of a stillness that could almost be felt he said, substantially: "Mr. President, I will tell the senator from Texas what I would do about it. I speak only for myself. But if I were President, as James Buchanan today is, and as Abraham Lincoln tomorrow will be, I would arrest the senator and his friends on the charge of high treason; I would have them tried by a jury of their countrymen, and, if convicted, by the eternal God, I would hang them!" He sat down as if shot, and for a minute or so the silence was even profounder than before.

Then away up in one corner of the gallery an unknown man sprang to his feet and, waving his hat, shouted out: "Three cheers for Andrew Johnson!" Three thousand Northerners crowded the galleries, but we rose as one man and gave three mighty cheers, such as the American Senate had never heard before. Of course, it was a "breach of the privileges of the Senate," and John C. Breckenridge (a double-dyed traitor), who sat in the Vice President's chair, immediately ordered the galleries cleared. Again that unknown man called out:

"And now three cheers for the Union!" and we gave these even mightier than before, amid the tossing of hats and waving of handkerchiefs; and then we filed out into the corridors of the Capitol, men shouting and hurrahing, and some even crying like children. This was my first personal experience of Andrew Johnson, and, I confess, greatly impressed me in his favor.

Soon afterward he went home to Tennessee by way of Virginia, with his life threatened *en route* because he was a Union man; and I did not see him again until November, 1863, when I was ordered to Nashville, and found him there in office as military governor of Tennessee. He had his headquarters in the classic State Capitol there, which he had fortified and barricaded and filled with troops (loyal East Tennesseans); and stood ready for legislation or battle, as the day might bring forth.

From then on to February, 1865, when he left for Washington to be inaugurated as Vice President, I saw a great deal of him, and he always bore himself as a hero and a statesman. From early morning until late in the afternoon he was usually in the Executive Chamber, listening to the pathetic tales of the refugees and freedmen, who crowded to him for counsel or relief from all parts of Tennessee; or else he was devising ways and means for their shelter and subsistence, or providing for their due enrollment in Union regiments and batteries.

There was no one so humble or ragged or destitute, that he could not approach his excellency with his tale of woe, and no one left his presence without aid or comfort of some sort. He early recognized the importance of freeing the slaves, and enlisting them on the side of the Union, and our freedmen had no truer friend in Tennessee than Andrew Johnson during all those dark days.

In personal appearance and deportment he was a

model American statesman of those years, and was greatly honored and esteemed by all who came in contact with him—except rebels and traitors. Of course, these latter hated him bitterly, with an intensity of hatred inconceivable to Northerners. But, all the same, Andrew Johnson held on his course, and in the darkest hours there (as after Chickamauga and before Nashville, when the hearts of men like Stanton and Grant even misgave them) he

> " Bated no jot of heart or hope,
> But still bore up,
> And steered right forward."

It is enough to his credit to say that he possessed the absolute confidence of Rosecrans, of Thomas, of Sherman, of Grant—of all who commanded out there—as well as of President Lincoln; while the rank and file of our Union troops were enthusiastic in his behalf.

In February, 1865, he left for Washington, and I did not see him again until August of that year; when I happened to be in Washington, and called at the White House to pay my respects to him as President. He was apparently the same simple, affable, approachable American citizen as previously, patriotic and Union-loving to the core. How he afterward came to cast himself into the arms of his old enemies, during our baleful period of reconstruction, has always been to me a mystery and a puzzle.

In September or October, 1865, I was one of a committee of Jerseymen to call upon him, in the interest of our freedmen and of the Fifteenth Amendment, and he was still stanch and steadfast in their behalf. When afterward he turned his back upon them (though once posing as their "Moses"), and upon all his own Union record, it was as if the sun had gone out at midday or another star had fallen—like Lucifer, son of the morn-

## Andrew Johnson

ing, or Julian the Apostate, or Benedict Arnold. Indeed, human politics is a queer profession and often a sad business. How often a disappointed statesman in his declining years turns upon his life record, and seeks to rend it and his old friends to pieces, and to tear down and destroy what he was a lifetime in building up; as *vide* Webster, Seward, Sumner, Greeley, and Andrew Johnson—not to mention others elsewhere or of more recent times! God save any man from such a fate!

In 1866-67 I was absent, South and West, on long tours of army inspection, and did not see President Johnson again until September, 1867. Meanwhile he had become embroiled with Congress and General Grant, and had "swung around the circle" to the other side; while I had continued "steadfast in the faith" as a Republican. My army service was now ended, having resigned and been ordered mustered out, and I called at the White House to say "good-bye." He kindly asked about my future, and made proffer of his services; but we were now traveling on different roads, and, of course, I could not avail myself of his good offices.

I never saw him afterward, but can never forget his sterling patriotism and superb heroism in the days when they were most needed. Personally, he was certainly honest and incorruptible. He was loyal to his friends and true to his word. He had absolute faith in the people, and meant well by the republic. And with all his errors and mistakes (due largely to his time and section and education—or rather want of education), I have nevertheless always kept a warm place in my heart for Andrew Johnson. Abraham Lincoln loved and trusted him. And had Abraham Lincoln lived, Andrew Johnson would have turned out a different man.

## CHAPTER III
### George B. McClellan

WHEN the war began, in April, 1861, I had no fancy for soldiering, and after debating the question well concluded I would do my fighting best at home. But after Bull Run I thought I saw clearly we were in for a four years' job at least, and in August, 1861, decided to enter the service. Accordingly, I joined the Fifth New Jersey, as a first lieutenant, and in the last days of August found myself in camp at Washington.

General McClellan had already assumed command of the Army of the Potomac, and, fresh from his victories in West Virginia, was being heralded as our "Young Napoleon." We now know that these West Virginia victories did not amount to much, and that Rosecrans really did the business there—what there was of it. But compared with Big Bethel and Bull Run, and our other military exploits at that time, they loomed up like Marengo and Austerlitz. As McClellan was in chief command, of course he got the credit; and soon became the hero of the hour.

As my first commander, I saluted and honored him; and in many respects he was indeed the beau ideal of a soldier. He certainly took hold of the green and awkward Army of the Potomac with intelligence and skill, and soon put new life and vigor into it. Our demoralized regiments and brigades were reorganized and divisioned; our disorganized batteries were rehorsed and equipped and put to drill; our forts were overhauled; and our line of defenses extended and strengthened. Though his headquarters were in a house in the heart of

Gen. George B. McClellan, 1862.

## George B. McClellan

Washington (a military mistake, as I always thought), yet he was in the saddle a portion of each day, and all parts of the army soon became familiar with his presence and person. His inspections and reviews were of weekly occurrence, and, notwithstanding current criticisms, were a constant and valuable school of drill and discipline to both officers and men.

McClellan was then a moderate-sized man, apparently about thirty-five years of age, with a sharp, quick eye, a clear-cut nose, dark brown hair, mustache, and imperial; and he sat upon his handsome horse like a born centaur. His uniform and horse equipments were modest; his bearing was dignified and soldierly; and though his jaw and chin lacked massiveness and strength, yet, on the whole, it goes without saying, he made an excellent impression in all our camps.

This continued well into the fall—that superb fall of 1861. But when autumn was over and past, and a hundred thousand of us—the very flower of the North—all volunteers, not a drafted man or a substitute among us—now well drilled and disciplined, still lay idle within the defenses of Washington, while the Confederate flag floated unchallenged within view of the Capitol, it is not to be wondered at that we began to lose faith in our young Napoleon; and when winter wore on, and still nothing was attempted (except the fiasco of Ball's Bluff and the sacrifice of poor General Baker), we naturally grew impatient and disappointed.

His slow and uncertain movement in the early spring of 1862 against Centreville, where he found only "Quaker guns" instead of the impregnable fortifications he anticipated, did not help his waning reputation. And when afterward we sailed down the Potomac and landed in the mud before Yorktown, and settled down to a slow siege, instead of marching straight after the retreating enemy, a good many of us made up our minds that Richmond was yet a long way off under "Little Mac." A month's delay before Yorktown, where our fighting was chiefly with the spade and shovel, in bottomless mud, while a division or two of Confederates were permitted to hold our great army at bay, until they got ready to retire, did not add to our good humor.

Then came Williamsburg, with "Little Mac" fourteen miles to the rear,[1] "superintending the embarkation of troops," according to the Comte de Paris (Vol. II, page 18); which a brigade commander or an aid could have done quite as well or better! Here he allowed Hooker, with his single unsupported division, to engage the whole rear guard of the Confederate Army, much his superior, while the rest of our Army (one hundred and twenty thousand strong)[2] looked on; and only the timely arrival of Kearny, marching to the sound of the enemy's cannon, and full of first-class fighting qualities, saved us from rout and ruin there.

It is true, Hancock came in at the finish and occupied some redoubts near Fort Magruder. But his fighting was small and loss inconsiderable (only thirty-one men) compared with Hooker's, who here lost some fifteen hundred men in killed and wounded—the very flower of his division.[3] Yet McClellan telegraphed to Washington that Hancock was superb, "his conduct brilliant in the extreme;" and barely alluded to Hooker and Kearny —he believed they had done some fighting and "lost considerably on our left!"[4] It is true he corrected this a week afterward (May 11), and did them partial justice.[5] But they never forgave him for being "fourteen

[1] *War Records*, vol. xi, part i, p 22.
[2] Comte de Paris, vol. ii, p. 14. *War Records*, vol. xi, part iii, p. 130.
[3] *War Records*, vol. xi, part i, p. 22, 23.
[4] *Ibid.*, vol. xi, part i, p. 448.
[5] *Ibid.*, vol. xi, part iii, p. 164, 165.

## George B. McClellan

miles" in the rear, and ignorant of their terrific fighting and terrible losses. And, singularly, he repeats this injustice in his "Official Report of the Peninsular Campaign"[1] and also in his "*Own Story*," p. 33.

Williamsburg over, we crept up the Peninsula at the rate of four or five miles a day, when we ought to have made forced marches (twenty or thirty miles a day), and finally sat down at Fair Oaks, astride of the Chickahominy, as if specially inviting the attack we soon got. It was only God's Providence, and Sumner's pluck, and Hooker and Kearny's magnificent fighting, that saved us from utter ruin there. As it was, we got a thorough drubbing on Saturday, as we deserved; but recovered our ground on Sunday. And both Hooker and Kearny always said we could then have marched straight into Richmond, had McClellan but given the order. I remember seeing Hooker and Kearny in fierce conversation about this, soon after noon of that sweltering Sunday; Hooker on horseback and Kearny in his shirt sleeves, with his hat off and a red bandanna about his neck, standing under his tent-fly by the roadside and gesticulating violently with his remaining arm—both of them amazed and excited at McClellan's orders.

But instead of advancing and attacking Richmond, we halted at Fair Oaks and lay there over a month, in the heart of the Chickahominy Swamps; our only drinking water polluted with the dead and decaying bodies of both men and horses, and the very atmosphere fetid and heavy with miasma and malaria. We here lost more men from fever and disease than a pitched battle would have cost us. We buried our dead on the battlefield (nearly a thousand of them) in shallow graves, and burned the bodies of our dead horses, because the ground was too swampy to bury them, and our only

---
[1] *War Records*, vol. xi, part i, pp. 22, 23.

drinking water was from springs and swamp-holes vitiated by all these. *Fair* Oaks! it has always seemed to me rather like a synonym for Tophet or Purgatory. I always look back to my army life there as a hideous and horrible nightmare. Its only redeeming feature to me was, that while encamped there I received my first promotion (at the hands of Abraham Lincoln), and rejoiced in the double bars of a captain (June 11, 1862)!

Then came our "Seven Days' Battle," and "strategic change of base," so called, to Harrison's Landing, with our superb fighting at Savage Station, Glendale, and Malvern Hill, when we could again have gone straight to Richmond—the Confederates were so thoroughly used up—had anybody been present after Malvern Hill to give the order. But "Little Mac" was again absent —on a James River gunboat. Why was he not in the midst of his bleeding yet victorious army, and ready to lead it "On to Richmond?"

As we quitted our lines at Fair Oaks (monuments of labor and industry—great achievements with the spade) late at night, June 28, with orders to destroy our baggage, tents, and surplus stores, but not to burn them (lest we should disclose our movements to the enemy), one of the headquarters staff officers remarked to me:

"Why, Captain, this is only a strategic change of base!"

"Well, yes, Major," I replied, "I hope so. But it looks to me more like a *skedaddle.*"

And so it proved.

McClellan's original order for this movement—to the Third Corps at least, whether to the rest of the army or not—was a field telegram; and was handed to me to read by our Adjutant General, for my guidance and instruction. This was just after dark Saturday, June 28, 1862, about 8 p. m. In substance it said:

## George B. McClellan

"The general commanding directs that the trains be loaded with ammunition and subsistence, and dispatched as promptly as possible by Savage Station, across White Oak Swamp, in the direction of James River. All trunks and private baggage, and all camp equipage, will be abandoned and destroyed, but not burned. The general commanding trusts his brave troops will bear these privations with their wonted fortitude, as it will be but for a few days."

I had been up all the night before, and in the saddle for two days mostly, and had just "turned in" for a night's rest; but I dressed quickly, and was again soon on horseback. I was then Brigade Quartermaster (Third Brigade, Hooker's Division, Third Corps). We proceeded to carry out this order, and the other two brigades of our division did the same. We cut and slashed our tents with knives, and ripped them to pieces—many of them new Sibley and hospital tents. We chopped and broke the tent-poles. We knocked our trunks and valises to pieces with axes and spades. Our surplus clothing was cut and torn to rags. Our headquarter officers doffed their old uniforms, in which they had been campaigning so far, and donned their best ones—resolved that, if they had to abandon any, they would leave the old ones—and I did the same. But nothing was set on fire that night, lest the Johnnies should learn of our movement prematurely. Then we loaded up our wagons with ammunition and rations, as ordered, and started them for the James River, and in due time withdrew from our lines and followed after them. The next morning the rear guard set fire to our abandoned stores and property, and there was a general conflagration at Fair Oaks, etc.

I give these facts so precisely, because this "Baggage-destroying Order" was never published by General Mc-

Clellan, and his friends have ventured to deny it. The copies of it issued to our brigade, I have always understood, were burned up at Bristoe Station, in August, 1862, when Stonewall Jackson captured a train of cars there, containing among other things all the official desks and baggage of our brigade, and set fire to everything. But I recorded the substance of it in my private journal, for Saturday, June 28, 1862, and have the record still.[1]

In 1864, when McClellan was running for President, and this "Order" was denied, I published the above in the *New York Tribune*, and challenged contradiction; but it never came. I did the same in the *Century Magazine* for May, 1889, with like result. The only explanation I have ever heard is, that this order was issued to a part of the Army, but not to the rest, because of protests from leading officers that it might demoralize the troops, and so was afterward suppressed as uncanny, if not unmilitary. It is strange that no copy has ever been produced. Was none preserved by any officer? Or were all burned up at Bristoe, as aforesaid?[2]

At Harrison's Landing, of course, we were safe—under the secure shelter of our gunboats. Or, as "Little Mac" phrased it July 1, "I fear I shall be forced to abandon my material to save my men *under the cover of the gunboats.*" (*War Records,* Vol. XI, Part 3, p. 280.) The same day he telegraphed, "Rodgers will do all that can be done to cover my flanks (with his gunboats)." And again, "*More gunboats* are much needed." (*Ibid,* pp. 281, 282.) And still again, "I shall do my best to save the army. *Send more gunboats.*" (*Ibid,* p. 280.)

Lee certainly had the Army of the Potomac now where he wanted it—where it did not menace Rich-

---

[1] Also in my letters home. See chap. xv, p. 288.
[2] See Appendix, p. 359.

mond, and was fairly eliminated. How he must have laughed at "Little Mac," and his "strategic change of base!" To show his contempt for the whole business, garrisoning Richmond well, he marched leisurely down the Valley, hoping to take Washington by a *coup;* and he would have done so, had it not been for General Pope and his gallant if unsuccessful fighting.

Then came our promenade down the Peninsula and back to Yorktown again, after all our heavy fighting and frightful losses, and our tardy reëmbarkation back to Alexandria; with "Little Mac" in the rear, as usual, when he should have been at the front, hurrying his troops forward. He took "a savage satisfaction in being the last to leave" Harrison's Landing; he "remained constantly with the rear guard;" he "remained on the Chickahominy until the bridge was removed" (his "*Own Story,*" pp. 468-9); and was among the last to arrive at Yorktown, when he should have been among the first there, and hastening our reëmbarkation. He seems to have misconceived the entire "situation." Ordinarily his position in the rear would have been right, had our rear been in danger or even seriously menaced. But, once under way down the Peninsula, Lee paid no attention to our humiliating retreat—he was after "bigger game"—and, therefore, McClellan should have left the care of his rear guard to some good division or corps commander, and hastened back to Washington, to see how best he could help there. Had Lee taken Washington, no man can tell what would have happened—probably the recognition, if not the triumph, of the Confederacy. But, thanks to Hooker, Kearny, Reynolds, Heintzelman, McDowell, and others, who rushed their commands to the front, ready or not ready, Pope was saved; and *saving Pope* then and there meant *saving the republic.*

Hooker landed at Alexandria, and so eager was he to succor Pope, he marched immediately to the front, with his field officers on foot—their horses being yet on shipboard somewhere down the Potomac—and Kearny, I think, did the same. Franklin (one of McClellan's favorites) landed, and, after leisurely reëquipping his corps, called on Pope for cavalry to patrol his advance, and when he found Pope had not any, marched as far as Annandale, five or six miles out, August 29, and halted, because "detachments of the enemy's cavalry were reported" between Alexandria and Centreville, and McClellan did not deem it *"safe* for Franklin to march beyond," notwithstanding his splendid corps then numbered over ten thousand infantry, two squadrons of cavalry, and several batteries of artillery.[1] What did he want of cavalry to "patrol his advance?" He was strong enough to march anywhere there, with Pope all beyond him, and only "detachments of the enemy," if any, between. Had he pushed on to Centreville, August 29, as he should have done (and might have done), he would have arrived in time to save Pope possibly in his great battle of August 30. But, as it was, he "halted at Annandale," and did not reach Centreville until the evening of the 30th, after the battle was over.

Of course, there were wild reports of the enemy's cavalry being between Alexandria and Centreville at that time—McClellan's headquarters abounded with such rumors. And yet, about that time, I myself marched from Alexandria to Centreville, at the head of my brigade headquarters wagon train, without seeing or hearing of a Confederate soldier. I had been absent on "sick leave" from Harrison's Landing, and returning found this wag-

---
[1] Comte de Paris, vol. ii, p. 294; *War Records*, vol. xii, part 2, pp. 710, 722, 723, 739, 740. McClellan's *Own Story*, pp. 514, 516, 517. *War Records*, vol. xi, part 1, p. 99.

on train, with the horses of the field officers of my brigade, at Alexandria, while their owners were at the front, marching and fighting on foot. Knowing how trying this must be, I obtained an order from McClellan's headquarters to pass the lines, and hastened to Centreville, *via* Fairfax Court House. I was told at McClellan's headquarters that I could not get there; that the country was infested with Confederates; that Mosby's cavalry would "gobble" me up, and the like. But I said I would take the chances! And so, interrogating all "contrabands" *en route*, and scouting through all the dangerous-looking places, I arrived at Centreville, safe and sound; with only a handful of teamsters and camp followers! It is true, this was two or three days afterward; but the "situation" was still substantially the same, as reported then and there.

Pope certainly fought sturdily and gallantly, and was loyal to the core. But he was outnumbered at first; and his supports afterward came up by piecemeal, and he was beaten in detail, before he could get his incongruous commands together and weld them into one. The verdict of history must be, that neither FitzJohn Porter nor Franklin supported him cordially—refraining therefrom, either consciously or unconsciously, because of McClellan. Their telegrams and dispatches at that time, as well as their actions (and inactions), go to show this.[1]

I have always thought that both Porter and Franklin, as well as McClellan, should have been severely dealt with, because they then "failed to do their utmost" for the Union cause. For a less offense England shot Admiral Byng in 1757, and by that act did much to make her navy the greatest sea power of modern times. Porter, it is true, was court-martialed and dismissed—

---

[1] See Appendix, p. 360.

and afterward restored. But the judgment of his most thoughtful comrades was, that he was dealt with too leniently—many have always held he ought to have been "shot to death with musketry"—and they have regretfully seen little since in his "newly-discovered evidence," so called, to change their opinions. So, McClellan's telegrams and letters to both Lincoln and Stanton, from the Peninsula and afterward, bordered on insubordination, not to say mutiny; and how the President and Secretary endured their disrespect, not to say insolence, will astonish and amaze our future historians.[1]

Nevertheless, Pope was defeated, and now what was to be done? Poor Kearny had fallen at Chantilly, the idol of his division and the pride of the Army. Had he lived, doubtless he would have succeeded Pope. But Burnside was held inadequate, Hooker and Meade had not yet approved themselves; and so, as a *dernier ressort*, McClellan was allowed to drift into the command again. Then came Antietam—only a drawn battle, when it should have been a great and complete victory. By singular good luck (or kindly providence), Lee's "plan of campaign" fell into McClellan's hands;[2] and had he moved with celerity, Lee's army would have been struck while badly scattered, and beaten in detail—easily, if not overwhelmingly. But "Little Mac" sauntered along up into Maryland, at the rate of five or ten miles a day, after his manner, when he ought to have marched twenty or thirty; and when finally he struck the Confederates they had pulled themselves together, and just missed whipping him.

Nevertheless, Antietam was a victory, after a sort—Lee yielding the field at night and retiring into Virginia. It served to rehabilitate "Little Mac," and kept him in

---
[1] See Appendix, p. 361.
[2] *War Records*, vol. xix, part 2, p. 281. Comte de Paris, vol. ii, p. 318.

## George B. McClellan

command until his extraordinary delay afterward (when he ought to have been whacking and hammering away at Lee's retreating army) finally exhausted the patience of President Lincoln even, and relegated our "Young Napoleon" to the peaceful lines of Trenton, N. J., whence, singularly, he never emerged. In 1864, Grant, indeed, thought somewhat of calling him to a command again; but it never materialized.

And yet General McClellan was a brave man, a Christian gentleman, and an American of fine parts in many ways. I myself have seen him calm and erect and cheery in exposed positions, amidst a very storm of shot and shell, while everybody else was seeking cover. Notably did this occur on the left at Fair Oaks, Wednesday, June 25, 1862. There was a reconnoissance in force that day, chiefly by Hooker, to feel the enemy and advance our picket line. It was a superb June morning, with a slight breeze among the trees. The spectacle was magnificent, as Hooker swept down across the fields, his line half a mile long, his colors streaming in the breeze, his bayonets glittering in the sunlight; but without a drumbeat. The movement cost us, first and last, about three hundred men in killed and wounded, and resulted in nothing—a piece of useless slaughter—our line returning to where it started from. But, in the midst of our advance, McClellan and his staff (including the French princes)[1] rode over from headquarters, to view the affair from a redoubt to the left of the Williamsburg Road—called redoubt No. 3. Here also were General Heintzelman, and many staff officers of the Third Corps—myself included. The Confederates, from a lookout station on some lofty tree, saw

---

[1] They joined the Army of the Potomac in the autumn or winter of 1861, and left and returned to France soon after we reached Harrison's Landing, in July, 1862. "Rats leave a sinking ship," and evidently these gallant young Frenchmen did not want to be there, if the Army was going to be captured. Clearly they had lost faith in "Little Mac!"

this gathering of officers at redoubt No. 3, and soon began paying their compliments to us in the shape of shot and shell. At first the shells fell short or passed over us, exploding harmlessly in the air, or went wide of the redoubt. But presently they got our range, and pretty soon shell after shell came screaming straight at the redoubt, and every officer dodged or fell flat or leaped down into the ditch, except McClellan, who sat erect on the parapet, smoking a cigar and laughing heartily at our various misadventures. Fortunately the shells burst without injuring anybody; but McClellan's conduct throughout was fine, and nobody doubted his courage afterward.

Indeed, McClellan was popular with the army, as a whole, down to the very last. His manners were simple and unaffected. He was always in uniform, but readily approachable. His personal life and character were beyond reproach. He read Latin and Greek well, and spoke both French and Spanish like a native. He was a very connoisseur in art. He knew all West Point could teach him, and indeed was an adept in all branches of the military profession, except the last and most important one of all, and that is, *how to fight and conquer*.

As an organizer, and drillmaster, and disciplinarian, we did not produce McClellan's equal during the war. The Army of the Potomac was far and away the best drilled and disciplined and equipped army we had. But there he seems to have ended—with no power of getting on his legs and marching straight after the enemy and whipping him. He never knew when to take the initiative, and lacked aggressiveness and fighting energy; and so he never "got there," when he ought to have won every time, or nearly so. He never seemed to know the value of time—a vital element in campaigns and battles. He always underestimated himself, and overestimated

## George B. McClellan

his antagonist[1]—a capital mistake in military affairs. And so he finally acquired the sobriquet of McClellan the Unready, or our Little Napoleon.

I think history will declare, when she comes to sum him up finally, that he would have made an excellent Chief of Staff or perhaps a good Corps commander. But as commander in chief of the army, where he had to think and plan and act for himself and compel others to act, and where at times he had to take tremendous risks, clearly he was not a success; and it is amazing how tender contemporary history has been of him and his deeds, or rather want of deeds—if not misdeeds.

As a candidate for the Presidency against Abraham Lincoln, he was, of course, a war man on a peace platform; and bound to be defeated, after the signal success of Sherman at Atlanta, and the brilliant victories of Sheridan in the Valley. As Governor of New Jersey he did fairly well. His administration, of course, was free from scandals; but it was marked by the same limitations as his army career, and not even his best friends accounted him a Napoleon in civil affairs.

I regret to say these plain things of my first commander—he was so good a soldier and so nice a gentleman. But I must state the truth of history, as we then lived and made it; and this is how General McClellan always impressed me (and many others of his comrades) in those historic war days. Our Southern friends still account him the "greatest Yankee general." But when you ask them how soon he would have conquered their rebellion, and ended our war for the Union, they only look wise and venture no reply.

His losses on the Peninsula were certainly appalling:

---
[1] As at Yorktown and Fair Oaks, where he reported the Confederates as 120,000 to 180,000 or 200,000 strong, when they never had half that number. Where were his spies and scouts, and Secret Service funds? Comte de Paris, vol. ii, p. 83 ; McClellan's *Own Story*. p. 437, 442, 444, etc. ; *War Records*, vol. vi. part 1, p. 28-51, etc.; vol. xi, part 3, p. 71, 86, 102, 115, 143, 259 266, 280, 281, 282, 286, 292, 299, 315, 338. A good many references, but very interesting reading !

but it appears difficult to present them accurately. His "Official Report," August 4, 1863, does not agree with his "Army Returns" in 1862; and the War Department does not seem able to give the facts precisely. At least, this is the reply I received to two different letters sent there in February, 1898. He reached the Peninsula April 2, 1862. His "Return" for April 30, 1862 (before Yorktown), shows his strength present for duty, including Franklin's division (still on transports), as 112,-392; his special duty, sick, and in arrest, 5,850; being a total of 118,242 present, besides 12,136 absent, making a total aggregate of 130,378. About June 12 he was reinforced by McCall's division of Pennsylvania Reserves, 9,501 strong, increasing his total to 139,879.

His losses, in action, April 5 to June 24, including Yorktown, Williamsburg, Fair Oaks, etc., were 1,513 killed, 5,746 wounded, and 1,217 captured or missing; a total of 8,476. His losses, in action, from June 25 to August 23 (the date he left the Peninsula), including the "Seven Days' Battle," etc., is given by the War Department as 1,750 killed, 8,122 wounded, and 6,100 captured or missing; a total of 15,972. This would make his total losses, in action, 24,448.

His "Tri-Monthly Return" for July 10, 1862 (at Harrison's Landing),[1] gives his present for July as 99,776, and his total aggregate (present and absent) as 157,038. Add to this "99,776 present," his losses in action, as above given, and we have a total of 124,224. But his total strength on the Peninsula, or men received in all while there, as above given, was 139,879; which would leave only 15,655 as his losses from sickness and disease. This seems small, when one remembers our frightful sickness both at Yorktown and Fair Oaks, as well as Harrison's Landing. However, even this

[1] *War Records*, vol. xi, part 3, p. 312.

would make his total losses both from battle and disease 40,103.

On July 13, 1862, Mr. Lincoln telegraphed him from Washington: "I am told that over 160,000 men have gone into your army. When I was with you the other day (at Harrison's Landing) we made out 86,500 remaining, leaving 73,500 to be accounted for. I believe 23,500 will cover all the killed, wounded, and missing in all your battles and skirmishes; leaving 50,000 who have left otherwise. Not more than 5,000 of these have died, leaving 45,000 of your army still alive and not with it.[1]

On July 15 General McClellan answered this from Harrison's Landing, questioning whether he had received "160,000" men present in all; but giving his then present for duty as 88,665, and his present and absent as 144,407. He gave his sick as 16,619, and his absentees as "about 40,000."[2]

These figures, it will be noticed, differ from his "Return" of July 10 (above quoted) by about 11,000 men present. But Mr. Lincoln's estimate of "23,500" as his losses in action does not vary much from mine above (24,448); though I think his guess of "5,000" as having died from disease is more than twice too small. The "absentees" were not all deserters, by a long shot. But thousands of them were good officers and men, who had gone home on furlough or "sick leave," or otherwise, after our bloody and exhausting battles, etc., on the Peninsula, because of the want of hospital accommodations, medical attendance, etc.; and they never returned because of death or prolonged disability, incapacitating them for further service.

From all which, after much searching of the records

---
[1] *War Records*, vol. xi, part 3, p. 319.
[2] *Ibid*, p. 321.

and my own actual experience there, and much talk with others there, I think it fair to conclude as follows:

| | |
|---|---:|
| McClellan's total strength on the Peninsula, or men actually received, at least.............. | [1]160,000 |
| His losses in action..... 25,000 | |
| His losses from disease..... 25,000 | |
| | 50,000 |
| Remaining ........ | 110,000 |
| Present July 15, as per his above report to Mr. Lincoln........ | 88,665 |
| Absentees .............. | 21,335 |

It is true that Mr. Lincoln puts these "absentees" at "45,000," and McClellan at "about 40,000." But it is believed that, with the foregoing explanations, the above figures of 21,335 are more nearly accurate.

This makes his total losses, then, from both battle and disease, as 50,000, instead of "40,103," as above figured out; and this it is believed cannot be far wrong. In other words, General McClellan lost *one third* of his army on the Peninsula, and *gained nothing* whatever; the Army of the Potomac returning again to Alexandria in August, whence it moved late in March.

Even as, ingloriously,

> "The King of France, with fifty thousand men,
> Marched up the hill, and then marched down again."

Well might Robert E. Lee air his sometime Latin, and serenely sing, *"Parturiunt montes nascitur ridiculus mus!"*

---

[1] His "Return," July 10, gives his aggregate, present and absent, as 157,038, even then Mr. Lincoln's estimate of "160,000" of course was furnished him by the Adjutant-General, U. S. A., and made up from actual "Returns" in the War Department.

Gen. Ambrose E. Burnside, 1862.

## CHAPTER IV

### AMBROSE E. BURNSIDE

My next commander was General Burnside. Antietam was fought September 16 and 17, 1862; and Lee, dazed but not defeated, fell back into Virginia again. Here he was allowed to rest and recuperate, *ad libitum*, until November 1, or thereabouts, before McClellan got ready to pursue him—a delay inexcusable from every point of view. It is true, that "Little Mac" alleged his army was terribly bad off: short of horses, short of wagons, short of rations, clothing, shoes, and about everything. But if he whipped Lee at Antietam, the Confederates, beaten and retreating, must certainly have been far worse off; as was indeed the fact, of course.

Lee recrossed the Potomac on the night of September 18, without McClellan knowing much about it, if indeed suspecting it. Nevertheless, September 19, he telegraphed the general in chief (Halleck) at Washington as follows:[1]

"I have the honor to report that Maryland is entirely freed from the presence of the enemy, who *has been driven across the Potomac.* \* \* \*

"G. B. MCCLELLAN, Major General Commanding."

"Driven" by *whom, and when?* Certainly not by McClellan; for in his *"Own Story,"* page 620, he says: "On the night of the eighteenth the enemy, after passing troops in the latter part of the day *from the Virginia shore* to their position *behind Sharpsburg* [Maryland], as seen

---

[1] McClellan's *Own Story*, p. 621.

## Men and Things I Saw in Civil War Days

by our officers [evidently to mislead McClellan], suddenly formed the design of abandoning their position and retreating across the river. [And this] was effected *before daylight"* [apparently without his knowledge].

So Lee was back safe into Virginia again, and of course both Lincoln and Stanton (and the country) expected to see McClellan cross the Potomac *instanter* and march sharply after him. They both wrote and telegraphed him accordingly, but without result. The weather was superb—the exquisite autumnal weather of Virginia—and they daily became more urgent. Finally, October 1—two weeks of invaluable time having been lost—Mr. Lincoln himself paid him a visit, and patiently queried why he did not hasten after Lee. History will be surprised to learn that nothing came of this, even. And so, at last, as a *dernier ressort,* on October 6, Halleck telegraphed him as follows:

"The President directs, that you cross the Potomac and give battle to the enemy, or drive him South. * * * He is very desirous that your army move as soon as possible. * * * I am directed to add, that the Secretary of War and the general in chief fully concur with the President in these instructions."[1]

Did he go now? O, no! He still complained of his equipage, supplies, horses, etc.; and *two weeks* afterward —two weeks of golden opportunity—on October 21 was again ordered as follows:

"Your telegram has been submitted to the President. He directs me to say, that he has no change to make in his order of the 6th instant. * * * The President does not expect impossibilities, but he is very anxious that

---
[1] McClellan's *Own Story*, p. 628.

## Ambrose E. Burnside

all this good weather should not be wasted in inactivity. Telegraph *when* you will move."[1]

Did he move now? No, not yet! But on October 25 was again prodded as follows (in reply to a telegram that some of his horses were worn down, "fatigued," etc.):

"To MAJOR GENERAL MCCLELLAN: I have just received your dispatch about sore-tongued and fatigued horses. Will you pardon me for asking what the horses of your army have done since the battle of Antietam, that fatigues anything? A. LINCOLN."[2]

Did he move now? No, he did not budge yet! It seems incredible, but he actually did not cross the Potomac himself until November 1,[3] although he did, indeed, start some of his divisions across October 26—the day after Mr. Lincoln's characteristic and laconic dispatch. But the Sixth Corps—the last one over—did not cross until November 2;[4] and it was not until November 7 that "Little Mac" finally reached Rectortown, near Warrenton, Va.[5] Here he received orders from President Lincoln—his titanic patience at last exhausted, and no wonder—to turn the Army of the Potomac over to General Burnside, who was already present in command of the Ninth Army Corps, and his second in command as next ranking officer.

This change of our commanders, it must be admitted, was not altogether satisfactory; and there was some talk of making General McClellan military dictator, and of "marching upon Washington and taking possession of the government," and of pitching Lincoln and his Cabinet and Congress into the Potomac, etc.[6] But this was confined to a few favorites and "feather-heads" of "Lit-

[1] McClellan's *Own Story*, p. 640.  [2] *Ibid.*, p. 643.  [3] *Ibid.*, p. 658.  [4] *Ibid.*, p. 646.
[5] Mark these dates—Sept. 18th, Lee defeated and "driven" across the Potomac; but McClellan did not cross until Nov. 1—*six weeks* wasted!
[6] McClellan's *Own Story*, p. 652.

tle Mac's" (the army, as a whole, was thoroughly loyal), and duly evaporated with the early departure of General McClellan for the historic lines of Trenton, N. J.

It must be confessed, General Burnside was not welcome to us; but we accepted him and awaited his orders, as the best Mr. Lincoln could do under the circumstances. He had served creditably at first Bull Run, and won distinction at Roanoke Island, without much real fighting or actual generalship; and had just fought bravely at Antietam, if not very skillfully. And here he was now in command of the Army of the Potomac—one hundred and twenty-five thousand strong—a job requiring first-class brains. Now, what was to be done, and how was he to do it?

Burnside sat still a few days, studying the situation and gathering up the reins, and then suddenly decided to change the plan of campaign and make a dash at Fredericksburg, and beat Lee into Richmond that way. It was not a bad move, and held the potency and promise of success if rapidly executed. But Lee beat him in the foot race to Fredericksburg, and soon had his ragged Confederates in a stronger position than ever at Marye's Heights and elsewhere there, with the broad and unfordable Rappahannock flowing between us.

Of course, Burnside blamed somebody else for not getting our pontoons there in time to cross the river before Lee arrived. But he was the responsible commander, with ample powers and officers, and should himself have known how to make things "come to pass."

My own division did not get to Antietam; it was too much used up by the Peninsula and Pope campaigns, and was left at Alexandria to recruit and help man the defenses of Washington. Nor did we get up to Warrenton. But we marched first from Alexandria (I received my second promotion here, to division headquarters, October 15, 1862) to Manassas Junction, where we guarded the rear of the army while it switched over to Fredericksburg, and then joined it at Falmouth, by way of Fairfax Court House and Wolf Run Shoals, early in December.

I think this was the worst march I made during the war. Much of it was in the midst of a wild December storm of wind and rain and sleet, through fathomless Virginia mud, and the sufferings of the troops were indescribable. After the first day or so, many of our poor fellows became barefoot, and for a week or more after we arrived on the heights of Stafford I saw hundreds of our men standing guard or walking their weary rounds as sentries in the snow, with their feet bound up in grain bags or coffee sacks. Valley Forge (the Americans were in winter quarters and had good log huts there) could not have been much worse than Falmouth, in those early December days before our supplies got up. But the Quartermaster Department bestirred itself, and soon the army was again thoroughly equipped, and in superb fighting trim.

Of course, we had to have our inevitable "Review," and Burnside—portly and handsome, smiling and courteous, with his side-whiskers, mustache, and beautiful white teeth, but without dash or grip in his face—sat erect on his dark-brown bobtail horse, while a hundred thousand of us marched past, scanning him closely. I do not think there was an officer or a man of us that felt safe in his hands. But we were there to "obey orders," and to do and die, if need be, for the Union.

Now came the so-called battle of Fredericksburg. It was rather a foreordained slaughterhouse, and our brave boys the predestined victims. Lee had been given all the time he wanted, to fortify every hill and flood every ravine; and so all he had to do was to sit still and see us march into his traps, or knock our heads against his works.

We belonged to the Left Grand Division (Franklin's), and crossed the Rappahannock December 12, about three miles below Fredericksburg, while the Center and Right Grand Divisions crossed at Fredericksburg. Our crossing was not seriously opposed, because Lee wanted us to come over to his side, to save him the trouble of crossing over to ours. We had fifty thousand men there on the left, as good soldiers as ever fought. But Franklin lacked either inclination or ability to handle them, or had not precise orders as to when and how he should attack (as he always claimed—something was always at fault when Franklin had to *act*), and so little came of our movement there. Our only possible hope of success was to attack at once, before Lee's supports there got up. But we lay quiet all that day and night, while the Confederates (Hill and Ewell) marched day and night to reinforce that part of their line. When on the 13th we tardily advanced we found fifty cannon in position, and Stonewall Jackson and Longstreet confronting us.

Meade, with his gallant Pennsylvanians (he had only about five thousand men), accomplished something— he always was a good soldier—but he was left to be enfiladed by Confederate artillery and crushed by Confederate infantry—while the rest of us stood idly by for want of fighting orders. Franklin was far in the rear, as usual, with no real grasp of the battlefield, and Burnside miles away at Falmouth, and losing his head there. Of course, we fell back after heavy losses, and the Confederates did not pursue; they wanted us to try it again. Here poor General Bayard perished, struck by a passing Confederate shell while sitting under a tree in the midst of his staff, awaiting orders. He was a gallant Jerseyman; my own old school friend; already distinguished as a cavalry leader, and worthy to rank with Sheridan, had he lived. He was to have been married shortly, and his last moments were spent in speaking of his fiancée and of his beloved parents.

Meanwhile, the rest of the army had attacked in front of Fredericksburg. A mist hung over the river and the valley all the morning; but toward noon this lifted, revealing the Confederate heights bristling with bayonets and cannon, and swarming with soldiers. The key of the position was Marye's Hill, just back of Fredericksburg, and we were ordered to assault that impregnable height at all hazards and whatever cost.

During the morning I had been sent with a report or dispatch to Burnside's headquarters, and while galloping through a wood road my horse slipped on a root extending across the road, and fell heavily upon me. He was a large, jet black, handsome fellow, captured at Fair Oaks in June, in the rush of the battle there, and we both came down so hard I thought my right leg broken and done for, for sure. Neither of us could rise. But, fortunately, a squad of stragglers happened to be near, cooking a pot of coffee, and, rushing to our assistance, they soon got us on our feet again. I was badly shaken up and in great pain; but presently managed to climb into the saddle again, and ride on to headquarters. Here all was confusion and indecision, and I was detained considerably. But as I rode back over the brow of a hill overlooking the Rappahannock, *en route* to my division, as the fog lifted and the sun came out bright and clear, across the river I beheld our lines in motion— French and Hancock—and soon on the double-quick with a rush and a cheer they attacked the whole Confederate front there.

It was indeed a gallant sight; never one more so. Without a glass I could count the banners and distinguish the brigades from where I sat on my horse. How the muskets gleamed, and the bayonets flashed, and the flags streamed in the glorious sunlight! But scarcely had they started forward before the whole Confederate heights were a circle of fire. A hundred cannon were in skillful position there, and shot and shell opened great gaps through our regiments. But still our lines swept onward till the Confederate infantry opened, and then suddenly a cloud of smoke like the breath of hell rolled over the battlefield, and our brave boys disappeared from sight. It was a constant earthquake. It was a live volcano. The roar of battle was deafening and continuous even from where I sat; but it did not last. In twenty minutes or so it was all over. The cloud slowly lifted, and our men were back in their lines again—what were left of them. The field was strewn with the dead, and the dying. Riderless horses galloped wildly at will. The wounded were being borne to the rear. Thousands of men had become cripples for life; and thousands of firesides were desolate forever. Ah, me! but it was a pitiful spectacle; and I turned and rode on to my division, sick at heart over such useless slaughter of brave men.

But Burnside was not yet satisfied. He thought French and Hancock did not know how to do it; though they had sacrificed one third of their men. Down at the Phillips House, on the opposite or Stafford side of the river, a mile or more away from the battlefield, he strode up and down the terrace, and, shaking his fist at Marye's Hill, still thundering with artillery, insanely declared: "That height must be carried before nightfall!" So he sent for Fighting Joe Hooker, and ordered him to take it.

A smaller man than General Hooker would have blindly obeyed the order; but he first sent an aid to inquire about it, and then he himself (ever thoughtful of his men) recrossed the river under a heavy artillery fire, and endeavored to dissuade Burnside from such a useless butchery. His only answer was "to obey orders," and so, of course, Hooker went in, with all his accustomed ardor and intrepidity. But he might as well have stormed the fiery mouth of hell. Night came on in the midst of the furious fighting.

> "Cannon to right of them,
> Cannon to left of them,
> Cannon in front of them,
>   Volleyed and thundered;"

but Hooker did not give it up until thousands more of our brave boys were *hors de combat*.

First and last, we left over six thousand men at the foot of Marye's Hill and up its bloody slope; and, altogether, lost at Fredericksburg over twelve thousand men;[1] while the Confederate loss was about half as much more. Burnside, however, was not yet content, and meditated another attack next day at the head of his own old corps (he was no coward), but was finally persuaded to give this up.

We lay still the next day, and the next, with only occasional artillery firing and skirmishing; and finally on the night of the fifteenth Burnside made up his mind to withdraw, and before morning we had recrossed the Rappahannock and were back in our old camps again, or well on the way to them. Why Lee did not attack and destroy us and our pontoon bridges, in the midst of our night retreat, I do not know. Suppose he had trained his artillery on our bridges or bridge-heads? If he did not know of our retreat, he must have been kept poorly informed by his pickets. If unable to profit by

---

[1] Our exact losses were 12,353 men, of whom 1,180 were killed, 9,028 wounded, and 2,145 taken prisoners.—Comte de Paris, vol. ii, p. 596.

it, he must have been used up worse than we knew, or else have "lost his head" also in the magnitude of his victory.

Now what was to be done? Evidently, General Burnside did not know. But after pondering various projects, he finally decided to cross the Rappahannock again, above Fredericksburg, and try conclusions again with the Confederates. This was his famous "Mud March" in January, 1863. The campaign began all right—it was splendid weather; but a general thaw and rain set in soon afterward—the bottoms dropped out of the Virginia roads—and our pontoons and artillery seemed bound for China. After floundering around for three or four days in fathomless mud, with scores or hundreds of men attempting to haul a single piece of artillery, besides the horses, the advance was countermanded, and back we went to our old camps again. Of course, his generals (and the army) by this time were criticising him considerably, and his only plan to meet this was to request the President to dismiss General Hooker and others from the service, and relieve General Franklin and others from their commands. A brilliant idea, surely—magnificent strategy, splendid tactics—worthy of such a commander in chief! And Mr. Lincoln responded by relieving Burnside himself, and placing the gallant Hooker in command!

I do not want to be unfair or unkind to poor General Burnside. He was certainly loyal and patriotic, and meant to do his best. But I think history will declare he was utterly incompetent for such a great command, and ought never to have accepted it. It is true, he distrusted himself, and was averse to accepting it. But then no man ought ever to accept such a job, if he thinks he cannot accomplish it. A due self-confidence is essential to success in any line of business, but in none

## Ambrose E. Burnside

more so than in military affairs. A favorite maxim of Frederick the Great was: "The tools to him who can use them." But he never will use them, if he thinks he cannot. Grant selected Sherman as his right arm and Sheridan as his left, because they *believed* they could *whip the enemy.* It is to General Burnside's credit, that he did not disappear when relieved, like General McClellan, but later on went out to Tennessee and tried it again with a smaller command. But here also he got into trouble, and would have been compelled to capitulate to Longstreet at Knoxville, had not Sherman marched promptly to his relief the very day Grant and he finished up Bragg at Chattanooga. Sherman, indeed, knew well the value of *time.* He did not even ride into Chattanooga (to see and enjoy the victory a little, as most generals would have done), but instantly put his column in motion, with orders to make forced marches to East Tennessee (without overcoats or blankets even, though late in November, and bitter cold), and thus saved the day at Knoxville.

General Burnside no doubt would have done well as a brigade or division commander, where he would have had somebody else to do his thinking and furnish him orders. But to swing an army of one hundred and twenty-five thousand men; to think and plan and execute great things on a great scale, sometimes *instanter*—in short, to take the initiative and win against such a Confederate gamecock as Robert E. Lee—evidently this was a job beyond his caliber; and good and clean as he was in many respects, yet history will find it hard to forgive him for the Slaughter House at Fredericksburg.

## CHAPTER V
### Joseph Hooker

My next commander, and personally most beloved of all, was General Hooker; or "Fighting Joe Hooker," as we used to call him. I first saw him in December, 1861, when my brigade reported to him in lower Maryland. He was already in command of a New England brigade and a New York brigade there, and our brigade (Second New Jersey—his Third Brigade) completed his division, that became so well known afterward as Second Division, Third Corps, or "Hooker's Division," Army of the Potomac.

General Hooker was then in the prime of manhood, with steel-blue eyes, sandy hair, and clear-cut features— well set-up, but not corpulent—about six feet high; soldierly in his bearing and movements, and the béau ideal of a division commander. His talk was brilliant and incisive, and instinctively he impressed all who came in contact with him as an officer who knew *what* to do and *how* to do it, and confident of accomplishing it. I well remember his first inspection of our brigade, and how thoroughly he overhauled us. It was on a bright Sunday morning in December, 1861, at Rum Point, Md., opposite the Confederate batteries at Cockpit Point, Va. And as he went through us, regiment by regiment, there did not seem to be a defect in a uniform or gun or knapsack or mule team, that his eagle eye did not detect, nor a well set-up officer or soldier that he did not compliment and praise.

He was a West Pointer; he had distinguished himself in Mexico; and it was fair to expect great things of him

Gen. Joseph Hooker, 1863.

## Joseph Hooker

in the future. The winter of 1861-62 he devoted to drill and discipline—everybody had to "toe the mark"—and to winning the confidence and affection of his officers and men; and it is safe to say, that when we landed on the Peninsula in the spring of 1862, there was no finer division in the Army of the Potomac. It approved itself at Williamsburg in May, where it received its "baptism of fire."[1] It distinguished itself at Fair Oaks in June, where it helped greatly to save the day. It marched and fought like a Macedonian phalanx or a Roman legion, with bent brow and firm front, in the memorable "Seven Days' Battle" from front of Richmond to James River, in June and July, 1862. Indeed, in all the Peninsula campaign, there was no hard marching or heavy fighting that Hooker did not participate in, and everybody felt that, whatever else happened, his division at least was sure to be bravely and skillfully commanded. Hooker himself was always present on the field, alert and vigilant, conspicuously mounted on a white horse—with flaming eyes, florid face, and high shirt collar, that soon wilted down when we got engaged—but as cool and collected under fire as if directing a parade or a picnic.

In every engagement he always seemed to know exactly *what* to do and *when* to do it; and it goes without saying, his men always went into action with alacrity and intrepidity, because they knew he would not put them in improperly, or fight them blunderingly, or imperil them unnecessarily. He was never ordered to attack, that he did not obey promptly and intelligently. He was never called on for support, that he did not respond cheerfully and gallantly. Ever ready, ever willing and eager, always equal to the occasion, he never missed a battle or skirmish in the Peninsula campaign

---
[1] See p. 26.

when it was his duty to be present, and hence early acquired the sobriquet of "Fighting Joe Hooker," and well deserved it. He did not fancy this himself, as he said it implied mere brute courage, whereas he claimed capacity for command. But the name, nevertheless, came and "stuck" all through the war, because it aptly described his surface characteristics; that is, his readiness to fight and ability as a fighter.

When we were ordered back from the Peninsula, Hooker's division was one of the first to reach Alexandria, and, heeding the call and distress of poor Pope, with gallant Phil Kearny's division hastened loyally to the front, while Porter's and Franklin's divisions lagged lamentably behind. Had they moved as promptly as Hooker's and Kearny's, our second Bull Run might have resulted quite differently. Hooker, indeed, did not even wait for his private baggage, nor for the horses of his field and staff officers, but, recognizing the great need of General Pope, marched at once to Warrenton and fought gallantly by his side at both Bristoe and Manassas. Poor Kearny (peace to his ashes and tears to his memory!) did the same, and then fell at Chantilly the next day but one afterward, in the midst of a twilight reconnoissance (September 1). But, all the same, he baffled Lee's plans and headed off Stonewall Jackson on the march for Fairfax Court House, and thus saved our line of retreat to Alexandria and Washington.

Hooker was deeply touched when he heard Kearny had fallen (they were close friends and dear to each other), and we were all whelmed in a common grief. He was our Chevalier de Bayard, the idol of his division and pride of the army; our Phil. Sheridan of 1862, with a great career before him. I was only a short distance away when he fell; and I think Chantilly (fought in an evening thunderstorm) was the saddest hour I saw in

## Joseph Hooker

the service, before the supreme tragedy of Lincoln's assassination. General Lee showed the gentleman and chivalrous foe he was by sending Kearny's body into our lines under a flag of truce (September 2), "thinking the possession of his remains may be a consolation to his family."[1] And in this he only voiced the common sentiment of both armies toward the heroic Kearny. Subsequently he also sent his sword, horse, and saddle by request of Mrs. Kearny.[2]

Hooker's division did not make the Antietam campaign—it was too much used up—but was left behind at Alexandria to recruit its thinned ranks and worn energies. Mr. Lincoln, however, would not dispense with Hooker himself, and so he promoted him to the command of the First Corps, *vice* McDowell, relegated to Washington. Here General Hooker also acquitted himself well, but was severely wounded and borne off the field in the very hour of victory.[3] He was unable to report for duty again, until we reached Falmouth (December, 1862), but here he was assigned to the command of the Centre Grand Division—one third of the whole army—and still further demonstrated his ability by handling it ably and skillfully at the bloody battle of Fredericksburg.

Hence when, after Fredericksburg and the "Mud March," Burnside was inevitably relieved, Mr. Lincoln naturally appointed General Hooker to succeed him. What else, indeed, was there to do? Kearny was dead, or doubtless he would have been called to the command; Hancock and Meade had not yet "won their spurs;" Sumner (of the Right Grand Division) was too old and obstinate, and had never yet

---
[1] *War Records*, vol. xii, part iii. p. 807.
[2] *Ibid.*, vol. xix, part ii, p. 281. See also Appendix, p. 369.
[3] There is a story that the corps commanders at Antietam, disgusted with McClellan, were about putting Hooper in command over his head, but the messenger found Hooker too badly wounded to sit his horse, and so the whole scheme came to naught.

shown much head on his shoulders; Franklin (of the Left Grand Division) had again shown only irresolution and indecision, if not disinclination; and therefore the only thing to do was to place General Hooker in command. He had some enemies, it is true, chiefly because of his sharp criticisms of McClellan and Burnside. But he had also ardent and enthusiastic friends, who believed in him thoroughly, as both officer and man. And above all, he believed thoroughly in himself, and this in military affairs (and all human affairs) is often more than "half the battle."

General Hooker at once assumed command (about February 1, 1863), and none too soon. The Army of the Potomac was, indeed, then in a bad way. It had not been paid for six months. It had lost heavily in killed and wounded at Fredericksburg, with no adequate results. Above all, it had lost its *morale*, and was fast losing its organization. General Hooker officially reported he found nearly *three thousand officers* and over *eighty thousand soldiers* on the rolls "absent, with or without leave." The Proclamation of Emancipation (just previously issued), while all right *per se*, had, nevertheless, caused bitter dissensions, particularly among the line officers, and these he quickly stopped by prompt court-martial and dismissal. I knew of many who publicly declared, that "they did not enlist to fight for the niggers, and they were going to resign and go home." But a few courts-martial soon ended all that. The desertions he cured by "shooting to death with musketry" in a few of the more flagrant cases, and then getting Mr. Lincoln to issue a proclamation of pardon to all who returned voluntarily to the ranks by a given date.

He devised a system of furloughs, whereby all of us in turn might spend a few days at home. He abolished the clumsy organization by Grand Divisions—an invention

## Joseph Hooker

of Burnside, and worthy of him—and returned to the simple and more effective organization by army corps, as instituted by McClellan and practiced by Grant and Sherman. He invented the corps "badges," or, rather, adopted the invention of poor Kearny, who first instituted them on the Peninsula, in order to identify his own troops as the "Red Patch Division," and Hooker now wisely diversified and extended these to the whole army. My own Division soon became known as the "White Diamonds."

He increased and improved the rations. He set up brigade bakeries—to give us fresh bread, in lieu of "hardtack." He reëquipped and reclothed all who needed it; he weeded out incompetent and unworthy officers; he looked sharply after everything that could make for drill and discipline and organization; he rode constantly through our camps and hospitals and among our batteries and wagon trains, and saw everything that was going on (and *not* going on), and thus it was not long before everybody felt that the eye and hand of a masterful commander was upon him. And so, when in May, with the Virginia dogwoods all in bloom, we set out for Chancellorsville, it was a common remark by shrewd observers, that the Army of the Potomac was never in better heart and trim.

At Chancellorsville, General Hooker's strategy was good, but his tactics failed. His plan, indeed, was excellent, and his generalship of a high order, until the surprise and rout of the Eleventh Corps (indifferently commanded by Howard, and badly handled by Sigel, Schurz, and others) and his own grievous disability ruined everything. In the very crisis of the battle there —in the very pinch of the campaign—while standing on the porch of the Chancellor House, overlooking the hotly contested field, a Confederate cannon ball struck a pillar of the porch against which he was leaning, and the pillar in falling knocked him senseless. I saw and talked with him myself shortly before this, and he was alert and confident as usual. But now he was unconscious or helpless for hours—dazed, half paralyzed, not a tithe of himself—just when his brain and hand were most required, and his next in command (Couch) knew not how to gather up the reins suddenly and direct the battle. Hence things drifted, and hence we fought Chancellorsville by piecemeal, and did not put in half our troops, and hence were worsted there (notwithstanding John Sedgwick's brilliant work down at Fredericksburg), when we ought to have won a great and telling victory. Its only comfort to me personally was, that it brought me another promotion (Lt. Col. and Chief Q. M. 3d Corps, May 27, 1863).

But bad as Chancellorsville was, and in some respects it was really melancholy, it nevertheless was not a blunder and a disaster like Fredericksburg. If baffled and defeated, at least we were not discouraged and demoralized, and soon were ready to try conclusions again with our Confederate friends. Grievous as were our losses, they did not begin to compare with Lee's; for he there lost his great lieutenant, Stonewall Jackson, his right arm hitherto, and was never able to replace him afterward. Hooker still held the respect and esteem of the army, if not its full confidence, and the masterly way in which he followed up and checkmated Lee in June, 1863, from the Rappahannock to the Potomac, in the beginning of the great Gettysburg campaign, won our hearty admiration. Indeed, Hooker always claimed that Meade only followed out his plans substantially, in fighting as he did at Gettysburg. It must be remembered that Meade was only three days in command before our great battle of Gettysburg, with much to learn

## Joseph Hooker

in many ways; and had Hooker been there and succeeded so well, it is hardly credible that, with his energy and self-reliance, Lee would have got back into Virginia again so easily, after being whipped so thoroughly up there in Pennsylvania.

I saw a good deal of General Hooker after he was relieved from the command of the Army of the Potomac, and he always chafed bitterly over it and scolded much, but he did not sulk. He was still ready for duty, there or elsewhere, and when, after Chickamauga (September 19, 1863), he was ordered West with the Eleventh and Twelfth Corps (soon after consolidated into the Twentieth), he showed his accustomed intelligence and energy by moving his entire command—over twenty thousand strong, with their artillery, ammunition, baggage, etc.—by rail from Washington, D. C., to Bridgeport, Ala.—*nearly a thousand miles in six days*—a feat unparalleled during the war.

He asked for me to accompany him (I was then serving as Inspector at Army headquarters), but Stanton was still angry with him, and characteristically replied: "I will give General Hooker no more officers until he *gets* West and *does* something!" Hooker then went in person to the White House, but Mr. Lincoln gave him a like reply. And so he went West. Here he was prompt to report to Thomas and Grant, and did much to relieve Chattanooga, and fought his famous "Battle Above the Clouds"—the very poetry of the war—at Lookout Mountain. His actual fighting at Lookout did not amount to very much; but it was scenic and dramatic—"Above the Clouds"—and gave him a worldwide and historic fame.

In the spring and summer of 1864, he participated actively in the great campaign and battles of General Sherman from Chattanooga to Atlanta, and there was hardly an important engagement from the Tennessee to the Chattahoochee, that he did not have a hearty and heavy hand in. His last battle was at Peach Tree Creek, in front of Atlanta, where the gallant McPherson fell—young in years, but full of honors. Sherman now made the mistake (as I have always thought) of putting Howard in McPherson's place, over the head of Hooker—his superior in rank as well as large military qualities; and Hooker unfortunately committed the still greater mistake—the error of his lifetime—by instantly resigning and retiring to Cincinnati. Howard then commanded the Fourth Corps, and was commanding it well. But he had failed Hooker at Chancellorsville, and I suppose Hooker, conscious of rectitude and of his own greater qualities, could not endure to see Howard (his junior in rank also) thus promoted over him. Of course, it was human to refuse to submit to such treatment. But it was not war, nor good military politics, and I think Hooker keenly regretted it always afterward.

Unquestionably, Sherman was a little jealous of Hooker, or, at least, was not fair to him in this assignment of commands after his loyal and brilliant services both East and West. But, all the same, Hooker would have stood better in history had he "accepted the situation," and fought the war through to its finish. Suppose he had stuck to it, and gone on to Savannah, and up through the Carolinas, and been in at the final surrender of Joe Johnston, and appeared in the Grand Review at Washington? He would indeed have been welcomed as "Fighting Joe Hooker;" and what an ovation he would have been given by the Army and the nation!

Altogether, I confess, I have always thought well of General Hooker, and have tried to say it here. His intellect was of a high order—broad, keen, alert, vigorous—and what he did not know of the art of war and practical soldiering is hardly worth knowing. He was open and accessible to everybody; but he also knew how to assume authority and exercise command. One could not be long in his presence without feeling the mastery of his mind and will, while the charm of his manner was something indescribable. As a division commander, he certainly did not have his superior in the Army of the Potomac. As a corps commander, his conduct at Antietam speaks for itself. As an army commander, he was unfortunate at Chancellorsville; but otherwise and elsewhere he showed high military qualities, and I sincerely think deserves higher rank in history than he has hitherto received.

In his later years, after the war ended, he was paralyzed both mentally and physically, and so was unable to "write himself up," in the *Century* and otherwise, as others did. Had he lived and been himself, unquestionably we would have heard the other side of the story; for he held "the pen of a ready writer." But, all the same, he was a great and illustrious American soldier, and I dare to lay this tribute upon his grave. He was my comrade and good friend always, from 1861 to his decease, and I honored and loved him much. And every officer and soldier of "Hooker's Old Division," at least, will hurrah for him forever!

As illustrative of his chivalric nature and fine soldierly character, I beg to add the following. In the winter of 1861-62, on the lower Potomac, our camps soon became places of refuge for Maryland slaves, and their aristocratic owners (largely disloyal) procured a general order from McClellan to retake them wherever found, and commanding officers were instructed accordingly. A party of slave owners rode up to Hooker's headquarters one day, and reported several of their slaves in the camp of a Massachusetts regiment in his division, and, citing

General McClellan's order, demanded the surrender of their "property."

"Yes," said Hooker, "I have seen the order, and yonder is the Massachusetts camp. And if your slaves are there and choose to go with you, and the Massachusetts boys are content, I have no objections. But if they refuse, and a row occurs over there, I fear you will get into the guardhouse—the same as any other marauders."

"But, General Hooker, are you not going to apprehend our slaves for us?"

"Why, bless my soul, no! I am Brigadier General U. S. Vols., and no 'nigger-catcher!' I was born and bred in New England!"

It is needless to say, that the poor fugitives were safe, and McClellan's famous (or rather infamous) "Maryland slave order" soon became a dead-letter in all Hooker's camps.

So, in December, 1861, he sent for me one day, and when I reported in person said he thought of putting me under arrest, for "disobedience of orders." But when I explained it was only *quasi* disobedience, and that I was right and the order wrong, he complimented me on my non-compliance with it, and wound up by inviting me to "take a little commissary" and to dine with him! This was my first interview with General Hooker, and it goes without saying we remained friends ever afterward.

So, after the bloody battle of Williamsburg in May, 1862, where Hooker lost fifteen hundred men in killed and wounded, and Hancock only thirty-one, and yet McClellan gave the credit chiefly to Hancock,[1] Hooker rode over to our headquarters one night, and sitting around our Jersey camp fire, with Lieutenant Colo-

---
[1] See p. 26.

nel Mott, of the Fifth New Jersey (afterward General Mott), and myself, and others, after discussing McClellan's extraordinary dispatch considerably—some of us quite excitedly—he summed it all up humorously thus: "I say, Mott, it seems to me you and I, and your Jersey Blues and the Excelsior Brigade, were not at Williamsburg at all! Hancock did the business!" And he laughed gayly and rode homeward.

So, in September, 1862, after his cruel wound at Antietam, when he lay at Washington, out at the Asylum (the superintendent of which was his old friend, and so had invited him there for rest and treatment), a party of us rode over from Alexandria one day to call upon him, and among other things urged him to recommend Colonel ——, of a certain New Jersey regiment, for promotion to brigadier generalship. He heard us all through patiently, and then burst out wrathfully with: "I will not do it! I will never do it! He is a good officer and a gallant man, as you say. But he is not fit to be trusted with the good name and fame of his brother officers, and I will never recommend him for brigadier general."

We continued to urge him, when again he answered: "Why, of all men, you are the last ones to recommend him. Do you know he once reported you for 'absence without leave,' when he hadn't anything to do with you —out of spite and pure ugliness—when you were really 'absent on sick leave' by my orders and General Heintzelman's? I never said anything about it; but when his report passed through my hands (at Harrison's Landing), I took good care to exonerate you. And the 'Old Pirate' is not fit to be trusted with the reputations of my officers; and he never shall be, more than he is now, with my consent."

Naturally, we were astounded, as this was the first we knew of this business. But, all the same, we urged:

"Well, that was long ago—is now ancient history—and it didn't harm anybody! Promote him anyhow—he is so good a soldier and so capable an officer."

But Hooker would not listen to us, and promoted three other colonels of our brigade (Mott, Revere, and Carr) over his head, and Colonel —— never did get to be brigadier general to the end of the war! This was very like General Hooker. He had a keen sense of justice and great affection for his officers and men, and in return they believed in and trusted him, and would follow him to the cannon's mouth—and over the cannon!

So, also, I remember another experience with him in January, 1863. A Lieutenant V——, in a New Jersey regiment, was ill with typhoid or some other camp fever, and his father, a leading citizen of Trenton, N. J., came down to look after him. The next day he called to see me, and said his son was sure to die if he remained in camp, but that if he could get a "leave of absence" he would take him home, and thought he might save him. I told him this was next to impossible, under existing orders. He said he had just lain all night by the side of his son, to keep him warm (the weather was so raw and cold), and a few more such nights in a tent would kill his boy, and couldn't I do something to help him in the premises? His distress was so great, I said I would try, but warned him against overconfidence, as few "leaves" were being granted, and they had all to go through regimental, brigade, division, corps, and grand division headquarters, and be approved by all these, before they would be considered by Army headquarters.

However, I drew up an application for "leave," and had the lieutenant sign it, and got it approved at regimental, brigade, and division headquarters, and then mounting our horses we rode over to corps headquarters, where it was also cheerfully approved. Much elated, we rode on to grand division headquarters, and reached there soon after dark. I called on the adjutant general, and stated our business, but he said it was after office hours, and General —— (our grand division commander) had given orders not to be disturbed—he was engaged. I asked him where the general was—our business was urgent—involved life or death, probably—and couldn't we possibly see him? He pointed us to a large tent, and said we could do as we pleased, but he advised us to return next day. As this would involve staying at Acquia Creek or Washington over Sunday, and cost two or three days, and might prove fatal to his son, the father objected, and so we made bold to approach the general's tent and knock, when we found him "engaged" in a game of cards with two other major generals, and a bottle of "commissary" between them, of course!

I apologized for the interruption, and, introducing myself and the father, stated our business briefly, but I was cut short with the curt reply that it was too late for business, and we must return next day. I tried to explain, and persisted, but was again rebuffed; and as we retired from "the presence" of this distinguished major general, the father's heart sank within him. We mounted our horses and rode dejectedly away—all our hard work for nothing! But, suddenly, I remembered Hooker, and broke out with: "Let's go up to headquarters, and see General Hooker. I know it is unmilitary to go there without the approval of the grand division commander. But let's go up there and see Hooker anyhow, and see if he won't cut 'red tape' and grant this 'leave,' under the circumstances."

And so we rode on to headquarters—got there along toward midnight of a dark and dismal night—and found General Hooker still in his office tent, hard at work over his correspondence. As his sentry halted us, Hooker recognized my voice, and called out through the tent door cheerily: "Come in, Rusling! Sentry, it is all right! Let 'em come in!" And so we went in, and told our story briefly, pretty much as above—"with naught extenuate and naught set down in malice"—and when we got through, the grand old man—his face flushed and eyes blazing—exclaimed: "Where is the paper? Let me have it. I'll show General —— a 'leave' can be granted without his approval, in a case like this."

And so he took the application, and indorsed the "leave" upon it, in his own handwriting, with verbal orders to report it to the adjutant general (poor Seth Williams). Thanking him for his kindness, we bowed ourselves out and rode happily back to our own headquarters.

And *this*, too, was "just like General Hooker." And it was just such fine acts of chivalry and courtesy, that endeared him to everybody that came in contact with him—civilians as well as soldiers.

Perhaps I should add, that Lieutenant V—— left next morning, carried on a stretcher to the railroad at Falmouth, and, after an absence of a month or so, recovered and returned to duty; but soon had to resign, and subsequently died of this same army disability, or its sequences.

And so, O General Hooker—good friend, brave heart, generous soul, great commander—hail and farewell!

Gen. Meade, 1863.

## CHAPTER VI

### George G. Meade

My next commander, and always highly esteemed, was General Meade. He was a West Pointer also, and by birth a Pennsylvanian. He had served with credit in Mexico, and stood high in the Engineer Corps of the Regular Army. His first command during the Civil War, I think, was a brigade of Pennsylvania Reserves, from which he was duly promoted to division and corps commander and rank of major general. He fought well on the Peninsula, he distinguished himself at Fredericksburg and Chancellorsville, and when in June, 1863, Lee was invading Pennsylvania, and it was decided to relieve General Hooker, Mr. Lincoln naturally turned to Meade, because, in addition to other qualifications, he was also a Pennsylvanian. Evidently "Old Abe" thought there was going to be hard fighting up there in Pennsylvania, and who so likely to defend her well as a gallant son of her own soil?

General Meade was then tall and slender, gaunt and sad of visage, with iron-gray hair and beard, ensconced behind a pair of spectacles, and with few popular traits about him, but with a keen and well-disciplined intellect, a cool and sound judgment, and by both education and temperament was every inch a soldier. He surely had need to be all this; for in three days after assuming command, Gettysburg was precipitated upon him, with all its awful cares and tremendous responsibilities. How well he met these, and how much he deserved the proud title of "Conqueror of Gettysburg," is now matter of history. His stout fight there is one of the great battles of history, and will rank forever with Marathon, Platæa, Waterloo, and the other great fields whereon the destinies of the human race have been staked and won. The mere fact that he there faced Robert E. Lee, and whipped him, in a square stand-up fight of three days' duration—their two armies not greatly differing in actual strength "present for duty"—alone settles his fame forever as a military commander, discuss him otherwise as we may.

The first day at Gettysburg Lee struck our right, and, elated by Fredericksburg and Chancellorsville, thought he was going to have things pretty much his own way, but was amazed at our stubborn resistance—all honor to John Buford and John F. Reynolds, and much honor to Howard and Hancock! Poor Reynolds fell—to the grief of the whole army—a brilliant and capable officer, who had already been offered the command and declined it, but doubtless would have succeeded to it, had he lived and Meade have fallen or proved incapable. The second day Lee struck our left, and made a terrific struggle for the mastery there (called by many the real battle of Gettysburg, because the Confederates lost so heavily and were so badly shaken up), but gained nothing of substantial value—thanks to Sickles, Humphrey, Warren, and the gallant Third Corps. The third day, still confident, Lee aimed straight at our center, believing he could pierce it and ruin us, hazarding everything on the cast of a die—on that superb charge of Pickett's division, one of the finest exploits in military annals, far surpassing "The Charge of the Light Brigade" at Balaclava, immortalized by Alfred Tennyson; but was himself bloodily repulsed and reduced to the verge of ruin.

For all this General Meade deserves the highest credit. How well he swung the Army of the Potomac, about eighty thousand strong then, and fought it right, left, center, and all together as it had never been fought before! History will not permit anyone to detract from his just deserts on those three great days at Gettysburg—especially on that last great day, when three hundred cannon shook both earth and sky, and the whole countryside from Seminary Ridge to Cemetery Hill was as the gaping mouth of hell. How magnificent, how terrific it all was, and how superbly Meade held the reins and guided us safely through!

But after Pickett's awful repulse, or rather his annihilation—for out of his five thousand men less than one thousand got back to the Confederate lines, and out of twenty-two mounted officers, only two—it is not so clear that Meade ought not to have made a "counter-thrust" (Lee and his great lieutenant, Longstreet, expected this), and he certainly was in fault in not following the Confederates up more sharply, hacking and whacking away at them as they fell back from Gettysburg to Williamsport, with a baggage and supply train "seventeen miles long" literally filled with their wounded and dying—"one long wail of misery and anguish for seventeen miles," as the Confederate General Imboden, in command of it, wrote afterward.

Here at Williamsport, Lee found the Potomac at freshet height from July rains, impossible to ford, and with his pontoons swept away, and had Meade hit him promptly and heavily, as he was well able to do with his victorious and reinforced army, it is hard to say what might not have happened. It is clear that Mr. Lincoln and his Cabinet expected much just then, and had good reason to do so.[1] It was certainly a great opportunity, big with vast possibilities, such as come to men but once in a century or so. For had Lee been compelled to sur-

---
[1] *War Records*, vol. xxvii, part iii, pp. 529-553, 567-605, 612, 645, etc.

render then and there, the war would have ended in 1863, instead of 1865, and there would have been no Wilderness campaign, and no Sheridan in the Valley, and no Sherman's March down to the Sea in 1864. But Meade called a council of war, which, of course, did nothing, as usual. Then he reconnoitered a week, and called another council of war, and then decided to advance next morning, notwithstanding his council of war advised otherwise.[1]

But "next morning" Lee was not there! Like the shrewd and capable commander he was, on arriving at Williamsport and finding the Potomac unfordable, Lee did not sit down in despair (as a lesser man might well have done), but he promptly set to work to collect canal boats and to improvise pontoon bridges out of these and other materials, pulling down houses, tearing down mills, cutting down trees, etc., and by thus taking advantage of our tardiness, the very night Meade made up his mind to attack (July 13), Lee crossed the Potomac successfully, and was safe back in Virginia again. How it must have delighted his Confederate soul—even as Antæus gained new vitality and strength whenever he touched his mother earth!

But Meade, disgusted—as he might well have been, seeing how he had been "euchred" and the country disappointed—now tendered his resignation, like the man he was. But he was continued in command, and promptly crossed the Potomac also, and followed Lee down to the Rapidan (warding him off from Washington and Alexandria), with now and then a brisk attack, but no serious action, and there both armies came to a mutual halt.

I saw much of General Meade during his delay at Williamsport (being on duty temporarily at Army headquarters), and know he was greatly anxious and

---

[1] *War Records*, vol. xxvii, part iii, p. 703.

troubled over what to do and how to do it. Halleck was urging him to attack every day—almost every hour —"hit or miss."[1] But Halleck was safe in the War Department at Washington, eighty miles away, while Meade was in the field at the head of the army, and keenly alive to his duties and responsibilities.

This must be said for General Meade, that if he sat still, Washington at least was safe beyond peradventure, and this was an important factor in the game he was then playing. He had just fought a great battle and won a great victory, and was it now wise to hazard all this by another great battle, which might go wrong, as battles sometimes do and will? Besides, he would now have to attack, and Lee would be on the defense, on interior lines, and he might give us another Fredericksburg over again, which would have been most disastrous there and then. No doubt Meade weighed all these things well. But the fact that he at last decided to attack, when it was a week too late, I think history will hold as due proof that he ought to have attacked immediately, when he found Lee in such desperate straits, with a defeated and depleted army, and the unfordable Potomac at his back, and had he done so the chances are he would have covered himself and the army with imperishable renown. Had Meade been a greater or a lesser soldier, unquestionably he would have done so. As it is, let us be thankful he was what he was, and at least conquered at Gettysburg.

I well remember that week or so at Williamsport. At Army headquarters we were all on the *qui vive* every day, and eager for action. Each day we expected something big to happen, but nothing came of it. On the night Lee escaped (July 13) we were ordered to breakfast at dawn, and to be in the saddle by 7 A. M. But next morn-

---
[1] *War Records*, vol. xxvii, part iii, p. 605, etc.

ing, as we mounted, a dispatch was received from Howard, that the Confederate works in his front "were evacuated;" and soon an officer came galloping down the road, with the news that Kilpatrick had entered Williamsport at 8 A. M., and the Confederates were already safe across the Potomac. Lee had begun his movement at midnight,[1] leaving Jeb Stuart to cover his withdrawal and retreat with his cavalry; and by daylight was mostly over. Our advance struck his rearguard at Falling Waters, and captured some two thousand prisoners, etc.[2] But what might we not have accomplished had we struck Lee the day before or a week before?

At headquarters, I am sure, there was a general feeling of disappointment and regret, not to say chagrin. Having nothing better to do, with two or three other officers, however, I rode on up the Williamsport road, exploring the beautiful country there and inspecting Lee's abandoned works, etc., quite down to the river, and thought then, and have always thought, that Meade here missed a great and golden opportunity.

About August 1, 1863, I was assigned regularly to duty at headquarters, Army of the Potomac, and continued there until about November 10. I saw much of General Meade during this period, and came to have a high appreciation of his mind and character. I found him to be a conscientious and hard worker; as a rule, rising early and retiring late. He did not seem to care much for "Reviews," but believed greatly in reports and inspections, and by means of these and his own keen observations kept himself well informed as to the character and condition of all parts of the army. He was not social—had few, indeed, of the popular arts that Hooker possessed—was habitually grave and reticent. But he

---

[1] *War Records*, vol. xxvii, part iii, p. 1001.
[2] *Ibid.*, p. 698.

was accessible for all needed purposes, and constantly grew in the estimation of capable and worthy officers.

Of course, we lived in tents, and as the autumn came on our huge headquarter camp fire became a point of reunion for all headquarter officers, especially after nightfall. Here every evening you would find Meade, with his hands clasped behind him and his head bent forward, with his fatigue cap or old slouch hat well down over his eyes, chatting gravely with Humphrey, his chief of staff, or Seth Williams, his adjutant general, or Ingalls, his chief quartermaster, or Hunt, his chief of artillery, or Warren, his chief engineer, or other general officers that happened along, and midnight often found his solitary candle still burning in his tent and the commander in chief hard at work there.

As a rule, he was a better listener than talker. Ingalls and Hunt were the great talkers there, and they both talked exceedingly well, and Warren, too, was keen and bright. What campaigns they planned and unplanned! How they outwitted Lee and ended the rebellion again and again! What camp stories they told! What old soldier "yarns" they spun! But no space for them here. Meade's sense of humor was not large, but he was keen and intelligent, his mind worked broadly and comprehensively, his patriotism was perfect, his sense of duty intense; and he would willingly have laid down his life at any time had our cause required it. In manner he was often sharp and peremptory, but this was because of his utter absorption in great affairs.

While thus serving here in October, 1863, we had our famous "see-saw" campaign, from Culpeper to Centreville, and back again. Lee suddenly advanced to turn our right, with about forty thousand men, and we immediately retired behind the Rappahannock, and kept it up until we reached the heights of Centreville, though we numbered over sixty thousand men.[1] Here we halted two or three days, with Bull Run in our front, inviting Lee to attack us, but he was too wary to take such risks. Evidently Gettysburg had been enough for him! Then he retired again behind the Rappahannock, and we "chasséed" back after him, and were both soon in our old camps again near Warrenton and Culpeper, without much hard fighting on either side. This campaign has been much criticised, but if Meade erred at all it was on the safe side, and in war as in civil life prudence is often "the better part of valor." Clearly he did not want to fight a third Bull Run, on the same unlucky ground substantially of McDowell and Pope's sad reverses, but preferred the safer and infinitely stronger line of Centreville. So, Lee knew better than to "butt his brains out" against the heights of Centreville, and wisely retreated when he found he could not catch Meade napping nor decoy him into a losing battle.

During this movement to the rear, on October 13, as we neared the Rappahannock, General Meade ordered me to take charge of our immense wagon trains, and hasten their crossing below Rappahannock Station. The consolidated trains of the Army of the Potomac then averaged about fifty miles. I found them all crossing by a single ford, and at once directed new fords to be constructed, by cutting down the banks of the river, etc., and soon had several trains crossing simultaneously and rapidly, and at dusk rode into headquarters near Catlett's Station, and reported our trains practically over. But I was myself thoroughly exhausted, having been in the saddle all day and most of the previous night and day, and after a meager supper was soon sound asleep. In an hour or so, however, along about nine o'clock, an orderly roused me with:

---
[1] See Appendix, p. 368.

"General Meade's compliments, and he wants to see you immediately."

Reporting to him, he said our trains had gone into park for the night at Brentsville, about ten or twelve miles distant, with orders to move on next day to Fairfax Station, to the rear of Centreville; but that the Confederate cavalry were working round in that direction, and he feared that they might raid or "gobble up" our trains, unless they were started at once for Fairfax, and he wished me to proceed immediately to Brentsville and take charge of affairs there. I hesitated; hinted I was used up, dead-beat with fatigue, etc.; but he cut me short by saying I had managed the trains so well at the Rappahannock that day, that he was going to intrust me with this Brentsville job also. And then he added, by way of parting benediction:

"Good-bye, Rusling! The Rebs are reported off in that direction, and you may bring up in Richmond before I see you again!"

"No, I won't either, General," I rejoined, kindling up (evidently as he intended); "I will go through all right, and put the trains through, too."

He gave me his hand, and smiled gravely down from behind his glasses (I was only a young fellow then, and of moderate stature compared with Meade's), and bade me take what escort I wanted. But I chose only four cavalrymen, for secrecy and speed, and was soon in the saddle again and off for Brentsville.

Once out of camp, we abandoned the main road, and struck straight for Brentsville by the byways and plantation roads, depending on an "intelligent contraband" as guide, that I picked up at the first cabin, with a promise of five dollars if he piloted us safe through, or a bullet through his head if he misled or betrayed us.

"All right, massa," he answered, displaying **his**

ivories; "I'll take dat five dollars; fer I was gwine wid you Yankees, anyway!"

I mounted him behind one of the cavalrymen, and though the night was pitch dark we reached Brentsville safely before midnight. Here we found the teams ungeared and everybody fast asleep; but soon had the trains on the road again and off briskly for Fairfax Station. With the trains thus well in motion, and their corps quartermasters well instructed, I threw myself on the ground by a flickering camp fire, and went heavily to sleep, and slept till after sunrise of a superb October morning, and, then waking up, found our vast trains still rolling on and on. I breakfasted with some officers on a cup of coffee, hard-tack, and fried pork, and then smoked a pipe and lounged on the porch of the Brentsville tavern (its proprietor, of course, in the Confederate service) until the last train was well on its way, and then, mounting my horse, started for Centreville.

I struck the railroad again at Bristoe about noon, and with my little escort (minus the "contraband," whom I had turned over to the trains as a teamster—no doubt he made a good one) was jogging leisurely along toward Manassas, but had not got a mile away from Bristoe before I heard brisk firing back there, and found the Confederates under A. P. Hill had swooped in just to my rear, and would certainly have "gobbled" me up had I been only a few minutes later. It was a narrow escape —a rather "close call," as old soldiers say—but an escape, nevertheless. As it was, they ran into the Second Corps, and struck it heavily. But Warren handled them so roughly, and showed such good generalship by posting his men in a railroad cut and some old earthworks there, that they were soon glad to withdraw, with a severe loss both in killed and wounded.

Of course, I was cut off and could not reach Warren,

## George G. Meade

and so I rode on to headquarters at Centreville and reported to Meade that same afternoon. He seemed glad, and congratulated me on my safe return, and I was glad to find my tent pitched, and to get a good "square meal" and a night's unbroken rest again. This was on October 14, 1863. The Comte de Paris, in his admirable *History of the Civil War in America* (the best yet written), Vol. III, pages 777, 778, in speaking of our trains here, says: "They were retarded and not able to reach Brentsville (October 15), and were thus greatly exposed." But he is mistaken, as our last wagon left Brentsville before noon of the fourteenth, and rolled into Fairfax Station safe and sound before nightfall, as above stated. Meade's order, "The trains will move to the vicinity of Brentsville," is dated October 13, 1 P. M. (*War Records,* Vol. XXIX, part II, page 305), and that same night I rode to Brentsville and hastened thence to Fairfax Station as above stated.

We got back to Warrenton and Warrenton Junction again about November 1, and both armies practically resumed their old lines. Lee had gained his object, which evidently was to baffle and bully Meade and lead him to waste a month of magnificent weather, in which he should have been campaigning and fighting. Doubtless Lee thought we would now go into winter quarters; but after about a week Meade decided on a new movement against Lee's right, by way of Kelly's Ford and Mine Run, hoping ultimately to seize the heights of Fredericksburg by surprise and move on Richmond by that route.[1] In the early morning of the day we moved, as I was about mounting my horse to accompany headquarters—we had breakfasted about daylight—I was

---

[1] Meade could not divest himself of the idea that Fredericksburg was the true route to Richmond. Soon after arriving at Warrenton he recommended this and urged it repeatedly. But Mr. Lincoln replied: "I have constantly desired the Army of the Potomac to make Lee's Army and not Richmond its objective point." And Grant afterward adopted the same phraseology.—*War Records,* vol. xxix, part iii, pp. 201, 202, 207, 208, 361, 409, etc.

handed a telegram from the War Department, directing me to proceed at once to Tennessee and report to General George H. Thomas. I sought General Meade, and handing him the telegram, asked him what it meant? Expressing surprise, he said he "hardly knew what; was sorry to lose me, etc.; but it is a safe rule always to obey orders—especially when they are signed by Secretary Stanton!" And then he added, as a crumb of comfort (for I was reluctant to go West—all my friends were in the East): "It will likely lead to promotion, young man! George Thomas needs good officers out there!"

And so, shaking hands and kindly bidding me "good-bye," and "good luck to you!" he mounted his horse and rode to the front, while I, shaking hands with the staff and bidding everybody good-bye, within an hour took the cars at the nearest railroad station, with my horses and baggage, and before noon was back in Washington and *en route* to Nashville.

This seemed to me at the time a great misfortune—one of the most untoward events of my life—as if I was "banished to Botany Bay"—and I could not understand it. It caused me many a bitter hour, as I traveled westward. But in the end it made me full colonel, and brigadier general (by brevet), and on the whole was the luckiest thing that could have happened to me. It brought me into contact with Grant and Sherman and Thomas, and their great operations in the West, and broadened and helped me on many lines and in many ways ever afterward. And so, "Hail and thanks" to Edwin M. Stanton, after all!

I never saw General Meade again. I did not get East again until August, 1865, and it so happened our paths never crossed each other afterward. The affair at Mine Run (November, 1863), above alluded to, though at first big with promise, ended in a *fiasco*, and we were soon back at Brandy Station and Warrenton, with the two armies facing each other, like grim gladiators, on the line of the Rapidan again (December, 1863).[1] Here the Army of the Potomac went into winter quarters, the weather getting to be bad, and Meade not knowing what better to do. Clearly Lee had outmaneuvered and outwitted him, and the campaign of 1863 closed with the honors in Lee's favor, notwithstanding his ghastly repulse at Gettysburg.

Nevertheless Meade was continued in command of the Army of the Potomac in 1864 and until the close of the war; and on the whole, history will declare he commanded it well. It is true, his command in 1864-65 was mainly nominal; for Grant was there himself, and in supreme command—overseeing and directing everything—with his eye and hand on everybody, and vowed to victory. But Meade must have shown high qualities, of both loyalty and generalship, or Grant surely would not have tolerated him even thus. He was certainly a great and able commander, if just a little too prudent at times; and as the conqueror of Gettysburg, and last commander of the Army of the Potomac, his fame is secure forever. To Pennsylvanians, at least, he will always be a hero and an idol; and to all others, a great and illustrious American, while time lasts or history endures.

---

[1] How disappointing this was to Mr. Stanton is shown by his following brief telegram to General Butler, at Fortress Monroe, Dec. 2: "Meade is on the back track again without a fight."—*War Records*, vol. xxix, part ii, p. 537.

## CHAPTER VII
### GEORGE H. THOMAS

MY next commander, and always greatly honored and esteemed, was General Thomas. Not Lorenzo Thomas, Adjutant General United States Army, but George H. Thomas, Major General United States Army, and Commander in Chief of the Army of the Cumberland. They differed considerably. The one was a Delawarian, and worthy of Delaware—the home of the whipping post still—smoothbore and narrow-gauge, a master of red tape. The other was a Virginian, and worthy of the home of George Washington and Thomas Jefferson— big-souled, broad-gauged, built on the plan of Plutarch's men. Large-framed, clear-headed, judgmatical, I think George H. Thomas resembled George Washington in body, brain, and soul more than any officer I met during the civil war. In some respects, indeed, he was an abler man than our American Fabius; but whether, on the whole, he could have swung things so well as George Washington did during our American Revolution may, of course, be doubted.

Though a Virginian, "native and to the manor born," and with the air and bearing of a real Virginian, Thomas, unlike Robert E. Lee, did not resign his commission and desert his colors when Virginia seceded (or tried to). He had graduated well at West Point, and served honorably and creditably in Mexico, and now stood loyally by the United States, though tempted much to accept a Virginia or Confederate commission. Doubtless the fact that he had married a New Yorker had something to do with it. A good wife always anchors

Gen. George H. Thomas, 1864.

a good man to good things. But, however this may be, in the dark winter and spring of 1861, when Southern-born officers by the score were resigning and flocking over to Jefferson Davis, Thomas was always "faithful among the faithless found," and certainly this was remembered to his credit in after years by Abraham Lincoln and Edwin M. Stanton.

At first, in 1861, he was only a colonel of regulars under General Patterson, at Harper's Ferry, Va. Think of his masquerading there as colonel, when he ought to have been major general and commander in chief! Had he been so, in the light of his subsequent career, it is not too much to say that Joseph E. Johnston would never have slipped away from his vigilant eyes and firm fingers to reinforce Beauregard at Manassas, and our first Bull Run would likely have resulted the other way.

Later, in August, 1861, he was made Brigadier General of Volunteers and ordered West, and there soon distinguished himself by the handsome victory of Mill Springs, Ky., January, 1862. This was the beginning of his long and uninterrupted career of successes, until ultimately he became celebrated as "the Union general who never lost a battle." It was no fault of his that his fine division did not get up at Shiloh or Pittsburg Landing in time to do much service. But at Stone River, or Murfreesboro (December 31, 1862, to January 2, 1863), he commanded our center, and bore the brunt of the awful conflict there, and shared with Sheridan and Hazen the honors of that bloody field—such as they were. When Rosecrans, dispirited (as well he might be) at the close of the first day's fight, summoned a council of war and submitted the question as to whether they should retreat or try it again, Thomas's sturdy answer was, "This army cannot retreat," and wrapping himself in his blanket he turned over and went calmly to sleep, and thus assured our subsequent substantial victory there. It was, indeed, a "bloody field." We lost 12,000 out of 43,000 men engaged, and Bragg 10,000 out of 47,000. But Bragg held twenty-eight of our guns captured in action; and it was only sheer pluck and "clear grit" on our side, that induced the Confederates to yield the field at last.

In the masterly advance from Murfreesboro to Chickamauga, Thomas was ever vigilant and gallant, and on that fateful field (September 19-23, 1863), when Rosecrans, Crittenden, McCook, and others had drifted to the rear (Rosecrans, indeed, into Chattanooga—more shame to him), Thomas still stood like a lion at bay in command of our center and left wing, and saved the Army of the Cumberland from ruin and dishonor, and, indeed, then and there well won the sobriquet of the "Rock of Chickamauga." Chickamauga, in some respects, was not unlike Gettysburg, as anyone can see who visits the field there now. When Thomas at last stumbled back on Snodgrass Hill there, his position was much akin to that of Meade's at Cemetery Ridge, and Longstreet ought to have recognized this—having been whipped at Gettysburg only the July before. No Confederate power on earth could have driven Thomas from Snodgrass Hill, had the rest of the army here rallied to his support.

Of course, Rosecrans, having lost his head, was now relieved, and also, of course, by common consent, the command at Chattanooga was now turned over to Thomas, and right well did he vindicate his promotion. He had been tendered the same when Buell was relieved in October, 1862, but declined it. To Grant's anxious telegram from Louisville, *en route* from Vicksburg to Chattanooga, "Hold on to Chattanooga at all hazards. Will be with you myself in three days," his heroic reply was (so characteristic of the man), "We will hold the town *till we starve!*" And they did come pretty nearly to starving—lost over ten thousand horses and mules, and the troops reduced to half rations—before Sherman arrived with relief and Grant got things well straightened out there.

In our final struggle about Chattanooga (November 23-25, 1863), Thomas commanded our center, and with Sheridan, Wood, and others swept magnificently up the heights of Missionary Ridge, stormed the Confederate center, charged their apparently impregnable artillery, crushed their gallant infantry, and whelmed Bragg in one universal ruin. Poor old Bragg—obstinate and chuckle-headed to the last! He thought he had us "Yanks" in a trap there, sure, and was going to bag us all for sure! But what more could he expect, with four such adversaries as Grant, Sherman, Thomas, and Sheridan all present on the field, and all four "pulling true" as a team of thoroughbreds against him.

In the great Atlanta campaign of 1864 Thomas commanded the Army of the Cumberland still, and how much Sherman depended on and was indebted to him will be seen when I say that, out of the ninety-eight thousand seven hundred and ninety-seven men composing Sherman's triple army (of the Cumberland, the Ohio, and the Tennessee), Thomas commanded sixty thousand seven hundred and seventy-three. In all the operations and actions from Chattanooga to Atlanta, indeed, Thomas handled his troops with consummate ability and conspicuous gallantry, and had the full confidence of that great soldier, General Sherman. Indeed, Sherman took no important step there without first consulting Thomas, and trusted him fully as to both strategy and tactics. He never had to give him precise orders and detailed instructions as lesser lieutenants, but only indicated his objective points, and then with general suggestions left him large liberty of action—a wise course with such a lieutenant. And Thomas never abused this confidence, but rather amply justified it by sound judgment and soldierly conduct, that endeared him more and more to his men every mile of the campaign from Chattanooga to Atlanta.

With the capture of Atlanta (September 2, 1864)[1]— a genuine and great feat of arms that saved the fortunes of the war and reëlected Abraham Lincoln—Sherman decided to strike next at Savannah; but he must needs also take care of Tennessee and Kentucky, and this grave task he now intrusted unreservedly to General Thomas. Thomas, of course, would have preferred to go "Marching through Georgia" by the side of his illustrious chief. But, good soldier that he was, he uncomplainingly retraced his steps, first to Chattanooga, and then back to Nashville. Here he took upon himself the conduct of the memorable campaign and battle of Nashville—his first independent command—and disclosed qualities, I venture to say, that placed him in the very forefront of military commanders. He was the one colossal figure in all that region, during all that period; and now let us see *what* he did and *how* he went about it.

His first duty here, of course, was to watch Hood, and divine where he was going to strike, and then to checkmate and destroy him, if possible. Hood, gallant and prompt soldier that he was, quickly gathered up his Confederates, and, feigning first to attack Chattanooga, nevertheless aimed straight for Nashville. This handsome city, the Athens of the South, was then our great depot of supplies for all that region—what Washington was to us in the East—and Hood hoped to capture this and push the war back to the Ohio, as a good set-off to

---

[1] "Atlanta is ours and fairly won," as Sherman telegraphed.

Sherman's audacity. Had he succeeded, Sherman's superb march down to the sea would have been largely neutralized, and his own great campaign of 1864 have gone down to history as "magnificent" indeed, "but not war." Sherman, gifted with genius, was not unconscious of this. But, great soldier that he was, he trusted Providence and "took the chances." But this was only because he had first taken the measure of Thomas, and held his chosen lieutenant assuredly equal to the grave business in hand.

Meanwhile, General Thomas, once back at Nashville (October, 1864), and sure of Hood's objective point, first pushed Schofield out with the best troops he had—the Fourth and Twenty-third Corps and Wilson's Cavalry, all good troops—to watch and worry Hood and retard his advance—and then set to work himself with herculean energies to reinforce and further fortify Nashville. Had he had his own old Army of the Cumberland complete, which he had done so much to drill and discipline, he would have been supremely confident. But Sherman had taken the flower of this with him, and it was now Thomas's hard duty to pick up the odds and ends at the rear—scattered garrisons of posts and depots, railroad guards, white and colored troops, green regiments *en route* from the North, etc.—and to fuse and weld these into one homogeneous and fighting whole, in aid of Schofield's hard-pressed force.[1] Without a grumble or complaint (*vide* McClellan on the Peninsula), he quickly concentrated all these at Nashville, and next armed five thousand out of the fourteen thousand quartermaster employees then there (many of them old soldiers), and sent them into the trenches. Then he called out the citizens, white and colored, Union and Confederate, and set them to work on his extended lines. But his "Morning

---

[1] *War Records*, vol. xlv, part ii, p. 17.

Reports" showed he still lacked numbers; and so he called on his old chief, Rosecrans (then commanding in Missouri), to lend him A. J. Smith's corps—eleven thousand as fine troops as ever marched or fought—and on the arrival of these his mind and heart cleared fairly up.

I had seen and talked with him daily (some days several times a day) from his arrival at Nashville October 3, and a cloud of anxious care rested always on his brow. Habitually, during all that period, he wore his military hat pulled down over his grave gray eyes—was reticent and gloomy; but now his hat lifted, his broad brow cleared up, and his strong and massive face began to shine with the fierce light of impending battle. I happened in his quarters the night General A. J. Smith arrived at Nashville, by way of the Cumberland, from St. Louis, with thirteen transports and eight armored gunboats swarming with veteran soldiers, and I shall never forget the scene. It was the night of the battle of Franklin (November 30), and our news of matters there was as yet uncertain.[1] Judge Campbell, of the United States Supreme Court, then residing at Nashville, gave a reception that night, and on my way to it I dropped into General Thomas's headquarters (about nine o'clock), to inquire more about Franklin. Thomas, his hat up and face all aglow, handed me a telegram from Schofield, announcing that he had defeated Hood; putting *thirteen* of his *general officers* alone and over *six thousand* of his men *hors de combat*—a terrific blow to the Confederates—but was now falling back on Nashville in pursuance of his orders. Thomas eagerly inquired if I had any news from A. J. Smith. I answered, no; that I had sent a swift steamer down the Cumberland early in the afternoon to hurry him forward, but it was not yet time for his arrival.

---
[1] *War Records*, vol. xlv, part I, p. 34; part ii, p. 17.

## George H. Thomas

"Well," he said, "if Smith does not get here tonight, he will not get here at all; for tomorrow Hood will strike the Cumberland and close it against all transports."

I replied, he need not fear, for Smith would certainly "arrive soon;" and went on to Judge Campbell's.

About midnight I left Judge Campbell's, and on my way back dropped in at Thomas's headquarters again, and there I found Schofield and T. J. Wood just arrived from Franklin, and all three in conference over what was to be done next day. Wood was still on crutches, from a wound received in the Atlanta campaign; but in command of his corps, and handling it ably and gallantly. Thomas introduced me to the other two, and again eagerly inquired about A. J. Smith.

"O," I replied, "he is all right. Just as I came in I heard his steamers tooting along the levee!"

And, even as I spake, the door opened, and in strode General A. J. Smith, a grizzled old veteran but a soldier all through. They all four greeted each other eagerly; but Thomas (undemonstrative as he was) literally took Smith in his arms and hugged him; for he now felt absolutely sure of coping with Hood, and defeating him duly. They first discussed Franklin, and rejoiced over it, and then Thomas spread his maps on the floor and pointed out his Nashville lines, explaining their bearings and significance. I left them at 1 a. m., all four down on their knees and examining attentively the positions to be assumed next morning, as Schofield and Wood fell back on Nashville and Smith marched out from the Cumberland.

The next morning I rode down to the levee, to take a look at our new friends. They were a rough-looking set, bivouacked all along the levee, and cooking coffee. I rode up to a group, and asked who they were and where they were from.

"We are 'Smith's guerrillas!'"[1] the answer was. "We have been to Vicksburg, Red River, Missouri, and about everywhere else down South and out West, and now we are going to Hades, if old 'A. J.' orders us!"

Now came the siege of Nashville proper. Nashville is beautifully situated on the Cumberland River, which here makes a sharp bend north, and within this bend, on the southerly side of the river, lies the goodly city itself. Hood at once stretched his forces across this bend, occupying the crests of a series of hills, three or four miles from the city—his flanks covered by cavalry—and thus boldly confronted Thomas, who occupied a similar but better series of hills, nearer, of course, to Nashville. Thomas had the advantage of position, as his line was shorter, and many of his hills were also heavily fortified, and had been for a year or two. Their fighting strength, however, was not dissimilar, about fifty thousand men each—Thomas rather less, all told, of real effectives, though reported more. But Hood had the advantage here, as his troops were mainly well-seasoned veterans, the flower of the Southwest, toughened and tried by arduous campaigns and bloody battles, the survivals substantially of the Atlanta campaign; while Thomas's were many of them green and mixed troops, as I have heretofore stated.

Hood thus sat down seriously before Nashville, cutting our communications with everything south and west, and immediately began feeling our lines, as if meaning to attack. Next he planted batteries on the Cumberland, and thus closed that artery for supplies to everything but armored gunboats. Our only line of communication still left open was the Louisville and Nashville Railroad to the north, already overwhelmed

---

[1] This was their usual name, because of their wide service and rapid work. *War Records*, vol. xlv, part ii, p. 235.

with locomotives and cars withdrawn from Nashville and below, and a slender and precarious line at best; a single track road, nearly two hundred miles long, liable to be cut by guerrillas at any moment, and which Forrest was only waiting for the Cumberland to fall to cross and smash at his pleasure.

We were thus pretty thoroughly cooped up and penned in for a time; and people at a distance, who knew little about our strength or the state of our supplies, naturally enough grew nervous.[1] There was, however, no real cause for alarm at any time, especially after Hood let his first forty-eight hours slip by without assaulting. Had he attacked at once on arriving, and massed heavily on our right—the weakest point in our line at that time, though afterward made one of the strongest—he might have given Thomas some trouble; though he could hardly have succeeded in his enterprise.

In fact, our last reinforcements (Smith from St. Louis and Steedman from Chattanooga) gave us such a happy preponderance of both infantry and artillery, that, from the hour they were both safely in, nobody there who knew much of affairs ever seriously doubted our ability to hold Nashville at all hazards and against all contingencies.[2] Steedman, indeed, like Smith, got in just in the nick of time "to save his bacon." In truth, Steedman did not *save* his entirely, as a few of his last cars, loaded with troops, were attacked and captured by the daring Forrest, almost within sight of Nashville. General N. B. Forrest, though an uneducated man, was yet one of the most distinguished and successful of all the Confederate cavalry leaders. He it was who, when asked one day the secret of success in war, replied: "To git thar fustest with the mostest men!"

---

[1] *War Records*, vol. xlv, part ii, pp. 16, 17.
[2] See chap. xv, p. 376, 383.

## Men and Things I Saw in Civil War Days

And so, with our forces all up, with everybody at work and all in good heart and trim, we soon had two goodly lines of works constructed, encircling Nashville on the south and west; frowning with forts and redoubts, and bristling with rifle pits, and covering our whole outlying hills, as I have said, from the Cumberland around to the Cumberland again. We were thus ready to receive Hood, and prepared at all points to meet his attack, so early as December 5 or 6—Franklin being fought November 30.

Thomas now waited; but Hood did not come. He tempted him with reconnoissances, but he would not respond; he peppered him with round shot, but he would not answer; he complimented him with shell, but he did not reply. Hood evidently had the strange notion that Thomas would either evacuate without fighting, or would be starved into a surrender by the cutting of his communications; and, therefore, that all he had to do was to make good his investment, and strike as he was able at the Louisville Railroad, *a la* Sherman at Jonesboro when aiming at Atlanta.

He singularly mistook his man. He forgot he was dealing with "The Rock of Chickamauga." A novice in warfare might have known Thomas better. His forces all in hand and his works well completed, with fair supplies of all kinds on hand and abundance of most, Thomas's once anxious brow had long since cleared thoroughly up; and it was now apparent to all, who happened much at headquarters, that "Old Pap Tom," as his soldiers were fond of calling him, prudent commander as he was, would soon be "spoiling for a fight!"

The battle of Nashville would have been delivered now, instead of later; for General Thomas was now fully ready. He was confident of his men, and knew his men to be confident of him; but one thing more was yet needed, to make his anticipated victory double sure, and that was cavalry.[1] He had plenty of cavalrymen, and tolerably good cavalrymen, too, but only about half enough horses; their animals having broken down and been used up in the hard campaign so far from Georgia and Alabama back into Tennessee, and others were not to be had anywhere, in the regular way, within the required time. To get them from the North, by purchase and requisition, might take a month or longer, and this would never do. So he issued an order to seize and impress all serviceable horses within our lines, in Tennessee and Kentucky,[2] at all hazards and whatever cost; leaving the government to settle for them afterward.

Within a week he had his dismounted cavalrymen remounted and ready for business. I think this "seizure" resulted in over seven thousand fresh horses, but I am not sure as to the exact figures. But Thomas, and Wilson, his chief of cavalry, I personally know, were greatly delighted to secure these "mounts."

Now, at last, General Thomas was ready and eager to move; but unluckily a heavy rain now set in, and Jack Frost happened along, and soon the whole Nashville hills were aglare with ice—impracticable for cavalry, artillery, and infantry alike.

"Both armies were ice-bound," said Thomas in his Report.[3] Neither man nor beast could now keep his feet, and so Thomas for some days yet was still further compelled to "nurse his wrath to keep it warm." Grant in the East, a thousand miles away, could not understand this, and impatient at what seemed Thomas's indecision and delay, telegraphed him repeatedly from

---

[1] *War Records*, vol. xlv, part ii, p. 17.
[2] He did this December 2. It was authorized by Secretary of War December 2, but ordered by Thomas before his authority arrived. *War Records*, vol. xlv, part ii, p. 29. See also *ibid.*, pp. 16-18.
[3] *War Records*, vol. xlv, part ii, pp. 114, 120, 155; also part i, p. 37.

City Point to attack Hood at once, with all his forces.[1] But Thomas, wary and wise, and understanding the situation better, answered back that he had done and was doing "everything in his power," and if dissatisfied they might relieve him, and if relieved he "would submit without a murmur." But he could not move against his judgment.[2]

Grant, well knowing Thomas's value, was reluctant to relieve him; but finally ordered Schofield to take command (December 9), and then, quickly repenting of it, suspended the order before it was issued.[3] But, growing more impatient, December 13, he ordered Logan West to take command at Nashville, and then questioning the wisdom of this too (as well he might), on December 14, he hastened himself to Washington *en route* to Nashville. But that very day a general thaw set in at Nashville, with evidence at sundown of an early break-up. Thomas at once issued his orders for attack on Thursday (December 15) at early dawn—the very day Grant arrived at Washington and Logan started for Louisville—and before nightfall of the same eventful day he had struck Hood a tremendous, if not fatal blow.

His plan of battle was simple, yet well matured, and will well bear consideration. The future historian, judging it by its rich results, will pronounce it superb. As I have said, the right of his line rested on the Cumberland, covered by gunboats, and extended thence in order as follows: Sixteenth Army Corps. Brevet Major General A. J. Smith commanding; Fourth Army Corps, Brigadier General Wood commanding; Twenty-third Army Corps, Major General Schofield commanding; and a provisional organization of white and colored troops, Major General Steedman commanding; thus

[1] *War Records*, vol. xlv, pp. 70, 97, 143, etc.; Grant's *Memoirs*, vol. ii, pp. 380, 382, etc.
[2] *War Records*, vol. xlv, part ii, pp. 114, 115.
[3] *Ibid.*, vol. xlv, part ii, pp. 114-116.

around to the Cumberland again—his left also covered by gunboats.[1] His plan was to demonstrate boldly on our left, where the enemy was strongest; while he in reality massed everything on the right, where the enemy was actually weakest, and thus with the gunboats covering to overwhelm Hood's left, mash in his line, and roll it back on the center, and, having thus got well upon his flank and rear, to crush his center too, if possible, as the result of his first day's work. This having been done, the job assigned for the second day was to smash Hood's right, and then either to envelop him with our victorious wings, or, at all events, to bruise and hammer him so roundly, that he would be glad to pull up stakes and hasten back to the Tennessee.

In pursuance of this plan, then, A. J. Smith was ordered to advance at daylight, December 15, his right covered by Wilson's cavalry, the gunboats also coöperating as required. Wood was ordered to leave only a heavy curtain of skirmishers in front of his works, to mass everything else compactly on Smith's left, and thus to hold himself in readiness to support Smith's attack, at a moment's notice. Schofield received like orders, but to mass instead on Wood's left, and to hold himself rather in reserve. Steedman, in addition to holding our extreme left, was also placed in charge of our inner line of works, with a force composed of the garrison proper of Nashville, Brigadier General Miller commanding; a provisional division of white and colored troops, Brigadier General Cruft commanding; and the Military Organization of the Quartermaster's Department, Brevet Brigadier General Donaldson commanding (with myself as adjutant general and chief of staff).[2]

In accordance with his orders, before dawn Steedman

---

[1] *War Records*, vol. xlv, part ii, p. 183.
[2] *Ibid.*, vol. lxxii, part i, Supplement, pp. 635, 688.

on our left developed a heavy line of skirmishers, consisting principally of excellent colored troops; and soon after daylight he pushed his line up to and across the Murfreesboro Pike. The enemy's pickets resisted stoutly; but presently fell back. Steedman pursued, until he came plump up against a Confederate battery, planted beyond a deep rocky cut of the Chattanooga Railroad—too long for his line to flank and impossible for it to cross. Not knowing this at first, his men eagerly charged the battery, and would probably have carried it, had not the deep cut aforesaid prevented them from reaching it. As it was, they fell back with considerable loss; but their attack had been so eager and vehement, that Hood was misled to believe that our whole army was there in force for our main attack, and proceeded to weaken his left accordingly, in order to reinforce his endangered right, as he supposed.

A fatal mistake, as he soon learned to his grievous cost. For, almost immediately, Thomas opened in full blast on our right; A. J. Smith, supported by Wood and covered by Wilson's cavalry, swept forward like an avalanche on Hood's enfeebled left; and almost before Hood knew we were advancing, we were upon him and over him, were crushing his line, storming his batteries, and flanking his positions. And in a trice, so to speak, his whole left wing was hopelessly doubled up and gone forever.

This let our cavalry loose; and now Wilson swept around and past our right like a thunderbolt. One division, under General Johnson, he sent down the Cumberland to look after the Confederate General Chalmers, and a battery there, which was duly taken; with the other two, Croxton's and Hatch's, he covered Smith's right and hung like an avenging cloud on the flank and rear of the Confederates, as they fell sullenly back on their center. Our infantry, indeed, here struck the Confederate left like a battering ram, while our cavalry turned and enveloped their extreme left, and threshed it as with a flail.

Hood now saw his mistake of the early morning, and from the heights about Nashville his long lines of infantry and artillery could be distinctly seen in the distance, hurrying over from his right to support his imperiled center. His position was still a strong one, stretching along the wooded sides and crests of a series of high hills, covered with breastworks, fringed with rifle pits and abattis, and bristling with cannon that swept all the sides and ravines; and Hood now bent all his energies to hold it to the last.

A. J. Smith, though brave as a lion, was too good a soldier to butt his brains out against such a position; and so he halted to reconnoiter and report. As the result of his observations, Wood was brought well up on Smith's left, and Schofield, who had hitherto been chafing in reserve, was moved out and swung around on Smith's right; while Wilson was pushed out still farther to the right, so as to outflank and gain the rear of Hood's new position, if he found it practicable. Hood's line was now thoroughly felt, by both artillery and infantry, from point to point, and though there were some successes here and there, yet Hood held his ground so stubbornly, that little was effected until just at nightfall, when Wood charged a battery that had been shelling his line much of the afternoon, and carried it with a rush in the handsomest style.

This closed our operations on the first day, and our troops bivouacked on the field thus so manfully won. Sixteen pieces of artillery and about two thousand prisoners were the fruits of this first day's work. Then Thomas rode home to his Nashville headquarters at dark, to telegraph to Washington and Grant that his movement had begun.

As he left the place he had occupied most of the day, he remarked to a staff officer:

"So far, I think we have done pretty well. Unless Hood decamps to-night, to-morrow Steedman will double up his right, Wood will hold his center, Smith and Schofield will again strike his left; while the cavalry work away at his rear."

His words had the prescience of a prophecy; for nearly this exact movement took place next day. Under cover of the night Hood drew back his right center and right, so as to straighten the new line he had been forced to assume, and on the morning of December 16 was found in position along the Overton Hills, some two miles or so to the rear of his original line.

It will be noticed, that Hood had thus shortened his line, by drawing in and concentrating his forces. He now planted himself squarely across the Granny White and Franklin Pikes to cover his trains, that were already fast hurrying to the rear. All his strong lines of works nearer Nashville, upon which he had bestowed a vast deal of labor and care, were thus wholly abandoned, because obviously untenable after the thorough smashing and turning of his left on Thursday (December 15), and it was soon evident to all, that his present stand was now only in desperation.

Indeed, everybody now felt that Hood was in fact already well whipped; and that, if let alone, he would of his own accord soon depart whence he came. But Thomas, sturdy old hero, had not the least idea of letting him alone! He had given "old Pap" too much trouble! And so, with the break of day, our skirmishers were up to and over and through Hood's old works. Thence our lines swept easily and steadily forward, on our center and left; until a thick curtain of Confederate skirmishers and the opening of their artillery warned us to halt and consider. Hood's new position, when reconnoitered, proved to be one of much strength, as already indicated, and had been selected and well fortified by him days before, in wary anticipation of all possible contingencies. For Hood was no fool, as proved by his fine record at Gettysburg and elsewhere.

His line on Thursday had been originally over six miles long; until his left was doubled up, or rather battered in, when it was reduced to about four. But here, on Friday, he occupied a line scarcely three miles in length, running along the wooded crests of closely connecting hills; and which even a better commander than Hood might well have regarded with complacency.

The two keys to his position were commanding elevations directly on and covering the Granny White and Franklin Pikes—two splendid roads leading to Franklin, Columbia, Pulaski, and so down the country to the Tennessee and Alabama. Both of these hills were admirably adapted for defense, as well by nature as by Hood's industrious axes and shovels. Here now the Confederates stood grimly at bay prepared to deliver a final battle, that was to decide for that war the fate of Tennessee and perhaps also of Kentucky.

If successful here, Hood could retire at his leisure, his trains intact, sweeping the country as he marched; or, for that matter, if he chose, could return to Nashville and try another bout with "the chuckle-headed Thomas" (as a Confederate general dubbed him, because of his obstinate fighting at Chickamauga); or, possibly, he might cross the Cumberland and make a dash at Louisville, and push the war back to the Ohio. On the other hand, if unsuccessful, his trains were menaced, his army endangered, Tennessee in effect lost; and a rapid retreat down the country and across the Tennessee into Alabama, with Thomas whacking and thundering at his heels, his only alternative.

A more prudent commander would have thought twice and hesitated long, before accepting such perilous chances. But Hood never was a prudent commander, although a gallant soldier, and Thomas now was only too glad to grapple with such an audacious adversary.

Accordingly, as indicated the night before, Thomas now at once pushed forward his left; and as Steedman advanced he found the Murfreesboro and Nolensville Pikes, as had been expected, comparatively free of the enemy. A few cavalrymen disputed his advance, here and there; but their resistance was feeble and practically amounted to nothing. As he came up to the Overton Hills, however, and stretched across to connect with Wood, the enemy opened on him with an advanced battery; and, in pursuance of his instructions, Steedman halted now and awaited orders.

Wood meanwhile had come up early on the Franklin Pike, and was now engaged in shelling the enemy's lines on Overton Knob; though meaning only to hold him in position there. Both he and Steedman, as yet, were acting only as foils; and they were both directed now to await the further development of movements off on the right. There, massed on or about the Granny White Pike and extending well to the right of it, were A. J. Smith and Schofield, with the Sixteenth and Twenty-third Corps, with Croxton and Hatch of Wilson's cavalry eagerly coöperating, feeling briskly all points of the enemy's position there; but unable as yet to discover the vulnerable point they desired.

The day thus wore on apace. Noon came, with but little valuable result, as yet. Smith and Schofield were both chafing, and eager to assault; confident of their ability to carry the opposing lines. But Thomas, as yet, refused his consent. He was not yet fully ready. He had sent the cavalry well around to our right, to gain Hood's flank and menace his rear; and he was still waiting to hear from them, before he launched at Hood's head these twin thunderbolts of war.[1]

Now, however, well on to four o'clock in the afternoon, news from our cavalry came suddenly, in a prolonged fire of carbines and rifles, that swept around Hood's left and crept up along his rear. Then the hour had struck and the time had come.

"Now tell Generals Schofield and Smith to advance," was Thomas's quiet order.

Away sped his aids, spurring like the wind. But before the order could reach either Smith or Schofield, they had both already caught the meaning of the fierce fire along the Confederate flank and rear; and, without waiting to hear from their imperturbable old chief, they both ordered a general assault; and, simultaneously, with leveled bayonets and ringing cheers, their lines swept superbly forward, up to and over and around the Confederate works; while Wood and Steedman on their left, catching up the inspiration, pressed gallantly forward. And almost before Hood had time to think (or swear) our general movement struck him like a cyclone, and carried all before it.

For a time, of course, there was hot work there. The whole Confederate line, from end to end, was ablaze with musketry and aroar with cannon. How those lovely Nashville hills did roar and quake with musketry and artillery, on both of those great historic days there—"a

---

[1] The query will doubtless occur to the reader: "*Where* was Forrest all this time?" The answer is: Hood had previously scattered his cavalry, a part being sent off down the Cumberland after our transports, where they accomplished little, and the rest on a raid around Murfreesboro, where they got well drubbed about the same time Hood was being pummelled on Thursday. Thomas, it was reported, knew of Forrest's absence, before ordering our attack.

part of which I was, and all of which I saw!" How the artillery went "Bang! Bang! Bang!" with shot and shell! How the grape and canister shrieked and whizzed! How the bullets went "Zip! Zip!" in perfect hailstorms at times!

How anybody there escaped alive seems a miracle now. On this second day, especially, the whole battlefield at times was like the grisly mouth of hell, agape and aflame with fire and smoke, and alive with thunder and death-dealing shots. The hills and slopes were strewn with the dead; the ravines and gorges crowded with the wounded. I saw men with their heads or limbs shot off; others with their bodies blown to pieces—only their limbs left. I rode by a tree on the Overton Knobs, behind which a Confederate had dodged for safety, and a Union shell had gone clear through both tree and soldier, and exploded among his comrades.

The actual conflict did not last long. In an hour or so it was mainly over, and what was left of the Confederates were in full retreat down the Franklin and Granny White Pikes, and so away for Dixie. Some few stood their ground bravely and fought desperately to the last, until killed or captured. But many abandoned their muskets, where they rested between the logs of their breastworks, and others threw muskets, knapsacks, blankets, everything aside that would impede their locomotion, as they fled wildly and panic-stricken away from the battlefield—"for Dixie's land, *away, away!*"

Said a captured Confederate brigadier general to me that evening, in speaking of this final Union charge and Confederate rout:

"Why, sir, it was the most wonderful thing I ever witnessed. I saw your men coming and held my fire—a full brigade, too—until they were in close range, we could almost see the 'whites of their eyes,' and then poured my volley right into their faces. I supposed, of course, when the smoke lifted, your line would be broken and your men gone. But, it is surprising, sir, it never even staggered them. Why, they did not even 'double-quick' or 'rush,' but right along, as cool as fate, your line swung up the hill, and your men marched right up to and over my works and around my brigade, before we knew they were upon us. It was astonishing, sir, such fighting. If I must say it, it was really splendid!"

'I thanked him for this hearty tribute to Yankee pluck and heroism, and proffered him some friendly cigars and my pocket-flask, both of which he accepted; and so we parted, he for the provost marshal's, and I for my command. Two other Confederate brigadiers, *en route* from the front to the rear as prisoners, dined with our mess that night on the field. We found them penniless, our boys having "gone through" them when captured, as usual on both sides. We tendered them loans, which they gratefully accepted; and, subsequently, when the was was over, they both repaid the money duly. Of course, after all, they were yet American soldiers and gentlemen.

But to return to the battle. As I have already indicated, General Hood's whole army, once so exultant and defiant, was now and here thus thoroughly routed. Over three thousand prisoners, including one major general, three brigadier generals, and over two hundred other officers, here threw down their arms, in addition to the killed and wounded. The day's work produced besides some forty pieces of artillery, many battle flags, and small arms almost innumerable. The total results of both days' battles footed up as follows: about five thousand prisoners, including one major general, four brigadier generals, nearly three hundred other officers, one headquarter wagon train, fifty-six pieces of artillery, many battle flags, killed and wounded by the thousands, and small arms and ammunition by the fieldful nearly.

Night did not close the conflict; but all night long of that second day and the next day and the next, for nearly two weeks, though it rained heavily and the roads became execrable, Thomas went hacking and whacking away at Hood's army with both cavalry and infantry (his fresh horses stood him in good stead now), as it retreated pell-mell through Tennessee into Alabama; and substantially wiped it out and destroyed it[1]—just as McClellan and Meade should have done with Lee's army after Antietam and Gettysburg, had they been built on the plan of George H. Thomas. For all military purposes, Hood's army was practically extinguished, and never figured as a fighting force seriously again during the war. It would have been completely eliminated, if not captured, had not Thomas's main pontoon train got on the wrong road, through a misunderstanding of his orders, and so reached Duck River twenty-four hours too late. Hood had destroyed the bridges there, and Thomas could not cross in pursuit, until his pontoons came up.

Indeed, Nashville was the cleanest and completest campaign and battle of our great Civil War on either side, as I think all military critics are now agreed, and it stamped Thomas henceforth as a really great commander. He had worked it all out like a problem in mathematics, and executed it like a fine piece of engineering; and Nashville is studied to-day as a model at West Point and Woolwich, at St. Cyr and Berlin.

His total operations against Hood, during November and December, including Franklin, Nashville, etc., re-

---
[1] See Appendix, pp. 373, 377.

sulted in thirteen thousand one hundred and eighty-nine prisoners of war, including seven general officers and nearly one thousand other officers of all grades, exclusive of killed and wounded, seventy-two pieces of serviceable artillery, and battle flags and small arms almost beyond mention. During the same period he received over two thousand Confederate deserters. Our own loss in killed, wounded, and missing, did not exceed ten thousand.[1]

Poor Hood! He was really an able and gallant soldier; and his army was incomparable—the same substantially that was pitted against Sherman all summer. But he ought to have known better than to butt his brains out against "The Rock of Chickamauga." It was like the whiffet against the mastiff, or the panther against the lion, or the tiger against the elephant. But I doubt if there was a single Confederate general, not excepting Longstreet and Joe Johnston, but perhaps excepting Robert E. Lee, who would have succeeded much better against glorious George H. Thomas.

Of course, General Logan halted at Louisville, when on his arrival there, on the morning of December 17, he got the news of Thomas's great battle; and, gifted eminently with common sense (as he certainly was), he returned quietly to Washington. Logan has been called "generous" and "magnanimous" for doing this, instead of proceeding on to Nashville and assuming command there; but, of course, he could do nothing else. Had he gone on to Nashville, President Lincoln would have quickly recalled him, and history would never have forgiven him—would have hooted him down the ages—for attempting to take the command from Thomas in the hour of his signal victories. Besides, Grant wired him

---

[1] *War Records*, vol. xlv, part ii, p. 46.

to come back; and moreover his original orders were to do nothing, "if Thomas had moved."[1]

As it was, Stanton hastened to telegraph Thomas his hearty congratulations, and ordered a salute of one hundred guns by all our armies. Grant did the same, but ordered two hundred shotted guns instead; and they were fired with a will all up and down our lines in front of Petersburg, amidst the music of our bands and the hurrahs of our rejoicing soldiers. And Meade and Sheridan did the same.[2] But Sherman was a little *in laches* here. It is true, in his *Memoirs* (Vol. II, page 219) he says, that "upon receiving official information of the victory" he, through his chief of staff, General Webster, "wrote Thomas congratulating him in the highest terms;" but the letter in question hardly bears this out. However, he said "Thomas gave Hood a good whaling," and in a special field order declared it to be "an achievement that entitles it to a place in the military history of the world."[3]

Congress also gave him a vote of thanks, and Mr. Lincoln shortly afterward promoted him Major General U. S. A. (December 24—a Christmas gift!)[4] Of course, this was some solace and satisfaction to Thomas. But I think he never quite forgave Grant for sending Logan to relieve him, when he was doing his whole duty at Nashville.

While modest and unassuming beyond most men, Thomas was also conscious of his own great qualities, and knew that as a commander he was head and shoulders above Logan, or any other volunteer officer. So, when his commission as Major General U. S. A. reached him, while in pursuit of Hood, according to an officer present, he cast it aside in his tent with the remark: "I earned that a year ago at Chattanooga;" alluding to Sherman's promotion

[1] *War Records*, vol. xlv, part ii, pp. 230-264; also, Grant's *Memoirs*, vol. ii, pp. 382, 383.
[2] See Appendix, p. 371; also pp. 372-375.
[3] *War Records*, vol. xliv, pp. 738 and 17.   [4] See Appendix, pp. 376, 377.

## George H. Thomas

there over his head, which he never quite forgave either. I saw much of General Thomas during all this Nashville campaign and afterward (1865-66). He was an upright Christian gentleman, as well as great soldier. And a purer patriot, or nobler officer, or worthier American, this republic has not yet produced, since the days of George Washington.[1]

Perhaps I may add, without immodesty, Nashville made me a full colonel (thanks to General Thomas and Andrew Johnson), though my commission did not reach me until May following. "But that is another story," as Kipling would say!

---

[1] See Appendix, p. 371.

## CHAPTER VIII

### WILLIAM TECUMSEH SHERMAN

My next commander was General Sherman; or, rather, I also served under him while serving with Thomas—the one commanding the other.

I first met Sherman personally not long after our momentous victory at Chattanooga (November 25, 1863), when he came up to Nashville to discuss and settle the great campaign of 1864 with General Grant. Later (March, 1864) Grant became commander in chief of all our armies and went to Washington, and Sherman became his successor in the Military Division of the Mississippi, embracing all of the United States from the Alleghanies to the Rocky Mountains.

General Sherman was then in the prime of life—a tall, brisk, wiry man; with dark reddish hair, inclining to baldness; sharp blue eyes, kindly as a rule, but cold and hard as steel sometimes; an aggressive, fighting nose and mouth; considerable of a jaw; and a face a mass of wrinkles. I have his photograph still, taken at his headquarters in the spring of 1864, which is so full of wrinkles he ordered it suppressed. But I begged it of his photographer and preserved it, because so faithful and lifelike, and present an engraving of it.

Habitually he wore a Western slouch hat, with a simple gold cord around it, and a rusty blue uniform indicative of his rank (Major General U. S. A.); but with his coat open and the lapels buttoned back. Indeed, this was the first thing that struck me on meeting both Grant and Sherman; they hardly ever wore their coats buttoned up to the throat; whereas our Eastern generals (McClellan, Hook-

Gen. Sherman, 1864.

er, Meade, etc.) hardly ever wore theirs otherwise. In campaigning he usually wore only a simple blouse, but with his proper shoulder straps, of course. Like Hooker, he was noted for his high shirt collars, and also like him, was distinguished for his "gamey" qualities at all times and everywhere. He impressed you at once as a keen, wide-awake man of affairs, with a mind and will of his own; bookish, but greater than his books; a master of his profession; alert, decided, far-sighted; knowing well what was needed, and resolute to do it, and also resolved everybody about and under him should know and do the same. I think he had absolutely no patience with incompetence or imbecility, and a harder man for a humbug to impose upon or a coward to deceive never breathed.

Like all our great commanders on both sides, of course, he was a West Pointer, *ex necessitate;* for education tells everywhere, but nowhere more than in "War Days." Bravery—mere brute courage—is not an uncommon quality among men. Said General Sir Henry Havelock: "In my experience, in any British regiment there are always a hundred men who would storm the gates of hell; eight hundred who, if they did, would follow in; one hundred who want to skulk in the ditches; and about thirty who do skulk there or elsewhere." But military brains—a natural aptitude for arms and the best culture West Point can give him—that is what an army commander needs, and Sherman was well dowered in that way. He was a native of Ohio, and came from good parentage there. Like all (or nearly all) who rose to prominence during the civil war, on both sides, he served in the Mexican War, but only in California, where he distinguished himself as a quartermaster and commissary merely, there being no fighting worth mentioning there.

Afterward he resigned from the army, and failed as a banker in San Francisco and as a lawyer at Leavenworth

—evidently having few gifts that way. When Sumter was fired upon (April, 1861) he was superintendent of a State Military Academy down in Louisiana, on a comfortable salary, but promptly resigned, with the frank and manly declaration:

"On no earthly account will I do any act or think any thought hostile to or in defiance of the old Government of the United States."[1]

Aided by his great brother, Hon. John Sherman, then and long afterward United States Senator from Ohio (also Secretary of the Treasury and Secretary of State), he was early appointed Colonel of the Thirteenth United States Infantry (he had been previously offered the "chief clerkship" of the War Department!),[2] and served with credit at our first Bull Run, July 21, 1861, commanding a brigade there. Soon afterward he was appointed brigadier general of volunteers, and ordered to Kentucky, August 24, 1861, and here took such large views of the rebellion, and of the force required to subdue it in the West, that the then Secretary of War (Cameron) thought him "insane," and relieved him of his command.[3] His estimate was that we needed two hundred thousand men to conquer and hold the Southwest; but subsequently, in 1864, he himself commanded over three hundred and fifty thousand men there.

However, events soon convinced the government of his thorough sanity; and April 6, 1862, found him at Shiloh or Pittsburg Landing, under Grant, in command of our advance division there. Here he suffered severely (I think was really surprised, though he would never admit that, technically); but fought gallantly and skillfully, and on the whole did much to retrieve our hard fortunes there. Next he campaigned with Grant down the Mississippi and

---
[1] See Appendix, p. 380.   [2] Sherman's *Memoirs*, vol. i, p. 170.
[3] Sherman's *Memoirs*, vol. i, pp. 214, 216, 217.

around Vicksburg (1862-63), and though not always successful, yet he won and deserved the full trust and confidence of that incomparable soldier. It is not true, that he "protested" against Grant's final campaign against Vicksburg. It is true he criticised it, and submitted his criticism, as he himself told me. But he also pledged his hearty and loyal support, and gave it unreservedly.

When, after the disastrous field of Chickamauga, Grant was summoned to Chattanooga—to take chief command there and smash Bragg, if possible—Sherman was at Memphis, but on orders from Grant gathered up all his Army of the Tennessee that could be spared, and hastened overland to Chattanooga by way of Eastport and Huntsville. He took the railroad, as far as it went, absorbing all its cars and locomotives, and then proceeded by forced marches eastward, at times mounting part of his men on horses and mules—did everything to speed his column to Chattanooga—arriving there in advance of the time anticipated, much to the delight of General Grant. It was such loyalty and devotion as this, without an atom of envy or jealousy, that endeared Sherman to the heart of his great chief, and it was no wonder that henceforth Grant trusted him absolutely and affectionately. Sherman well knew the value of *time*, and never wasted it—an item of prime importance in military affairs.

In the great operations that soon followed at Chattanooga (November 25, 1863) Sherman commanded our left wing; and crossing the Tennessee on pontoon bridges in the night, he attacked Bragg's right next day with vigor and fire. It is true he did not succeed in crushing it, as intended, because of the unknown and unfavorable features of the field there chiefly. But he attacked gallantly and skillfully, achieving important results; and, on the whole, it must be conceded, managed his part of affairs at Chattanooga with signal ability and credit. Immediately

—straight from the battlefield, hot from the pursuit of Bragg, without waiting to return to Chattanooga for their blankets and overcoats even, though cold and inclement weather had set in—his column set out for the relief of Knoxville, and by forced marches reached there just in time to save Burnside from Longstreet. Gordon Granger was ordered there first, because freshest and nearest to the line of march. But he was so slow in getting off, and grumbled so much, that Grant relieved him, and ordered Sherman instead "to assume command of all the forces now moving up the Tennessee;" and so saved the day at Knoxville. This was a piece of loyal and brilliant service that thrilled the country through and through at the time, and was never forgotten by President Lincoln; for Union-loving East Tennessee, with its "plain people," was always near and dear to his patriotic heart.

Said Sherman in his official report: "Of course, we had no provisions save what we gathered by the road, and were ill supplied for such a march. But we learned that twelve thousand of our fellow-soldiers were beleaguered in the mountain town of Knoxville, eighty-four miles distant; that they needed relief, and must have it in three days. This was enough—and it had to be done." How just like Sherman this reads now!

When Grant was ordered East to assume command of all our armies (March 3, 1864), doubtless he found it difficult to choose his successor in the West, as he well knew the great merits of both Sherman and Thomas. But as he knew Sherman better, had "summered and wintered" with him at Vicksburg and elsewhere, had seen his very heart and soul, indeed, and felt he could trust him all through, whatever happened, naturally he selected Sherman. It is certain Thomas did not like this, was much aggrieved thereby; as he then outranked Sherman, and commanded the Army of the Cumberland, a larger and more important command than Sherman's Army of the Tennessee. But he loyally "obeyed orders," nevertheless, and continued on in the service, the same sturdy patriot and gallant soldier as before (a good example for the Methodist preacher, who thinks he ought to be stationed at Jerusalem, but gets set down at Jericho instead).

Now came the great and memorable spring of 1864, with Grant commanding in the East and Sherman in the West; both resolved on victory, and *believing they could achieve it.* They had agreed to time their operations so as to give the Confederates no chance to reinforce anywhere. I heard Sherman myself say to the senior and supervising quartermaster at Nashville (General Donaldson) the day he left there for Chattanooga (about April 28):

"I am going to move on Joe Johnston the day General Grant telegraphs me he is going to hit Bobby Lee; and if you don't have my army supplied, and keep it supplied, we'll eat your mules up, sir—eat your mules up!"

Fortunately, he was not reduced to such rations; but it well shows his loyalty and spirit.[1]

His Atlanta campaign was a series of brilliant maneuvers and skillful battles that, I venture to say, alone will enroll him among the great masters of the military art forever. It was his first really independent command, and he conducted it magnificently. His strategy, it must be admitted, on the whole was faultless, and his tactics superb. It is true he outnumbered Johnston—his movable column averaged about ninety thousand, against Johnston's fifty thousand to seventy-five thousand; but then he was on the offensive and in the heart of the enemy's country, groping his way over rocky mountains and through wooded valleys, and with his army widely dispersed, while Johnston was on the defensive, at home, concentrated and

---

[1] He said the same afterward in substance. "If the worst came to the worst, we could live several months on the mules and horses of our trains." Sherman's *Memoirs*, vol. ii. p. 272.

largely fortified—a big and weighty difference in warfare. It is true, he did no heavy and serious fighting, except at Kenesaw Mountain and Peach Tree Creek; but that was because he believed in flanking more than battles, as Alexander, Napoleon, and every great commander always has. It is certain he never doubted his ability to take Atlanta; and all the cavalry raids, burning of railroad bridges, etc., in his rear never seriously disturbed him.

It was my good fortune to spend a day or two with him, on his lines in front of Atlanta, in August, 1864, about a fortnight before Atlanta fell; and he was then as "cool as a cucumber," notwithstanding the nervousness and apprehension prevailing throughout the North. He said he was only waiting, patiently as he could, for the extension and completion of his lines; and in due time "Atlanta will fall into our hands like a ripe apple." He sent his chief of artillery (General Barry, an old Army of the Potomac friend of mine) to show me his siege guns and batteries. We rode along the line amidst a perfect sprinkle of shells and bullets, at times. At one point, a mile or so from Atlanta, and about the same distance from Sherman's headquarters, a Confederate shell exploded in one of our batteries, literally knocking the right arm off an artilleryman near us—mortally wounding him, of course, and disabling several others. Our battery gallantly replied. The sharpshooters on each side from the rifle pits joined in the music. Soon the Confederate fire grew so warm—shells exploding at point-blank range, and Minie balls whizzing and buzzing about us like bees—that Barry suggested we had no business there, as we "were only sightseers!" and, therefore, would get no credit if we got killed or wounded! Had we been "on duty" or "under orders," of course we would have seen it out. So we retired presently through a ravine, and inspected another battery beyond the enemy's fire, from which we ourselves trained and sighted one of our largest siege guns, and sent our compliments into Atlanta in the shape of a Union shell. With a glass I could see it explode, and the people in the streets there scatter and run—which was as near as I got to the Confederate stronghold itself.

Returning to Sherman's headquarters, I accepted his invitation to dinner, which consisted chiefly of hardtack, bacon, sweet potatoes, and black coffee, served on a rough board table, evidently the recent handiwork of some camp carpenter, from a United States clothing box. For chairs we had rickety camp stools and United States cracker boxes. His headquarters consisted of tent-flies for himself and staff, and one or two wall tents for offices. His uniform was a gray flannel shirt, an old blue blouse, faded and weather-stained, and a pair of military trousers that apparently had done duty from Chattanooga down, if not much before. We spent but little time at dinner; as there was not much to eat, and he was too occupied and busy.

Retiring to his tent-fly, he produced a handful of cigars from somewhere, and, lighting one himself, smoked and talked incessantly while giving orders to officers coming and going, or dictating telegrams, letters, etc. With all his hard campaigning and awful responsibility, he was still bright and "chipper," alert and confident as when he left Nashville, if not more so. But while he talked much and interestingly of his past campaign, he was close as a mouse about the future. He was chiefly anxious about the state of his supplies—rations, clothing, ammunition, etc.—and ordered larger accumulations of these at Chattanooga and Nashville. But never a word or hint escaped him about Savannah, though doubtless his great march there was simmering in his mind, if not clear and definite.

While there, his three great subordinates, Generals Thomas, Schofield, and Howard, commanding the Armies of the Cumberland, the Ohio, and the Tennessee, respectively, called and held a consultation with him. It was easy to see that he held them all in high esteem and regard, as they did him. They were a fine sight to see—all great and distinguished soldiers—but Sherman easily dominated them all. His keen intelligence, incisive speech, prompt decision, and determined will readily made him chief everywhere.

Returning to Nashville, we just escaped capture by a division of Confederate cavalry, under Wheeler, off on a "raid." They waylaid and pursued our train all the way from Marietta to Dalton; but luckily we escaped, and got through to Chattanooga all right—the last train through for nearly a fortnight. This was on Sunday, August 14, 1864. We bade good-bye to Sherman on the evening of the thirteenth, and crossing the Chattahoochie ran up to Marietta; and here lay by until next morning, because of reports of Confederate raiders. We had a train-guard of fifty men or so, but Sherman advised us not to travel at night, and to proceed cautiously. He said we might get through all right, but the chances were "ticklish," and we would be safer to stop with him, until Wheeler was heard from more definitely. However, as our business with Sherman was over and we had been absent from Nashville longer than we anticipated, and knew we were needed there, we decided to start and push through, if possible.

Accordingly, after halting at Marietta Saturday night, we left there early Sunday morning, and ran cautiously along, feeling our way from station to station, until an hour or so after sunrise, when we discovered the track ahead of us on fire and the rails torn up. Of course, we slowed down and reconnoitered things carefully, and then moved cautiously ahead; when we found that a squad of Confederates had left there but a few minutes before. They had dashed in, cut the telegraph wire, tore up the railroad track, piled fence rails on it, and set the whole on fire; and then quickly decamped. We were told there was a regiment of them, with two pieces of artillery, a mile or two away, moving north; that they had already "gobbled up" a herd of two thousand cattle *en route* to the front, and were now after the railroad, and would be only too happy to "gobble" us also. This was not a very encouraging prospect for Sunday morning. We would have preferred being somewhere North, within the sound of any kind of "church-going bells" instead.

However, with some railroad men and tools we had along with us, we roughly repaired the road in an hour or so, and then ran slowly on for two or three miles farther, when again we found the rails torn up and the track all ablaze. The fence rails were piled up here prodigiously, for a hundred yards or so. But we had come upon the rascals so suddenly that they had only time to set fire to a portion, when they had to cut and run; and we saw them in the distance galloping "over the hills and far away." When we got the flames extinguished here and the fence rails removed, we found two of the iron rails gone, and of course could not proceed without these. The Johnnies had taken them up and hidden them, so as to make our delay and consequent capture sure. Hunting around, we found one of the rails secreted in a cornfield near by, but could not discover the other, and had to send a part of our men a mile back down the road till they found a spare rail and brought it forward.

By this time—along toward noon now—the chase began to be exciting. MacCallum[1] thought it was all up with us; but I bore it as philosophically as I could, resolved to see the thing out anyhow. The day was intensely hot, and we had put on light clothing in the morning; but we now removed this, and put on our heaviest woolen cloth-

---

[1] Gen. MacCallum, General Superintendent U. S. Military Railroads, Washington, D. C., my companion.

ing, so as to be better prepared for "roughing it," if captured; and also concealed our watches, money, etc. Our train-guard was well commanded by a plucky lieutenant, and we determined to fight it out, if attacked, if the Johnnies did not outnumber us too largely.

Having repaired the road again, we passed slowly on, hearing of small parties of Confederates near every station nearly; but were unmolested by any, until we reached Dalton about five o'clock in the afternoon. As we ran into the station there we saw the women and children scurrying about the streets, and the "contrabands" gathered in groups, and evidently greatly excited. The garrison, half a thousand strong, were marching up the hill and into their earthworks, and an unknown colonel on horseback (their commandant) hailed us and wanted to know where we came from. Suddenly, before we could reply, a shower of bullets came whizzing about the station, and another officer rode frantically up and reported that the head of Wheeler's cavalry had just struck Dalton and summoned it to surrender.

MacCallum and I "did not see it" just in that light. We held a brief "council of war," and decided Dalton was not a desirable place to halt in. We found the telegraph and railroad still working through to Chattanooga (thirty-eight miles distant), and we told the Dalton commandant to hold out, and we would rush into Chattanooga and send him back reinforcements. MacCallum himself, an old railroad man and a brave and determined officer, jumped upon the engine, and, getting up all possible steam, we thundered into Chattanooga at the rate of forty miles an hour, and soon had two thousand men and a battery of artillery on their way back to Dalton, where they arrived in time to repulse Wheeler and send his column flying.

Altogether it was rather an exciting Sunday, and I did not care to be quite so near being "gobbled" by the Johnnies again during the war. At Chattanooga they had us reported as captured sure, and a mile or two of track torn up, bridges burned, etc.; and I found a very alarming telegram from Nashville inquiring anxiously about us. The same night I sent a full report by telegraph, which was duly forwarded to Washington as the latest and most authentic news from Sherman and Atlanta, and gave much satisfaction there, comforting the hearts of both Stanton and Lincoln.

The next day we ran up to Nashville, and got through safely. The same day, or the next, Wheeler swept around Chattanooga, and crossing the Tennessee struck the railroad and broke it up so thoroughly that our train was the last one through, as I have said, for a fortnight or thereabouts.

This did not disconcert General Sherman, however, or tempt him to raise the siege of Atlanta. He had sagaciously foreseen all such "raids" before moving out from Chattanooga, and provided for them. He kept ten days' rations constantly in his wagons, and had a railroad construction corps of two thousand men always on hand, ready to repair his roads and rebuild his bridges; and days before his rations were exhausted his locomotives were again tooting across the Chattahoochie and well into his camps.

And so, notwithstanding all Joe Johnston and Hood could do (both gallant men and able commanders), Atlanta was doomed. Little by little, step by step, Sherman closed upon it, with his remorseless grip. At last, on September 2, 1864, he rejoiced President Lincoln and thrilled the country through and through with the characteristic telegram: "Atlanta is ours, and fairly won!"

With the fall of Atlanta he resolved to cut loose from everything and march down to the sea; and thus prove to the world that the Confederacy was only an eggshell after all. He was somewhat undecided at first whether to move on Savannah or Mobile, but finally resolved on Savannah. Of his great march there, and capture of Savannah, and tender of it as a "Christmas gift" to Mr. Lincoln, with two hundred and fifty cannon and thirty thousand bales of cotton (besides lesser booty), and his subsequent marvelous march through the Carolinas—along railroads, across rivers, through swamps and forests—and the final surrender to him at Raleigh of Joe Johnston and the Southern Confederacy, I can only say a word or two here. I make bold to say that it was as gallant and scientific a piece of soldiering as any general ever conceived or executed. He reduced his army to sixty thousand men, double-horsed his batteries, reorganized his cavalry, put twenty days' rations in his wagons, took beef along "upon the hoof," and then bidding good-bye to Lincoln and Grant, swung clear of his base at Atlanta and plunged into the heart of Georgia, resolved to forage upon the enemy—first taking the precaution, however, to study the United States Census Reports (shrewd soldier that he was), and thus ascertain the population and resources of every county he was to pass through. How well, how intrepidly, he did all this; how skillfully he concealed his movements; how gallantly he defeated all opposing forces; how resolutely he overcame every obstacle; and at last how magnificently, how gloriously he conquered—all this is now matter of history, and will constitute one of the brightest pages in American history for ages to come.[1]

His whole march, through the very heart of the Confederacy, was over one thousand miles long—extending over half a continent nearly—surpassing in many respects even Napoleon's great march on Moscow. Napoleon's ended in disaster and ruin; but no such fate befell our American gamecock—William Tecumseh Sherman—

---

[1] See Appendix, pp. 380, 381.

though often predicted by Jefferson Davis and his friends, South and North. Had Lee not surrendered in advance, Sherman meant, of course, duly to shake hands with Grant in front of Petersburg, and the two together—it goes without saying—would unquestionably have made quick work of that distinguished Virginian—fine soldier as he was.

After such multiplied and illustrious services ("the like of which is not read of in past history," as General Grant deliberately wrote),[1] it is no wonder Sherman was astounded at Mr. Stanton's reprimand for his terms to Johnston. Of course, Sherman erred in these, but it was on the side of generosity and magnanimity, as might have been expected of him, the war being over. Fortunately Grant,

"Greatest captain of them all,
Rich in saving common sense,"

was on hand to set things straight, protecting his great lieutenant, of course, as he was bound and sure to do. But Sherman never forgave Stanton, and I think history will excuse his just wrath and righteous indignation when he disdained to recognize him at our "Great Review" a few weeks afterward—War Secretary though he was.

I never saw Sherman again, after parting with him in front of Atlanta, until September, 1866, when we met in Colorado, both on tours of inspection there. Then we joined "outfits," and campaigned together for nearly a month along and through the Rocky Mountains, inspecting Kit Carson and the Ute Indians, exploring the vast "parks" there, camping out at night by some quiet lake or foaming torrent, and building high our camp fires from the fallen pines and cedars there. He was a prodigious talker and smoker, and stretched upon his blankets before the fire, with a cigar between his teeth or fingers, often

---

[1] Grant's *Memoirs*, vol. ii, p. 589.

talked half the night away. What great days and nights those were beneath the shadow or in the very heart of those mighty mountains! How he discussed his great comrades—Grant, Thomas, McPherson, Sheridan, etc.—and their great campaigns and battles together, or Lee, Johnston, Hood, and the rest; and what a flood of light he poured upon them all! Or, turning aside to other times, he would rattle away about Alexander, Cæsar, Napoleon, Cromwell, Wellington, and Washington, and their campaigns; and roam over the whole field of ancient and modern wars with keen eye and incisive tongue. Would we had had a stenographer there to take it all down, and a typewriter now to write it out! As a rule, he was the last one to sleep and the first one to awake, tending camp fires faithfully, and seemed literally never to tire of talking and smoking.

Altogether General Sherman was certainly a great and brilliant American, of original and striking genius, and made his mark deep and broad upon his times. He was the soul of honor, of spotless integrity, a royal friend, and a knightly gentleman. Clearly he was a born soldier; more showy than Meade or McClellan, less popular than Hooker or Rosecrans, not so safe, perhaps, as Thomas, but unquestionably a greater commander than either; and, I submit, one of the greatest masters of the art of war that ever lived. The nation certainly owes him a debt of gratitude that never can be paid. As the great companion and friend of Lincoln and Grant, his place in history is secure forever. Lincoln loved him, and Grant trusted him as "the other half of his own soul." And what more can I say?

Having mentioned "Kit Carson" above, our great American explorer and Indian fighter, it may not be amiss to add that he and Sherman were old friends. We visited him at Fort Garland, Colorado, and accompanied him to a council with the Ute Indians on the head-waters of the Rio Grande, in San Luis Park. "Kit" was then colonel of a regiment of New Mexicans and brevet brigadier general of United States Volunteers. When the Rebellion broke out, and most of our United States troops were ordered East, "Kit" applied to President Lincoln for permission to raise a regiment of New Mexico Volunteers; and he had done excellent service with it against the Indians. On one occasion he had taken nine thousand Navajoes prisoners, with less than six hundred of his men. At the close of the war he was ordered to Fort Garland and given command of a wide region there.

We found him in log quarters, rough but comfortable, and with his New Mexican wife and half-breed children around him. I had expected to see a small and wiry man, weather-beaten and reticent; but met a medium-sized, rather stoutish, florid, and quite talkative person instead. He certainly bore the marks of exposure, but none of that extreme "roughing it" that I had anticipated. In age, he seemed to be about forty-five. His head was a remarkably good one, with the organs of benevolence and reflections well developed. His eye was mild and blue, the very type of good nature, while his voice was as soft and sympathetic as a woman's. He impressed you at once as a man of rare courtesy and charity, such as a brave man ought always to be. As simple as a child, but brave as a lion, he soon took our hearts by storm, and grew upon our regard all the while we were with him. He talked and smoked homemade cigarettes (folding them himself as he talked) far into the night each evening we were there, and I have no room here for a tithe of what he said. In talking, I noticed, he frequently hesitated for the right English word—he had been so much among the Indians and Mexicans. But when speaking bastard Spanish (Mexican) or Indian he was as fluent as a native. Both

Spanish and Indian, however, are largely pantomime, which may have helped him along somewhat. The Utes seemed to have the greatest possible confidence in him, and invariably called him simply "Kit."

"These redskins," said Sherman, "think Kit twice as big a man as me. Why, his integrity is simply perfect. The Utes know it, and they would believe him and trust him any day before me!"

Kit returned this confidence by being their steadfast and unswerving friend.

The head chief of the Utes then was Ooray, who afterward proved himself to be a veritable Logan or Red Jacket of the Rocky Mountains. He was a medium-sized, athletic-looking man of about forty, with as fine an eye and head as you will see anywhere. Moreover, he was neat and clean in his person, as if he believed in the saving virtues of soap and water—something remarkable for a redskin. In manner he was dignified, in speech acute and sagacious, and he prided himself even then on being "a friend to the white man."

We spent several days and nights with Kit Carson and the Utes, and Sherman seemed to enjoy the time hugely, as a schoolboy let loose. He threw off all reserve as general of the Army, and entered fully into the life of the pioneer and Indian. He asked a thousand questions of everybody, and was never at a loss for a story or a joke, and added to the effect of these by the twinkle of his eye, the toss of his head, and the serio-comic twitch of his many-wrinkled features, in a way indescribable. Meanwhile he smoked constantly, and kept up that everlasting long stride of his up and down the floor or ground, with his hands deep in his trousers pockets, as if he would never weary. Beyond doubt, he was a great man and original thinker in many ways, and deservedly has taken his place in the American Valhalla.

Gen. Sheridan, 1864.

Philip H. Sheridan

## CHAPTER IX
### PHILIP H. SHERIDAN

IT was not my fortune to serve under General Sheridan, but I saw something of him, and came to esteem him very highly. He also was a West Pointer, and an Ohioan like Sherman; but was too young to have served in Mexico. He had distinguished himself, however, in our Indian troubles in Texas, Oregon, and Washington prior to the war.

In the autumn of 1861 he was ordered East from the Pacific coast at his own request for active duty against the Rebellion. In December, 1861 (being then captain of the Thirteenth United States Infantry), he reported to General Halleck at St. Louis, and was assigned to duty as chief quartermaster and chief commissary of the Army of Southwest Missouri. Of course, this did not last long. He was too "gamey" and mettlesome a man for such routine staff duties, though he knew much about horses, mules, wagons, rations, etc., and in due time—as naturally as water runs or grass grows—became colonel of the Second Michigan Cavalry, and was ordered to the Army of the Tennessee (May, 1862), then before Corinth, Miss.

Here, by changes and promotions incident to active service, he soon became commander of a brigade of cavalry, and handled it so well that in July, 1862, he was appointed brigadier general on the recommendation of his associate and superior officers, and in September, 1862, was transferred to the Army of the Cumberland, then operating in Kentucky, and assigned to an infantry division there. By steady drill and discipline he soon got this into excellent shape, and at the battle of Stone River or

Murfreesboro, Tenn. (December, 1862), he fought it with gallantry and skill, and certainly shared with Thomas and Hazen the honors of that bloody field—such as they were. For his good conduct here he was presently and rightly appointed major general of volunteers.

From Murfreesboro to Chickamauga (September, 1863) he served ably and creditably. But at Chickamauga, in the whirl and confusion of the chaotic conflict there—at best a dubious battle, which just escaped being an awful Union defeat—he lost his head, like Rosecrans and others, and fell back when he ought to have advanced, or at least have held his ground like the sturdy Thomas. However, this was amply atoned for by his general good conduct there and elsewhere, and in the titanic conflict at Chattanooga (November 25, 1863) he led in the grand assault on Missionary Ridge, under the immediate eye of Thomas and Grant, and conducted his attack so skillfully and spiritedly—with such alacrity and celerity—that Grant at once marked him for his own.

Hence, in the spring of 1864, when Grant assumed general charge of the Army of the Potomac, and was casting about for a new chief of cavalry there, his mind settled down on Sheridan, and "Little Phil" was promptly ordered East. He was then in East Tennessee, but he hastened to Washington by way of Chattanooga and Nashville, and while elated to go East and serve with Grant, was full of regret at parting with Thomas and Sherman—and especially with his old division. His officers and men spontaneously assembled at the station to see him off, and as his train rolled out they waved him farewell with every demonstration of sorrow and affection.[1]

He was then, I think, the youngest and certainly the smallest major general in the service. He had just passed

---
[1] Sheridan's *Memoirs*, vol. i, p. 340.

## Philip H. Sheridan

thirty-three years of age, was five feet five inches high, and weighed only a hundred and fifteen pounds. He was thin even to emaciation, and on first glance looked more like a lieutenant or a cadet than a major general. But a second glance gave better and more assurance. He had dark grayish-blue eyes, that looked right through you; a fighting nose and face; short neck, dark hair; was quick and energetic in his movements, full of confidence and conceit —in short, was the beau ideal of a fighting Irish-American of the better sort. He impressed you as an officer who would charge a square, or storm a battery, or shoot a deserter, or drink a cup of coffee (or something stronger) with equal *sang-froid*. But withal, there was little of the braggadocio or swashbuckler about him. He could be stern and dignified, as well as jolly and vivacious, and while everybody called him "Little Phil" (and he liked the patronymic,) his friends West, in bidding him good-by and Godspeed, confidently predicted that before the war closed he would "make a spoon or spoil a horn" somewhere East.

He assumed command of the cavalry corps of the Army of the Potomac May 5, 1864, and immediately began to reorganize and consolidate it. Heretofore it had been largely dispersed in outpost, picket, and guard duty; but he aimed to hold it in hand as one body, and swing it as a saber or a thunderbolt when needed.

With the opening of the Wilderness campaign events moved rapidly, and he soon began to show what stuff there was in him. Jeb Stuart, Lee's crack cavalry commander (and a splendid one he was), had been making trouble, as usual, the previous two years, when he rode around the Army of the Potomac and raided pretty much *ad libitum* (*vide* the Antietam and Gettysburg campaigns); and Meade and Sheridan were in consultation about him and his doings.

"Suppose you let me try my hand on him," suggested Sheridan.

Meade, tall and gray-bearded, from his greater height looked down on "Little Phil," and answered in his cautious way:

"You had better let Jeb Stuart alone! He is a dangerous man to fool with!"

This nettled Sheridan, and he hotly replied:

"O, bother Jeb Stuart! I know him well, and can whip him to pieces, if you will only let me!"

Meade reported this to Grant, and that great commander wisely and characteristically decided instantly:

"Did Sheridan say that? Well, then, let him go out and do it!"[1]

And the very next day Sheridan was off, and rode around Lee's right, and rode straight after Stuart until he found him in the environs of Richmond, and in less than a week smashed his redoubtable horsemen and killed Stuart himself, destroying the prestige of the Confederate cavalry forever. Then, shrewdly avoiding Richmond and eluding the forces sent in pursuit of him, he made a wide detour to the White House, crossed the Pamunkey on a broken-down railroad bridge there, which he had quickly repaired, and in a fortnight after leaving was back again by the side of Grant, ready for another blow, having severed most of Lee's important railroads and destroyed a vast amount of *materiel* and supplies. Doubtless Grant keenly enjoyed this as an object lesson to the Army of the Potomac as well as to Lee, and as an example to our Eastern cavalry chiefs especially.

Subsequently, early in June, Sheridan rode around Lee's left, and fought his cavalry and infantry at Trevillian, on the Virginia Central Railroad; breaking the road and seriously damaging Lee's communications and sup-

---

[1] Sheridan's *Memoirs*, vol. i, pp. 368, 369.

plies, and, drawing the Confederate cavalry off in that direction, thus opened the way for Grant's advance to the James.

Grant's Wilderness campaign as a whole, it must be confessed, was bloody and disappointing. But he had grimly made up his mind "to fight it out on that line, if it took all summer," and pluckily stuck to it, as he ought to have done. About the middle of June he crossed the James and sat down before Petersburg, holding Lee as in a vise, but unable to compel his surrender.

Secure within his marvelous lines, Lee soon began to play his old game of menacing Washington, by way of the Shenandoah Valley, hoping thus to induce Grant to relax his hold or finally to retire like McClellan. But this time he mistook his adversary. Grant retained his deathlike grip on Petersburg; but, detaching Sheridan, sent his young lieutenant to the Valley, with orders to clean it of Confederates and destroy all military supplies there, and thus close that back door to Washington for the rest of the war.

This was Sheridan's first independent command. He had fairly earned it by his gallantry and good sense, and right well did he justify it. He no longer had Rosecrans, or Thomas, or Grant to lean on or consult with; but now, widely separated from army headquarters, had to think and plan and act for himself. Mr. Stanton, looking him all over through his imperious spectacles, thought him too young for such a grave command;[1] but yielded his opinion to the joint and wiser opinions of Halleck and Grant. He was given a mixed command of infantry, cavalry, and artillery, amounting to about twenty-five thousand men, against the Confederate force of, say, twenty thousand. It is true Jubal Early afterward alleged he had only about eight thousand men altogether in the Valley; but Sheridan

---
[1] Sheridan's *Memoirs*, vol. i, p. 463.

answered by publishing the provost marshal general's receipts for *over thirteen thousand prisoners* he had captured from Early.

Once in the saddle, he quickly assembled his command in the lower valley, with headquarters at Hall Town, near Harper's Ferry. As a whole, it was not a very satisfactory command. For much of it had been ridden over and around and through, pretty much as the Confederate chiefs had willed. But Sheridan immediately set to work to reorganize and discipline it—changing officers, inspecting regiments, consolidating brigades—until he knew *what* he had and *whom* he could depend upon, and *how much* he could depend upon them. Then, about the middle of August, he advanced cautiously to Cedar Creek, but presently retired again to Hall Town, because the enemy seemed too strong, and he was still uncertain of his men, and could find no good defensive position farther up the Valley.

This retrograde movement, so like its predecessors, and so disappointing to Mr. Lincoln, filled Stanton and Halleck with dismay, and even Grant became impatient, and finally left Petersburg and came up to Washington himself, resolved to force the fighting in the Valley. He even proceeded as far as Charlestown, with a prepared plan of campaign in his pocket. But Sheridan easily satisfied him his own "plan" was right, and in reply to Grant's eager inquiries answered that he had completed his preparations, and was now all ready to go in. Grant characteristically pocketed his "plan of campaign"[1]—never even alluded to it—and tersely bade him "Go in;" and immediately Sheridan moved out from his lines and advanced upon the enemy like a thunderbolt.

He struck the Confederates first at Opequan (or Winchester) September 19, and again at Fisher's Hill Septem-

---
[1] Grant's *Memoirs*, vol. ii, p. 328.

## Philip H. Sheridan

ber 22, and "sent Early whirling up the Valley," with the loss of over five thousand killed, wounded, and prisoners, five pieces of artillery, and nine battle flags. He struck them again at Cedar Creek October 19, and, although his command had been surprised and routed in the early morning under General Wright, and was in full retreat on his arrival from Washington (whither he had rightfully gone under orders hastily to confer with Stanton and Halleck on imperative matters he could not otherwise settle[1]—being absent but three days, with *only four hours* in Washington, something extraordinary), he stopped the retreat, reformed his lines, and before nightfall attacked and routed Early in turn—recapturing our old camps, and all the artillery, camp equipage, and transportation Wright had lost, and also taking over twelve hundred prisoners, twenty-four pieces of artillery, and many battle flags from the Confederates, now routed and fleeing like chaff before the wind.

This was by all odds the most brilliant victory of the war, of its size and kind, and has well been immortalized by Thomas Buchanan Read in his stirring lyric, "Sheridan's Ride." It captured the imagination and aroused the enthusiasm of the loyal North as few victories did; and out of the very depths of his soul President Lincoln wrote him: "I tender to you and your brave army the thanks of the nation, and my own personal admiration and gratitude, for your month's operations in the Shenandoah Valley;" and (what was dearer to Sheridan) immediately promoted him to be Major General U. S. A. Stanton, as I have said, had thought him too young to command in the Valley; but now he also wrote, commending him unreservedly for "his personal gallantry and military skill, whereby, under the blessing of Providence, his routed army was reorganized, a great national disaster averted,

---
[1] See Appendix, p. 381.

and a brilliant victory achieved over the rebels for the third time in pitched battle within thirty days."

Sheridan now set to work to clean out the Valley as a field for Confederate operations, and, it must be conceded, made thorough work of it. He stretched his cavalry from mountain ridge to mountain ridge, and then moved down the Valley, driving all horses, cattle, sheep, and swine before him, and capturing or destroying all grain, hay, and other military supplies, and burning all grist mills, until that paradise of Virginia was one wild scene of devastation and desolation; or, as he himself wrote General Grant: "We have cleaned out the Valley so completely, that if a crow wants to cross it, he will have to carry his rations with him." Of course, this was not relished by the inhabitants there; but it was war, pure and simple, stern and awful, and closed that "back door to Washington" effectually for the remainder of the Rebellion.

Late in February following he entered upon his final campaign in the Valley. Early in the winter he had sent his infantry mainly to Grant, and now took ten thousand cavalry and swept up the Valley, and swooped down on James River above Richmond, intending to cross it and join either Grant or Sherman. But he found the James swollen and impassable, because of spring freshets; with its bridges gone and his own pontoons insufficient. So he contented himself with destroying canals and smashing railroads there, and then swept back around Richmond with superb disdain; threshing as with a flail all forces sent in pursuit of him; and, crossing the James below Richmond on March 26, reported in person to Grant again in front of Petersburg. How it must have delighted General Grant to receive him and his column back, and what a welcome he must have given to his brave and capable young lieutenant!

Clearly here was an officer after Grant's own heart, who

had vindicated his judgment and sagacity—whom he could trust all through—and he hastened to set him to work again. Lincoln came down from Washington, Sherman came up from North Carolina, and they all four met in council at City Point. Grant's first thought was to send Sheridan down to Sherman, and then for them both to march up and join him before Petersburg, and Sherman also favored this plan. But Sheridan hotly opposed it, and insisted that the Army of the Potomac alone was well able to whip Lee, and would be dishonored if helped by Sherman.[1] Finally Grant yielded. Sherman went back to North Carolina, and March 28 Sheridan got his orders to move out and "reach the right and rear" of Lee, and "force him out of his intrenched lines," if possible.

"Should he come out and attack us, or get himself where he can be attacked, *move in with your entire force in your own way*, with the full reliance that the army will engage or follow the enemy, as circumstances dictate!" These were the final orders of General Grant, that led to Lee's surrender—the beginning of his end—and they well show how much Grant relied upon and trusted Sheridan.

The very next morning Sheridan was in the saddle again, and our whole cavalry moved out, with the infantry following in part. But now a vicious rain set in, and the bottoms dropped out of the Virginia roads. Both horses and soldiers became stalled in the mud and quicksands, and March 30 Grant ordered a halt and partial return to the railroad again.

This disgusted Sheridan, and mounting a powerful gray (captured at Missionary Ridge) he rode six miles through the mud and rain, from Dinwiddie Court House to Grant's headquarters at Gravelly Run, and earnestly protested that they would all be ridiculed and ruined, if

---

[1] Sheridan's *Memoirs*, vol. ii, p. 128-132.

they did not go ahead—just as Burnside was after his famous Mud March (January, 1863), as "Burnside stuck in the mud!" He said the roads were just as bad for Lee as they were for us, and if he could move we could; that he would set every man to work "corduroying" them; and if Grant would let him alone, he would go on and break in on Lee's right at Five Forks, and force him out of his lines and whip him, mud or no mud.

Rawlins, Grant's chief of staff, was of the same opinion and insistent, until Grant quietly suggested: "Well, Rawlins, I think you had better take command!" But he paid more attention to Sheridan, and finally decided: "Well, we will go on"—a momentous decision.[1] Back Sheridan delighted rode, still through the mud and rain, bespattered from head to foot, and the next day but one afterward he did strike Lee at Five Forks, and forced him out of his lines, and whipped him; taking six pieces of artillery, thirteen battle flags, and nearly six thousand prisoners.

This brilliant victory, conceived and executed wholly by Sheridan, compelled Lee to let go his hold on Richmond and Petersburg and move out of his fortified lines, and from there on to Appomattox Court House and his final surrender (April 9) it was mainly a rout and a foot race. At Sailor's Creek, April 6, Sheridan again hit the Confederates, and took six generals and ten thousand prisoners, and wired Grant (back with the main army): "If the thing is pressed, I think Lee will surrender." Grant's laconic reply was: "Press things!" Then Sheridan did press things to such excellent purpose, that he outmarched Lee with both his cavalry and infantry, and on the morning of April 9, when Lee broke camp at Appomattox, intending to retreat still farther, suddenly Sheridan appeared ahead, blocking his way, with Meade hur-

---

[1] Sheridan's *Memoirs*, vol. ii, p. 142-144.

rying up in his rear. And then and there to him and the Confederacy came the end of all things.

Of Lee's surrender it is not necessary to speak more here. But it is the truth of history that in all the operations leading up to it, Sheridan was literally the right hand of Grant, hitting like a flail or striking like a battering ram, and what this spring campaign of 1865 would have been without him, I do not venture to say. It is enough to say, that without him the campaign of 1864 before Petersburg availed but little, and that with him the campaign of 1865 resulted gloriously. He certainly must have a large share of the credit, whatever is due to Meade and Grant; and his illustrious commander in chief would be the last to deny this. On the whole, I submit there was glory enough to go around for all. But all honor to Philip H. Sheridan!

To conclude, clearly he was not a popinjay, like Wheeler; nor a partisan, like Forrest—a slave driver turned soldier; nor a Prince Rupert, like Jeb Stuart; but he was a veritable Henry of Navarre, a plumed knight for the Union, and will rank among great commanders; if not of the first rank, yet well up among the first; and, unquestionably, would have risen higher had the war lasted and opportunity occurred. He had force and fire, and knew how to lead men and to inspire them. But he had also prudence and patience, and knew how to command men and conduct great operations as well, and few soldiers have shown both qualities in so large a degree. He has been compared to Kearny, but he had more breadth and keenness than Kearny, though less military learning and culture. He has been compared to Murat, but that *beau sabreur* had not half of Sheridan's brains, nor a tithe of his integrity and patriotism. In some respects he was to Grant what Stonewall Jackson, and after him Longstreet, were to Lee. But he was abler and nimbler than either, and Grant did not hesitate to declare that, take him all in all, he was second to no general our civil war produced on either side. "As a soldier," he said, "there is no man living greater than Sheridan. He belongs to the very first rank of captains, not only of our army, but of the world. I rank him with Napoleon and Frederick and the great commanders of history." That was Grant's sober opinion, long after the war closed; and who was or is a better judge?

Clearly he was one of Providence's picked men, required then and there for the salvation of the Republic. His name was a flag. His opportunity was large. His duty was great. And he was equal to both. He began life as the son of a poor Irish farmer. He rose to be General of the United States Army—the very highest rank in the Regular Army—in the most critical period of American history, a rank attained by Grant and Sherman only. Well, then, I say:

> "Hurrah, hurrah for Sheridan!
> Hurrah for Sheridan, horse and man!
> And when their statues are placed on high,
> Under the dome of the Union sky,
> The American soldiers' Temple of Fame,"

let every American boy study his great and heroic career; and may we all profit by his manly life and glorious example![1]

---

[1] See Appendix, p. 383.

Gen. U. S. Grant, 1864.

## CHAPTER X

### ULYSSES S. GRANT

MY last commander, and clearly greatest of them all—one of the greatest soldiers that ever lived (I say it advisedly)—was General Grant. I first met him in January, 1864, at Nashville, Tenn., after the victory at Chattanooga and the relief of Knoxville. He had gone from Chattanooga to Knoxville; and, when he found Burnside safe and sound, had ridden with part of his staff in raw winter weather, with the thermometer at zero, through Cumberland Gap to Lexington, Ky., and there taken the railroad to Louisville; whence he had come down to Nashville, then headquarters of the Military Division of the Mississippi, which embraced all that region from the Alleghanies to the Rocky Mountains, and from the Lakes to the Gulf of Mexico.

I need scarcely add that he arrived in Nashville weather-stained and travel-worn. He was then about forty years of age, and looked it easily. He had dark sandy hair, light blue eyes, a bearded face, and a general indifference but not slouchiness of figure, anything but soldierly, as Eastern officers understood things. It is true he wore a major general's uniform (and right well had he earned it); but it was rusty and seedy. His coat was open, and the lapels were buttoned back; his hat bore a gold cord, but was battered and worn; he went about unattended, with his head down and hands much in his pockets; and he looked for all the world more like a country storekeeper or Western farmer, than the illustrious conqueror of Vicksburg and Chattanooga, and the commander in chief now of half a million of men.

He was a West Pointer, indeed, and had distinguished himself in Mexico as a lieutenant. But he looked little like our traditional cadet, natty and "well set up," or usual regular officer; and to my Eastern eye was a decided disappointment. I had been accustomed to such trim and soldierly figures as McClellan, Burnside, Hooker, and Meade, all of whom looked the officer and army commander. But here was a man of different caliber, evidently intent on everything but show.

On second glance, however, he clearly improved. As you caught his eye, you found it clear and penetrating, and saw it could be hard as flint as well as soft as dew, and it was easy to perceive that there was a grip and grit in his face and jaw that would enable him to dare great things, and hold on mightily, and toil terribly, "when the hour had struck and the time had come." When he came to talk, you found him few of words and slow of speech; but he knew exactly *what* he wanted, and *why* and *when* he wanted it. And when you left his presence you could not help feeling, that here was a man of grave and serious purpose, gentle in manner, but bent on great things; cast in the mold of a Cromwell or Wellington rather than a Napoleon. And you instinctively felt he would be loyal to the end, and could be trusted all through.

He took a rebel house at Nashville, and was soon settled down and hard at work. His staff was small and his headquarters void of show. He attended few parades and reviews. He hated long letters and prolix reports. But he had the telegraph brought into his quarters, and every day with a telegrapher by his side would talk all over his great military division and with Washington, and every night he knew precisely where the enemy was, and what he was doing, and what we were able to do and dare. In other words, he knew the *value of time*, and in an hour or so would accomplish by telegraph what some other commanders would waste days in doing by pen and paper. So, also, he knew how *to decide.*

One day my chief, General Donaldson, went to him with a report and estimate, relating to the campaign of 1864, that involved millions of money and property, and when he had glanced it over he silently approved and ordered it. Hesitating, because of the vast expense, General Donaldson ventured to call his attention again to the figures, and to inquire whether he was quite sure he was right?

"No, I am not," was Grant's reply; "but in war anything is better than indecision. We *must decide.* If I am wrong, we shall soon find it out, and can do the other thing. But *not to decide* wastes both time and money, and may ruin everything."

Here unquestionably was one great secret of his immense success, and the key to many of his brilliant achievements.

Soon Mrs. Grant came down from "God's country," as we then called all north of the Ohio, and spent several weeks at Nashville. She did not see much of General Grant during the week—he was too busily engaged at headquarters, or was off in the saddle inspecting troops and forts or hospitals. But on Sunday they went regularly to the humble Methodist Episcopal church there together, and his devout example told for righteousness on all our forces in his Military Division. Before and after church he was often at headquarters, indeed; but not unless "the situation" demanded it, and his aids and orderlies were early excused from Sunday duty, unless their further presence was imperatively required.

As a military commander, his success was so phenomenal and his career so great that I hardly know how to speak of him further, within the limits of a chapter like this. He resigned from the regular army as captain in

1854, for want of something to do in our then "piping times of peace." First he tried farming near St. Louis, and then tanning at Galena, and barely earned a scanty support for himself and family. His total income was only about eight hundred dollars per year when the war broke out, with poor prospect of increase. Now he raised a company of volunteers, and hastened with it to Springfield, but failed of a command. Next he went to Cincinnati, and sought service under McClellan (then commanding there, and whom he had known in Mexico); but failed even to see him. Then he wrote to the War Department, and tendered his services there or anywhere, but was not even answered. But now, at last, Illinois had a regiment, mutinous and insubordinate, that she knew not what to do with, and tendered him its command; and then he began to show the real grip and temper of his mind and character. That regiment, it goes without saying, soon learned to "obey orders!"

His first great opportunity came in February, 1862, when he got tardy permission from Halleck (then commanding at St. Louis) to move on Forts Henry and Donelson, and the results were his signal victories there—over fifteen thousand prisoners, sixty-five cannon, and seventeen thousand muskets—that so thrilled the North at the time, and wrote his name down in history forever as "Unconditional Surrender Grant." I remember that his telegram announcing the surrender there was signed simply "U. S. Grant," and our adjutant in the Army of the Potomac the next evening at dress parade inadvertently read it "*United States* Grant," because that was our usual meaning of "U. S." then, and we had never heard of him otherwise! But we got to know his name better afterward.

His next affair, at Pittsburg Landing or Shiloh, was unfortunate—a drawn battle, or at best a barren victory—and some clamor arose for his removal; but Mr. Lincoln sagely replied: "We can't spare this man. He fights! he fights!" thus contrasting his vigor and virility with the inaction and supineness of McClellan and Buell. Next he moved on Vicksburg from the north, by way of the Mobile and Ohio Railroad, and failed (November-December, 1862). Then he tried it by way of the Mississippi, with Sherman and Porter assisting, and again he failed (January-March, 1863). But disappointments and failures only whet the resolution of great men, while they dismay and defeat small men; and hence Grant, more determined than ever, now boldly resolved to cross the Mississippi below Vicksburg, cut loose from his base, and attack that Confederate Gibraltar from the east and rear, and to the amazement of everybody succeeded magnificently.

This was our first really great Union success, clear and significant, and coupled with Gettysburg on the same day (that ever memorable Fourth of July, 1863), raised our national fortunes to a pitch of prestige that nothing afterward could much diminish. Our other campaigns consisted largely of long marches or hard-fought battles; but Vicksburg was brilliant strategy as well as gallant tactics, and placed Grant in the very front rank of great commanders. It freed the Mississippi from Cairo to the gulf; it bisected the Confederacy as with a knife; and it really sounded the death knell of the Rebellion, had its doughty chiefs only had "ears to hear." And the honor and glory of it all belonged to Grant, and to Grant alone. For, as Sherman said to me with his own lips, one night in the fall of 1866, as we lay bivouacked by a blazing fire in the shadow of the Rocky Mountains: "Yes, it was Grant's plan, and nobody else's. I objected to it—did not 'protest,' as has been said—but tried to dissuade him from it as too big and risky. But Grant stuck to it, nevertheless, and now deserves the credit of it all. I wrote him, it is true, but nevertheless pledged him my 'zealous coöperation and energetic support,' if he decided to go ahead; and I kept my word.[1] After we cut loose from our base, I never saw him again until we reached the Big Black. There we halted to rebuild a bridge, that the Rebs had destroyed, and I lay down in a contraband's cabin near the bridge-head to get a wink of sleep while the work went on, when about midnight Grant rode up with some of his staff, and I rushed out bareheaded, and taking him by the hand said, 'General Grant, I want to congratulate you on the success of your great plan. And it is "your plan," too, by heaven, and nobody else's. For nobody else believed in it!'"

The mere figures as to Vicksburg alone are immense. See how they read: thirty-one thousand six hundred prisoners; one hundred and seventy-two cannon; over sixty thousand muskets; and a vast amount of *materiel* and stores. But these, indeed, only half tell the story!

It will always remain one of the mysteries of our Civil War why Grant was not now allowed to keep his Vicksburg veterans together, and ordered to strike somewhere else. He himself wanted to move on Mobile, in conjunction with Porter and Farragut. But Halleck and Stanton between them now managed to scatter his forces, where they accomplished next to nothing. Subsequently he himself drifted down to New Orleans; where, returning from a review, he was thrown from an unruly horse and gravely disabled—was insensible at first and lame for many weeks afterward.[2]

Now came Chickamauga (which likely never would have happened had Grant moved on Mobile), and Stanton and Halleck, frantic at the impending consequences, now hurried Grant to Chattanooga, disabled as he was. I

---

[1] See Sherman's *Memoirs*, vol. i, p. 317; also *War Records*, vol. xxiv, part iii, pp. 179, 180.  [2] Grant's *Memoirs*, vol. i, p. 581. See Appendix, p. 384.

know of no more dramatic or pathetic spectacle during the war than Thomas cooped up at Chattanooga, the nation fearing his retreat or surrender, and Grant hastening to his relief by railroad and on horseback, by night and by day, lame as he was. He had been on crutches for weeks, and was still so lame that his staff had to carry him over hard places in the roads, where it was not safe to ride on horseback, when crossing the mountains between Bridgeport and Chattanooga (sometimes by torchlight); but he got there nevertheless. It was one man on crutches against Bragg and his beleaguering army; but our reinforcement was adequate, as the event soon proved. In reply to Grant's anxious telegram from Louisville, "Hold Chattanooga at all hazards, I will be there as soon as possible," Thomas had telegraphed him, "*I will hold the town till we starve;*" and right well did he keep his soldierly promise.[1]

With Grant once in Chattanooga everybody felt safe, and all there braced up and showed fight. What Thomas would have accomplished without him it is, of course, impossible to say. But it is certain that Grant's very presence, when it became known, was an inspiration; it soon put a new aspect on affairs there; and when Sherman also arrived with his succoring army, it required no prophet to foretell the result. As the stars in their courses "fought against Sisera," so the fates now were plainly against Bragg, and his overwhelming defeat was only a matter of time, and of brief time. This came November 24 and 25, when Grant struck him like a cyclone—with Sherman and Sheridan, Thomas and Hooker, all combined—and literally "smote him hip and thigh;" inflicting a loss of over five thousand killed and wounded, over six thousand prisoners, fifty pieces of artillery, and seven thousand stands of small arms; while the remainder of his

---

[1] *War Records*, vol. xxx, part iv, p. 479.

army (beaten and half panic-stricken) retreated sullenly into Georgia. It is such great and stunning victories as these—Donelson, Vicksburg, and Chattanooga—at decisive hours or at great strategic points, that determine human wars and settle the fate of nations. All minor battles and campaigns are mere stage thunder or side scenes. But such actions as these, if they do not end the drama, at least mark the march of its successive and bloody steps, and point significantly to the coming catastrophe.

The relief of Knoxville now followed, as a matter of course, and this ended the campaign of 1863 in Tennessee and all that region. Grant now returned to Nashville, as the natural center and brain of his great Military Division, and soon began to plan for the campaign of 1864. He resolved to strike next at Atlanta, with subsequent blows at Mobile or Savannah; but in March, 1864, was appointed Lieutenant General, and put in supreme command of all our armies, then over a million strong. This did not spoil him, but with rare good sense he decided to go East and take command there, while he left Sherman to "swing things" in the West, as he was well able to do. He did not deem it right or wise to remove Meade, in view of his great record at Gettysburg and elsewhere; but he made his own headquarters with the Army of the Potomac, and soon substantially directed all its movements.

He lost no time, but early in May, as soon as the roads dried up, moved out of our winter camps with an army (including Burnside) one hundred and twenty thousand strong, well seasoned and veteranized, and over three hundred guns. Opposed stood Lee, with about seventy-five thousand men, better veteranized, and over two hundred guns. Not unevenly balanced, though these figures seem otherwise; for Lee was on the defensive and on his native soil, with every foot of which he was familiar (over which he had already campaigned three years), and in the midst of his devoted friends; while Grant was on the offensive, and in a new and unknown country, and surrounded by a hostile people—conditions indeed gravely affecting campaigns and battles.

So began his great campaign against Richmond, with all the world looking on and all history attentive. He was tempted to move his army first by water to the James, like McClellan, and there attack Richmond from the South; and he has been criticised and scolded by McClellan's friends and admirers ever since, because he did not do this. But, after mature reflection, his common sense and wise answer was that the Confederacy rested on Lee's bayonets; that there could be no peace until Lee's veterans—the gallant Army of Northern Virginia—were first conquered or ground to powder; and, therefore, that his "true objective was first Lee's army." Had he gone to the James immediately, he would have found Lee and his brave veterans confronting him there just the same; and as we had to fight it out anyhow, he reasoned, why not fight on the Rapidan as well as on the James? Besides, this would cover and protect the national capital, and Mr. Lincoln, with good reason and his usual good sense, always made this a *sine qua non* of every Virginia campaign.

So we had the bloody and desperate battles of the Wilderness, of Spottsylvania, and Cold Harbor; not very scientific, not very strategic, not very tactical always; and they could not be, because of the conditions of the country (heavily wooded), and of the contending armies (both American), both armed and drilled alike, and both ably officered and commanded. But Grant hammered continuously away, as if the very sledge hammer of Thor, resolved to "fight it out on this line, if it takes all summer," and daily moved by the left flank grimly forward, like the march of doom.

I can imagine Lee's amazement, his disgust and dismay,

when he found Grant did not retreat after the awful carnage of the Wilderness. The Army of the Potomac had always fought bravely and then retreated, in like circumstances, under its previous commanders; and Meade evidently expected this now, too. But Grant smoked his cigar, and sternly ordered the army again "by the left flank, forward!" and Lee, in the depths of his soul, must have realized that the end was indeed now come, or surely coming. It is true our losses from the Rapidan to the James were enormous—fifty-four thousand nine hundred and twenty-six men in killed, wounded, and missing. But the fighting had to be done—sometime, somewhere—and Lee's army ground to pieces; and Grant alone had the nerve to do it then and there. In my judgment, now thirty-five years afterward, after a full review of all the facts, it was a great "job of work," as Carlyle says, greatly done; and history will justify his sagacity and vindicate his generalship, despite his maligners and slanderers.[1]

Once across the James, he sat down before Petersburg; and though he found Lee there, alert and vigilant, it was no longer Lee's army of old, but one for which "both the cradle and the grave had been robbed;" and its final defeat and surrender were now only a question of time. What mattered a few months, more or less? He held Lee and the Confederacy now in a vise, as with the grip of destiny, while his great lieutenant moved on Atlanta and Savannah, and the bells of Appomattox were already beginning to toll, if one did but listen. When Lee essayed to threaten Washington, to divert Grant from Petersburg and Richmond, by his usual back-door route of the Shenandoah, Grant dispatched Phil Sheridan to lock that door forever by his brilliant victories at Opequan and Cedar Creek. And Lee must now have felt another coil of destiny tightening surely around him.

---

[1] See Appendix, p. 385.

Then, at last, came the ever memorable spring of 1865, with Sheridan again in the saddle, and again triumphant at Five Forks and Sailor's Creek, with Petersburg doomed, Richmond abandoned, and Appomattox as the end of all things. Here Lee—baffled, beaten, broken-hearted—now at last grounded arms, with all his army and *materiel* of war, and the Southern Confederacy passed into history as a hideous nightmare—a political blunder and crime—never to recur. It is the fashion with some to say, "Lee hadn't much left." But the official records show that between March 29 and April 9 he surrendered forty-seven thousand four hundred and eighty-eight men and six hundred and eighty-nine cannon, besides his killed, wounded, and missing.[1]

Donelson, Vicksburg, Chattanooga, Appomattox—these, I say, were great and memorable victories, either of them enough for one man's fame; but Grant achieved them all, and so wrote his name down in history imperishable as the stars. Criticism is always cheap and easy, provided one be far enough away from the battlefield. But history looks only at results, and the substantial fact remains that Grant *succeeded where all others failed*. As Mr. Lincoln once said of him, "Grant is the only one of our generals who has fought twenty-eight great battles and won twenty-eight great victories." Verily he knew how to "make things come to pass!" He was not an Alexander, nor a Cæsar, nor a Napoleon; but I venture to say that he was a greater commander than either of them, under the changed conditions of warfare as they existed here from 1861 to 1865; and an infinitely better man; and his fame is secure for all the long centuries to come.

Said Sherman to me (and he was a good judge) one evening in 1866, after the war was over, while chatting around our camp fire in the shadow of the Rockies:

---

[1] Grant's *Memoirs*, vol. ii, pp. 500, 501.

"Grant is the greatest soldier of our time, if not of all times. He does not know as much about books and strict military art and science as some others, but he possesses the last quality of great generalship; he knows, he *divines,* when the supreme hour has come in a campaign or battle, and always boldly seizes it. When he begins a campaign, he fixes in his mind what is the true objective point, and abandons all minor ones; holding that he will recover these afterward easily enough, if only successful at the main point! So he dismisses all possibility of defeat. He believes in himself and in victory, as absolutely as the Christian believes in his Saviour. If his plan works wrong, he is never disconcerted, but promptly devises a new one, and is sure he will win in the end.

"In every engagement there comes a supreme moment, when both sides are well whipped, and whichever commander first *divines* this and puts forth all his strength, hazarding everything for success, he is sure to 'get there!' and Grant never failed to divine and seize it. As for example, at Shiloh and Pittsburg Landing we were pretty roughly handled—not exactly 'surprised,' but the next thing to it—and at the end of the first day's fight, along after dark, Grant rode over to my headquarters, and asked me what I thought about the battle. I answered, that I thought we were 'pretty well whipped.'

" 'Yes,' said Grant, 'I think so too. But haven't you observed, during the last hour or so, the enemy has made no progress? That means his force is spent. One of our flanks is covered by an impassable ravine; the other by gunboats. Our riffraff have gone to the rear. What are left are good soldiers. And whichever side takes the initiative in the morning, the other will retire. And Beauregard will be mighty smart, if he attacks before I do!"

"I told him there was sense in this, and he rode away.

But about midnight I received his written order to attack at daylight with all my force, and the whole army would support me. I did, and after a feeble resistance the Johnnies went skedaddling back to Corinth, and the field was ours.

So also at Chattanooga, I was ordered to attack on the left—Bragg's right—and I did with all my force, but soon found the ground impassable, and was repulsed. I was ordered to attack again, and did, with like result; and halted for orders. These came, 'Attack again,' and I thought the old man daft, and sent a staff officer to inquire if there wasn't a mistake. But his reply was, 'No! Attack as ordered!' And I did, vehemently; and, simultaneously, he hurled Thomas and Sheridan against Bragg's center, piercing and crushing it, and rolling his wings up both ways, and the campaign was ended. Now what Grant did was this: by my attacks so often on the left, he made Bragg believe our main attack was to be there, and so he weakened his center to reinforce his right, and when Grant 'divined' he had done this sufficiently, he hurled Thomas forward as a battering ram, and smashed him completely. It was a great victory—the neatest and cleanest battle I was ever in—and Grant deserves the credit of it all."

"Yes," he added, characteristically, "some others of us on both sides were pretty good generals; but not one of us could compare with Grant, nor begin to compare with him!"

Of course, I do not give Sherman's precise words, but I give his precise ideas, and almost his exact words. For they impressed me deeply, and have been repeated often since then, both privately and publicly.

As a mere organizer and drillmaster, Grant certainly did not compare with McClellan or Meade or Hooker; but when it came to aggressive campaigning and fighting, or to taking a large and comprehensive view of affairs—such as seeing the end of a campaign or a battle even from the beginning and holding steadfastly on, despite everybody and everything, no matter what happened, provided we succeeded—he was worth all three of them rolled into one, and more. Clearly, he knew officers well, and his judgment of subordinates was unerring, as witness Sherman, McPherson, and Sheridan—all his chosen lieutenants. And as the most illustrious soldier of American history (much exceeding Robert E. Lee, as I humbly think), let us take off our hats to him, and in the fine lines of Alfred Tennyson, in his superb "Ode on the Duke of Wellington," devoutly say:

> "Let his great example stand,
> Colossal, seen of every land;
>    And make the soldier firm, the statesman pure,
> Till in all lands, and through all human story,
> The path of duty be the way to glory.
>
> "And let the land whose hearths he saved from shame,
> For many and many an age proclaim,
> At civic revel and pomp and game,
> And when our long-illumined cities flame,
> Our ever loyal iron leader's fame,
>    With honor, honor, honor, honor to him—
> Eternal honor to his name!"

And as for believers in Methodism, let them also say: "All hail to this modest man of Methodist faith and Methodist origin!" Born in a Methodist home, bred in a Methodist Sunday school, trained in the Methodist Church, and married to a Methodist wife, right worthily did he become the first Methodist President of the Republic. And as the great conqueror of the Rebellion, and twice President of the United States, he will descend to history an honor and a credit to the Methodist Episcopal Church, while time lasts or history endures.

Gen. Robert E. Lee, 1864.

## CHAPTER XI

### ROBERT E. LEE

I DID not serve under General Lee, and am glad I did not; but may I venture to write a chapter on General Lee also? It may be dangerous business, but has not the time come to marshal the facts and try to arrive at some just estimate of General Lee also? It has become the fashion to place General Lee on a pedestal, and worship him afar off—at the expense of our Union generals, particularly of General Grant—as *vide* General Lord Wolseley and others. But let us take the scales of history, and see how they balance. I will at least try to hold them level, whichever "kicks the beam." I beg pardon of his Confederate friends in advance, if I seem to be unfair. But really I do not mean to be so, if I can help it.

Of course, Secession was a sophism, and the Southern Confederacy from the first a thing doomed. It was an anachronism in the nineteenth century—a pirate ship still afloat, but sure to sink or be sunk in due time. How could they expect a government to succeed or endure, "whose corner stone was slavery," as its Vice President Stephens himself boasted? Every American of real clear-headedness, I submit, saw this from the beginning, and why a man of Robert E. Lee's conceded caliber did not, or could not, or would not see it (as his brother Virginian, George H. Thomas, readily did) is one of the puzzles of human nature. But without discussing the right or wrong of General Lee's conduct in joining the Southern Confederacy, of which much might be said; for he owed his education, his career, and his allegiance to the United States —he had so sworn; or his responsibility, direct or indirect, for the horrors of Libby and Andersonville, which he certainly knew all about and could have stopped, had he so chosen; or the moral character of the Rebellion, about which, I suppose, men will long differ—let us, notwithstanding, now proceed to weigh and measure him as a military commander alone.

Lee's first independent command, it will be recollected, was in West Virginia early in 1861; and it will not be denied that even Rosecrans was enough for him then and there. Next he succeeded to the command of the Army of Northern Virginia at Fair Oaks in June, 1862, after Joseph E. Johnston was wounded on the first day there; and it must be admitted, that the second day at Fair Oaks was not a Confederate success. Then came the "Seven Days' Battle," so called, with McClellan; and though his great lieutenants, Jackson and Longstreet, fought superbly, yet General Lee failed to detect or divine our "change of base" to the James, but sent Jackson off on a wild goose chase toward the White House, at right angles to our line of retreat, when he ought to have been hammering hard at our affrighted rear—no, not "affrighted," but stunned and bleeding rear. The Army of the Potomac never became affrighted; in its *personnel* it was incapable of fear. At Malvern Hill he put in his troops "by piecemeal," and was bloodily repulsed, as he deserved, and only his good luck saved Richmond then from dangerous attack, had not McClellan lost his head. Of course, I admit General Lee was too much for our "Little Mac," as a rule; but does that entitle him to rank as a first-class commander?

At second Bull Run, of course, he beat Pope, because Pope never had much head, and it is conceded Porter and Franklin both failed him. But at Antietam, it must be admitted, even McClellan worsted him, or at least persuaded him to fall back into Virginia, from which history will aver he ought never to have moved. At Fredericksburg he certainly made a superb defense, but he had only Burnside against him, and all the advantages of position with him. But when, after the awful slaughter there, we lay beaten—left, right, and center—why did he not give us a counter-thrust, or at least attempt it? Or, more significantly still, why did he allow our defeated and demoralized army there to recross the Rappahannock at night, free and unmolested? Why did he not detect or divine our retrograde movement of despair, and strike us suddenly and furiously, like Thomas struck Hood after Nashville? A well-ordered night attack there, while we were crossing the few pontoon bridges, or waiting to cross them, our columns halting, mixed up, and all crowding to the bridge-heads, with the chances incalculably on his side, might have resulted in a great and unspeakable calamity to us there—probably would have so resulted.

At Chancellorsville, it is conceded, he whipped Hooker well. But why did he let Hooker escape so easily? I don't know how it was down on the left with Sedgwick, for I was not there; but upon our right, our main army, we expected grave trouble in crossing the river again, but were practically unmolested. He had lost Stonewall Jackson, and Longstreet was absent, it is true. But why did he not send "Billy" Mahone, or McLaws, or Anderson to smite us "hip and thigh," while we were crowding over like sheep at United States Ford, and marching thence dispirited, back to our old Stafford camps again?

At Gettysburg, it will not now be denied, Lee was well whipped by Meade, and only his good luck and Meade's overprudence saved him from ruin. He certainly "lost his head" somewhat there; and had Meade divined how dazed Lee was by Pickett's awful defeat, he would have ordered a "counter-thrust" immediately, as Lee expected, or, at least, would have hammered and whacked away at his rear so vigorously, as he staggered back to the Potomac, that he would never have got across it into Virginia again.

I think history will declare that Lee's two invasions of both Maryland (1862) and Pennsylvania (1863) were military mistakes, as well as political blunders. Of what possible good could they be to the Southern Confederacy? Did he suppose he (Robert E. Lee) could dictate terms of peace to Abraham Lincoln, even if he penetrated to Philadelphia or New York temporarily? Did he not *know*, could he not *perceive*, that the North had only begun to fight, and would never, never permit the American Republic to be divided, least of all on the line of slavery? Both of these invasions, I submit, will seem to history as huge wastes of time and blood and treasure, hard to be excused. They were certainly military failures. Politically they consolidated the North. Clearly they did not help the South, and they cost General Lee thousands upon thousands of gallant men he could never replace.

In the Wilderness, and from the Rapidan to the James, it will be admitted he fought magnificently, with bent brows and flashing eyes, like a Roman gladiator. But, it must be remembered, his arena there—also like a Roman gladiator's—was all his own. Like MacGregor, "his foot was on his native heather" there. He was easily familiar with every mile of it. He had just campaigned over it, for three years in succession, against McClellan, Pope, Burnside, and Hooker, and he knew every wood path, as well as turnpike and crossroad; while to Grant, who had never been there before, it was all a *terra incognita*. So the inhabitants there were friendly and devoted to him, while to Grant they were savagely hostile. So, also, the country as a whole was horribly wooded—a veritable tangled wilderness of Virginia pines, scrub oaks, underbrush, etc.—so that while Grant, it is true, largely outnumbered Lee, yet numbers counted for but little there, seldom over one third or even one fourth of our forces being actually engaged. So, again, it must be remembered that Lee was constantly operating on interior lines, while Grant had to fight on exterior lines, and the rule of attack and defense under such circumstances, in such a country, and under like conditions, is held to be at least three or four to one; whereas Grant never mustered quite two to one. And yet day by day, week by week, General Lee was forced backward by Grant's everlasting order, "By the left flank, forward!" and during that whole campaign never gave us one resolute, determined, successful "counter-thrust." Sheridan rode around him twice. Grant hammered away at him continuously, with fearful losses —fifty-four thousand nine hundred and twenty-six men. But the best General Lee could do, fought he never so skillfully and bravely, was to fall back at last stubbornly and defiantly on Richmond and Petersburg.

At Petersburg he certainly made a gallant defense, and fought General Grant for all it was worth. It was a grip of two giants. It was a wrestle between two Titans. It was, indeed, a veritable " tug-of-war." But Grant never had enough troops to invest the place completely, and with back doors open to both Richmond and Danville (for reinforcements and supplies), it is not to be wondered at that General Lee held out so long and well. A military siege is a slow thing at best. Think of Antwerp and Dantzic, of Saragossa and Metz. Remember Sebastopol. Sedan is not a case in point, because the Germans far outnumbered the French, and practically surrounded them; and were better organized and armed, and much more ably commanded. But fight as he would and could, when Grant once got his hand firmly on Lee's throat (as when Sheridan triumphed at Five Forks), Petersburg and Richmond were doomed, and Appomattox followed logically as the end of all things.

So much by way of general observation. Now, suppose we weigh him a little more particularly. In the first place, please remember, Lee seldom took the initiative, and when he did he often got badly worsted; as at Malvern Hill, Antietam, and Gettysburg. Next, what campaign of his much exceeded, if equaled, in completeness and finish that of Thomas's at Nashville? So, what one compared with Sherman's great march on Atlanta and Savannah, and thence up through the Carolinas—over a thousand miles of marching and fighting, through the very heart of an enemy's country? And so especially, I beg to ask, what one can begin to compare with Grant's masterly operations down the Mississippi and around Vicksburg, or his magnificent relief of Chattanooga, or his superb siege of Petersburg—in all extending over half a continent nearly?

Again, is it not true that General Lee never conducted a great siege successfully, nor compelled the surrender of a single army? While Grant conducted Donelson, Vicksburg, and Petersburg, and captured at each place an entire army—at Donelson fifteen thousand men, at Vicksburg thirty-one thousand six hundred men, at Petersburg (or Appomattox), between March 29 and April 9, 1865, forty-seven thousand four hundred and eighty-eight men and six hundred and eighty-nine cannon. Just think of these figures, pray—ninety-four thousand and eighty-eight men. They will well bear pondering. Now, to stand on the defensive and strike only from the shoulder, I submit, is a greatly different thing, and calls for far less bigness and fineness of brain and soul, than to conceive and execute great aggressive campaigns and battles like these; and Lee and Grant must be weighed accordingly, if we would be just and fair. Of course, it is conceded that the rank and file on both sides were much the same, with the difference rather in favor of Lee, because more of the Confederates in proportion were native-born Americans.

Again, consider, pray, who General Lee's antagonists were: McClellan the unready, Pope the overbold, Burnside the blunderer, Hooker "Fighting Joe" and a good deal more, Meade a good safe commander ranking high; but not one of them a man of first-rate abilities, and some barely third-rate. Of course, Lee ought to have beaten such antagonists, or most of them. But when he became pitted against Grant, his plans soon went awry, and *a single campaign ended him*. Now *why*, pray *why*, if he measured up to this simple man from the prairies of Illinois?

General Lee was, indeed, the true type of the Southern oligarchs—proud, haughty, pure, upright (in their way), self-centered, well poised; as Grant was the true type of our Northern democracy, the consummate flower of our American civilization, and in the end was bound to win, because he embodied the moral and spiritual forces of his age and time, and was the best representative of them. Lee was, indeed, a man of excellent parts, but not of the greatest parts. He was a gentleman, a patriot, and a Christian—after his kind, the Confederate slaveholding kind. Indeed, I concede, as Shakespeare says:

> "His soul was gentle, and the elements so mixed in him,
> That nature might stand up, and say to all the world,
> Behold a man "—

a Southern slaveholding man. But I respectfully submit, he was not Grant's superior as a soldier, nor, indeed, his equal, nor nearly so, as I think history will hold in her final analysis; and he will be lucky if he maintains even second place on the world's roll of great commanders.

Clearly General Lee cannot rank with Alexander, Cæsar, Napoleon, and Von Moltke—all of whom were great aggressive commanders, all of whom conducted great aggressive campaigns and battles successfully, all of whom managed great sieges and compelled large surrenders, like Ulysses S. Grant. All these must welcome General Grant to their distinguished and illustrious company—to the Valhalla of the world's greatest commanders and conquerors. But as for Robert E. Lee—hold the scales never so level—I respectfully and regretfully submit (for he also was an American), they must deny him *entrée* there. Conceding all that is claimed as to his paucity of numbers, resources, etc., he yet fails to meet the supreme tests, and his friends and worshipers are unwise to challenge such comparison.

Let Lee abide in his own place. It is a large place, and he fills it well. For he was a gallant gentleman and an accomplished soldier, intelligent, alert, vigilant, brave, resolute, determined, devoted to his State, and dedicated to his cause—a hero worthy of any age or any land (of his kind). But nevertheless I must maintain Grant clearly out-tops him, as the oak out-tops the cedar or the pine; and Grant's sturdy name and fame will grow and broaden like the oak as the years roll on. Grant's supreme mission to mankind—his chief business on the earth—was to conquer the Rebellion, and he did it thoroughly.

Lee's supreme mission was to defend the Confederacy, and it ended in the " Lost Cause " and was ground to powder. Does not this estimate of Lee belittle Grant and his great deeds? By no means! Each fought in his own place, and fought well. But Grant's was the weightier sword, and finer-tempered. It was Cromwell against Rupert—the Puritan against the Cavalier—the nineteenth century against the eighteenth, or seventeenth, and the result could not be doubtful!

What would Grant have done in Lee's place? Really, I don't know, but presumably great things. Grant was bold, aggressive, enterprising, far-sighted, level-headed, broad-minded, patient, tenacious, full of grip and grit, and evidently would have "made a spoon or spoiled a horn" (most likely have "made a spoon," or several of them), even on the Confederate side. Let us be thankful he fought on our side! He was the soul of honor and truthfulness. His uprightness and integrity were perfect. And in generosity and magnanimity and clemency, he has never been surpassed, if equaled. He let the Confederates take their horses home after Appomattox " to help them make a crop to carry themselves and their families through the next winter," though they had surrendered and forfeited everything. He refrained from visiting Richmond after its fall—Von Moltke and his generals insisted on marching through Paris. And when Andrew Johnson afterward sought to arrest General Lee, Grant claimed him as his own paroled prisoner of war, and would not suffer a hair of his head to be touched.[1]

What would Lee have done in Grant's place? Evidently, with our numbers and resources and our cause, he would have succeeded magnificently. With his ancestral ties, he would have gone down to history as our second Washington. A great future opened up before him, but he did not or could not see it, and so missed his true place. Clearly the Confederacy produced no man equal nor nearly equal to him. "Stonewall" Jackson, Longstreet, and Joe Johnston were well enough in their way; but none of them could hold a candle to Robert E. Lee. But had General Lee been on our side and successful, I think he would have marched through Richmond! Of all on both sides, only Grant was equal to the self-abnegation and self-effacement of not doing so. And so he wound up his last official report with these memorable words, which every Union soldier will now heartily reiterate: " Let us hope for perpetual peace and harmony with that enemy, whose man-

---

[1] Grant's *Memoirs*, vol. ii, p. 493, etc. ; *War Records*, vol. xlvi, part iii, p. 665, 667.

hood, however mistaken the cause, drew forth such herculean deeds of valor."[1]

Washington, Lincoln, Grant! What a superb triumvirate they make! What a crowning glory they are to America and to human nature! If the American Republic, with all its faults, can produce three such men in the first century of its existence, while we are yet crude and awkward—the " raw recruit " of the nations—what shall we not do, under Christ, in the fullness of time and the maturity of our powers, when we become thoroughly drilled and disciplined? Clearly great men, and great things, yet await us. We are just getting our eyes open, and beginning to look around us, and to see *who* and *where* and *what* we are. God bless and speed the United States of America![2]

---
[1] Grant's *Memoirs*, vol. ii, p. 632; *War Records*, vol. xlvi, part i, p. 60.
[2] See Appendix, p. 385.

## CHAPTER XII

### Campaigning and Soldiering

Heretofore I have discoursed about our great commanders chiefly. Now let me say something about our rank and file. I fancy few civilians have much idea of what army life really is or consists of. They see only the rainbows on the outside. They hear only the rolling drums and sounding bugles. They see only " the pride, pomp, and circumstance of glorious war "—the marching regiments, the shining muskets, the gleaming bayonets, the flashing sabers, the streaming colors—and they think that magnificent. It is superb. It stirs one's blood. And the first exclamation that leaps to one's lips is, " Who wouldn't be a soldier!" But a little practical campaigning and soldiering changes this considerably, and many a patriot who enlisted enthusiastically early in 1861 soon wished himself home again—and wished it eagerly.

Let us see if we can realize just a little what army life really is. To begin with, a soldier must first bid good-bye to home and family or friends, perhaps never to return; and that is a little dampening to one's ardor. Next he must be mustered in and sworn to " obey orders "—good or bad, wise or otherwise—no matter who the officer over him—and that is not always agreeable to an American citizen. Next he must don heavy woolen clothing, that usually fits (or misfits) him wretchedly; because made according to average size, without reference to the individual wearer. It is good in cold and stormy weather, but suffocating and intolerable in hot days and nights, especially in the latitude of Virginia and Tennessee, or farther south.

Then he must learn the "manual of arms," to march and drill, and drill and march. And he is marched and drilled, and drilled and marched by the hour daily, until every muscle aches and every bone seems ready to break. Or he is put to policing the camp, which is not "police" duty in common parlance at all, but is the menial and degrading duty of sweeping and cleaning up the dirt and refuse, that gather naturally about a regiment or home of a thousand men. All soldiers detest this, especially raw recruits, because they say they enlisted to march and fight, not to "police!"

Then he must draw his rations and cook them—such as he can get and when he can get them. Sometimes good, often bad. Sometimes "full" rations, when he has enough and to spare; sometimes "light," when he has to eke them out the best he can. No cook stoves, of course; only rude fires on the ground, with green logs usually (except when he can find "top" fence rails—*vide* one of McClellan's orders on the Peninsula, which allowed us to take the "top rail;" but soon, of course, there wasn't any "top" rail), and in rainy weather more smoke than fire.

If ordered suddenly on a march or into battle, he moves with three or five days' cooked rations (or none at all, it may be) in his soiled and greasy haversack, to last twice said time, if need be. If a veteran, he knows how to make these last until he gets more, whether the days be more or less. He has learned how to "forage," and to find a stray pig or chicken, or a hidden ham or potatoes. But if a raw recruit, he eats his rations up speedily, as a rule, and takes a lesson in how to starve. In due time he learns the best part of the ration to be coffee, sugar, hard-tack, and "beef on the hoof," and husbands these while he throws all the rest away, as *impedimenta*, as Cæsar would say.

To drill or march all day, heavily loaded down with arms and accouterments, ammunition and rations, in heat and cold, in sunshine and shower, in dust or mud, is bad enough; but then comes night, with no beds or shelter, as a rule, in active campaigning. The best one can expect is an armful of grass or broken twigs or bushes under the open sky—*al fresco*. More often only the soft side of a rail or the damp ground; sometimes only mud or slush. If he has marched or fought all day, any rest is welcome; and he is only too eager for the order, "Halt! Stack arms!" to drop down by the roadside wherever he may be. Of course, at post or in winter quarters he can make himself comfortable. Tents can be drawn, huts can be built, bunks constructed, etc. But in campaigning and soldiering generally, all these have to be left behind (except our little " shelter tents," so called, which amounted to but little real shelter), and the actual hardships, exposures, privations, and miseries of the average private soldier and company officer are simply inconceivable to our stay-at-home civilians.

I remember a march that my division (Second Division, Third Corps—"Hooker's Old Division") made late in November, 1862, from Manassas Junction to Fairfax Court House, *en route* to Falmouth or Fredericksburg, in the midst of a wild, wintry storm of wind and rain, that took us all day to make twelve or fifteen miles; and at nightfall we bivouacked or camped down by the roadside in mud and rain and hail and sleet, to sleep the best we could. Nothing but green and wet wood for camp fires, and everybody ready to perish with fatigue, exhaustion, and cold. It was an awful, horrible experience for over ten thousand of us, and I shudder at its recollection even yet.

Or in the midst of some such horrible march he may be ordered to "corduroy" the road, by chopping trees and carrying them through the mud and water to the worst places; or to help lift the stalled wagons out of the swamp holes; or to take spades and "double quick" to the front or flanks to throw up hasty intrenchments; or to help build redoubts and forts—pure digging—a kind of "fatigue" work all soldiers hate, and I do not wonder. The Confederates made their Negroes do this, as a rule. But our soldiers had to " dig " for themselves.

But, worse yet, when the day's march or battle is ended, he may be ordered on guard as sentry, or on post as picket, and while his companions sleep off their fatigues and anxieties, he must tramp his weary round or stand his "two hours on and four off " all night, and the next morning must " fall in " with his company, and again march or fight all day, it may be. If, overcome by fatigue or exhaustion, he falls out and drops to sleep by the wayside, he is liable to arrest and court-martial, with prospect of " ball and chain " or to be " shot to death by musketry," or he is likely to be " gobbled up " by the enemy, and to find his way to Libby or Andersonville at last.

Or, worse yet, he may be ordered into the trenches, and must there dig or fight under fire of the artillery or musketry of the enemy; and must crawl or lie there all day, in all kinds of weather; or take the chances of having his head knocked off by a shell or his body " plugged " by Minie balls, if he dares to show himself above the earthworks. At nightfall he may be relieved and allowed to retire to better and safer quarters; or he may have to stay there, and "see it out" for a week or longer.

Or, still worse yet, the enemy may make a sortie, or we may be ordered to attack, and a partial or general engagement result; with fierce struggles and desperate onsets and bloody combats, which may leave him minus an arm or a leg, or with a hole or two through his body. If not killed outright, then comes the hospital, with its dreaded life and maybe awful death; and then the "Dead March in Saul " and farewell volley of musketry end all things.

## Campaigning and Soldiering

Or, if there be no serious fighting, that direful scourge of the camp and siege, chronic diarrhœa or typhoid fever, may ensue, and thousands of brave fellows waste away into shadows, gaunt and saffron-hued—many thousands more than by bullets, as *vide* McClellan's soldiers on the Peninsula and Grant's before Vicksburg. I think we lost more men on the lines before Richmond in June, 1862, in the heart of the Chickahominy swamps, from diarrhœa and fever, than a pitched battle would have cost us—ay, twice over, or more. Grant's soldiers suffered in the same way on the malarial levees and among the fever-cursed bayous of the Mississippi. The mysteries and miseries, the awful horrors, of human life under such circumstances are simply indescribable. To say that men sickened and died there " like sheep," by the thousands and tens of thousands, but feebly tells the story. And that was not all. For the seeds of disease then and there sown endured through after years; and thousands and tens of thousands more were thus afterward brought to a soldier's disabled life or to a soldier's grave as really and truly as if they had sickened and died before Richmond and Vicksburg. And the same is alike true of those who campaigned and soldiered in the Carolinas, in Tennessee, in Georgia, in Louisiana, in Texas, and elsewhere during the war.

Our losses in actual battle, however, were not so great as popularly supposed. Of course, the rush and roar of battle and the awful carnage of the battlefield, first and last, it goes without saying, cannot be overdrawn. Thucydides, Cæsar, Thiers, Napier, Comte de Paris, Swinton, and Badeau, all have tried it, and failed. As Mr. Lincoln once said in my presence:

"People not there would think everybody was going to get killed. It's like a runaway I once saw out in Illinois, during a political parade. The two horses bolted through the 'shanghai' fence, and ran alongside of it for a quarter of a mile or more, and then bolted back into the procession again. But there was not a buckle broken, nor a trace gone, nor a horse much hurt!"

Our Union regiment which suffered the most during the war (Fifth New Hampshire Infantry) lost only two hundred and ninety-five men in actually killed and mortally wounded, from 1861 to 1865, out of one thousand or so originally enlisted; and others, of course, still less. As a rule, "it takes a man's weight in lead to kill him in battle," and in even such severe engagements as Murfreesboro or Stone River it took twenty thousand rounds of artillery to hit seven hundred and twenty-eight men, and two million rounds of musketry to hit thirteen thousand eight hundred and thirty-two men. In other words, only one shot told in every one hundred and forty-four fired. In the Franco-German War, it took ninety-one and one half bullets and one and one half cannon shots on an average to even hit a Frenchman. Of the actually killed in battle, there was only one chance in about two hundred and fifty. In the Crimean War the British fired fifteen million shots and killed twenty-one thousand Russians, or one to every seven hundred shots. The French fired twenty-nine million shots and killed fifty-one thousand Russians, or one to every five hundred and ninety shots. The Russians fired forty-five million shots, at both British and French, and killed forty-eight thousand, or one to every nine hundred and ten shots.

During the war we fought over two thousand pitched battles and skirmishes—many of them really great engagements—averaging over one every day in the week, Sundays included. We had over three hundred battles in which our loss exceeded one hundred men each. We fought over one hundred such engagements as Bunker Hill, New Orleans, and Buena Vista. The Army of the Potomac lost more men in many a morning picket firing than the losses on both sides at the battles of both Trenton and Princeton. Nearly every army corps lost more men than George Washington lost in the whole of the Revolution. Our losses in the whole War of 1812 and with Mexico did not equal a single day's fighting at Gettysburg or Chattanooga. The Crimean campaign did not begin to compare with that of Grant against Vicksburg, nor the siege of Sebastopol with the siege of Petersburg. And Germany's total losses in the Franco-German War did not equal ours in the single campaign of 1864 against Richmond.

Our total number of enlistments was two million eight hundred and sixty-five thousand and twenty-eight, but as many of our men enlisted two or three times (for different terms of service), our total number of soldiers and sailors was probably about two million. Of these, we lost something over one hundred thousand in killed and mortally wounded, which was bad enough. But we lost nearly three hundred thousand from disease during the war, and have been losing largely from the sequences thereof every year since. Our ratio of killed was only about five per cent, but of deaths from other causes nearly fifteen per cent. So that the arrows of disease, invisible and stealthy though they be—apparently of small account—were nevertheless about three times as fatal and deadly as round shot and shells, grape and canister, bullets, bayonets, and sabers. Our losses in killed and wounded, however, exceeded those of any other modern war. For in the Crimea these were only about three per cent; in Austria in 1866, only about two and a half per cent; in the Franco-German war, 1870-71, only about three per cent; while in our great Civil War we lost nearly five per cent, and the Confederates over nine per cent.[1]

An army is really a city on legs, thoroughly organized

---

[1] See Appendix, p. 387. Also p. 395.

and commanded, complete within itself and a law unto itself. Our great armies East and West seldom moved less than a hundred thousand strong, often more, and they were as if a whole city, say, like Albany or Columbus or Indianapolis, rose up each morning and walked off complete in everything—clothing, food, medicine, ammunition, etc.—and each night camped down again complete in all things. The mere organization and command of such a body of men, so that everything will work like clockwork and "obey orders," is itself an immense job of work, requiring first-class brains. Then transportation, clothing, and feeding is another great task, requiring an almost divine providence and care. And hence a great quartermaster or a great commissary must also be a man of brains as well as a great commander.

Patriotism is a good thing, but the history of all wars shows that the soldier must be well clothed, well fed, and well paid to be gallant and efficient. Hence the great Frederick said: "An army is like a snake; it moves upon its belly!" And hence Grant and Sherman, Hooker and Meade, Thomas and Sheridan, always looked sharp after their quartermaster and commissary departments. So, too, they were alike careful of their medical department. If wounded or sick, soldiers must be well attended, and hence ambulances, stretchers, hospitals, etc., were always amply provided. There never was a war in which more care or better care was given to these humanities than in ours. And no great commander omitted to visit his hospitals regularly. So, also, the pay department was important. Men liked to get their "pay," and to send it to their families—in whole or part.

But all these were only preliminary and preparatory, so to speak, to the ordnance or arms department, which supplied the cannon, muskets, sabers, accouterments, ammunition, etc., which are the last analysis of war, and must be most looked after. The whole constituted a magnificent and terrible fighting machine—designed and built for battle, grim and to the death, savage and barbarous, of course, as war is[1]—controlled by one eye, directed by one hand, commanded by one will, supreme in all things, and when that was Grant's, or Sherman's, or Thomas's, or Sheridan's, something was certain to happen soon and somebody sure to get hurt.

In thinking it all over now and recalling what we passed through, in our four long and terrible years from Sumter to Appomattox, it really does seem amazing that we were not all either killed or wounded, or so disabled by battle or disease that any of us still survive. If anybody questions this, let him go out and rough it in our fields or forests or swamps for four years, with only a blanket (often we hadn't any or only a poor "shoddy" one) ; and go barefoot for days in fall or winter or spring, as many of us often had to when campaigning and soldiering down in Dixie. Often have I seen soldiers on the march or standing guard with only grain sacks or the remains of old blankets about their feet. (Valley Forge was bad, but they had log huts there and were in a friendly country; but often we had only "shelter tents" in winter, as at Fredericksburg, and were in the midst of bitter enemies.) This would be bad enough of itself; but add to this the chances of earthquake and volcano, of shot and shell, of bayonets and sabers and death-dealing strokes from every hill and valley, ravine and stream, and then see whether

> "A soldier's life is always gay,
> So why be melancholy, boys,
> So why be melancholy?"

as we used to sing around our camp fires or on the march, when we hadn't anything better to do or sing.

"I do not believe a man ever stood guard in front of

---

[1] Or, as Sherman once said, " War is hell!"

the enemy at night," said General Sherman on one occasion, "or passed through the crash of battle, without in a measure its telling upon his physical system. Nor did any man ever carry a knapsack, haversack, gun, and ammunition on those long marches, sleeping on the ground at night, exposed to all kinds of weather, living upon hardtack and other army fare, without injury to him. It may not show its effects in ten years or twenty years, but the results are sure to come."

For all this glorious life—such as it was—we paid our soldier boys the munificent sum of forty cents a day, in green backs, worth fifty cents or less to the dollar, most of the war! Why, we pay our common laborers on the streets a dollar and a half a day in gold, even in "hard times," and they don't take the risk of any such little accidents as shot and shell, bayonets and sabers, either. And they do not work in bad weather, and are sure of full rations and fair quarters every night, too.

Why, what is it that we do not owe 'the Men of 1861" and their widows and orphans? Is it any wonder we now have a large pension roll? Or is it not more wonderful that our old soldiers are not all on the pension roll? And should they not all be there soon, because of what they have been and done and suffered for the Republic? Or are they now all "frauds" and "dead beats" and mere "pension grabbers," as our anti-pension, latter-day patriots now allege? Or, rather, have we not now fallen on evil days unworthy of the Republic; days whose humor will presently pass away, and the nation turn again to honor and gratitude?

But are we, therefore, sorry we enlisted under the stars and stripes and fought for the Union? No, I think not. Hardly an officer or soldier would admit that. Though we would like a little more appreciation sometimes! Even our dead had but one regret, and that was, like poor

Nathan Hale's in the days of '76, "that they had but one life to give for their country." No, we are not sorry. We remember the good fellowship of the camp, the joy of the march, the first sight of the enemy, the excitement of the skirmish, the fierceness of the battle, the fury of the charge, the glory and satisfaction of the victory, the triumph of the flag, the salvation of the Republic—and our chances of promotion. No, we are not sorry. We are glad we enlisted. We are proud to be known as Lincoln's boys and Grant's old soldiers, even as Cromwell's men in after years were proud to be known as "Cromwell's old soldiers." God bless the flag! Long live the Republic! And thanks be to Almighty God (I speak it reverently and with bowed head),

> "The good ship Union's voyage is o'er,
>   At anchor safe she swings,
>     While loud and clear,
>     With cheer on cheer,
>   Her joyous welcome rings.
>
> Hurrah! Hurrah! It shakes the wave,
>   It thunders on the shore,
>     One flag, one land,
>     One heart, one hand,
>   One nation evermore."

In concluding this chapter on "Campaigning and Soldiering," I do not think I can do better than to quote the following remarks of General Sherman in 1875—his mature opinion of things after the war was well over. They will be found keen and incisive, as usual with him, and eminently suggestive and instructive:

"Very few of the battles in which I have participated were fought as described in European text-books, namely, in great masses, in perfect order, maneuvering by corps, divisions, and brigades. We were generally in a wooded country, and, though our lines were deployed according to tactics, the men generally fought in strong skirmish lines, taking the advantage of the shape of ground and of every cover. We were generally the assailants, and in wooded and broken countries the 'defensive' had a positive advantage over us, for they were always ready, had cover, and always knew the ground to their immediate front; whereas we, their assailants, had to grope our way over unknown ground, and generally found a clear field or prepared entanglements, that held us for a time under a close and withering fire. Rarely did the opposing lines in compact order come into actual contact, but when, as at Peach Tree Creek and Atlanta, the lines did become commingled, the men fought individually in every possible style, more frequently with the musket clubbed than with the bayonet, and in some instances the men clinched like wrestlers, and went to the ground together. Europeans frequently criticised our war, because we did not always take full advantage of a victory; the true reason was that habitually the woods served as a screen, and we often did not realize the fact that our enemy had retreated till he was already miles away and was again intrenched, having left a mere skirmish line to cover the movement, in turn to fall back to the new position. * * *

"When a regiment is deployed as skirmishers, and crosses an open field or wood under heavy fire, if each man runs forward from tree to tree, or stump to stump, and yet preserves a good general alignment, it gives great confidence to the men themselves, for they always keep their eyes well to the right and left, and watch their comrades; but when some few hold back, stick too close or too long to a comfortable log, it often stops the line and defeats the whole object. Therefore, the more we improve the firearm, the more will be the necessity for good organization, good discipline, and intelligence on the part of the individual soldier and officer. There is, of course, such a thing as individual courage, which has a value in war; but familiarity with danger, experience in war and its common attendants, and personal habit, are equally valuable traits, and these are the qualities with which we usually have to deal in war. All men naturally shrink from pain and danger, and only incur their risk from some higher motive, or from habit; so that I would define true courage to be a perfect sensibility of the measure of danger, and a mental willingness to incur it, rather than insensibility of danger, of which I have heard far more than I have seen. The most courageous men are generally unconscious of possessing the quality; therefore, when one professes it too openly, by words or bearing, there is reason to mistrust it. I would further illustrate my meaning by describing a man of true courage to be one who possesses all his faculties and senses perfectly when serious danger is actually present. * * *

"It is related of Napoleon that his last words were, 'Tête-d'armée!' Doubtless as the shadow of death obscured his memory, the last thought that remained for speech was of some event when he was directing an important 'head of column.' I believe that every general who has handled armies in battle must recall from his own experience the intensity of thought on some similar occasion, when by a single command he had given the finishing stroke to some complicated action; but to me recurs another thought that is worthy of record, and may encourage others who are to follow us in our profession. I never saw the rear of an army engaged in battle but I feared that some calamity had happened at the front—the apparent confusion, broken wagons, crippled horses, men lying about dead and maimed, parties hastening to and fro in seeming disorder, and a general apprehension of something dreadful about to ensue; all these signs, however, lessened as I neared the front, and there the contrast was complete—perfect order, men and horses full of confidence, and it was not unusual for general hilarity, laughing and cheering. Although cannon might be firing, the musketry clattering, and the enemy's shot hitting close, there reigned a general feeling of strength and security that bore a marked contrast to the bloody signs that had drifted rapidly to the rear; therefore, for comfort and safety, I surely would rather be at the front than the rear line of battle. So also on the march, the head of a column moves on steadily, while the rear is alternately halting and then rushing forward to close up the gap; and all sorts of rumors, especially the worst, float back to the rear. Old troops invariably deem it a special privilege to be in the front—to be at the 'head of column'—because experience has taught them that it is the easiest and most comfortable place, and danger only adds zest and stimulus to this fact.

"The hardest task in war is to lie in support of some position or battery, under fire without the privilege of returning it; or to guard some train left in the rear, within hearing but out of danger; or to provide for the wounded and dead of some corps which is too busy ahead to care for its own.

"To be at the head of a strong column of troops, in the execution of some task that requires brain, is the highest pleasure of war—a grim one and terrible, but which leaves on the mind and memory the strongest mark; to detect the weak point of an enemy's line; to break through with vehemence and thus lead to victory; or to discover some key-point and hold it with tenacity; or to do some other distinct act which is afterward recognized as the real cause of success. These all become matters that are never forgotten. Other great difficulties, experienced by every general, are to measure truly the thousand and one reports that come to him in the midst of conflict; to preserve a clear and well-defined purpose at every instant of time, and to cause all efforts to converge to that end.

"To do these things he must know perfectly the strength and quality of each part of his own army, as well as that of his opponent's, and must be where he can personally see and observe with his own eyes, and judge with his own mind. No man can properly command an army from the rear, he must be 'at its front;' and when a detachment is made the commander thereof should be informed of the object to be accomplished, and left as free as possible to execute it in his own way; and when an army is divided up into several parts, the superior should always attend that one which he regards as most important. Some men think that modern armies may be so regulated that a general can sit in an office and play on his several columns as on the keys of a piano; this is a fearful mistake. The directing mind must be at the very head of the army—must be seen there, and the effect of his mind and personal energy must be felt by every officer and man present with it, to secure the best results. Every attempt to make war easy and safe will result in humiliation and disaster."—Sherman's *Memoirs*, Vol. II, pages 394, 395, 406-408.

## CHAPTER XIII

### A GREAT QUARTERMASTER

IN the previous chapters I have several times alluded to the importance of the quartermaster's department. This is the department that supplies quarters, barracks, storehouses, hospitals, clothing, camp and garrison equipage, horses, mules, harness, wagons, ambulances, forage, transportation generally, and the thousand and one other things wherein the other departments fail or fall short. In short, this is the great business department of an army, as distinguished from its mere fighting department, and one is essential to the other.

A good quartermaster is expected to be "sufficient unto himself," and to make good the deficiencies of everybody else. I think it safe to say, were the secret history of our great campaigns in the Civil War known, no great commander on either side succeeded without a good quartermaster. In marked instances they themselves had previously been quartermasters—as Grant, Sherman, Sheridan, Joe Johnston, and others.

A signal instance of such an officer, conspicuous in many ways and for many things, was General Robert Allen, U. S. A., whom I venture to call a great quartermaster. In vindication of the brainy staff, as against the fighting line, let us see if we can arrive at some estimate of his work and worth, and thus rescue at least one staff officer from unmerited oblivion. A West Pointer of the class of '36, he performed various duty until the war with Mexico, when he was appointed quartermaster of the Kentucky Cavalry in Taylor's column, that moved *via* Monterey; but subsequently was assigned to Twiggs's Division

Gen. Robert Allen, 1864.

in Scott's column, that moved *via* Vera Cruz to the City of Mexico. This was a good position for that war, and Allen must have shown sterling qualities already, or General Twiggs (himself an old quartermaster) would not have selected him for the place. As it was, Allen—then a captain only—conducted affairs with marked ability; and it was the common remark of Twiggs that his division was "the best supplied of any in the army" there.

The secret of it was that his quartermaster, though gifted with a wholesome respect for red tape, was yet not afraid to cut it, when the occasion demanded. With much native tact and sagacity, he readily adapted himself to the changed condition of men and things in Mexico, and thus availed himself of all the resources of the country as Scott advanced. Scouring the *haciendas* far and wide, he found no lack of transport and rations, where other officers reported little; and when one method failed his fertile intellect soon devised another. After the fall of the City of Mexico he was placed in charge of our main depot there, and continued in charge of it until our final evacuation of the country.

That war left him a brevet major (a high rank in those days), "for gallant and meritorious conduct" at Cerro Gordo and elsewhere. Soon afterward he was ordered to California. Of course, when Sumter fell, and our Army jumped suddenly from thirteen thousand men to over half a million, with nearly a quarter of our old officers gone—"seceded" to Jeff Davis and the Confederacy—a quartermaster of such character and efficiency could not be allowed to fossilize on the Pacific Coast. Accordingly Allen, like Sheridan (then also on the Pacific Coast), was soon ordered East, and in October, 1861, was assigned to duty at St. Louis.

Fremont was still there, but his quartermaster (McKinstry) had already been relieved, and he himself was beginning to grow dimly conscious of his coming collapse. He attempted to combat his fate; and, regarding Allen as probably hostile, sought his removal. But Allen was backed up too strongly from Washington, and was himself too fertile of expedients to be caught napping. It was related at the time, and doubtless truly, that Fremont maintained such absolute control and espionage of the mails and telegraphs that no communication conflicting with his wishes could leave St. Louis. His new quartermaster, however, "flanked" this arrangement, by dispatching his letters and telegrams by special messengers to Springfield, Ill., and Indianapolis, Ind., to be forwarded from there!

In due time, however, Fremont reached his level, and was succeeded by Halleck, "Old Brains," as he was then called. With true military sagacity he called in and concentrated the scattered forces of Fremont's command, and soon brought to bear upon the unshapely masses his undoubted talent for organization and discipline. The "note of preparation" resounded everywhere throughout his department, but was especially audible at St. Louis and Cairo, which in the hands of Allen soon became great beehives of industry and energy. Into these two depots men and *matériel* poured from all quarters, and they early took rank as the Washington and Fortress Monroe of the West.

In February, 1862, General Halleck authorized Grant's movements up the Tennessee and the Cumberland, that resulted soon in the fall of Forts Henry and Donelson. The thrilling effects of these great victories history will never forget, appalled as we were by the dreary inaction or sickening disasters of our armies elsewhere. In these important movements, Allen (now a full colonel) shared largely. It will be noted that these movements were entirely by water, so that in addition to the general outfit and supply of the troops—no small job then—he had also to

## A Great Quartermaster

provide river transportation for about everything. When it is recollected that our forces thus equipped and moved were at least double the number of our total old Regular Army, it will be seen that his task was no easy one for that period of the war. How great it was then, it is now hard to comprehend.

We had four years of huge experience in war matters after that, during which our quartermaster's department was educated up, from its former petty work, to the supplying and moving of a million of men. But then (February, 1862) everything was new and cranky. Our lines of supply even had not yet been determined. Our resources were unknown; our contractors still untried. Barracks, storehouses, hospitals were to be built; corrals started; repair shops inaugurated; steamboats and railroads acquired; and horses, mules, wagons, ambulances, harness, forage, clothing, tents, equipage—everything, provided.

The "Volunteers" themselves as yet were an experiment; and the newly-fledged quartermasters, as a rule, did not know a "requisition" from an "invoice," nor an "abstract" from a "property return." It was under such conditions, raw and unformed, that the depots at St. Louis, Cairo, etc., had literally to be *created*—built up from nothing—and Grant's heavy force equipped, moved, and followed up, as he advanced into Kentucky and Tennessee. Yet the official reports show that Allen did the job well, and was warmly commended for his ability and judgment, his vigor and efficiency.[1]

Some idea of what our quartermaster's department was, prior to the Civil War, may be formed from the following extract from Report of Quartermaster General, 1860, page 189 of the volume of "President's Message and Accompanying Documents" for that year. He says: "At the

---
[1] Reports of Secretary of War and Quartermaster General, 1862, etc.

end of the last fiscal year, the number of clerks employed in this office was reduced from *thirteen* to eleven." (!) That is, less than many a post quartermaster had to employ in the years 1861 to 1865. Joseph E. Johnston, afterward lieutenant general, C. S. A., was then quartermaster general, U. S. A., and he begged for *"two* more" (!) clerks to bring up certain back "claims of quartermaster employees for military bounty land." As contrasted with these *eleven clerks*, in 1860, in December, 1865, the quartermaster general's office reported over *five hundred clerks*, and its work was still in arrears.[1]

Subsequently, after Pittsburg Landing, or Shiloh, when Halleck himself went to the front and advanced on Corinth, he took Allen along and advised freely with him. Halleck, while a prodigy of industry and an encyclopedia of knowledge, it goes without saying now, was a great red tapist, believing in the "circumlocution office," but he was soldier enough to know his own defects as a commander in the field.

Allen, on the contrary, always had a dislike for mere forms; and was gifted besides with that consummate comprehension and knowledge of affairs, seemingly intuitive, which Mr. Lincoln used to define so well by that homely phrase "horse-sense."

Of really poetic tastes and liberal culture—few Army officers being so well versed in letters—Allen yet possessed enough common sense as to all practical matters to make the fortunes of half a dozen brigadiers—as they run. Had he chosen command instead of logistics, there is good reason to believe he would have made one of our most successful generals. As it was, his union with Halleck in the West, as his chief quartermaster and trusted friend, gave our army there the benefit of their mutual gifts, and resulted altogether most favorably for the country.

[1] Report of General M. C. Meigs, Quartermaster General, U. S. A., 1865.

## A Great Quartermaster

When Halleck was ordered East, later in 1862, as a sort of general in chief or confidential adviser to the War Department, Colonel Allen was sent back to St. Louis, as the then natural brain of the quartermaster's department in the great West. From there he directed the supplies, that followed up and sustained the army of General Curtis, in its arduous campaign through Missouri and Arkansas, which resulted in the victory of Pea Ridge and occupancy of Helena. At the same time he kept the Cumberland, the Tennessee, and the Mississippi swarming with transports, bearing men and supplies to Rosecrans, Grant, Sherman, and Pope, as they operated in turn against Murfreesboro, Island No. 10, Memphis, Chickasaw Bluffs, and down the Mississippi generally. When at last, in 1863, Grant withdrew from all minor points, and concentrating his forces sat down with the grimness of destiny before Vicksburg, convinced, like Scipio before Carthage, that Vicksburg *must be taken* ("*Delenda est Carthago*") as the vital condition of success in the Mississippi Valley, the quartermaster's department in the West was, indeed, put upon its mettle.

Our force operating about Vicksburg, when Grant got fairly to work, was never much less than one hundred thousand men, and, say, fifty thousand animals—private, artillery, cavalry, draught, all included. To these must be added, say, fifty thousand men and twenty-five thousand animals more, that were scattered from Vicksburg to St. Louis, along the Mississippi, and through the States of Tennessee, Kentucky, Missouri, and Arkansas. All of these were depending on St. Louis, directly or indirectly, for almost everything they used or consumed. Not only clothing, camp and garrison equipage, forage, and general quartermaster supplies had to be provided and pushed forward; but subsistence, ordnance, medical stores, etc., also must go; and the quartermaster's department, of course, was charged with the duty of forwarding the whole.

When it is remembered that Vicksburg is over eight hundred miles from St. Louis, and that all troops and supplies had to be collected and forwarded either from that base or from Cairo or Cincinnati—its two outlying dependencies—and that all the unserviceable *matériel*, broken-down animals, and sick and wounded men that were constantly accumulating at the front, had to be re-transported to the rear and disposed of somehow, some idea may be formed of the kind of brain and nerve then required by the chief quartermaster at St. Louis. Yet our official reports show that Allen managed affairs there so ably and skillfully that our army before Vicksburg and in all that military division never wanted long or materially for anything.[1]

Indeed, the quartermaster's department in the West, from almost nothing in 1861, had grown into a vast and potent machine, with a weak wheel here, perhaps, and a rotten cog there, yet, as a whole, its operations were amazing in extent and wonderful for general excellence. As its chief, Allen presided over everything, remaining mostly at St. Louis, but taking flying trips also to Cincinnati, Louisville, Cairo, and down the Mississippi generally, to see how matters fared. St. Louis was the primary base, but he established a secondary depot at Memphis, which ultimately grew into large proportions; and, of course, still another at the front, which shifted its position as the front itself shifted. Both of these were placed in charge of able and efficient chiefs; but the immediate charge of the great depot at St. Louis was retained by himself, assisted by a corps of subordinate quartermasters.

A most difficult and widespread organization was thus

---

[1] Reports of Secretary of War, General Grant, and General Meigs (quartermaster general), 1863.

created and commanded, and supplies of all kinds pushed forward to Vicksburg and elsewhere, with almost the beneficence of Providence and certainty of fate. To the casual observer much may have—must have—seemed chaotic and confused. But there was a governing mind controlling the whole; and the result was a generous abundance at the front of all necessary things, that must have delighted the heart of General Grant and put life into his gallant army.

Of course, with such a general as Grant to command and fight—sagacious, intrepid, resourceful, unyielding as fate—and such a quartermaster as Allen to back his operations, Vicksburg was bound to fall, and with its fall the Mississippi flowed "unvexed" from Cairo to the Gulf. This was our first really *great success* of the war, and verily "bisected the Confederacy." It was really another death wound, like Gettysburg in the East on the same day (July 4, 1863), and those two great victories taken together made that Fourth of July memorable in history forever.

With the fall of Vicksburg there was a lull in affairs in the valley of the Mississippi. But soon again "the note of preparation" sounded, and transportation and supplies were called for, for the troops that moved in various directions; and, subsequently, for Sherman's heavy column that moved first from Meridian to Memphis, strengthening as it moved, and then struck boldly off across the country, through the heart of Tennessee, to succor the Army of the Cumberland, then beleaguered by Bragg at Chattanooga.

Without notice or requisition from Sherman (so secretly did he move), General Allen nevertheless "divined" the march of this column, and on his own responsibility *hurried steamers up the Tennessee, that met the column at Eastport, and ferried it over without delay.* This foresight much facilitated this great march, and speeded Sherman to Chattanooga in time to share in the signal victories of Lookout Mountain and Missionary Ridge.

These were conspicuous events, known to everybody in the West. But, meanwhile, as a part of his lesser duties, Allen was also furnishing transportation and supplies to the troops in New Mexico, Utah, and across the plains generally, and he also fitted out and followed up various Indian expeditions operating in what are now Dakota, Wyoming, and Montana. The troops engaged in these, to be sure, were not numerous; but their lines of supply were extended and hazardous (no railroad west of the Missouri then), and the work required both forethought and sagacity.

Now, however, came a change, and a still larger sphere of duty. In fact, a little before this, early in the fall of 1863, Allen was ordered to move his station from St. Louis to Louisville; but not to release his hold upon St. Louis.[1] Chickamauga had been fought, Rosecrans had retreated to Chattanooga, where he was closely besieged, and disaster and gloom impended over our cause in the Southwest generally. Our successes down the Mississippi were being overclouded by these more recent events in Tennessee and Georgia; and the problem was how to restore our prestige and advance our arms in that important quarter. General Grant himself, "the hero of Donelson and Vicksburg," as he was then chiefly known, was ordered posthaste from New Orleans to Chattanooga (though lame and on crutches, from the fall of his horse)—the Secretary of War meeting him at Louisville *en route*. And Allen was directed to grapple with the question of supplies,

---

[1] The immediate charge of St. Louis he now committed to General William Myers, U. S. A., of whom he afterward said with characteristic generosity: "More work, with less pretension, has been accomplished at that point than any other under my control, and I accord to General Myers the chief merit of its performance. He has never been appalled by the magnitude or complication of his duties, but has done his work with cheerfulness and alacrity."—"Annual Report" of General Allen, 1865.

as Nashville and points below called for them. Quartermaster General Meigs himself hastened from Washington to Chattanooga, to watch matters in person, so critical was the situation.

Evidently there was now heavy work to be done at Louisville, Nashville, and beyond; both as to organization and management. For our troops at Chattanooga, though already on half rations and their animals starving by the thousands, were soon to be nearly or quite doubled by those moving to their relief. The problem looked not merely to the succor and relief of Chattanooga, which was a *fait accompli* by the superb victory of Missionary Ridge, November, 1863; but also to the equipment and supply of Sherman's formidable column, consolidated from the armies of the Ohio, the Cumberland, and the Tennessee, that it was proposed in the spring of 1864 to direct on Atlanta and beyond, if possible.

Here was work of itself sufficient to overwhelm, if not appall, most brigadiers. For it was computed that Sherman's total force for his great campaign, to wind up with his "March down to the Sea," including those to be left behind in Tennessee and Kentucky to hold the country and guard his railroads back to the Ohio, would seldom fall much, if any, below one hundred and fifty thousand men and, say, seventy-five thousand animals. And this was found to be the case afterward. But, in addition to this, as if to see how much could be heaped upon one pair of shoulders, General Allen was also charged with the supply of all our troops up and down the Mississippi and across the plains and through our Territories, the same as before; and his "reports" and "property returns" (1864-65) show, that in the aggregate this "job" was not greatly inferior to the other.

To meet the demands of his new position, he was now designated "Chief Quartermaster" of the valley of the Mississippi" (he had already been promoted to the rank of brigadier general); and vested with the necessary authority, accordingly. This did not suit General Sherman, however, who now insisted upon Allen's joining him in the field, as chief quartermaster of his combined armies, and applied for him with that view, proposing to confide to him a wide discretion. Allen, also, was now desirous of active field service, as he had been tied down to depots in the rear for so large a part of the war, and so he proceeded to join General Sherman, then near Kingston, Ga.; supposing that Sherman's application would, of course, be granted. But it was refused by Secretary Stanton, on the ground that General Allen's services were of more value to the government at Louisville—in fact, indispensable—in the position he then occupied, as chief quartermaster of the valley of the Mississippi, "in which *several armies* were operating," rather than merely "directing the transportation and supplies of *one army* in the field, already equipped and provided."

The really colossal work Allen was now called on to grapple with is thus summed up, in part, in his "Annual Report" for 1865:

"It (Nashville) drew heavily upon the resources of the country, already partially exhausted by requisition from other quarters. The heaviest items were purchased at remote points—remote, I mean, from the base of operations —and their transportation monopolized and taxed to their utmost *all the steamboats on the Western waters, and all the rolling stock on the Western and Southwestern railroads*. It was a herculean task to collect, transfer, and concentrate at one point horses and mules by the hundreds of thousands, corn and oats by the million of bushels, hay by the tens of thousands of tons, wagons and ambulances by the tens of thousands—fitted out with harness, etc.— subsistence stores by the hundreds of thousands of tons, and miscellaneous articles in the aggregate proportionably large. At the same time, immense trains of railroad stock, engines, cars, etc., were brought from the East, crossed over the Ohio River at Louisville,[1] and sent forward to transfer the stores from Nashville to the front."

In this terse but graphic statement, it will be observed, he says nothing about clothing, camp and garrison equipage, nor ordnance stores, nor medical supplies—all very large for such a campaign—nor about troops, well and disabled, whose transportation alone, to and from the front, must have constituted a huge item likewise.

In brief, to make up his supplies and keep them up, he had to lay the whole North under contribution. He resolved to sustain Sherman, at all hazards and at whatever cost, if there was power and money enough in the government to do it; and right well did he keep his resolution. He drew heavily on all the chief depots East, as far indeed as Boston, for clothing, equipage, and general quartermaster stores; and literally ransacked the Northwest for horses, mules, corn, oats, hay, and whatever else it possessed that Sherman needed. The whole was concentrated on the Ohio and Mississippi, and thence poured into Nashville and other points as required, by railroad and steamboat *via* the Cumberland and the Tennessee, until all such dependencies were duly supplied and kept supplied. Nashville became one vast storehouse and corral, with warehouses covering whole blocks, one of them over a quarter of a mile long, with corrals and stables by the ten and twenty acres each, and repair shops by the fieldful.

Thus Sherman's great campaign became preeminently a success; primarily, of course, because of his own great genius as a military commander, born soldier that he was; but also largely *because his Quartermaster's Department throughout sustained itself so excellently*. Before his

---

[1] There was no bridge there then.

campaign began, it was scarcely believed, in high quarters, that this could be done. To supply an army of such a magnitude, over a single line of faulty railroad, hundreds of miles from its true base, was a new and untried thing.[1]

The best soldiers in Europe pronounced the attempt quixotic, and the War Department and Mr. Lincoln, it must be confessed, grew more and more nervous, as Sherman plunged deeper and deeper into Georgia. The Army of the Potomac, not much more numerous as a whole, professed to be baffled by it, again and again; it never got a hundred miles away from its base at Washington on a single-track railroad; and experienced quartermasters East and West, of acknowledged capacity, were dubious as to the result. But Allen and his subordinates, at Nashville, Chattanooga, and elsewhere, accepted the task, and not only "filled the bill," but did it magnificently.[2]

In his "Official Report of the Atlanta Campaign" Sherman said: "From that day to this (May 1 to September 15, 1864) stores have been brought forward in *wonderful abundance*, with a *surplus* that has enabled me to feed the army well during the *whole period* of time." It is not often that the quartermaster's department gets such generous recognition. But Sherman could well afford it; for the whole problem of his campaign was wrapped up in this one question of *transportation and supplies*, as no one more willingly conceded than that great captain himself always.[3]

With the fall of Atlanta and Sherman's departure for

---

[1] It is true he had river transportation also, *via* the Cumberland and the Tennessee to Nashville part of the year. But from Louisville south there was only a single track road to Nashville about two hundred miles, and it was one hundred and fifty-one miles more to Chattanooga, and one hundred and thirty-eight more to Atlanta, or nearly five hundred in all from the Ohio—his true base.

[2] Several of his officers were of great ability and singular devotion—particularly the Senior and Supervising Quartermaster at Nashville, General J. L. Donaldson, another West Pointer of rare gifts and superior merit—but it does not come within the scope of this chapter to particularize further.

[3] In his "Official Report of Atlanta Campaign," speaking of this, Sherman frankly says: "I know more solicitude was felt by the Lieutenant General commanding, and by the military world at large, on this, than on any other one problem involved in the success of the campaign.—*War Records*, vol. xxxviii, part i, p. 84.

Savannah, General Thomas soon coupled the defeat and almost annihilation of Hood before Nashville. This ended the war, practically, in the West; and though General Allen continued to send large supplies to Nashville, and down the Mississippi generally, until after the surrender of Lee and Johnston, yet his chief work was over.

It is true, he "lent a hand" in the transportation East of the Twenty-third Corps, in the spring of 1865; and had considerable to do in fitting out and following up various cavalry expeditions into East Tennessee and West Virginia soon afterward; and also was somewhat busy again later in the season, when Sherman's and Thomas's veterans returned to Louisville for muster out and retransportation to their homes. But all this was "child's play," compared with the multiplied and herculean labors he had performed throughout the war, and for which he was duly brevetted major general to date from March 13, 1865.

To present some of his work a little more specifically, I give the following figures from official reports; which, it is submitted, speak for themselves. From October 1, 1861, to June 30, 1865, he received and disbursed himself, on account of the United States, $106,694,657.24. During the same period there was disbursed at St. Louis, under his direction, $90,799,435.88 in addition. That is to say, during the said period, he made and controlled an aggregate expenditure of $197,494,093.12 of the public funds. His total disbursements during the Civil War, including those prior to October 1, 1861, and subsequent to June 30, 1865, exceeded $200,000,000—a greater sum, I venture to say, than was ever handled by a single quartermaster in this or any other country, during an equal period of time. *And not a dollar of it stolen or misappropriated.* To gain some idea of the magnitude of this amount, and what it represents, and what the Civil War cost us, it may not be amiss to add, that the total disbursements of the quartermaster's department for 1860 by all its officers—from Boston to San Francisco, and from the Lakes to the Gulf—were only about $6,000,000!

To enumerate the supplies purchased and transported by this great sum of money is, of course, impracticable. But a few of the principal items are suggestive, to wit: 26,234,423 bushels of oats; 8,864,173 bushels of corn; 337,518 tons of hay; 100,364 horses; 75,329 mules; 60,854 sets of harness; 6,638 wagons; 1,269 ambulances.

Other heavy items will occur to the reader, but those above cited are difficult to realize, so vast are the figures. Suppose we try to. For example, if you hitch six mules to each of his wagons, the usual army team, and allow sixty feet to each team and wagon, the usual marching distance when teams are well "closed up," they would extend about seventy-five miles. If you hitch two more of the mules to each of his ambulances, and allow forty feet to each team and ambulance, their usual marching distance, they would extend about ten miles more. This would still leave about forty thousand of his mules ungeared. If you put these in column, two by two, and allow fifteen feet to each span, which is as close as they can well travel, they would stretch out about forty-eight miles farther. If to these we add the surplus horses, at the same rate, they would extend one hundred and fifty miles more. That is, altogether, they would constitute an army train or traveling caravan two hundred and eighty-three miles long; which is forty-three miles farther than from New York to Washington; or, to turn the other way, the train would reach from New York, through Connecticut, Massachusetts, and New Hampshire, to Portsmouth.

If now his wagons are driven up to his huge pile of forage, and loaded at the rate of two thousand pounds to each wagon, the usual marching load, it would take one million eighty-seven thousand one hundred and seventy-eight wagons more to move the remainder of his oats, corn, and hay. These wagons all put in line, with teams in marching order, would extend to the enormous distance of twelve thousand two hundred and fifty-seven miles, or more than half around the earth. If, in addition, we were to load up the clothing and the tentage which he received and issued, of which no figures are given above, we would require several thousands of wagons more.

To load up the rest of his quartermaster stores, such as iron, coal, lumber, lime, hardware, paints, oils, rope, etc., would complete a wagon train that, altogether, would belt the globe. If now at the head of this grand column we were to place his garrison equipage, in the hands of his numerous civilian employees (clerks, mechanics, teamsters, laborers, etc.), amounting to the many thousands—at Nashville alone over twelve thousand in 1865—with orders to "Forward, march!" what a blare of bugles, and what a flutter and waving of guidons and colors there would be!

Such was Robert Allen: soldier, gentleman, Christian —a great staff officer; an American and a quartermaster of whom we may well be proud. I had the honor to serve under him nearly two years (1863-65), chiefly at Nashville, Tenn.

Other good quartermasters we had, such as Rucker, at Washington; Donaldson, at Nashville; Ingalls, in the Army of the Potomac; and Easton, in the Army of the Mississippi. All these were great and brainy officers, too —all old West Pointers, of course. I knew and honored them all. But Allen, I think, outtopped them all, and will live in history as the Great Quartermaster of our Civil War.

## CHAPTER XIV
### THE ANGEL OF THE THIRD CORPS

It is true that our mothers and sisters, our wives and sweethearts, did not do any fighting during the war. They did not carry muskets, nor swing sabers, nor storm batteries, nor even campaign and march with us. But they did pretty much everything else; and in many instances and on frequent occasions they felt the war even more keenly than the average officer and soldier did. They scraped lint; they made havelocks and hospital bandages; they packed our knapsacks; they cheered us as we left; they prayed for us while absent; and they welcomed our return. They were our faithful allies in the rear, and with cheerful hearts sent their bravest and best to the front for four long years, though certain of heart-breaking news sooner or later. Alas, how "long" they were to many a poor lady!

So, too, these allies thronged our hospitals and hospital boats, both at the front and in the rear; and by their angelic presence and divine sympathy saved many a poor fellow's life, or eased and comforted his dying hours. So, too, they organized "Soldiers' Children's Homes" all over the North, where the orphan children of our soldiers would be tenderly cared for and educated, and future homes provided for them. What nobler work could there be than this?

I did not meet "Mother Bickerdyke," of Western memory; but I did meet Miss Gilson, of Eastern memory, and beg to record some recollections of her here. For over two years she came under my frequent observation in the Army of the Potomac; and I personally knew her, and

## The Angel of the Third Corps

esteemed her greatly. Her full name was Helen L. Gilson, and she was from Chelsea, near Boston. She was a young lady of beauty and culture, bred in the best New England ways—and there are no better ways anywhere. She came down to the army and entered upon hospital life, solely because of her intense New England patriotism and high sense of Christian duty.

She did not linger at Washington or Alexandria, as many other nurses did; but joined the army, ready for field duty, with her own stout wagons and horses, camp equipage, etc., complete, at her own charge and expense. She had her carriage, for bad weather, but generally rode on horseback—a perfect horsewoman—and a handsome picture she made on the background of army life; well but never showily attired, and reining her thoroughbred well in hand. She was never alone, but always accompanied by an elderly gentleman—I think the mayor of Chelsea or some other old home friend.

At parades and reviews she was often in evidence, and apparently enjoyed such military spectacles; but did not affect the society of our brigadiers and their staff officers, charmed as many were with her. Nor did she repel our gold-laced Hotspurs, but went on her own sweet way among both officers and men, wherever her chosen hospital work took her. Many a young aid and surgeon or assistant surgeon fell desperately in love with her, but all their sighings and pleadings were in vain—she seemed to be as cold as Minerva and as chaste as Diana; or as if already vowed to another, and meaning to keep her vow.

I met her first at the White House, Virginia, on the Peninsula, in June, 1862, where she was serving on a hospital boat, nursing our sick and wounded, after the battle of Fair Oaks, or Seven Pines, as the Confederates call it. We were lying in front of Richmond, and I had been sent back to the White House for clothing, camp equipage, etc., and not getting through with my requisitions had to stay all night there. There was no hotel there—the White House was merely an army depot; and I was given quarters on her boat for the night, with some other like officers. After supper we gathered on deck and chatted for a long time, on that mild June evening, rehearsing our various experiences—Miss Gilson among us. She spun her "yarns" with the rest of us; but all so modestly and intelligently, that everybody was delighted with her. We parted reluctantly, all expressing a hope we might some time meet again.

A month or so afterward, along early in July, after McClellan's famous "change of base" to Harrison's Landing, or "the Seven Days' Battle," as it was euphemistically called, I was going down the James River on a hospital boat myself, burning up with the Chickahominy fever (about as bad as the "Santiago fever," I guess!), when the door of my stateroom quietly opened and in stepped Miss Gilson, with a bowl of iced lemonade—the first "ice" I had seen that summer. She did not recognize me at first, I was so sallow and wan and fever-stricken, and used up. But I quickly recognized her, and really thought her an angel or something akin to one, and I have never drunk a draught that seemed half so good as that iced lemonade! Then she sopped my head with ice water, and bathed my face and hands, and presently also recognized me. But I soon dropped into a deep sleep, from which I did not awake until we reached Fortress Monroe. Ill as I was, I had been in the saddle, for two or three days and nights most of the time, as necessitated by that strategic "change of base;" and now was *en route* for home on sick leave. I had read about "the angel of the camp," etc. But here was one *in propria persona*.

Afterward I often saw her riding and driving through the army, but remember her particularly in the great field hospitals at Potomac Creek, after the bloody battles of Fredericksburg and Chancellorsville, Va., 1862-63. She was dressing wounds and nursing the sick there, a good Samaritan in very deed. In the intervals of this Christ-like work she would read religious and patriotic pieces to our poor fellows, or sing like a seraph. She was never careless in her dress, but was always simply and tastefully habited, if the only lady present; and she usually wore a white veil twined about her head to hold back her abundant chestnut hair.

During all those dark days of the winter and spring of 1862-63, she made her headquarters with the Third Corps, and moved about our vast hospital tents there a vision of grace and beauty, as well as of charity and mercy. It is no wonder that our Boys in Blue of the old Third Army Corps christened her our "Angel of the Corps;" our American "Florence Nightingale;" and, like the British heroes of the Crimea, with the original Florence Nightingale, "turned to kiss her shadow on the wall," as she passed along the hospital wards.

During the winter of 1862-63, while we lay near Falmouth, Va., many colored people were also brought into our hospitals; poor abandoned slaves, broken down and used up and abandoned because no longer of any use to their masters; all suffering from unspeakable hardships and exposures. But Miss Gilson cared for these poor fellow-creatures, just as gently and tenderly as for our Union soldiers. For they were all God's creatures in her eyes; and should they not all have the same kindly care?

I remember one poor slave boy, thirteen or fourteen years old, that was brought into our camp while we lay at Boscobel, near Falmouth (a former plantation of George Washington's, I believe). He had been abused and neglected, and his limbs were so frost-bitten and injured that he had to have both feet amputated, and thus be made a helpless cripple for life. But Miss Gilson cheered and comforted him, sat by his side for days, taught him to read and write, read and sang to him by the hour, as well as prayed for him and taught him how to pray; and thus charmed his pains and sorrows away. I never knew what became of him afterward; but I suppose that some kind man or woman got him North into a good "Home," after the war closed.

After Chancellorsville, she went to Gettysburg with the Army of the Potomac, I believe, or joined it soon afterward, and continued with it until 1864, or thereabouts. Then she went down to South Carolina, to look after the freedmen there; believing that they needed her most. She continued there, nursing and teaching in the camps and hospitals and on the plantations there, until the close of the war. But I was ordered West in November, 1863, and never saw her afterward. After the war, she married some worthy Massachusetts man; but she is now many years deceased. The "Third Army Corps Union," I am glad to say, subsequently erected a handsome monument to her, at Chelsea, Mass.; but her life-record is her own best monument. No purer patriot, or nobler lady, or truer American lived during our great Civil War; and I beg to lay upon her distant New England grave this passing tribute to her memory.

## CHAPTER XV

### SOME ARMY LETTERS

WHILE in the Army, it was my habit to write home every Sunday. Not models of literature and philosophy; but simple army letters, such as many an officer and soldier wrote home at that time. My people preserved most of them, and when I got home handed them back to me; and here follow many of them. They are given substantially as written, except some privacies of no account to the general reader. If dull at times, they are at least true and faithful pictures of army life, as we lived it at the time; and I trust they will not be without some historic value. They were not written for publication, but for the private perusal of my own family and friends; and doubtless will prove all the more interesting and welcome to many on that account. At all events, I commit them to the reader for what they may be worth, as genuine and real experiences of campaigning and soldiering from 1861 to 1865, in both the Army of the Potomac and the Department of the Cumberland. I beg pardon in advance for many shortcomings, and especially for constant "egoism"—inseparable, of course, from such letters.

My regiment left Trenton, N. J., Thursday, August 29, 1861,[1] and reached Washington, D. C., next day. We went into camp on Capitol Hill, a mile or so east of the capitol, and here follow said letters in order:

"CAMP BURLINGTON, WASHINGTON, D. C.
Sept. 8, 1861. Sunday afternoon.

"DEAR BROTHER: Yours of fourth was duly received. I intended to write home ere this, but a multiplicity of matters has prevented.

---
[1] Was commissioned August 24, 1861.

"I am very well, and very content. Am pleased far better than I expected to be. Have already got the camp into working order, and this coming week will have little to do. Last week I worked very hard. Think I must have averaged from six to ten hours in the saddle every day. My resolve was to complete our equipments at once, while here at headquarters, and so save harder work hereafter. The field and staff all say I have succeeded well. * * * I should not write it here, had they not come and volunteered it. It is at least certain, that there is no other camp near us, in which the soldiers are as well off as the Fifth New Jersey. A half mile away is a —— regiment, and hard by them a —— regiment, and both live like pigs. Our men shall not, if I can help it; and I believe I can.

"The morals of the camp are good. * * * There are many noble fellows among them; a large number are Methodists. We have had a prayer meeting every night since last Sunday, and two hopeful conversions. We need a chaplain badly. * * * We have had no preaching to-day, but a prayer meeting is called for this evening.

"Our wagon train arrived safely on Friday. Now we are all right. I had already secured three four-horse teams from the government; New Jersey sent me eleven, and two ambulances. This makes us fourteen four-horse teams, and two two-horse ambulances—all that we want for the transportation of the regiment anywhere.

"My horse stands camp life splendidly. * * * Have got another horse, a little pony, and so have two to ride now. * * * You ought to see the pony; he is about as big as a rat, and is the greatest little fellow to canter you ever saw! My own horse suits me, in every respect; and I shall save him all I can.

"Surgeon Fisher and I rode into Washington to service

this morning, and I have allowed no work in my department all day. It is my resolve, that there shall be no Sunday work with us, if it can be avoided.

"We live well. The lieutenant colonel (Mott), the major (Truax), and I mess together; and we have every comfort we could desire. Plenty of meat; plenty of vegetables; and tolerable chickens (if we pay well for them). Have no fears of Washington. We have fifty thousand men here—too strong for any force the rebels can bring against us."

"ALEXANDRIA, VA.
Sept. 22, 1861. Sunday evening.

"DEAR FATHER AND FAMILY: Here we are in 'Dixie's Land,' encamped upon the 'sacred soil!' We left Camp Burlington, near Washington, yesterday about 2 P. M. and arrived here about 8 P. M. last night. The troops came by steamboat; the baggage train went by land. The colonel proffered me permission to come with the troops; but I preferred to accompany our train. I left Washington with a train of seventeen wagons about 5 P. M. Crossed Long Bridge, and entered upon the 'sacred soil' about 5.30 P. M. Shortly after, it began to rain, and it poured incessantly all the way here, and far into the night. Fortunately, I had been thoughtful enough to strap my waterproofs on my horse; and donning these, came through dry as a feather. I had a rear guard of twenty men, all of whom I put aboard the wagons. Then with my wagon-master in the rear, with my quartermaster's sergeant by my side, at the head of our column, we marched gallantly down to Alexandria!

"About halfway here, whom should we meet but Colonel Jonathan Cook and a carriage load of other Jerseymen, returning from Alexandria to Washington. I had come upon a squad of soldiers, guarding the road, and had rode up to their watch fire to obtain a cup of coffee, while the train was halted to rest, when Johnty hailed me with, 'Hello, New Jersey, how are you!'

"Entering Alexandria, an officer met us, and conducted me to the camping ground. Here I drew the wagons up in line, posted my guard, with orders to remain geared up, until further orders; and then through the pouring rain went off in quest of the regiment. A corporal was sent to conduct me through the town. We went first to the wharf. Here we found part of the troops, comfortably quartered in the warehouses, and the other part quartered in the famous, or rather infamous, *Marshall House*, where Ellsworth fell. Thence I rode to General Montgomery's headquarters, where I found our staff. The general received me like a prince, ordered supper for us all, and quartered us in an adjoining hotel for the night. Thence I sent orders to the wagons to ungear, feed, and make themselves as comfortable as possible till morning.

"This (Sunday) morning we moved out to camp. All day, till near nightfall, we have been busy pitching tents and arranging matters. Now, once more, we are pretty well settled. Our camp is just on the outskirts of Alexandria, not more than a half a mile from General Montgomery's headquarters. The probability is, that we shall remain here for some time as a guard to the city. Our camp is high and dry; infinitely more pleasant than the former one. Very likely we shall remain here all winter, quartered in town. * * *

"Fortunately, my boy Charley has consented to remain, at least until next spring, and he is invaluable. He is the best boy in camp, and I don't know what I would do without him. He can cook, wash, mend, clean horses, pitch and strike tents, and in short do anything he has a mind to. Above all, he is faithful and honest, as a hot day is long."

## Some Army Letters

"ALEXANDRIA, VA.
Sept. 29, 1861. Sunday evening.

"DEAR FATHER AND FRIENDS: We have been in high glee here all day. The much-feared and widely announced Munson's Hill is ours, without firing a gun. Yesterday afternoon our troops advanced upon it in two columns, and the rebels fled in all directions. This morning I rode out to see it, with General Montgomery and staff. We started at 10 A. M., and were gone all day; making a wide reconnoissance of the forts, the pickets, and the general lines of the Union Army.

"The works at Munson's Hill were of the most absurd character. There has never been a single cannon mounted there. The whole thing has been a grand humbug and bugaboo! Naturally, it is a strong position; and our men will soon make it impregnable. Inclosed you will find a twig of a tree, growing on the peak of Munson's Hill.

"I am weary with the long ride, and must close. The Rev. Thomas Sovereign is here, and has been appointed chaplain to the regiment." * * *

"ALEXANDRIA, VA.
Oct. 6, 1861. Sunday afternoon.

"DEAR BROTHER AND FRIENDS: I write you today, not from 'Camp near Alexandria,' but from Alexandria itself. We broke up camp and moved into Alexandria on Friday afternoon. Eight companies of our regiment are now here, quartered in town: one at the Slave Pen, in charge of political prisoners; one at the Provost Marshal's, as City Police; one on an adjoining street to assist them; and three in the Marshall House, where Ellsworth fell, as general garrison. Our other two companies are stationed at Fort Ellsworth, with some eight hundred marines, about two miles from the colonel's quarters. At present they are detached from our command, and report to Captain Wainwright, who commands the fort. The staff are quartered in two handsome Secesh brick houses, on Prince Street, about two squares from General Montgomery's headquarters.

"My own room is a large fine parlor, on the ground floor. The door opens into the hall; two windows in front, opening on the street; two in rear, opening down to the floor, and so out to a piazza and large yard. My bed —feather bed and hair mattress, with rosewood bedstead —stands in one corner; in another stands a mahogany sideboard; near that a rosewood sofa; next, a mahogany wall table; next, a handsome piano (!); next, a splendid stove; next, a mahogany clothespress; next, a stylish hat-rack; next, a mahogany washstand, with bowl, pitcher, soap-dish, and brush-dish complete. I am writing on a mahogany center-table, covered with a blue and yellow damask tablecloth; and overhead is a handsome chandelier, with four gas-burners and cut glass shades! I forgot to say that I have in addition a half dozen sofa-bottom chairs, and one large rocking-chair! If this be war, 'who would not be a soldier?' Abandoned and confiscated Secesh property, of course.

"We found two 'contrabands' in our house, who last June were abandoned by their master, and told to take care of the house and themselves the best way they could. No provisions, and not a cent of money. Such is 'chivalry!'

"The colonel has relieved me of the whole commissary, or provision department, by appointing Lieutenant W—— to the place, and leaving me to my quartermaster's duties proper—fuel, forage, tents, quarters, transportation, etc. The appointment was at my instance, and relieves me of unpleasant duties.

"For some reason, I know not why, I seldom get the Trenton papers. Am much obliged for *The Christian Advocate,* and hope you will send it regularly.

"Was at the Methodist church this morning. A good sermon, on the resurrection, with sacrament."

"ALEXANDRIA, VA.
Oct. 13, 1861.

"DEAR FATHER AND FRIENDS: This has been an eventful day with us. About ten o'clock a party of us; namely, the colonel, lieutenant colonel, major, surgeon, commissary, adjutant, Captain Sewell, and myself, together with a daughter of the colonel now visiting the regiment, started from here on horseback for Mount Vernon. It is about ten miles distant. For seven miles we found our pickets constantly in view, but at the end of that distance, as we crossed a little run, we left the last of our troops behind. From there to Mount Vernon we were without our lines, and in the enemy's country. Nothing, however, happened to us, and the ride was most exhilarating. The day was magnificent, one of those grand and gorgeous October days, when the sun looks down from an unclouded sky, and summer seems lingering in the lap of autumn.

"We were a gay and gallant party; seven of us on horseback, and all armed to the teeth. Small as our party was, we were good for at least seventy shots. We rode up to Mount Vernon about noon, dismounted, hitched our horses; and then wandered all over its historic grounds. We went down to the tomb, and there with heads uncovered, in the presence of Washington's remains, swore anew allegiance to our country and her laws. Thence we went to the house, saw Washington's mess-chest and camp table, his surveyor's staff, his library, the room in which he died, and so on. Then we went out into his yard and garden.

"It is a most delightful spot, on the brow of a hill, that juts down to the Potomac. Don't wonder that Washington loved it.  I collected a number of relics, which I forward by this mail.  The small snail shell sent in this was picked up at the mouth of Washington's grave.  We remained there about two hours, saw everything, and mounted for our return about two o'clock.  Got home safe about four.  We were very lucky; for there was danger in such venturing.  Yet I would not have missed the trip for a great deal.[1]

"In a day or two we expect to leave Alexandria.  We return to Washington for awhile, and then go I don't know where.  There are rumors of our being sent West or South, but they are unreliable.  We are content.  Such is a soldier's life.

"P. S.—This is a piece of the Marshall House, cut from the stairway, just where Ellsworth fell."

"MERIDIAN HILL, NEAR WASHINGTON, D. C.
        Oct. 20, 1861.

"DEAR FATHER AND FRIENDS: We are here once more north of the Potomac.  We left Alexandria last Thursday, about 11 A. M., and marched here, about two miles and a half north of Washington; a distance of twelve miles in all.  Arrived here about 2.30 P. M.; and by dark had camp pitched, and all complete.  Fortunate men we were; for in less than a half hour afterward it began to rain, and poured steadily all night.  My tents behaved admirably, and kept me dry as a pin.  Expected to take cold in moving from our comfortable and even luxurious quarters to the field again; but was not affected at all.  Camp life is really enchanting; and I love it better every week.  Of course, we have a few annoyances; but they are not worth mentioning.

"This morning I was at church in Washington.

---

[1] A few days afterward another party of officers ventured there and were captured by the Confederates, and then dismissed by our Secretary of War for being outside of the lines without orders.

Heard my old college chum (Rev. John R. Effinger) preach, and afterward dined with him. Poor fellow! He is a Virginian, and a true Union man; but his brother is an adjutant in the Rebel Army.

"We are here with the Sixth, Seventh, and Eighth New Jersey Regiments just alongside of us. We are at last brigaded under General Silas Casey, a New England man, a West Pointer, who was through the Florida and Mexican Wars, and has been thirty years in the United States Regular Army. He is perhaps fifty-five years of age; but his head is white as snow. Hale, hearty, robust, however; and 'every inch a soldier,' they say. I think we'll like him. Called at his headquarters yesterday morning, and had a satisfactory interview. 'Twixt ourselves—I think I shall be *brigade quartermaster.*'

"Don't know how long we shall stay here. Think we shall remain a week or two. Am perfectly content to move any day. Strange how camp life inures a man to changes.

"I intended to tell you about a Union speech I made in Alexandria, the night before we left, but my sheet is full. Our field and staff attended a meeting of the 'Union Association' there, and I was called out. General Montgomery, who was present, commended me considerably. Ah, it was my old trade!"

"CHARLOTTE HALL, MD.
Nov. 7, 1861.

"DEAR FATHER: I have only time this (Thursday) morning to write a line. We came here on Tuesday afternoon. Left Washington Sunday morning. Distance forty miles. We expect to return to Washington next Sunday. Are here to protect Union men at the election."

---
[1] I was appointed acting brigade quartermaster about November 30.

"WASHINGTON, D. C.
Nov. 14, 1861.

"DEAR FATHER: We got back here last Sunday afternoon. We had a tolerably pleasant expedition. Met with no enemy. Marched about one hundred miles in four days, and rested four. Our men stood the march admirably. The weather was mostly pleasant, though one or two days it rained very hard. We were glad to get back to our camp again, and our tents seemed as fine as parlors. I caught a cold, and felt badly for a few days, but am now quite as well as usual.

"We have glorious news from South Carolina this morning, and the camp is wild with enthusiasm. There is a rumor of our being sent there, but I guess we shall be let alone for a week or two. If, however, we do go South, you may be sure New Jersey will not be dishonored by her sons."

"CAMP ON MERIDIAN HILL.
Nov. 16, 1861.

"DEAR BROTHER: This army life suits me. But I want *you* to promise me one thing, and that is, if I fall in this war don't leave my bones here in Rebeldom. I don't want to rise in the resurrection in the midst of this people. Take me home to Jersey, and bury me with the rest of you; that we may rise together.

"There is some talk of our going to South Carolina; but as yet all is uncertain. We are very tired of resting here, in inglorious ease. The order to strike tents for Charleston would be received by the regiment with a shout of joy. For my part, I have thought the matter all over, and *am ready*. If we conquer there, we shall cover ourselves with glory; if we fall, we shall fall fighting bravely. In either case, the country will be served.

"Our brigade is attaining some degree of discipline and skill, and the spirit of the men is admirable. Of course, all are overjoyed at the great success of the fleet. How singular that the news at this date from all points should be equally glorious! It seems almost like the hand of Providence. I trust it is a full turning of the tide, that is to roll speedily on to victory.

"It has been pretty rough weather for a week or two back, but I have stood it admirably. Those bedclothes you sent me are now invaluable. Besides, I have plenty of blankets, and a gay little *stove* in the corner of my tent that makes all very comfortable. 'Charley' has gone home, but I have one of the best of servants in his place— an Ethiopian ('Moses'), worth his weight in gold. Our march down into Maryland was very severe. One day it rained for hours, and we bivouacked in the midst of it, in an open field, that was soon ankle deep with mud. Four thousand men and one hundred teams tramping through soft ground soon make a mortar bed. We soon had blazing fires, and managed to keep warm; but it rained far into the night, and the experience was dismal. The field and staff ate supper in a pouring rain, that melted the very sugar and salt on the camp table." * * *

"WASHINGTON, D. C.
Nov. 24, 1861.

"DEAR HENRY: You see we are still here. The report of our going South is now contradicted. The strong probability is that we shall remain here all winter. I am at least tired of the uncertainty of going, and to-morrow shall set myself about building stables for our horses. We have some eighty horses in the regiment, and the cold weather is beginning to tell on them. The government, as yet, has refused lumber for stables; but I believe I can 'bore' it out of the officials. At least, I shall try! My own horse and the pony I keep blanketed, and they are both looking well.

"I don't think our weather can have been so severe as yours. We have had no snow yet, and but little frost. The men build ovens in their tents, and most of the officers have small stoves. For my own part, I was never more comfortable, nor so healthy. The general health of the regiment is excellent. Out of nearly nine hundred men we have only eight or ten in hospital.

"Our paymaster was around last week; and, in consequence, the 'boys' are flush and jolly. The most of them have sent large remittances home. Some companies have sent home as much as fifteen hundred and two thousand dollars.

"Herewith you will find the photograph you desired. I had it taken in all my 'toggery,' on purpose to please you. Hope it is satisfactory. I inclose others for the rest of the family. Cost twenty-five cents; *dirt cheap* for Washington.

"Heard a sermon this morning by Rev. Mr. Edwards, of our Church. Text: 'Enoch walked with God, and he was not; for God took him.' A good, sensible discourse, clear and logical. * * * Bishop Simpson preached in town this morning; but I did not know of it, until after service was over. I think I shall call upon him this afternoon and hear him this evening."

"NEAR WASHINGTON, D. C.
Nov. 30, 1861. Saturday.

"DEAR FATHER: I have only time to write you a single line. We are under orders to move this afternoon or to-morrow morning. We go down the Potomac on steamboats, to Budd's Ferry. Land there on the Maryland side, and join the division of General Hooker. The Fifth, Sixth, Seventh, and Eighth New Jersey Regiments all go; under the command of Colonel Starr, as acting brigadier general. I suppose it is intended for Hooker's division to cross the Potomac and storm the Rebel batteries. Am already acting brigade quartermaster.

"Am very busy in making preparations to leave. All is confusion and clamor. * * * Good-bye, and God bless you all." * * *

"CAMP ON LOWER POTOMAC, MD.
Dec. 9, 1861.

"DEAR FATHER AND FRIENDS: * * * The weather is magnificent. The days calm and clear and warm; the nights still and starlight. To-day the air was almost like a day in May. We had a grand review and inspection of the whole Jersey brigade by General Hooker and staff. Four thousand Jersey Blues stood in line, their muskets flashing defiance to the Rebels across the river. We are directly opposite the Rebel batteries; and from the hills above they must have seen us plainly.

"Shortly after noon to-day the Union fleet just above us moved down to Freestone Point, about a mile above us on the other side, and began shelling the batteries there. Six of them lay off the batteries and pounded away at them in splendid style. For a time the fire was returned, but the Rebels soon deserted their guns, and fled in all directions. Then off went boats from our gallant ships, and soon all the buildings on the Point were wrapped in flames. This to prevent them sheltering the Rebels, in case we wished to land a force there. The sight was grand. I witnessed it from the top of a lofty pine, just back of our camp. When the Rebels broke and ran, scattering over the Virginia hills like frightened sheep, our whole regiment broke out into spontaneous cheers that made the old river ring again.

"As if to make a big day of it, to-night we had a furious cannonading. Just below us on the Virginia side is Shipping Point: here lies the heaviest battery the rebels have. Opposite we also have a splendid one. Every day almost they exchange shots by way of variety. To-night, however—a bright moonlight night—about 9 P. M., a large vessel attempted to run the blockade. Wafted along by a slight but steady breeze, along she came, until almost opposite Shipping Point, when flash! whiz! bang! bang! went a shot and then a shell, right across her pathway. She paid no attention to the warning, but with a saucy air, as if indifferent to their bellowings, on she went in gallant style. The Rebels seemed maddened by her audacity, and shortly every gun they had opened a terrific fire. My! how tremendously they roared! For full half an hour they blazed away in magnificent style. The flash of the guns; the whiz and whir of the shots; and the bombs, with their long line of light bursting in air, altogether made a spectacle truly grand and imposing. Hundreds of our boys lined the high bluffs just back of our camp, and when at last through the dull gray of the night they saw the vessel safely past, and the Rebel batteries again in sullen silence, they broke out into uproarious cheers. * * *

"You *may* send me some things, if you will take the trouble. I shall not get home Christmas, and you had better send me a present! If you send it by express, it will take only about ten days or two weeks to reach me. If you send it otherwise, I shall never get it. * * * The expressage will cost a dollar or two, but the box will be worth to me many times that. Also send me some long and warm woolen stockings."

"CAMP ON LOWER POTOMAC, MD.
Dec. 16, 1861.

"DEAR FRIENDS: How rapidly time flies! Another week gone, and I scarcely know it. It is over three months, almost four, since I left home; and yet it seems but yesterday. Have been sad and pensive all day, and have thought more of home than for a long time. I suppose it has been caused by the death yesterday of one of our men. He was a German, with no friends in America. Was taken with typhoid fever; lay some time, and yesterday afternoon dropped off before anybody knew it. *Hard drink* was principal cause. Of all other places, drunkards should shun the army, and yet we have 'lots' of them. Nine tenths of the sickness and suffering in camp comes from habitual drunkenness, either directly or indirectly. Poor fellow! We made him a rough board coffin; and hard by a little country chapel, a mile away, we buried him beneath the trees, to await the resurrection morning. Our men hardly seemed to notice it. Such is the hardening and dehumanizing effect of camp life.

> "'*Where* one goes, and *how* he fares,
> Nobody knows and nobody cares.'

"Have nothing of especial interest to communicate. It is very dull here. The Rebels are right across the river, and we see them every day; but the river is too wide for either of us to harm the other. Nearly every day they pop away at some passing steamboat; but, as out of two thousand shots only *one* (!) has hit a vessel, we pay but little regard to them.

"I was down to our battery the other day, and had the pleasure of a shot at the Confeds. The gun was loaded, and I sighted it and touched it off. Whiz! screech! went the shell; and the next moment two miles away the Rebels were scampering uphill, and off to the bushes. I don't know that I did them any harm. But I frightened the fellows awfully, and it was my first shot at Secesh and slavery!" * * *

"WASHINGTON, D. C.
Dec. 20, 1861. Friday afternoon.

"DEAR FATHER: As you see by the above, I am here in Washington. Left camp yesterday morning, and arrived here yesterday afternoon about three o'clock. Came up on business in my department. Worked hard yesterday afternoon and late last night. Also, to-day until 3 P. M., when I got through and got my stores all aboard the transport. The transport is a Government steamer, loading with hay, grain, provisions, etc., for our division of the army. It does not leave here until to-morrow at 10 A. M. * * *

"It is definitely certain now that I shall not get home Christmas. Have given up all hope of it, and have almost made up my mind not to come home at all, until the war is over. I don't want to make 'two bites of a cherry!' My mind is fully made up to fight it out to the bitter end, and I fear if I should come home you would unman me.

"It is not to be disguised that we have much to suffer, which you in Jersey would call hardships; but we have made up our minds to endure the worst, in the sacred cause of Liberty and Union, and so we manage to weather it somehow. We have become *soldiers;* we love peace, but accept war, and are not afraid to die in support of so great a cause. We are battling, father, not merely for the present nor for ourselves, but for the future and forever, and for all the vast generations of men everywhere and through all time. The Union must not fall, though millions perish; for with its fall would be extinguished all the highest and holiest hopes of mankind the world over, and for generations to come.

"We don't care for England. If she wants to fight, let her come. We would prefer her friendship, but if she won't be quiet, let her come on. She is all wrong on the law and justice of the case;[1] and, if she dares to fight, will be overwhelmed with the execration and scorn of mankind. She had better mind her own business. Russia is watching her. And at her first step forward, the Russian bear will place his paws—one on Constantinople, and the other

---

[1] The "Mason and Slidell" case.

on Hindustan. Nevertheless, I don't think this 'Trent' affair will lead to war." * * *

"CAMP ON LOWER POTOMAC, MD.
Dec. 28, 1861.

"DEAR BROTHER: Your letter came welcomely; likewise the list of articles contained in box; though the box itself is still somewhere on the road. I presume it will arrive in time for New Year's, or shortly after, which will do just as well.

"These have been dreary holidays to me. For a week past, like Job, I have been afflicted with 'sore boils.' As usual, they have come in the wrong place. * * *

"Have had a bad cold, but am getting over it. Has been cold here this week. Real Christmas weather. To-day it is bright and pleasant; but the air is raw. * * *

"Cousin Will Rusling, of Salem, arrived in camp the other day. He enlisted as a *private* in Company F, and thinks he'll like soldiering! O, dear! He has a prospect, however, of being promoted to a sergeantcy. * * *

"The Rebels have been very quiet this week. Scarcely any firing. No prospect of a fight. Our boys are eager for one. I believe they'd fight well." * * *

"CAMP ON LOWER POTOMAC, MD.
Jan. 5, 1862. Sunday night.

"DEAR BROTHER AND FRIENDS: It gives me pleasure to say, that at last my box and contents have arrived safely. They came on the last day of the old year, and were welcomed exceedingly. On New Year's night I gave a little party, and we—the field and staff of the Fifth—ate and drank to the health of 'our friends at home!' Everything was in excellent condition, except the sweet potatoes. The dampness of the apples had communicated itself to them, and three fourths were already decayed. The apples were fine, the doughnuts excellent, and the cakes—both ginger and fruit—quite superb. To all my friends, many thanks! * * *

"Most welcome of all, however, were the two flannel night shirts. You can't imagine how nice they are these cold nights. I wrap up in them, neck and heels, and sleep 'warm as toast.' They are the best 'institutions' about camp; and several officers are already taking pattern by them. * * *

"The weather here has become sharp and bracing, but we do not feel it. We all have stoves or fireplaces; and, with plenty to eat and plenty to wear, we get along very comfortably. Man is very largely an animal, and soon accommodates himself to circumstances. We have got used to Nature, and don't mind her winds and storms. People visiting here affect to pity us, and ask if we don't suffer? We laugh, and point to our ruddy cheeks and swelling bodies. I have gained twenty pounds, and my trousers and vests are all too small!" * * *

"CAMP ON LOWER POTOMAC, MD.
Jan. 12, 1862. Sunday evening.

"DEAR FRIENDS: This has been a great Sabbath. Have worked hard all day, and am greatly fatigued. For a week past, we had been blockaded by ice. The river froze over last Monday night, and we had no mail and no communication with Washington from then until last night. Forty-eight hours ago it began to rain, and then came the thaw. To-day the thermometer stands at seventy degrees in the shade, and the weather is like late April or early May. Yesterday the ice disappeared; and last night Rum Point was crowded with arriving transports, laden heavily with army stores.

"Notified my wagon-master and quartermaster sergeant last night, and this morning early we were off with eight teams to the landing. There by nine o'clock, and such a scene! Three whole companies had been detailed to unload the steamers, and there they were tramping up and down the beach, over their ankles in Maryland mud, and no brain anywhere to give them method and directions. Head on to the beach lay a barge, which contained the most of my stores. Poor old boat! Two days before, in attempting to reach Rum Point, she was cut through by the ice and sank off Alexandria. Yesterday a tugboat pumped her out and gave her a friendly tow down here. I had thirteen large boxes of clothing, etc., aboard of her; and after a deal of trouble and labor succeeded in getting them ashore. Loading our wagons, about 1 P. M. we started for camp; and, of course, came through! The Fifth New Jersey will always 'come through!' But O such roads! Mud! mud! mud! Mortar, mud, and quagmires!

"Arriving here, we got some dinner, and then called a board of survey, to examine the condition of the goods. They were all thoroughly soaked, having been in the water forty-eight hours; but we found nothing seriously damaged, except some two hundred and fifty caps. These were condemned, and ordered to be issued at half price. The rest we shall try to dry to-morrow. The examination was long and tedious, and it was nightfall before the day's business was done. Have been in the saddle about four hours; and on my legs all the rest of the day. I reckon I am tired! I would not write a line, only I know you are anxious to hear regularly from here, and will be impatient if you don't.

"Nothing important here. The 'Pensacola' passed down last night. The Rebels popped away at her, and broke our slumbers; but that was all. To-day they have been firing more than usual. They pitched one shell right over onto our parade ground, about three hundred yards from my tent. My! what a commotion it made. The boys ran straight to the spot, and picked up every piece as a relic. We have got used to such noisy and fussy 'playthings,' and don't care for them."

"Camp on Lower Potomac, Md.<br>Jan. 19, 1862.

"Dear Friends: I thought I would not write you to-day, inasmuch as my quartermaster sergeant, S——, has gone to Trenton, and will probably see you ere this can reach Jersey. Nevertheless, have concluded to. For, you see, when one is off this way, and life grows weary, it is almost as good as a talk to write a letter. It acts as a safety valve, to let off one's superfluous thoughts and feelings. I suppose the writing of a letter often saves a young person from crying. And as for old persons (like me), why, if they are accustomed to the pen, oftentimes they *must* write, or 'bust.'

"As I write, I sit eating one of your apples. They are almost the 'least and last remains' of my Christmas box. How delicious they are! Each bite seems better than the others; first, because the apples are intrinsically good, and second, because they have come from the paternal mansion. Home! home! 'Though ever so humble, there is *no* place like home!' And if it happens to be a good one; then there is a heaven begun below, which that one above shall not far surpass.

"Am very well for me, as Mr. S—— will tell you, though not as hearty as I was in the fall. The wretched weather we have had lately affects me somewhat. Yesterday it drizzled and rained all day; and to-day there is a constant fog and rain, that are just making our camp a mortar bed. The soil is a heavy, slippery clay; and though in the woods, and on a side hill, our ground is becoming a quagmire. You have no idea of the roads.

They are perfectly execrable. I wonder every day more and more how our poor teams manage to navigate them. Yet our horses and mules continue in splendid condition so far, and are the admiration of all who see them.

"Yesterday I had a heavy job. I distributed some eight hundred stand of arms, and received some seven hundred old ones from the companies. Also received some thirty thousand rounds of cartridges, and issued forty thousand. In addition to this, I packed all the old arms ready for transportation. It was about two days' work, crowded into one; and we went straight through it, in spite of the rain. It was a disagreeable, wet, and muddy job; but we got through by sundown. Was much fatigued; but feel tolerable again this morning. No inspection this morning; too wet and muddy. No church, of course. * * *

"I think I shall get home some time next month. Don't expect me, however, till you see me."

"WASHINGTON, D. C.
Jan. 28, 1862.

"DEAR FATHER: Once more I write you, and again from Washington. I arrived here yesterday, or rather last night. Our boat stuck fast on a sand bar, just off of Rum Point; and we lay there four hours, waiting for the rise of the tide. This put us four hours back, so that we only arrived in Washington after dark.

"I had expected by this time to have obtained 'leave of absence,' and have been here on my way home. But, as the Fates would have it, about the time I was about making application, out came an order from McClellan, revoking all leaves of absence, and prohibiting any more. I sent my application in, however, but it was refused; and so I rest for the present."

"CAMP ON LOWER POTOMAC, MD.
 Feb. 2, 1862.   Sunday evening.

"DEAR BROTHER: * * * Another dull, plodding Sabbath. There was a little sunshine for three or four hours, almost the first in a month now; but the clouds have come back again, and the sky is threatening. Yesterday there was a cold, sleety rain, until long after noon. Was out in the most of it; and caught cold in my back, which last night and to-day was quite lame. This morning, however, was in the saddle again for several hours, and am better as I write.

"The mud is unfathomable; and we are about building a road. I laid it out yesterday and to-day; and to-morrow the whole brigade—four entire regiments, about thirty-six hundred men—will commence work upon it. It is only about two miles long; and we shall complete it in a few days. 'Many hands make light work.' Fortunately, I am brigade quartermaster, and have nothing further to do with it. My orders were to lay out the road; and the colonels of the regiments were instructed each to build a section and keep it in repair. For weeks past our roads have been horrible; and a 'corduroy' road has now become an absolute necessity.

"I think we shall lie here till April, because we can't get away. By that time we shall be comparatively 'veterans,' and shall doubtless see service. Hope so. Am inexpressibly tired and disgusted with McClellan's do-nothing policy, and want to fight or come home."

"CAMP ON LOWER POTOMAC, MD.
 Feb. 9, 1862.

"DEAR FRIENDS: Sunday has again come around; and now Sunday night. It has been a nice Sabbath. For a wonder—almost the first time for a month—the sun rose clear; and has mostly continued so all day. It has been warm, genial, pleasant—almost like late April or early May. At eleven o'clock our chaplain preached in one of the avenues, to a large congregation of just *seventeen* privates and two officers! All over the camp the men were lounging and talking, and it was sad to think how few he could really collect. * * * A good chaplain, a man of life and energy would draw out the whole regiment. Here are nine hundred men, hungering and thirsting for something to rouse and inspire them, something to relieve their minds of the monotony and dullness of camp in winter weather, and he brings out exactly nineteen men, another officer and myself included!

"Surely, if of ordinary capacity, a chaplain ought to preach well. The soldier himself, his perilous and holy calling, the glorious cause for which we are fighting, the inestimable principles at stake, his friends at home, the tender ties that bind him there, his wife, his children, future generations, and the whole world for which he is also battling—surely these are topics to arouse a chaplain's soul and inspire his tongue with words of fire, if so be that he have a 'soul' and possess a 'tongue.' * * * I think I could have *talked* myself this morning. The morning was so bright and cheery, and the men looked so glad to see the sun once more that it made one's heart beat and eyes flash to look upon them. But alas! I am only a quartermaster, and not supposed to have either a conscience or a tongue!

"For a month past we have had some most fearful weather here. Rain! rain! Fog! fog. Mud! mud! Yes; mud! mud! mud! Quagmires! Mortar beds! Roads with the bottom fallen out! For a week past, some regiments have been carrying their forage and provisions on the shoulders of their men. Friday, as I went down to Rum Point, I met a whole company of the Indiana Cavalry, trudging along, slop, slop, through the interminable mud; each with a huge bundle of hay on his shoulders.

The road was impassable for teams; and they were afraid to go on horseback, for fear of miring down. My long-legged gray, 'Uncle Abe,' carried me through safely; but once or twice I really thought we would go through to China.

"At Rum Point I succeeded in begging a boat—a long, flat scow. This we loaded down with hay and grain, put a horse to her, and then swung boldly down the beach—canal fashion—right in the face of the Rebel batteries, to within a half a mile of our camp. Our wagons were there waiting for us, and we were soon unloaded and all right. The Rebels took no notice of us. Perhaps they pitied us; though I rather think it was because they feared their guns wouldn't reach us. We have played the same game several times since, and by this means we shall probably be able to obtain all our supplies. Had I not by chance hit upon it, our men would have been compelled to march three miles to the landing, and then carry everything up the best they could.

"The roads are wholly impassable, and now at last a new one has been ordered. It leaves the left of our camp, and takes a 'bee line' to the landing. It is being built of brush, logs, and sand or gravel; and, when completed, will be a great gain. Our whole brigade has been at it for a week, and it will be nearly a week more before it is done.

"There is nothing new here. The general health of the brigade is good, though now and then one sickens and dies. We lost a man this morning by consumption. He would probably have died at home, as his lungs were all gone. It is such men that chiefly fill the hospitals; men worn out and debilitated, and who ought never to have been passed by the examining surgeon. Men of ordinary health at home get along well, even now, in the depth of winter, and here in this God-forsaken region. * * *

"I thank you heartily for *The Christian Advocate*. You

don't know how I have enjoyed it to-day. The *Tribune*—one day old—comes nearly every day, and *that* is good; but the *Advocate*, which I have read all my life since I was a child, is more welcome on Sunday." * * *

"HEADQUARTERS, 3D BRIGADE,
HOOKER'S DIVISION,
LOWER POTOMAC, MD.
Feb. 16, 1862.

"DEAR BROTHER: This has been quite a Sunday. In the morning, at eleven o'clock, I attended service at the Sixth Regiment, the chaplain of which—the Rev. S. T. Moore, of the Newark Conference—is an old fellow-student at Pennington Seminary. He had been receiving a large chapel tent, from some friends at Newark; and this morning we had the dedication. The usual dedicatory services were gone through with, and then we had a sermon from Dr. Rosé, the chaplain of the Seventh. His text was that brave one from Ecclesiastes, 'Whatsoever thy hand findeth to do, *do it* with all thy might.' It was a plain, good, earnest sermon; and told well.

"This afternoon, at half past two o'clock, the chaplain of the Sixth had an appointment to preach at a Methodist Episcopal church, some six miles down the country. A party of officers formed to accompany him, and invited me to ride along. Of course, I went; and such a time! The roads were horrible! The country miserable! And the congregation about thirty! And *such* a people! Nevertheless, I enjoyed sitting in a 'meeting house' once more, seeing that I hadn't been inside of one before in nearly three months.

"At Washington I used to attend church somewhere, whenever I had opportunity; but down here there are no churches, to speak of; and the roads and weather have been so execrable that it has been impossible to reach even such as there are. The church we were at this afternoon was a 'specimen,' with a little gallery at one end for the 'darkies,' two big stoves in the center, and sort of a box for a pulpit, and a *paper* fringe around the Bible cushion. It would have done you good to see the women-folks. Some came in wagons, some in carts, and some on horseback! They all wore 'store goods;' but then *such* goods have not been seen up North this many a day!

"We had a fine snow yesterday and last night; and to-day there is enough for good sleighing, if the roads had any bottom. Yet it is not cold. The air was a little raw yesterday; but to-day it is very agreeable. I suppose it will soon be gone. Thanks to hard work and plenty of it, our corduroy road is done, and already named the *'Jersey Turnpike!'* It is really a splendid road, leading straight from our camp to Rum Point, and will remain to astonish the benighted Marylanders long after the brigade has departed. It is built in a substantial manner, with brush at the bottom, then logs, and then a coating of clay and sand. General Hooker declares it a 'big thing,' and I think you would cordially concur. 'Abe,' who hates the mud awfully, neighs his satisfaction as soon as he reaches the turnpike, and canters cheerily along from end to end of it.

"No, I am not yet 'brigade quartermaster'—only acting. But I *shall* be. I have been performing all the duties of the office since last December (besides my regimental duties); and my application is backed up strongly by both Colonel Starr, who commands the brigade, and General Hooker, who commands the division. Then, besides, the post is mine by right of seniority. * * * The *pay* isn't very much more, but then it would promote me to a *captaincy*, and thus place another *bar* upon my shoulder straps. But I shall not stop there. If the war lasts and there is any sort of a chance, I am coming home at least a 'major,' or I shall not come home at all.

"We expect a fight here now any day. What glorious news from Kentucky! Isn't Foote a trump? And from Dupont! And Burnside! And isn't Fort Donelson a *'big thing?'* Hurrah for 'U. S.' Grant! I brought the news over from General Hooker's last evening, and you should have heard the 'boys' yell! The whole brigade went wild with excitement, and the bands all struck up 'Yankee Doodle' and 'John Brown' to help the thing along."

"CAMP ON LOWER POTOMAC, MD.
Feb. 23, 1862. Sunday.

"DEAR BROTHER: Another week has gone and we are still here on the Potomac. There was some talk early in the week of a movement ere this, but the continual rain has postponed it. O, such weather! Rain, rain, rain! If it were not for our corduroy 'turnpike,' we could never haul provisions; but would have to carry them on the backs of our men, or starve. As it is, however, we have plenty of everything, and get along very well. The weather, though, breaks up all military movements; for over a month, we have had scarcely a drill.

"It seems strange, this passing a whole winter in tents. I used to think it rather tough to pass it even in a house. I used to think father's frame house much colder than a brick one! Well, I have passed a winter in a canvas house down here; and, to tell the truth, have been almost as comfortable as I was at home. I have had plenty of blankets, plenty of clothing, and a good stove; and so have got through. But there is no mistake about the weather having been execrable. Even now we can scarcely stir out of our tents, without going into the mud up to our ankles.

"Some time this week I shall send to your address a box, containing various Secesh trophies. Among the rest is a Rebel knapsack from Alexandria, and several things from Mount Vernon. Among the latter is a *walnut*, a *chest-*

*nut,* and an *acorn,* which I want you to plant in the spring and see if you can't get them to grow. If not of use to us, they may be of interest to our posterity (when it comes!); because obtained by Uncle or Grandfather James, at Mount Vernon, during the Secession Rebellion!

"I saw a 'gay old' team here the other day. It was an old cart, with two little bulls to the tongue; and two little mules, with corn-husk collars and rope traces and lines, to the lead. A big 'contraband' was driving, and a Southern lady rode in state! What a figure she would have cut, going up State Street! And the saddest of it all was, that the poor creature didn't know how ineffably ridiculous she really was!

"I suppose you had a great time in Trenton yesterday. We did nothing here, as the orders for the celebration did not arrive till this morning. Nor could we, if they had; for it rained all day, as if the clouds had broken to pieces.

"Don't get crazy up North over the Union victories. I know they are rather 'big' things, but there is a lot of fighting to do yet."

" CAMP DETESTABLE, LOWER POTOMAC, MD.
March 2, 1862.

"DEAR BROTHER: Yours, inclosing our Western cousin's, came yesterday. He has evidently had a rough time of it. Should have known better than to enlist in the heart of winter. If a man enlists in the summer, he gets acclimated as the cold weather comes on, and so goes through. We haven't minded the winter at all. He says the gunboats were going up the river, and there would be a 'big fight soon.' His date was February 4, and so Forts Henry and Donelson, as well as Clarksville and Nashville, have all been since. Rather a 'big' fight, I reckon! The fellow seems to be plucky, though, in spite of his sickness, and when you write to him, give him a hearty 'Godspeed!' for me, as a voice from the Potomac!

"I head my letter 'Camp Detestable.' It is detestable, because we are doing nothing; it is detestable, because we are outside of all God's creation here; it is detestable, because of the mud when it storms; it is detestable, because it don't dry up soon enough; it is detestable, because it is clouded over this morning, and is going to snow again; and it is detestable, because here we lie idle month after month, while Grant and Buell and Burnside are winning great victories and covering themselves and their commands with glory. Faugh upon such soldiering!

"You caution me about my antislavery utterances. All right! Yes, I hate slavery just as much as I can; and shall hit it whenever I can. I am most profoundly convinced before God of its enormity and wickedness; and must speak out, if I would preserve my conscience clean. To my own mind, there is but one course to pursue; and men who now apologize for slavery will be ashamed to own it ten years hence. The war can have but one result, and when it is over, men will be astonished that they could ever have been anything else than 'antislavery.'

> "'John Brown's body lies moldering in the ground,
> But his soul goes marching on.'

"That is the song we sing down here, and as we shout it forth, we make these old Maryland pines ring again.

"At last, we expect to move. Some say this week. Hope and pray so. But I don't believe it. I predict we are good for another month here, come what may. Banks and McClellan will do all the fighting, and leave us to guard the Potomac. Possibly, we may cross and assist, but I don't believe it.

"Cousin Will was yesterday promoted to *first sergeantcy* of Company F. In December he was a private; then made fourth corporal. And now promoted over three corporals and four sergeants to be first or orderly sergeant. A 'big' thing! He now stands first on the list for a second lieutenancy, if his captain will be good enough to get shot or die!"

"HEADQUARTERS, 3D BRIGADE.
March 10, 1862.

"DEAR FRIENDS: Am weary and exhausted; yet I must write you a line. I suppose you have already heard the great good news from this point; still a word from me will 'make assurance doubly sure.'

"You know I wrote you last Friday from Washington. On Saturday I intended to return here, but found it impossible to find a boat going here. Was notified, however, that a government transport would leave at noon on Sunday, and, disagreeable as it was, deemed it my duty to avail myself of the opportunity. There was a stiff breeze against us, and it was quite sundown as we approached Mattewoman River. When within four or five miles of it, we were startled by the sight of the gunboat 'Anacostia,' lying quite under the guns of Cockpit Point, and pouring a terrific fire of shot and shell upon the Rebel intrenchments. As she floated farther down, and approached Shipping Point, her fire seemed to be redoubled in force, and we were astonished that throughout the Confeds seemed to make no reply whatever. Long before we had been amazed at the vast columns of smoke rising above the Rebel intrenchments, and our only conclusion was, that either the Rebels had evacuated or that the 'Anacostia' had dispersed them.

"Landing at the dock, I hastened up to camp, and there learned that the smoke had begun to arise about noon, *before* the 'Anacostia' had begun to throw her shells, and that it was rumored that the Confeds had set fire to their works, and absquatulated 'bag and baggage'—'horse, foot, and dragoons.' About three o'clock the 'Anacostia' had crept close in shore, landed two boat loads of sailors and marines, and in a quarter of an hour afterward up the Rebel flagstaff shot the Stars and Stripes. The whole proceedings were plainly visible from the Maryland shore; and it is needless to say that our whole brigade speedily went crazy. Such shouts and cheers as rent the air, you never heard.

"Throughout the division all was bustle and excitement. I went over to General Hooker's on business, and found his quarters crowded with officers, and that he had suddenly gone off to the gunboats. Full of excitement, when I got back to camp, I couldn't sleep; and it was nearly twelve o'clock before I thought of retiring. Then, just as I was undressing, an orderly came riding furiously into camp, and the next moment Lieutenant Colonel Mott, who now commands the Fifth, was summoned to Colonel Starr's tent. In a few minutes I heard him come back—his tent is next to mine—and going in, he handed me a written order. It was in substance, that at sunrise this morning he should report at Rum Point, with five hundred picked men, carrying one hundred spades and one hundred axes, as well as their arms, and there to go aboard a canal boat, which would be towed by a tug to Cockpit Point. Landing at or near the Point, he was to explore the woods on each side, throwing out pickets in advance as he proceeded, gain the Point, dismantle and destroy the fortifications there, and bring off with him such booty as he was able. The order was peremptory, and the job possibly dangerous; yet everybody wanted to go.

"I went straight to Colonel Starr, and with his permission offered my services to Colonel Mott, as volunteer aid-de-camp. He kindly accepted them, and told me to report to him at 5 A. M. It was then after 1 P. M., and I turned in, clothes and all. After a restless slumber of three or four hours, I was roused up by the hum of the camp; and, eating a hasty breakfast, at daybreak was in the saddle. We got to Rum Point just as the sun rose, and there we found five hundred men from the First Massachusetts, who had been detailed in like manner, to proceed to Shipping Point.

"After a deal of fussing, at last the men were finally embarked, and making fast to a little spider of a tug that came to us from the flotilla, at 8 A. M. we left Maryland for the 'Land of Dixie.' Meanwhile, a cold storm of wind and rain had set in, and the day promised to be vastly disagreeable. As we got out into the Potomac, which is there some three miles wide, we saw the flotilla all under steam, and coming gallantly down to protect our landing. The tug towed us within two hundred yards of shore, and then cast us off.

"We could get no nearer; and so, casting anchor, we proceeded to disembark by means of a long scow, which we had brought with us. The scow held about one hundred and fifty men, and the first load was soon landed. I landed with them, springing ashore with a half dozen others. The men were instantly formed and spread out as skirmishers. Our orders were to move slowly forward, scouring the banks and bushes; but not to proceed more than a mile inland, until the second load had landed. On we went, and as we approached Cockpit Point our hearts beat quick. We expected to find at least pickets there, if not the Rebels in force; and when we had gained the bluff and found ourselves within the batteries, with no signs of an enemy, we felt quite disappointed. Tarrying there a moment, to discover and destroy their contrivances to blow up their magazines and us with them, if we attempted to enter them, we once more proceeded cautiously forward, and subsequently our pickets were thrown out three miles in advance, without seeing a Rebel.

"We were informed by the inhabitants, that they had

commenced to evacuate as long ago as last Wednesday, and that the last of them had left Sunday afternoon. They said they were going to fall back on Fredericksburg, and I suppose they have. This is on the railroad to Richmond; and confirms us in the opinion that Manassas will soon be abandoned, if it be not evacuated already. They had evidently left in the greatest haste; as valises, trunks, boxes, axes, spades, and clothing lay around promiscuously. In several places were the remains of trunks and clothing, which they had burned, rather than abandon. O! I must stop. Will finish the rest to-morrow. Our expedition was entirely successful. Got back all safe, thank God, and so good night!"

"HEADQUARTERS, 3D BRIGADE,
HOOKER'S DIVISION,
LOWER POTOMAC, MD.
March 13, 1862.

"DEAR FRIENDS: It is only this morning, after two days' rest, that I feel able to resume my letter of the tenth. I fear that letter was much incoherent; for I was weary and excited, and I wrote it all after twelve o'clock. I believe I took you as far as reaching the *camp* of the Rebels. This was composed of log huts, covered with rough pine shingles; and was decidedly the filthiest place I was ever in. Dirt, grease, garbage, everywhere abounded; and in such weather as we have had all winter, living there must have been awful.

"Everything indicated that their forces had left precipitately and in great haste. Clothing, intrenching tools —such as spades, shovels, axes, and picks—mess-chests, trunks, valises, bedding, all lay around promiscuously, and in places great quantities had been burned. There was plenty of fresh beef and flour; nearly every cabin had a good supply of these two articles; but of vegetables there was absolutely none, and no remains of any. Some letters, printed in Secesh papers, that we found there, complained that they were short of vegetables, and I presume it was so. I inclose some writing I found there. Have a heavy bowie knife, but this I think I shall retain. There were several wagons, of fine character; but, before decamping, they had hewn them to pieces. The spokes were cut out, and the tongues cut in two.

"After exploring the camp thoroughly, I returned to the batteries. Meanwhile, the remainder of our expedition had disembarked, and another company had been thrown forward on the right, to scout the country as far as possible and prudent. At the batteries I met Lieutenant Colonel Mott and some three hundred men. They instantly set to work to dismount the cannon and hurl them over the bluff into the Potomac; the said bluff being at least a hundred feet high. There were four of them, all heavy pieces, and one a thirty-two-pound Parrott rifled gun, taken from us at Bull Run. Attaching long ropes to them, the men laid hold, and by main strength dragged them out of the earthworks, and over to the bluff; down which they crashed with terrific noise. We had intended to remove them, but a stiff breeze created so heavy a swell on the river, that it was impossible to load them on the boats. They lie now at the water's edge, and a floating derrick can at any time swing them on board a steamer. We then emptied the magazines, carrying the shot and shell down to the beach, whence boats conveyed them to the gunboats.

"We had finished all up and were about departing, when I had the following adventure: Said I to Dr. Sharp (a little fellow from Belvidere, who is assistant surgeon in the Sixth): 'Let us explore those bushes yonder, while the men are arranging to reëmbark.' The doctor agreed, and we started off first to a heap of brush, about two hundred yards in the rear of the main battery. As we passed, I observed a long heap of fresh earth beneath, and supposed it a grave; but examining it more closely, I found it rectangular instead of oblong. I called to the doctor to stop, and throwing off some brush, we soon discovered a hole about five feet broad, ten feet long, and three feet deep, crammed full of conical nine-inch shells! There were one hundred and sixty in all, part of them loaded and capped, ready to blow us up, if we had not been careful. Of course I shouted the discovery to Colonel Mott; and soon he and a hundred men were around the infernal projectiles. We lifted them carefully out, and transferred them to the charge of the gunboats.

"Then began the reëmbarkation, which kept us until sundown. We left thirty men in the scow, tied behind the canal boat, and then the gunboat 'Satellite' took us in tow; and we started for Rum Point, some four miles off, obliquely across the river. Meanwhile, the wind had risen until it blew a gale; the canal boat rolled and careened, until it was impossible to stand on deck; and behind, the poor old scow dipped water at almost every wave. The men became excited, and it required the utmost exertions of the officers to preserve order and thus insure safety. After a half hour of deep anxiety, during which I was uncertain whether we would not all founder in the Potomac, we got within the headlands of Mattewoman Creek; and soon after arrived safely at Rum Point. We got back at 8 P. M., having been absent on the expedition just twelve hours. Now commenced a weary march of three miles up to camp; but about halfway our servants met us with our horses, and the remaining distance was soon gone over. Arrived at camp, we had a hundred inquiries to answer, as nothing had been heard from us since morning; and you may be sure we were all 'lions' until late at night.

"I omitted to say, that we cut down the Rebel flagstaff; and by a real poetic justice used its pieces in tumbling the Rebel cannon into the Potomac. We planted the Stars and Stripes high above the fortifications, and gave them three good Jersey cheers, as the old banner rolled out upon the breeze. The First Massachusetts were detained at Shipping Point until late at night, and the next day were sent back again. To-day other detachments from the Sixth and Seventh New Jersey have been sent over there; and I presume we shall hold it permanently, preparatory to a general crossing of the division. Of course, all is excitement here. We are making every preparation for a general move; and the sick are getting well fast. Everybody 'spilin' for a fight!'"

"HEADQUARTERS 3D BRIGADE,
HOOKER'S DIVISION,
LOWER POTOMAC, MD.
March 19, 1862. Wednesday evening, 8:30|o'clock.

"DEAR FATHER AND FRIENDS: Our mail has just arrived, the first since Saturday, and I am disappointed in not receiving a letter from you. Have written you *three* within the last ten days, and have had a reply only to the *first,* which was sent from Washington. Our mails have become very irregular. All passenger boats were ordered off the river two weeks ago; and since then we have had to depend on government transports, which run only as occasion requires. The object, of course, was to conceal preparations and movements, which it was not proper for the public to know.

"Yesterday, I rode down to Port Tobacco, the county seat of this county. It is about fifteen miles from here. The country that way is much better. Some tolerable farms and farmhouses. Saw one house that was whitewashed and another with green blinds—the best evidence of civilization that I have met. Port Tobacco is a little village of six hundred or so inhabitants, and a pretty 'smart' place. We have a company there on picket; been there since January 20. The captain is an old friend of mine, and being a fine day, I went down to see him, as well as the country. There was a party in the town, to which the captain had been invited, and word was sent to bring us along—me and a friend who went down with me. Pleasant time. Nice people. But mostly 'Secesh.' Some nice young ladies; but they didn't know a single 'Union' song!

"Came back this morning, and found the brigade under orders to march at five minutes' notice. Bustle and confusion all day. Orderlies arriving and departing constantly. Have been packed up all the afternoon; but it has now set in to rain, and I guess we sha'n't go to-night. We march without tents or knapsacks, with two days' rations; and expect to cross at Acquia Creek, and take Fredericksburg in the rear. Probably you will hear of our victory before you get this. Yesterday nineteen steamboats, crowded with troops, went down the river; it is supposed to Fortress Monroe. Look out for stirring news.

"I send herewith a photograph of General Hooker. It was given to me by himself, and bears his autograph. Take care of it. I prize it very highly. I wish you to remember, that I have a *box* containing some books, official papers, etc., at the *Metropolitan* (formerly Brown's) Hotel, on *Pennsylvania Avenue*, Washington. I sent it up there Monday for safe-keeping. * * * The 'official papers' are the vouchers for my accounts with the government, down to January 1, 1862, and will be of use, if my accounts are ever disputed or anything happens to me. * * * My pay is drawn until the first of March; the balance can be drawn by father any time, if I fall.

"Pardon these instructions. Not pleasant to write, yet you may need them. On the eve of great and decisive events, which every aspiration of my heart and every conviction of my brain induces me to share, I have no right to expect exemption from that fate, which must befall some of us. Have counted the cost, and am not afraid to die for my country. To speak frankly, have somehow thought, from the first, that I would never return alive from the war, and it may be that I shall fall ere another week rolls around. * * * In my past life, I can see many errors, that I could wish to correct; yet I doubt if I could live it much better, if I had to do it again, and I confidently trust all to Jesus." * * *

"HEADQUARTERS 3D BRIGADE,
LOWER POTOMAC, MD.
March 23, 1862.

"DEAR FRIENDS: It is Sunday once more, and we are still here. Our orders to move were countermanded at the last moment, and our suspense is becoming painful. As you have seen by the papers, we are now attached to the army corps of General Heintzelman. He was here yesterday, on a little steamer; conferred with General Hooker for an hour or two, and then went on down the river. Two of his divisions have already passed down, and we expect to follow some time this week. We don't know *where*, but we expect to Fortress Monroe. Acquia Creek, as you know, has been abandoned, and we suppose our corps is ordered to Fortress Monroe, to coöperate with McClellan when he moves on Gordonsville and Richmond. Everything now is kept as secret as death; and nobody knows anything, until 'orders' come. I don't think we shall be off now before Thursday or Friday; but it is certain we shall not stay here. There is no enemy here to oppose, and there is enough force elsewhere in Maryland to keep her loyal.

"I suppose you have heard from Newbern? That disposes of the 'Hamilton Square' man's letter, that Burnside was reëmbarking. He did 'reëmbark,' but it was only to turn up at Newbern, and win another glorious victory for the Constitution and the Union!"

"WASHINGTON, D. C().
March 29, 1862.

"DEAR FATHER: Up here again, on a flying trip, to return to-morrow. Contrary to the expectations of everybody, we are still at our old camp near Rum Point, and I suppose we shall not leave for some days. Meanwhile, for two weeks past, the river has been thronged with transports loaded with troops all going down—down— nobody knows *where;* but we suppose to Fortress Monroe. We must have met at least ten thousand troops yesterday on their way down, of all branches of the service; infantry, cavalry, and artillery. The report here is, that McClellan and his staff embark to-morrow; and that the move on Richmond now is to be by way of Norfolk. We expected to lead the advance; but from present indications shall bring up the rear, if we are not left behind altogether. You see nothing of this in the papers, because it is prohibited; but tremendous events are preparing at the mouth of the James River, and look out for great and stirring news. * * *

"I would like to get home and see you very much; but have dismissed all thought of that now, and must wait till after McClellan has fought his long-promised battle. If successful, it will ultimately make him the greatest man in Christendom. If defeated, the public opinion of an indignant and infuriated North will compel the President to dismiss, if not otherwise punish him."

"HEADQUARTERS 3D BRIGADE,
LOWER POTOMAC, MD.
April 1, 1862.

"DEAR HENRY: Home again! Left Washington yesterday (Monday) morning, and reached here at dark. Came down in a sailboat. Brigade still here.

"On Sunday morning heard the Rev. Dr. Tefft, formerly editor of the *Repository,* preach in the Senate chamber. My! how he scored the Rebellion! He is now chaplain in the First Maine Cavalry.

"I write now to send home the inclosed lithographs and photographs, and because I feel like writing. It has been a lovely day. So calm, so warm, so bright! To-night clouds have come over the sky, but all is as still and pleasant as your nights in June. O how delicious such weather is here in camp! You walk, or rather lounge off, down through the camp, and away along the bluff, looking out over the river for many a mile; snuffing the pure air of the morning; or, if you choose, you mount your horse, his blood almost as buoyant as your own, and away you gallop, as if life was all a dream.

" 'Abe' has weathered the winter, and this spring has come up splendidly. O! how good he felt this morning, as I rode over to General Hooker's. Everybody else is afraid of him. But, with me, he will jump hedge, ditch, or fence, and can run like the wind. Good 'Uncle Abe!' How his heels flew this morning! The glory of *his* nostrils *was* terrible, and *his* neck *was* clothed with thunder!

"To-night I lit my pipe, and strolled off down through the tents and off upon the parade ground. Dark around, while on every side, far and near, gleamed the cheerful camp fires; the men spinning 'yarns,' or here and there singing their patriotic songs. I thought of you all, and just then our band struck up 'Sweet Home!' Ah, me! how I wished I was there—not that you could induce me to stay there, but just to see the old things, to tell you many things I cannot write, to see the old place and the old things. Such thoughts and such longings came over me, as I walked and smoked; but *you* are there and *I* am here, and must not leave. * * *

"In that 'box' at Brown's Hotel, Washington, I have

deposited the Rebel bowie knife I found at Cockpit Point, and a lot of other things.

"And so I close. Here for this week, I guess! Then to Norfolk. Direct your letters, as before."

"ON STEAMER 'ARROWSMITH,'
OFF RUM POINT, MD.
April 6, 1862. Sunday evening.

"DEAR BROTHER: Yours came a day or two ago. As to 'Rum Point,' I have to say, that the name is more amusing than significant. Why it is called *Rum* Point, I do not know; but suppose it is due to the general darkness and barbarism that this slavery-cursed region abounds in. Sure it is, that there is no 'Rum' here now, except what is smuggled in surreptitiously. The vile drink, in all its varieties, was prohibited by the most stringent orders, shortly after we came here.

"And so at last—*at last*—we are off! There is no mistake this time. We broke up camp yesterday (Saturday) morning at daylight, and proceeded to embark as rapidly as possible: the Second Brigade down the river at Liverpool Point, the First Brigade four miles this side at Budd's Ferry, and we, the Third Brigade, here at Rum Point. We were all aboard the transports here by 2 P. M., and here we have been lying ever since, awaiting the arrival of the schooners, which are to convey the teams and stores, and to be towed by our steamers. The brigade is embarked on five large North River steamboats; and the troops are as comfortable as could be expected. One of them, the 'John Brooks,' is a huge affair, and carries at least thirteen hundred men. The 'Arrowsmith' carries about six hundred of the Fifth and the headquarters of the brigade. We are much less crowded than the rest: and are indeed quite comfortable. The cabin is occupied by Colonel Starr and his staff, and a few of the officers of the

Fifth. A 'brigade' appointment has its dangers and responsibilities; but it also has its *privileges*—chief among which are better quarters and more authority.

"As I write, the teams are slowly embarking, and we expect to bid farewell to these dreary regions either to-night or early in the morning. The boats all have steam up, and have orders to get under way at a moment's notice. We leave behind us all of our teams save four to a regiment, and three for the brigade headquarters. So, we turned over to the quartermaster here all our tents, and received instead the little *shelter tents*, which the men will carry on their shoulders. The brigade staff, however, are each allowed a wall tent and a servant's tent, so that we shall be all right. * * *

"And now, you naturally ask, whither are we bound? Nobody knows *certainly*, except General Hooker; and he very properly—keeps his own counsel. Nevertheless, we all suppose that we are bound for Fortress Monroe, and thence to Richmond. There will be a great and bloody battle there. You people at home have no conception of the immense force that has been quietly, yet rapidly, concentrating there. McClellan went down a week ago, and for two weeks, or rather three, the river has been day and night crowded with the transports carrying troops thither and returning. The whole prodigious Army of the Potomac, with the exception of two or three small divisions, has gone there, and yet the papers have been silent as death, and few of you know anything about it. Keep this news *quiet*, but remember it in case you hear of any movements there. Be sure our force will be brave and overwhelming, and will prove invincible (if duly handled) by any force the Confeds can bring against it. We leave here a regiment of Indiana cavalry and the Fifty-sixth Pennsylvania, which arrived from Washington on Friday; which force is deemed sufficient to guard the Maryland shore.

"I regret to say, have been ill for twenty-four hours past, though now able to sit up and write. Our orders came on Thursday night, and all day Friday I was in the saddle, arranging and assigning the transports, and did not finish till late that night. Yesterday we were up before daylight; and about sunrise—as usual, indeed *always,* when the Fifth has moved—it set in to rain. A dull, heavy air, filled at times with rapid rain, and always with more or less, prevailed throughout the day; and when at 5 P. M. I came aboard the 'Arrowsmith,' was well worn out. An hour afterward, Colonel Starr wanted an important order to go ashore, and of course I volunteered. But when I returned it was long after dark, and I knew I should be ill. So I was, all last night, and all day to-day, until 5 P. M., when I began to rally. As I write, it is 8 P. M., and I feel my old cheerfulness returning. Have been sitting up for three hours, and trust by morning I shall be myself again. * * *

"It has not been much of a Sunday; yet I have read one chapter in the Psalms—that favorite one of mine beginning with 'God is our refuge and strength, a very present help in trouble.' Have not had as clear an indication of the Divine Presence for many months. How good God is at times, when we need *His* consolation most!" * * *

"JAMES RIVER, VA.
April 8, 1862.

"DEAR FATHER AND FRIENDS: We are here in Hampton Roads, just off Fortress Monroe. Left Rum Point Sunday night, and arrived here yesterday (Monday) about 4 P. M. A storm set in yesterday morning, and the bay became very rough. The storm still continues, and we are still on board the 'Arrowsmith.' We are to go up York River to a place called Ship Point; where we are to join our army corps—Heintzelman's. But three boats of the brigade have arrived; the rest, and all the rest of the division, are still somewhere up the bay or river.

"Great movements here. An immense amount of shipping, steamboats and sailing vessels. The little 'Monitor,' Ericsson's battery, lies off in the stream about one eighth of a mile from us. She looks precisely like what the Rebels called her, 'A Yankee cheese-box on a raft!'

"I write this hastily, late Tuesday afternoon, merely to say we are here safe. Will write more at length after we land."

"FORTRESS MONROE, VA.  
April 13, 1862.

"DEAR FRIENDS: * * * Our brigade left here Friday morning. All but one boat had arrived on Monday and Tuesday; but they were detained here by the storm until Friday. It was a wild and terrible storm; and our vessels were afraid to venture out. On our boat there was no stove in the cabin, and I suffered much. Wednesday the storm grew worse; and it was so disagreeable that Colonel Starr sent me aboard another boat, where there was a stove.

"Thursday morning, not being any better, he ordered me ashore, and placed in hospital. They expected to leave immediately, but were detained until Friday morning. Early that morning they all left for Ship Point; which you will observe by the inclosed map, is up York River, and only about six miles from Yorktown. Heard from them yesterday. They arrived at Ship Point the same day they left; and at once disembarked. Thence they marched two miles to Heintzelman's corps; where they encamped in the woods, about four miles from Yorktown.

"Am here at the United States Hospital, in the old Hygeia Hotel. It is a comfortable two-story frame building; right under the guns of Fortress Monroe. It contains about five hundred sick men, in all degrees of sickness. Am in a little room about twenty feet square, with two other officers. One is nearly well, and will soon leave; the other is very low with camp fever. We each have a little iron bedstead, with a comfortable bed. My colored boy, Moses, is with me, and takes the best of care of me. He never leaves me, night or day, and is as gentle as a woman. * * *

"Our forces have already invested Yorktown. If Yorktown surrenders, and I am not there, it seems to me I shall die with vexation. * * *

"I suppose I ought to say something about the 'Merrimac.' I saw her on Friday, when she first came out;[1] and from the top of the hospital, with my glass, watched her some time. She came out of Norfolk about 8 A. M., and steamed leisurely over about halfway to Newport News, when she stopped, as if reconnoitering. With her were two large black steamers, the 'Jamestown' and the 'Yorktown,' and a half dozen little tugs. The 'Yorktown' stopped a moment at the 'Merrimac,' and then put off toward Newport News; suddenly she tacked about, and came right down the north shore of the bay toward Hampton. Everybody was astounded. What could she mean? We soon found out. There were three little schooners there, like those in your canal; and she went down like a snake after toads, deliberately to gobble them up. With the utmost coolness, she fastened first one and then another to her, and then struck boldly off for Norfolk. The audacity of the thing struck everybody dumb. A gunboat was immediately ordered around to Hampton; but it was too late then to 'lock the door'—the horse was gone! The shipping at once took fright. Sloop after sloop, schooner after schooner, immediately hoisted sail, and soon a hundred of them were scampering down the Roads, and out into the bay, as if Old Nick was after them!

"Meanwhile the 'Merrimac' lay still, as if waiting for

---

[1] Her second appearance.

the return of her consort, 'Yorktown.' It was two hours before she returned. Then they laid their heads together, as if consulting; then they separated and lay to, like bulldogs watching. The 'Merrimac' was four miles off, and I could see her plainly. She looks exactly like the roof of a house, for all the world, except that there are four sides instead of two; and she has a big, black smokestack sticking up through the center. In front, just above the water's edge, I could see a projecting ram's head, which at that distance looked just like the head of a turtle poked out ahead as it paddles along. The whole thing is the hugest, most ungainly, and horrible looking monster you ever imagined. The 'Monitor' looks like a tadpole, when compared with her. A little, long, low, black thing—'a cheesebox on a raft,' is all I can call her.

"On Friday she lay quietly out in the stream, awaiting the onset of the 'Merrimac.' A short distance off lay the 'Naugatuck'—Stevens's battery. Just back of both, concealed behind the Fortress, was the 'Vanderbilt,' cased in cotton bales, and armed with a sharp steel bow; intended by her great speed and weight to run the 'Merrimac' down. Their plan was to draw the 'Merrimac' down to where they lay, so that the guns of the fort and also those of the Rip-Raps might all be brought to bear on her. She was evidently afraid. She floundered about for several hours, as if uncertain whether to advance or retreat; and, finally, by way of variety, pitched a shot at the 'Naugatuck,' which fell short. The little 'Naugatuck,' no bigger than a scow, promptly replied; and threw a two-hundred-and-forty-pound shot far beyond the 'Merrimac.' In two minutes she fired again, and her shot struck the water within twenty yards of the 'Merrimac.' A cheer burst from the crowd on shore here; and forthwith the 'Merrimac' turned tail and, with her consorts, paddled off for Norfolk, evidently quite disgusted. Yesterday she poked her nose around Sewall's Point, and to-day again; but she has not ventured out. Our people here have the greatest confidence in the 'Monitor,' the 'Naugatuck,' and their other defenses, and are eager and anxious for the 'Merrimac' to give them battle." * * *

"FORTRESS MONROE, VA.
April 24, 1862.

"DEAR FRIENDS: I did not write last Sunday. Was too unwell and too excited. Had been lying here a week and a half; sometimes worse and sometimes better. One bed had been occupied by three different officers; all of whom had recovered and returned to their regiments, and still here I lay in torment. The occupant of the other bed —a Captain Samuel Barstow, of Oswego, N. Y.—however, was far worse. He had come the same day I had, and was a little delirious then, poor fellow! He had the camp fever, which rapidly assumed a typhoidal character, and from the first we hadn't much hope of him. He thought he would soon be well; but all the time he grew worse, until last Sunday, when the surgeon gave him up. It was a terrible day. He was unconscious of everybody but his attendants; and writhed and raved in delirium, until wholly exhausted. Part of the time it took two men to hold him on his bed. He fancied there was a gang of men lurking about to kill him, and his shrieks at times were appalling. I couldn't bear to be in the room; yet I had to go there at night, and all the while he was dying. His struggles grew feeble, until about midnight, when he quietly yielded up the ghost. The hospital attendants were called, and he was soon removed to the 'dead room;' but you can form no idea how I felt the remainder of the night. My poor boy, Moses, lay quietly on the floor by my side; but neither of us slept a wink all night. Captain Barstow's father was in Washington, and was telegraphed immediately. He was refused a pass here; but he went to the Secretary of War in person, and wrung one from him. He arrived here Tuesday, and conveyed the remains of his son home.

"Such is another of my experiences! I think if I keep on, I shall be pretty well 'posted' in army life, ere the war is over. Thank heaven! I shall not be here much longer. Shall leave for the brigade to-day or to-morrow. It moved last week from Ship Point, up close to Yorktown, and is now with the advance.

"The chaplain was down to see me last week; he rode down on horseback, a distance of twenty-two miles—pretty good for an old man like him. Rode back, too, the same day. A brave and faithful man, after all.

"There is a terrific battle preparing there. Cannon and mortars, shot and shell, are leaving here every hour, in immense quantities. This morning a large train of ambulances went up. There will be some furious fighting there. It will be the second fight of the Army of the Potomac; and the great battle of the Rebellion, apparently.

"There is no more news of the 'Merrimac.' She hasn't come out for a week. Fort Wool, on the Rip-Raps, exchanges an occasional shot with Sewall's Point; but it amounts to little. Our people here repose implicit confidence in the 'Monitor;' though I must confess she hardly seems to deserve it."

"IN CAMP BEFORE YORKTOWN, VA.
April 27, 1862.

"DEAR FRIENDS: Arrived here last night about dark. Left Fortress Monroe yesterday about 2 P. M., and came by steamboat to Ship Point. Here I landed myself and horses. Fortunately, found a wagon that was coming up to headquarters, and put my trunk and bedding aboard that. Came near losing my gray horse, in landing him. The gangway was very narrow and steep, and when about halfway ashore he slipped and fell, both hindquarters falling over the dock. His head and forequarters being ashore, after a deal of work and pulling, we succeeded in getting him up and saving him. He was scratched pretty badly, and somewhat bruised; yet he carried me bravely up to camp, some six miles, over horrible roads.

"I say 'horrible'—most horrible! It has rained here for several days, and the bottom is all out. The soil is a light sandy loam, of no thickness; underlaid by quicksand. When the top gets wet, it cuts right through, and wagons sink to the axletrees. I think I must have passed at least a hundred scattered along the road, stuck fast.

"I took everybody by surprise last night. All crowded in to welcome me back; but I was tired and fatigued. They will take good care of me here. My friends hustled around this morning and got a floor for my tent, and a little sheet-iron stove, so that I am quite comfortable. Indeed, there is but one other stove in the whole brigade; and where they got mine from is a mystery.

"By the bye, should anything happen to me while in the army, and you come on to see after me, apply for information to either of the following persons: Colonel S. H. Starr (commanding brigade), Lieutenant Colonel Mott, Dr. James C. Fisher, Adjutant C. K. Hall, or Quartermaster Sergeant Sandt, all of the Fifth Regiment; or to Quartermaster Thomas P. Johnston, of the Seventh. All of these are my good friends, and will assist you every way. * * * If I get no better, shall be home soon. But I want to be here; and don't think it soldierly to leave, now that we are face to face with the enemy, on the eve of a great battle.

"Yorktown is about three miles away; our outposts, about two. The troops are laboring hard, and are much exposed; yet they are hilarious and enthusiastic. Our first parallel is already open, and every night thousands throng the trenches. It is a regular siege, just like Sebastopol. Everybody is wide awake. Reconnoissances, skirmishes, and sorties are continually occurring. Berdan's sharpshooters are performing prodigies. It will be a long time before the assault is made. Should not be surprised if weeks yet elapsed. A siege is always excessively slow; especially if it be a 'big thing' like this. * * *

"It is a very queer Sunday we are spending here, with cannon roaring and shells bursting every few minutes, all along the lines. But my trust is in God, and Him only will I serve."

"IN CAMP NEAR WILLIAMSBURG, VA. }
May 6, 1862.

"DEAR FRIENDS: It is Tuesday night, and I feel I ought to write you a line; though I hardly know how. * * *

"Of course, you have heard of the great battle here. Yorktown was evacuated Saturday night. We started in pursuit Sunday morning. Hooker's division led the advance, our brigade being third in order. Marched all day Sunday and all night Sunday night, with frequent halts, because of road obstructed, etc.; and at eight o'clock Monday morning overtook the enemy near here. Hooker formed line of battle, and attacked immediately. Our brigade held the left wing, which the Confeds tried to turn. Our division, about ten thousand strong, fought the whole rear guard of the Rebel Army, some thirty thousand, as reported, all day; and at 4 P. M. had gained and lost the battle ground no less than *four* times. Hooker had sent messenger after messenger for reinforcements, but the rain had made the road so horrible, that the troops could not get up.

"At last, at 4 P. M., as I have said, General Kearny, a Jerseyman, came up with his division. Our men were already giving way; fifteen minutes later he would have found them retreating. They had fought all day, had no ammunition left, had eaten nothing since morning, and were discouraged at being left to fight alone. But Kearny —God bless him!—arrived at the critical juncture, proclaimed himself a Jerseyman, rallied our wavering ranks, in the name of the Union, and with his bands playing 'The Star-Spangled Banner,' and his men yelling like savages, led his division to the attack on the double-quick. The effect was glorious; our division at once rallied, and the Confeds, falling back at all points, were soon fleeing everywhere.

"I can't say much more. Our loss has been heavy. The colonel of the Eighth was wounded and will probably die. His major was shot dead. The lieutenant colonel of the Seventh is severely wounded. The lieutenant colonel of the Sixth was killed; as also his adjutant, Lieutenant Wilkes, of Trenton. The colonel of the Fifth was slightly wounded. And now of ourselves at brigade headquarters. General Patterson[1] had his horse killed; Captain Freese, ditto; and Lieutenant Hall's horse wounded. Am safe myself, but used up.

"Of company officers many have fallen, and others are wounded. Lieutenant Lalor (of Trenton) is killed; his body will be sent home. We have many prisoners."

"CAMP NEAR WILLIAMSBURG, VA.
May 8, 1862.

"DEAR FRIENDS: Wrote you a hasty letter on Tuesday night. To-day, Thursday, have more leisure, and write again.

"The accounts I sent you of the fight here are absolutely true in fact; though the papers we have received so far do not even mention us. However, we have only Tuesday's papers, and their news is only down to early Monday. The fight was a gallant one, and only failed to be decisive be-

---

[1] He had been assigned to the command of the brigade only a few days previously.

cause of either the slowness or timidity of General Sumner. Our division, early in the day, obtained a position from which they could have advanced up a ravine, under good cover from the enemy's fire, and outflanking his right have gained his rear, had we been even *feebly* supported. This movement would have resulted either in bagging the whole Rebel Army, or in driving them panic-stricken back on Richmond. General Hooker sent messenger after messenger to Sumner to coöperate; but he stubbornly refused. All day he lay within two miles of our heroic men, in plain sight and sound of the Rebel guns, and let us fight on weary and alone. He was Hooker's superior officer, and could only be solicited. McClellan was miles back, somewhere lost in the woods, and could not be found.

"Fortunately Kearny came up, scouting around for himself, and seeing our perilous position, took the responsibility of ordering up his division; and came on at the double-quick. He rode up to a group of our men, that lay weary and exhausted by the roadside, and inquired who they were. They replied, 'Jerseymen!'

"'Well, then,' said he, 'in the name of God, follow a one-armed Jersey Blue back into the fight, and we'll whip them to pieces!'

"He had lost one arm in Mexico, and his heroic conduct now, as he sat coolly on horseback, at the head of his division, roused our boys to the wildest enthusiasm. They forgot their weariness, they forgot their exhaustion, they forgot their wounds, even; and with terrific cheers went back to the conflict with a spirit that proved irresistible. The Confeds soon fled at all points; and our men lay down to sleep on the battlefield.

"The spectacle on Tuesday morning as I rode along, was sickening. The dead yet lay upon the battlefield, and the wounded were being carried along in litters to the various hospitals. In a row of dead officers, that had been carried in near headquarters, I recognized poor De Klyn Lalor. He was hit in the forehead, early in the day, and soon expired. Subsequently his body fell into the hands of the Rebels, who bayoneted him through the foot, and then robbed and stripped him. Many of our dead, and a large number of our wounded fell into the hands of the Rebels at one time; but subsequently we drove the enemy back, and recovered most of them. We found a large number at Williamsburg, whither the Confeds had sent them.

"Our brigade loses in killed, wounded, and missing five hundred and thirty-four. We went into the fight with two thousand two hundred and fifty, so that we lose nearly one fourth—a very large proportion. The other brigades of the division suffered severely, though not so heavily. It was a hard-fought battle and a bravely won victory; and when the truth is all known, it will figure in history as one of the most closely contested engagements of the campaign or war.

"The weather has cleared up beautifully. The country about here seems to be a much better one than we have hitherto found. It is an old settled district of the State. Williamsburg is a town of some three thousand people; and in Colonial times was the capital of Virginia. Have not been out of camp to look around; but the reports are all favorable. We are encamped in a wheat stubble field, the soil of which is certainly fair.

"It is uncertain whether I shall get home or not. There are so many others, who are wounded, that ought to go, that I can illy be spared. Am on duty every day, and manage to 'pull through' somehow. So don't expect me till you see me.

"As I suppose you have heard, Colonel Starr has been relieved of the command of the brigade. His successor arrived on Saturday, as we marched on Sunday; and at once assumed command. His name is Frank Patterson, a son of General Robert Patterson, of Philadelphia. He is a brigadier general, and was appointed at the request of McClellan. He is more pleasant and affable than Starr; anybody can approach him; he is cool and quiet and says but little. In the fight, he was as calm as if on parade or drill, and fought the brigade splendidly. He says he never saw men and officers behave better under fire, and is enthusiastic in his praise of the Jerseymen. The troops are well pleased with him. He continued me in my appointment as acting brigade quartermaster; much against the wishes of Colonel Starr, who wanted me to return to the Fifth Regiment.

"P. S.—A mail just come, and I have a paper from home and a letter from E——! Good! Bless the post office!"

"CAMP NEAR WEST POINT, VA.
May 12, 1862.

"DEAR FRIENDS: I did not write you yesterday, because too weary. We left camp at Williamsburg Saturday morning, and marched some fifteen miles; when we encamped for the night. It was a warm day, and the men suffered severely. We encamped in an oat field; the general and his staff bivouacked under a large apple tree. Our poor horses had a good time on the young oats and a wheat field adjoining; and they needed it sadly. On this whole movement they have been worked cruelly and fed wretchedly. Some days we had no grain, and hardly ever any hay.

"Yesterday morning (Sunday) we took a late start, and marched leisurely along till 3 P. M., when we encamped here, where we are to stay for a day or so. We are about five miles from West Point, in the midst of a well-cultivated country. It is the best country I have seen in all *Secessia*. The houses, barns, fences, and fields all indicate a very considerable degree of prosperity. A few inhabitants remain, who are probably half loyal. We are encamped in a rolling clover field, on the farm of a man who claims to be Union, but hardly knows what *Union* means.

"Am getting quite well again, and thankful I am. The quartermaster of the Seventh is lying very ill at Yorktown, and is not expected to survive. The quartermasters of the Sixth and the Eighth are both sick here; and the quartermaster of the Fifth, the only one fit for duty, was only appointed last week, and is therefore *green*. Don't know what they would do without me. I manage everything, by pen and brain; and am writing orders and letters all day and half the night.

"We expect to go from here direct to Richmond. We have great good news from all quarters; from Norfolk, New Orleans, Corinth, etc.; and I guess the most of us will get home next fall or spring. Am very busy and must close. I wish merely to add, that the newspaper accounts of the battle of Williamsburg are meanly false. Our division lost one thousand five hundred men, in killed, wounded, and missing; and it is totally ignored. The whole thing was a useless sacrifice, and *McClellan is afraid to publish the truth.* General Patterson declares *justice* shall be done the Jersey brigade, or he will resign."

"CAMP NEAR NEW KENT COURT HOUSE, VA.
May 16, 1862.

"DEAR FRIENDS: * * * We moved here yesterday, marching some six miles. Breaking camp about 6 A. M., we made good time until 8 or 9 A. M., when it set in to rain, and poured pretty steadily. The road was full of troops and trains, and we made slow progress. At noon the roads had become so heavy, it was deemed advisable to halt and encamp; which we did in a heavy rain. You would think it hard to encamp in the mud; but we get used to such things. Having once pitched your tent, you send for a pile of wood, arrange this before the door of your tent, kindle a fire; and in an hour or two, let it rain as it will, you will be dry enough inside.

"To-day the roads are frightful. General Hooker pronounced them impassable, and forbade the division to move. I sent five four-horse teams six miles to draw four thousand pounds of forage! They left at 10.30 A. M., and got back at dark. We shall probably stop here a day or two, as the road ahead of us is so full of troops that it will be impossible to move. The whole Peninsula is crowded with soldiers, and heaven only knows what McClellan wants of them all!

"It has cleared off, and the night is beautiful. The sight outside my tent is one well worth seeing. The country for a mile around is rolling and fertile, and the whole space crowded with encampments. Immediately before me lies our whole division, of over ten thousand men; the lights gleaming up from the tents, and flickering from a hundred camp fires. Our headquarters is on a little ridge, just in the edge of a pine woods, and commands a fine view of everything around us. As we sit at the tent door, and smoke our evening pipes, the cheerful murmur of the camp floats up the hill; and our own voices chime in, as we talk of the friends at home. * * *

"There is no immediate prospect of a fight here, nor do I think we shall have much severe fighting. Richmond will be evacuated, and the whole concern 'shut up shop' and go South soon. However, it is impossible to say what a day or an hour may bring forth."

## Some Army Letters

"HEADQUARTERS 3D BRIGADE,
HOOKER'S DIVISION,
ON THE ROAD, 21 MILES FROM RICHMOND.
May 19, 1862.

"DEAR FRIENDS: It is now Monday night. I write now instead of yesterday, because I have *only now* the leisure. The past week has been a busy and laborious one. On Tuesday we moved about three miles, and camped for the night. On Thursday we moved again, in the midst of rain, and made some eight miles. Yesterday, Sunday, of course, we started again, and desecrated one of God's most beautiful Sabbaths by another march of some six miles. This morning we started again at nine o'clock, and at about four reached here—a distance of perhaps eight miles. It began to rain about ten o'clock, and poured pretty steadily until we reached camp, when it ceased, and it has since then cleared off very nicely.

"We are encamped just on the road, within the edge of a pine woods, in one of the most lovely sections of the country I ever saw. The land, for some seven hundred acres, belongs to a Dr. C——; he lives just across the road, perhaps an eighth of a mile from our headquarters, and has the finest house and the best looking farm that I have seen anywhere in Secessia. This evening General Patterson and staff took tea there. One week ago, he told us, General Joe Johnston, General Lee, General Magruder, General Longstreet, General Smith, and the redoubtable *Jeff. Davis* himself, sat down to tea in the same room, at the same table.

"To-day two Rebel generals came within our lines, carrying a flag of truce. They passed us blindfolded, on their way to McClellan's headquarters. They were large, thick-set, fine-looking men, dressed in the flashy gray cloth of their uniform. Of course, we are ignorant of their errand; though 'Little Mac' knows it by this time.

"I see that McClellan has at last found out that Hooker was at Williamsburg. It was high time. If he had not acknowledged our services there, it would have raised a storm, which would have blown him out of the commander in chiefship, like a feather. Hooker's report is yet to come in; he showed it to me the other day, and it will do the Jersey brigade some little justice. All the stories you see in the papers about our brigade 'breaking and running' there, you may, *in my name,* brand as infamous lies. It astounds us, beyond measure, how anybody *can* lie so. Out of two thousand two hundred and fifty, with which we began the fight, we lost five hundred and thirty-four, nearly twenty-five per cent, which is a large average for the bloodiest fight; it is more than the French lost at either Magenta or Solferino, and almost twice what they and the English lost at the storming of Sebastopol. Cowards don't sustain such losses. They are careful of their hides. It is only heroes and veterans who are strangers to fear and account death preferable to defeat and disgrace. It is but the truth of history, that if it had not been for the heroic valor and sublime courage of the Jersey brigade on that hard-fought day, Hooker's division would have been outflanked and the whole army rolled back upon Yorktown. * * *

"Much as I desire to see you all, and much as I know you desire to see me, I cannot reconcile it to my sense of duty to leave here now. Every quartermaster in the brigade, save one, is either sick or absent; and as a consequence my hands are full. * * * Pray excuse me; and I will come home, after we have fought and won at Richmond! I greatly need rest and a change, it is true; but this is no time to take either."

## Some Army Letters

"HEADQUARTERS 3D BRIGADE,
HOOKER'S DIVISION,
BOTTOM BRIDGE, VA.
May 24, 1862.

"DEAR FRIENDS: It is now Saturday afternoon; but I seize the opportunity of writing, as to-morrow we may not be here. We left camp at Baltimore Cross Roads yesterday, about 5 P. M., and reached here about 8 P. M.—a distance of perhaps five miles. The roads were very heavy, and the troops marched very slowly. The wagon-train stuck badly, and some of the teams did not get in till late this morning. We had supper at 9.30 P. M., and lay down to sleep, under the shelter of a grand old oak, a little after 10 P. M. Slept soundly till morning. After breakfast, it set in to rain, and that put us to pitching tents as rapidly as possible. It has rained quite steadily all day; a cold raw rain, that will play havoc with the men, if it continues long. We remain in camp to-day, as we cannot move; and shall probably be off again to-morrow, as it happens to be Sunday! Of course, we move 'On to Richmond!' We are now within thirteen miles of that Rebel nest, and shall certainly soon be there; even if we have to fight for it.

"At our last camp, Baltimore Cross Roads, we lay for several days, and it was a godsend to us. The weather was warm and pleasant, most of the time. Our camping ground was a sloping pine woods. The men and teams both had a fine chance to recruit their worn energies. The woods, together with a fine property of seven hundred acres adjoining, belongs to a Dr. C——. I believe I spoke of him in my last. He is a thorough Secessionist, and was a member of the Convention that voted Virginia out of the Union. He had some twenty slaves, of whom twelve 'skedaddled' to parts unknown, shortly after our encampment, and six more were sensible enough to follow their footsteps on Thursday night. He thought them very 'ungrateful,' one especially who was so foolish as to take along her baby. He didn't pretend to work his 'niggers' much, as he had only three hundred acres of cleared land; but he raised them regularly for the market, the same as he bred any other stock! He had a blacksmith shop, just in the corner of the woods, below our headquarters. Our men took possession of it, and proceeded to shoe up our horses, and repair wagons, harness, etc. We had our own tools and horseshoes; but used his forge, a little of his iron, and a small amount of coal. As we were leaving, he came to me, as brigade quartermaster, and wanted pay for the damage.

"'How much iron have our men used?'

"'I reckon, sir, about *five* pounds!'

"'How much coal?'

"'About half a bushel!'

"'And what are iron and coal worth in ordinary times?'

"'Well, sir, iron sells for about six cents a pound, and coal for about forty cents per bushel; though both are higher now!'

"'That is, you claim just fifty cents! And *you* own seven hundred acres, and twenty slaves, and are one of the F. F. V.'s! I'll tell what I'll do. If you will take the "oath of allegiance," and hang out the Stars and Stripes, I'll settle your claim instanter. Otherwise, I think it will have to rest!'

"Here was a man who deliberately trafficked in human flesh and blood, to the extent of thousands of dollars per year, and voted for Secession; and yet he had the audacity to present a claim against the United States for fifty cents! I asked him if he had been a Union man, and ours a Secesh Army, what would have been his treatment. 'O! sir, I suppose they would have taken *all my property* and *imprisoned me, too.*' Yet we 'protected' him carefully, and placed a guard at his house to keep marauders off!

"The country here is fine and would be beautiful, were it not for the ravages of war. God spare New Jersey from the horrors of the march of a hostile army! For miles on each side, the country is practically devastated. The fences are thrown down or destroyed. The young grain and clover are pastured off or trampled under foot. The cattle and horses, if not driven off, wander idly where they choose. The houses are deserted. The Negroes sometimes work and sometimes hold high carnival. And how in the world the population is to subsist, I really cannot tell. Fortunately, but few of them deserve to 'subsist' (they have been such wicked traitors); and these, I suppose, Uncle Sam will take care of!

"MONDAY, May 26.—We are two miles across the Chickahominy, and an order has just come to prepare for battle. Ere you get this, likely we shall either be in Richmond or badly defeated. Am out of postage stamps and can't get any here. Please send me a hundred when you write."

"ON THE ROAD, NEAR SAVAGE'S STATION,
TEN MILES FROM RICHMOND, VA.
Monday, June 2, 1862.

"DEAR FRIENDS: On Saturday afternoon at four o'clock, the brigade moved off hastily toward Richmond. We had heard heavy firing for three or four hours, and the news came that Casey's division had been surprised and driven back by the enemy. Kearny and Hooker moved up promptly to support; and the enemy were checked and driven back. When the brigade marched, I was ordered to take all the teams and baggage, with the least delay, back to the east side of the Chickahominy. The roads were horrible, yet we succeeded in getting all the trains and about three fourths of the baggage across by 10 P. M. It then set in to rain, and was so pitch dark that we suspended operations till morning.

"Sunday morning, at daylight, the battle was renewed. The teams were all sent back, before sunrise; and by 10 A. M. we had all across save a few loads. At this time, the battle was so dubious that I received orders to hold my trains in hand, east of the river, and to abandon the rest of the baggage, if necessary. By twelve noon affairs brightened, and at 1 P. M. I got orders to send the teams for the rest immediately. Sent them off, and at 3 P. M. got orders to recross the river and move to the front. Left orders for the absent teams, and at 4 P. M. recrossed, and at 8 P. M. found the brigade about six miles in advance. The battle was severe; the Rebels had been repulsed, but still showed a good front a mile or so away; and General Patterson ordered me to turn the trains and retire to a safe distance in the rear. Vexed with the multiplicity of orders, I yet cheerfully complied; and, each quartermaster leading his own regimental train, we were soon again in motion.

"We retired a half mile or so, and at 9.30 P. M. parked the wagons by the roadside. Had a cup of coffee, a hard cracker, and some cold meat, and at 11 P. M. lay down to sleep. At midnight a regiment in advance of my train (some Pennsylvanians, I hear) became *panic-stricken* by a loose horse galloping through its lines; and with the most awful cries of 'The Rebels are upon us! Their cavalry are butchering our men everywhere!' they stampeded through my trains, as if Old Nick was after them. I had just fallen into a doze, but springing up, I seized my pistol and saber, and rushing out of my tent, called upon everybody to 'halt.' You might as well have called to a herd of maddened steers. There was no stopping the dastards, till I formed my little wagon-guard—about fifty men—in line with fixed bayonets and orders to shoot the first man that attempted to pass.

"I knew it was a 'panic' from the first. In springing to

my feet, I was cool enough to reflect that nearly our whole Army lay before us, and that a dash of Rebel cavalry was impossible, without prolonged picket-firing. One fellow I collared and hurled to the ground, and another my good boy Moses deliberately knocked down with my saddle. Said Mose, 'Just to think of dem big soldiers runnin' dat way! Golly, dis nigger wouldn't be such a baby!'

"This morning, I received orders to fall back a mile farther; and now am here. There is some fighting in the advance, but it recedes; and the Rebels are doubtless falling back. Word has just come that our brigade has gone ahead, and I momentarily expect to advance again. I chafe very much under the necessity which compels me to be here; but the orders of McClellan are stringent, and require every division, brigade, and regimental quartermaster to remain with his train, under penalty of being court-martialed and dismissed from the service.

"The battle in front is yet undecided, but I have thought it best to write to you, as this is my time. Shall write you more fully, when all is over. I do hope that we shall get to Richmond soon."

"HEADQUARTERS 3D BRIGADE.
June 8, 1862.

"DEAR FRIENDS: * * * I have good news from Washington. Major Webb, our paymaster, arrived to-day, and he reports that the President nominated me for brigade quartermaster, so long ago as the middle of May. Should this nomination be confirmed, as it probably will be, I shall at least have made a sure step in my own department. This, however, is but little satisfaction to me now; as I have had all the *honor* of the place for six months past, and done all its duties.

"It is Sunday evening. Of course, we moved again to-day. About half a mile, 'On to Richmond,' but very slowly. Last Sunday we fought; to-day we marched. I wrote you a letter in lead pencil, I believe, last Monday. That stated something about a fight. It was a desperate one, on Saturday. The fact is, Casey was overwhelmed and badly whipped. We marched to his support at 5 P. M., and reached him at dark. The fight had ceased with his being driven back over a mile, and when night fell the Rebels occupied Casey's camp. Our supports poured in from all points that night; and on Sunday morning at six o'clock, when we moved to the attack, we drove the Rebels everywhere.

"Two of our regiments, the Seventh and Eighth, were back at Bottom's Bridge, guarding the Chickahominy. The Fifth and Sixth went in on Sunday, led by General Hooker in person. As they approached, with solid front, to a swamp, one of Casey's brigadiers suggested, that the ground was swampy in there, and the men couldn't get through.

"'Get out of the way,' was Hooker's response; 'I have two regiments here, that can go anywhere.'

"And they did. The Rebels fled before them, and by 9 A. M. we had driven them out of Casey's camp, and advanced to our old outposts. That was one week ago, and there we lie now. There has been no advance beyond Casey's old camp. The papers lie; they lie horribly. They are trying hard to make McClellan a great man; whereas I sometimes fear he is a great donkey. Our loss was very heavy, principally on Saturday. Casey lost everything but his own life: and he was a fool not to have thrown that away. I fear our loss will not fall short of two thousand killed, and six thousand wounded. The loss on Sunday was trifling—in our own brigade, but some sixty in both killed and wounded. There was no fight on Monday. The *Herald* is mistaken. It was all over on Sunday by 9 A. M., and the Jersey brigade ended it.

"The Rebel loss must have been enormous. Sumner

buried one thousand on his part of the field. Our division has been burying all the week, and the woods are still full of them. The stench from their decaying bodies fills the atmosphere; and life here in camp is simply horrible. On Monday afternoon, just up the road from here, I counted sixty-five dead Rebels in a place not so large as your house. They lay in heaps. Our artillery literally *mowed* them down. We estimate their total loss at at least fifteen thousand—say, five thousand killed and ten thousand wounded.

"O, how horrible is war! Do you know I have never had any thought of resigning until now? But now, I am so shocked and disgusted with the horrors I daily witness, that I can scarcely refrain from resigning. Nothing but a sense of duty keeps me here. You don't know the one half at home. When we finally get to Richmond this Army will send home a tale of suffering and hardship and horror, such as will make your very flesh crawl. Field and staff officers *can* get along; but O how I pity the poor fellows on foot!

"The enemy are perhaps a mile and a half from us: Richmond perhaps six miles. We can hear the shouts of their troops, and the whistle of their locomotives. Our position is an exceedingly strong one, and we are daily *receiving reinforcements.* Fifteen thousand have already come, and more are arriving every train. My own belief is that Richmond will be regularly besieged, unless it is soon evacuated. Should not be surprised, if it is Corinth and Yorktown over again. There are alarms every night, and we have scarcely any rest. This is telling fearfully on the troops, both officers and men.

"Cousin Will has been sick, but is about again. He was in the fight at Williamsburg; but was sick in my tent at Bottom's Bridge, during the fight last Saturday and Sunday. He is with his company now, and in fair health and spirits. His captain was wounded badly, in the thigh, on Sunday. * * *

"The weather has been frightful, and the whole country is now a swamp. But we hope for the future. * * *

"I am still, through God's blessing,

"Yours affectionately, J. F. R."

"CAMP NEAR FAIR OAKS, VA.
June 15, 1862.

"DEAR FRIENDS: You are not entitled to a letter to-day, as I wrote Wednesday—I think it was—from the White House. Nevertheless, I write just a line, to say I am well, and all continues quiet here. We have picket-firing, of course, and occasionally one side or the other opens with shot and shell; but mostly all is quiet, each army slowly collecting its energies for another terrific engagement.

"The other day, while writing, a shell came screaming down the whole length of our camp, and struck about twenty yards back of our headquarters. You would be surprised how little alarm it provoked. Nobody 'skedaddled.' Nobody seemed particularly to care. The cook, at his fire, went on as unconcernedly as if nothing had happened, though the shell fell within twenty feet of him.

"We shall have a great fight here, but not immediately. It promises to be a siege. In such a case, we shall undoubtedly whip them. There is no mistake about McClellan being a great digger! Though whether he is a great general, events not yet ripe will have to determine.

"It has been fearfully hot here both yesterday and to-day; but now at 3 P. M. a furious thunderstorm is raging, from which we expect relief. The lightning is most vivid, and the thunder really appalling; while the wind is a perfect hurricane."

## Some Army Letters

"HEADQUARTERS 3D BRIGADE,
HOOKER'S DIVISION,
CAMP NEAR FAIR OAKS, Va.
June 21, 1862.

"DEAR FRIENDS: Good news! All hail, Abraham Lincoln! Have just this moment received my commission, as 'Captain and Assistant Quartermaster,' U. S. Vols., and hasten to inform you. Shall go over to army headquarters, and get mustered promptly as possible. I regret exceedingly that father should worry about me. Am in the Lord's hands, as much here as anywhere, and am sure I could not be engaged in better work, at my time of life and in this present age, than in assisting to crush this infernal proslavery Rebellion. Party prejudice is apt to blind; partisan feeling is apt to falsify; but, I think, he is stupid and far behind his times, who does not now recognize that God is working in this war, and that his hand will surely bring us safely through. Just now, here in America, He is demonstrating to all the world, that freedom and justice are every man's birthright—that injustice and oppression do not pay—or, in other words, in the simple but sublime phraseology of the Declaration of Independence, that '*all* men are created equal, and endowed by their Creator with the inalienable rights of life, liberty, and the pursuit of happiness.' It matters not whether men be white or black or brown, so that they be men, and have souls to save. Now, I believe all this. I was *taught* to believe it. It is a part of my very life and blood and bones. And I ought to fight for it—to be ready to die for it. My ancestors did;[1] and their very ashes would rise up in judgment against us, if neither of us boys was willing to fight for the sacred principles they bequeathed to us. They would be ashamed of such degenerate progeny; and they ought to be.

---
[1] I had two great-grandfathers in the Revolution—Captain William McCullough and Colonel Aaron Hankinson, both of New Jersey.

"Though exposed to great hardships and many dangers, I nevertheless thank God daily that I am here; and here I hope to stay, until the flag floats triumphant from the Ohio to the Gulf. I want you all at home to think of the consequent responsibility devolving upon you. Brace yourselves for every emergency; and remember that God will only require that of you which is right and best. I think God has given those who live at this period great opportunities. There has been no such chance for pure patriotism, exalted heroism, and sublime self-sacrifice here in America for the last fifty years, if ever.

"Now don't fret! If I were to resign and come home, you would soon grow ashamed of me, and wish me back in the Army. I know you love me—I trust very dearly; but you also love the Republic, and must be willing to hazard *one* in its defense. I trust, I hope, I sincerely desire, that God will have me in his keeping, and restore me safely to your fireside again. If not, and I am fated to fall here, weep only as for one who knew his duty, and was not afraid to do it.

"As brigade quartermaster, I have nothing to do with *'feeding the men.'* That branch of the service belongs exclusively to the commissary. The regimental quartermasters are also regimental commissaries; but the *double* office stops there. Our brigade commissary is a captain, a cousin of Simon Cameron, and has been with us since last winter. My duties refer more particularly to all kinds of transportation, and include clothing, camp equipage, etc.

"I would rather be *regimental major,* because the rank and pay are both better; but then, I myself have my doubts whether I should be able to stand the fatigue and exposure of that position. When a regiment goes out on picket for twenty-four hours, as ours does twice a week, and has to lay there in the trenches, rain or shine, cold or hot, it is apt to use up officers who are even far heartier than I.

"It is very hot and oppressive here at times; but the nights are cool, sometimes cold.

"Things remain pretty much as they did. We are daily getting reinforcements, and our men are becoming more confident and cheerful. It is surprising how cool and indifferent they become to danger. Yesterday, about 2 P. M., I was up to the advance lines, on some duty, and suddenly a Rebel battery opened with great precision. The shells whizzed and burst all over the camp; but the only effect was to put the men to talking. I saw a party on their knees, playing cards; and they never even stopped playing. Subsequently, I was at a court-martial, as counsel for an officer; the shells burst all about us, but the trial went on as if nothing was the matter. The Rebels must have thrown a hundred shells at our camp; but not a single man was hurt. So singular is war!"

"HEADQUARTERS 3D BRIGADE,
HOOKER'S DIVISION,
CAMP AT HARRISON'S LANDING, VA.
July 3, 1862.

"DEAR FRIENDS: I believe it is Thursday night, and I should have written you on Sunday; but things have been so mixed up and confused here, that I hardly know what day it is. We have had a very sad time here. As yet, I don't know whether it is defeat or 'strategy.' McClellan's friends, or rather his devotees, say the latter; but to me, with my 'eyes open,' it seems like a great and terrible disaster.

"It has been a week and a half of stirring events. I have neither the time nor the strength left to tell you all, but will recapitulate a little. It began on Tuesday morning of last week, by an advance along the whole left wing. Kearny and Hooker advanced over a half mile; when they met the enemy, and a sharp fight ensued. The enemy fell back. Our loss was not heavy, and when night closed, we held the ground we had gained. The papers all err about it. The *Tribune's* account is the truest.

"Wednesday there was some fighting on the center and right. The same on Thursday. Late that afternoon, I went to the White House for supplies. Found everybody alarmed there, by a report that the Rebels had turned our right wing. Was tired and worn out; but got a good night's sleep on a hospital boat there. Friday morning left White House for camp; found all quiet there, until afternoon, when the sound of furious fighting reached us from the right. At 4 P. M. we received orders to move to the right, to support the center of Sumner's corps. We moved immediately, marched till dark, then straggled on, nobody knew where; and about 10 P. M. brought up in a swamp two or three miles beyond where the brigade was ordered to go. Such a piece of stupidity in the face of the enemy, was never heard of. It was all the fault of a wooden-headed brigadier (not of our corps), under whom we were ordered to report to Sumner. At daylight we were ordered back to Hooker; you may be sure everybody rejoiced to return to our old, well-tried, trusted commander.

"Got back and pitched camp about noon. At 4 P. M. ordered out on picket. No fighting all day, but the most profound silence all along the lines. No news of Friday's fight; which we construed to mean *bad* news. At dark on Saturday night, June 28, received an order from McClellan's headquarters, to pack the wagons with ammunition and rations, destroy all trunks, tents, and extra baggage, and move the trains as rapidly as possible across White Oak Swamp, in the direction of James River.

"We took this to mean 'skedaddle,' though some still thought it 'strategy.' I resolved to save a few tents for headquarters, and our trunks and official papers, if possible. The headquarters wagons were at once packed lightly, and sent to Savage Station, two miles to the rear, to await the regimental trains and myself in person. Supposing I might lose everything, I deliberately put on my best uniform; resolved that whether captured, killed, or escaping, I would at least be in 'harness!' The rest of us at brigade headquarters did the same; and you would be surprised to know how cheerful we were, even under these gloomy circumstances. Then I rode to all the regiments, hurrying up their trains; and at midnight reached Savage Station.

"The most of the trains of the brigade had arrived, and were there crowded in a hundred-acre field with about three thousand other teams. It had set in to rain, but I was so tired I threw myself on the ground, underneath an army wagon, and for an hour or two slept soundly. I awoke about 2 A. M., and finding a little opening in the teams, I started the brigade train, and by hard pushing and maneuvering had made a half a mile by sunrise. Here the road was so narrow that but one wagon could pass at a time, and all was a complete jam. Everybody had caught the idea that we were on a retreat; every officer was doing his best to force his own teams ahead; and the consequence was that nobody moved at all. At last General Fitz John Porter rode up, and with the genius of a true general produced order out of chaos. So many trains, however, were ahead of us, that it was long after noon before Hooker's got started at all. Then we moved slowly, crossed White Oak Swamp on two bridges our engineer corps had made, and parked for the night in a huge wheat field.

"Meanwhile there had been fighting all day in our rear, and our division was the rear guard. The enemy, of course, became aware of our 'skedaddle,' but Hooker was there, and held them sternly at bay. At daylight Monday morning, the whole train, the whole army, all the artillery, had passed successfully over, and then the bridges were committed to the flames. Meanwhile, Hooker had 'skedaddled' by another road, right from under the noses of the Rebels, and we were all safe on the way to James River. The rear guard formed along this side of the swamp, the infantry low down in the bushes, the artillery far up on the bluffs; and so awaited the enemy.

"Our train started at sunrise. By 10 A. M. we had made perhaps a mile. The road was full of wagons, two abreast. Some were still back in the wheat field. At this hour, suddenly, like concentrated thunder, "Stonewall" Jackson opened upon us at the destroyed bridges, with twenty pieces of artillery; and the wagons 'skedaddled' in all directions. Some mules and horses were killed, many wagons were overturned, and the rest galloped away for their lives. Meanwhile, our rear guard opened, and soon succeeded in silencing the enemy's cannon. This hurried up the main train. Our division quartermaster and myself discovered a new road, and into this we turned, and with a train over a mile long, we hurried along to our destination. The 'new' road ended in a swamp! We fetched up in this about dark, about two miles from James River, and there we were compelled to halt till morning. About 11 P. M. I got a cup of coffee and a piece of 'hard-tack,' and with this luxurious supper, lay down to rest under a large tree, and slept drearily until daylight. Then we cut our way out of the swamp, and by 8 A. M. encamped here in a wheat field, within a stone's throw of the welcome waters of James River.

"Not a wagon, nor a mule, nor a horse lost! All safe! At one time I fully expected to destroy everything. Had prepared axes to chop the wagons to pieces, and borrowed a box of matches, on purpose to burn them. I ordered my tent pitched at once, and spreading my blankets on the ground slept soundly until late in the afternoon. Then I went down to the River, and went in to bathe. O, the luxury of that bath! Tired, weary, dusty, dirty, it seemed like the very waters of Paradise!

"Meanwhile, there had been heavy firing at Malvern Hill and along our rear; but the enemy had been repulsed at all points. The army, however, had steadily fallen back, and now—Thursday night—it is all at or near James River. What it all means I cannot exactly tell. It has been a retreat by the flank, which is the most difficult of all movements, and so far has been successful. It has changed our base to James River, where it should have been in the first place. I think there is no doubt that it was a forced movement. McClellan's force was too small and scattered for his generalship. He couldn't protect his long line of communications. Ever since that raid at Tunstall's Station, he doubtless intended to shift his base here; but he was beaten so badly last Friday that he was compelled to hasten his operations. His right wing was whipped and turned, and he had to 'skedaddle.'

"The army is greatly worn out, and yet 'gamey.' It has rained for twelve hours, and all is mud ankle-deep; and yet we plod about cheerfully. The transports are here, the gunboats are here, and we hope yet to 'get to Richmond' soon. I send you a rough sketch of our movements, that you may understand better.

"Am 'played out' really, and coming home now, soon as matters straighten up a little. Quite sick yesterday, but improved to-day."[1]

"WASHINGTON, D. C.
Aug. 21, 1862. Thursday afternoon.

"DEAR FATHER: After a warm and dusty ride that never seemed so long before, I arrived here yesterday

---

[1] I was given a "leave" home soon afterward, and remained there about a month.

about 6 P. M. Was astonished at the amount of dirt that one can get upon himself in a few hours' ride. Eyes, nose, mouth, hair, ears—all stuffed with dust and cinders. Water never seemed so grateful; nor a bed so welcome!

"This morning I started out on a 'voyage of discovery,' to see if I could find out where our brigade is. Went first to the War Department, and was there referred to General Halleck. At General Halleck's they informed me it was at Yorktown, Fortress Monroe, or somewhere down the Bay or River—it mattered not *exactly* where—and then gave me orders to remain in Washington until the twenty-sixth, when they would send me on my way. Rather indefinite this. I construe it to mean that the army is on its way, by water, as fast as possible, for Acquia Creek, or about there; and that they deem it best for me to wait here, until it has reached its next field of operations. Wish I were home until then. However, I am here at Brown's Hotel, and am doing my best to 'kill time.' Now that I am once more fit for duty, it seems a long time until the twenty-sixth; but I presume it will soon pass away.

"Yesterday there arrived here a large number of officers, just released from Rebel prisons. Have talked with many of them; and they all tell the same story of suffering, starvation and wrong. Among others, I have met Captain Shellmire, First New Jersey Cavalry, of Buck's County, Pa., whom you will perhaps recollect. He was captured at the battle of Port Republic, in the Shenandoah Valley. He says they took him first to Richmond, and then to Salisbury, N. C. There they had no coffee, no sugar, no beans, no vegetables—nothing in the world but twelve ounces a day of sour bread, a little vinegar once in a while, some poor, tough, fresh beef once or twice a week, and for the rest of the time *pork* so alive with maggots that, when brought on the table, they had to harpoon it with their forks or it would have run away.

"He represents the condition of the imprisoned Union men, as still worse. He speaks of two old men whose only crime was their love for the Union, that dwindled away from their bad food, till they had to be carried to the hospital; and there the Rebels lay them without any bed or medicines, until they literally *died* from hunger and neglect. They wouldn't let our prisoners nurse them. One of the old men had a son in the Rebel garrison, and they even refused to let him nurse or see his dying father. This Captain Shellmire, by the way, is a quiet, sturdy, sensible man; not given to exaggeration; and, withal, is of the 'Democratic persuasion.'"

"ALEXANDRIA, VA.
Aug. 27, 1862. Wednesday evening.

"DEAR FRIENDS: Yesterday morning, on reporting to General Halleck, I received orders to proceed here, and rejoin the brigade wherever it might be. Reached here about 1 P. M., and found that the brigade had left for Warrenton Junction early in the morning! One of my horses went with the brigade; the other was left with the headquarters wagons, which left here to go by the turnpike, via Manassas, about 12 M. yesterday. It was 2 P. M. before I got the information, and then it was impossible to join either. I concluded to take the train at 4 P. M.; but afterward decided to wait until 11 this morning, as I would then reach the brigade before my horses, etc., arrived there.

"It was a lucky conclusion! For that railroad train was stopped by the Rebels at Manassas, and all made prisoners! The Rebel cavalry, reported at one thousand strong, with a battery of artillery, made an attack there last night, about eight o'clock, stopped two trains, and held the place as late as early this morning. This morning all was consternation here. No trains were sent out, and all the troops about here received marching orders forthwith. I concluded to make an effort to overtake our headquarters wagons, which I judged could not have got beyond Fairfax Court House. With two other officers belonging to our brigade, I chartered a carriage, and we drove almost to Fairfax Court House; when we met Banks's whole wagon train on the march for Alexandria! They had been at Bull Run, when the attack was made at Manassas, and having no guard, their corps quartermaster had ordered them back as above. We halted by the roadside, and waited until he came up. He said he had met our wagons, near Fairfax, and had advised them to return; which they probably did. He supposed they were in the rear of his train, and would arrive near Alexandria to-night.

"We held a 'council of war;' and, as the road was hilly and full of wagons and 'contrabands,' we concluded to turn back and await events here. The road was literally thronged with slaves, of all ages and both sexes; resolved to follow the wagons, wheresoever they might go. Some had horses, though the most were on foot. I saw one woman, with a child at her back, and another in her arms, mounted on a dilapidated old horse, which she was guiding with a strip of old muslin, passed through his mouth. We heard heavy firing in the direction of Manassas, until noon; and as Banks's train was not pursued or molested, we judge our forces are again in possession of that point.

"This is very perplexing. Hardly know what to do. If my horses were only *here*, I should be all right; but as it is, I am like a wagon without wheels or a locomotive without steam. Have ridden twenty-five miles to-day, and am quite worn out. To-morrow—I don't know what I shall do, though I suppose I must *try* to find my horses.

The town here is full of officers and soldiers. A great portion of the wagons and stores of the Army of the Potomac are still at Yorktown and Fortress Monroe, and many are here awaiting their arrival. Only our headquarters teams have arrived. The regimental trains are yet all behind, somewhere down the Potomac.

"Things are very unsettled. My own opinion is, that the whole army will fall back to the line of the Potomac. We have no generals with *heads* on their shoulders, and God alone can save the Republic. Therefore, let us do right and grant justice, that he may be inclined to uphold us by his everlasting arms."

"CAMP NEAR ALEXANDRIA, VA.
Aug. 31, 1862.

"DEAR FRIENDS: Wrote you a hasty line on Wednesday evening, which I suppose has already reached you. Had then just returned from a ride toward Fairfax Court House, in search of our headquarters wagons. The next morning I started out again, and about nine o'clock was so fortunate as to light upon them at Cloud's Mills. They had reached Fairfax Court House on Tuesday night, and on Wednesday morning had proceeded on toward Bull Run; when they met the head of Banks's train on its march for Alexandria. My wagon-master had the good sense to stop and turn around; and so, falling in behind said train, he drove back and arrived at Cloud's Mills on Wednesday night.

"I was more fortunate than I thought I would be. 'Fools for *luck!*' you know. Found *both* of my horses with the wagons, my saddle and equipments, and some other minor articles. The gray horse, 'Uncle Abe,' was pretty well used up. I fancy somebody has been riding him much of the time, but I shall soon bring him round.

The pony 'Jersey,' was all right. He is a hardy little fellow, and difficult to kill. In about five minutes, I had my saddle out and on the pony, and then as I sprang upon his back I felt that 'Richard was himself again.' Ordered the teams harnessed at once, and then conducted the train down here; where we are within the chain of forts, and comparatively secure.

"We are camped by a little brook, about half a mile from Alexandria, and within a quarter of a mile of where we were encamped when we were here last October. The regimental trains are all down the Potomac somewhere, between here and Yorktown. Two of our quartermasters are still at Yorktown, and I have two with me here. Our division is somewhere up the country, it is hard to say where. It left here last Monday and Tuesday for Warrenton Junction. On Thursday it was fighting at Bristoe Station, not far beyond Manassas. On Friday it was fighting at Manassas, on its way here, and yesterday all day there was a furious battle raging off toward Fairfax Court House or beyond, and I suppose Hooker was in it. If there is a battle anywhere, you may be sure *Fighting Joe'* will be there.

"No trains are permitted to leave Alexandria yet, and I suppose will not be until the road is fairly clear of Secesh. Am anxiously waiting for news, and expect to leave here any hour, to rejoin the brigade. The whole country around here is full of troops and thick with wagons. The wagons are chiefly from the front; but the troops come from Washington in an endless stream. So, also, from Yorktown and Fortress Monroe. Sumner arrived here on Thursday, landed on Friday, and at dark took up his line of march for Washington and Chain Bridge. To give you some idea of his forces, I will merely state, that the head of his column passed my camp at dark, and the last did not get by until after midnight.

Infantry, cavalry, artillery—it really seemed as if they would never cease tramping along.

"There has been furious and desperate fighting off toward Fairfax and Manassas; and all the definite news, so far, seems to be in our favor. I do not see how the Rebels can succeed, unless the Almighty so wills it, to punish us for not proclaiming 'Emancipation.' If we get whipped, that will be sure to come; but we may lose Alexandria, Washington, and the Potomac, as the inevitable result of the thrashing. I hope better things. God is good, though compelled to be just; and, I sincerely pray, he will now 'in wrath remember mercy!'

"It is now Sunday morning, and raining fast. Had hoped to get to church, but shall not leave my tent, unless it stops. Shall improve the occasion by writing to all the family."

"CAMP NEAR FORT LYON, VA.
Sept. 8, 1862.

"DEAR FRIENDS: I write this morning merely to say I am well, but very busy. Joined the brigade at Centreville, last Monday. Reported to Colonel Carr, who commands the brigade in absence of General Patterson; and went immediately on duty. That night we fell back on Fairfax Court House. Fought a battle at dark (Chantilly), in the midst of a furious storm of wind and rain; and poor Kearny fell. The thunder and lightning were so terrific, that we could scarcely hear the cannon at Fairfax Court House, and didn't hear the musketry at all. Next day, I started the train for Alexandria; arrived there toward night. The brigade got in Wednesday. Thursday we moved up here, on the extreme left, about half a mile from the Potomac, one mile in front of Fort Lyon, and three from Alexandria.

"Found the brigade in wretched condition—tentless,

ragged, and barefoot. Within forty-eight hours have issued no less than forty wagonloads of quartermasters' supplies—tents, shoes, stockings, blankets, etc. How I have worked! Had to go to Washington for everything! Yesterday, Sunday, I worked the whole day through; because we are liable to move again any hour, and our poor fellows were really suffering for necessities."

"HEADQUARTERS 3D BRIGADE,
NEAR ALEXANDRIA, PA.,
GROVER'S (LATE HOOKER'S) DIVISION.
Sept. 14, 1862.

"DEAR FRIENDS: * * * During the past week we have done nothing except move camp once, and that about half a mile. We move again to-morrow, about half a mile nearer to Alexandria. The troops are being drawn closely in around the works here on the left wing, and as many as possible are being sent off to the right and thence to Washington. The indications are that we shall lie here for some time, to recruit and refit. The division is sadly worn down and thinned out, and has received special permission to remain here for some time, unless extraordinary emergencies call for it elsewhere. We have won the reputation of being the 'fighting' division of the Army of the Potomac; but it has been at a fearful expense of health and life. Our splendid fighting qualities have made Hooker a major general, and a corps commander; and like a noble man, as he is, he has not forgotten us. He filed a special request with the War Department, that we might be let alone for a month, and Stanton has promised it, if possible.

"Meanwhile, Hooker has been transferred to McDowell's corps, and, at the head of it, is off somewhere up in Maryland, after the Rebels. When we get rested and recruited, we are to follow him; and still fight beneath his eye. For the present, the division is commanded by General Grover, the senior brigadier general, who is of the regular army, and a good officer; though not a man of such parts as Hooker. Our brigade is commanded temporarily by General Carr, formerly colonel of the Second New York—the senior regiment of the brigade—who has commanded it as senior colonel for the most of the time during the last three months. General Patterson is still absent, and it is uncertain whether or not he will return. If he does not, I suppose General Carr will become our permanent brigadier.

"Of course, we have no preaching in the brigade to-day! *Four* out of our *six* chaplains are at home. Of the *two* here, one is sick, and the other, Father S——, is so used up by the loss of his son, that he really isn't able to preach. Poor man! he found his son stretched dead, upon the battlefield of Bull Run; a ball had passed through both legs, severing the main arteries, and he had died almost instantly. He was a brave fellow, and a good officer. He had risen from the ranks to be adjutant of his regiment, and his father was exceedingly proud of him. The old man buried him on the battlefield, and then followed the brigade back to Centreville, almost heart-broken. Since we have been here, he has made application for a 'leave,' but has not yet received it. He has proved himself to be a brave and faithful officer; if not attractive as a preacher."

"HEADQUARTERS 3D BRIGADE,
GROVER'S DIVISION.
NEAR ALEXANDRIA, VA.,
Sept. 22, 1862.

"DEAR FRIENDS: * * * Have not been well for a week past. Am better to-day, and my whole heart goes out in ecstatic enjoyment of the glorious day, which the Almighty has poured athwart these hills and vales. We are encamped in front of Fort Lyon, a half mile nearer than when I last wrote you. Our left rests on the Potomac; our right rests on the hills, about half a mile west from the fort. Our camp ground is a high plateau, jutting down in bold bluffs toward the town and river; water is abundant and tolerably good.

"Our headquarters are established in a fine large Secesh house. The first floor is occupied by General Carr, and the office of the adjutant general. The parlor is appropriated to the latter, and to the telegraph office; and it also serves as a general lounging room for officers. Just over the parlor are two fine rooms, nearly as large as your parlors, and connected by a door; the front one is mine, and the back one my office. On the opposite side of the hall are the rooms of the adjutant general, aids-de-camp, etc.

"From my window is the most beautiful sight I have seen for a long day. The bluffs break abruptly down to the plain. Off in the plain lies Alexandria; just beyond flashes the Potomac; and beyond all, three miles or so away, rises the Maryland shore, swelling into slope, hill, and wooded mountain most beautiful to behold. Farther down lies Fort Washington. Farther up, seen distinctly at all times, but especially glorious in the gushing sunlight of the morning, lies Washington—the marble dome of its capitol 'a thing of beauty and a joy forever.' To the left, runs the line of forts—Ellsworth, Worth, Ward, Corcoran, etc.—which protect the city. Was there ever anything more enchanting?

"We are doing little except loaf. We have a strong picket out in front; and have been throwing up some rifle-pits, that's all. We had an 'alarm,' Saturday night. The pickets fell back and reported 'Rebels;' but I guess it was only 'John Barleycorn!' At any rate, nothing came of it."

## Some Army Letters

"HEADQUARTERS PATTERSON'S BRIGADE,
GROVER'S DIVISION.
Sept. 28, 1862.

"DEAR FRIENDS: * * * I had the pleasure of attending divine worship once more this morning, down in Alexandria. The preacher fired away about Paul, and his not being 'ashamed of the Gospel of Christ.' It was a prosy, old fogy, milk-and-water, shilly-shally, good-for-nothing affair; of which I am sure Paul would have been most heartily ashamed. Poor Paul! He was a great orator in his day, a bold, brave man, who hit heavily every abuse he came across; and it must wound his great heart sadly, to see how miserably some of his successors imitate him. I sat the service out, and enjoyed the singing and the prayer anyway; partly because I knew you were worshiping at the selfsame hour, and partly because I believed God was there.

"We have dull times here. General Hooker leaving us, our senior brigadier, General Grover, came into command of the division. Last week, General Sickles returned; and, by virtue of *his* seniority, assumed command. * * * Our brigade is now commanded by Colonel Johnson, of the Eighth New Jersey, who was so severely wounded at Williamsburg, reported mortally. He is still disabled for active duty; but is able to command while we lie here. General Patterson is here, hobbling about on crutches. His foot, sprained by the fall of his horse at Harrison's Landing, is still very lame; and he is unable to do anything. He looks badly; and, it is believed, will never resume command of the brigade. In that case, I presume, we shall have General Mott to command us. I am content."

"HEADQUARTERS PATTERSON'S BRIGADE,
NEAR ALEXANDRIA, VA.
Oct. 5, 1862.

"DEAR FRIENDS: * * * I was in Washington yesterday; started for camp at dark, but was overtaken by a gust of wind and rain, and remained all night. Left there this morning at sunrise, and galloped here, a distance of twelve or fourteen miles; and, arriving, found the brigade under arms and on the point of moving. Got a cold breakfast, with a cup of hot coffee, and then moved with brigade from near Fort Lyon, to this place, about two miles to the West, near Fort Worth. Again we are in tents, and it seems quite cozy; though not quite so warm these cold nights, as our good Secesh house. Headquarters are pitched near a large fine dwelling; but as it occupied, we do not feel justified in intruding. I do not know how long we shall stay here. We thought ourselves 'fixed' where we were; but it seemed we were not. However, we are still in the same chain of defenses, though farther to the West; and, I think, the probabilities are against our further removal.

"It has been a sad Sabbath. No dinner till 3 P. M. All the day consumed in removing and pitching camp. Even now, at dark, the din and noise of pitching tents and of lumbering wagons still continue. It has a bad effect upon the men. I don't know anything in all our experience so hardening as this work on Sunday. Yet many of our movements are ordered on Sunday (unnecessarily apparently); and it really seems as if all our heavy marching and fighting come on that day. Our 'general orders' to the contrary, notwithstanding!

"The President's 'Proclamation of Emancipation' gives me some comfort; only he should have issued it a year ago. I trust, most sincerely, it is not yet *too late*. I have no confidence whatever in McClellan's reputed victories.[1] His own official report of them condemns his Northern glorification. His battles are all *drawn* battles; or if he wins one, he fails to follow it up, and so loses its substantial fruits. We shall make no headway until he resigns or is removed. I place great faith in Hooker, and am inclined to believe that we have at last touched bottom.

"The 'Proclamation of Freedom' at last places things on their true and logical basis; and if the Government now only keeps its face Zionward, I believe all will yet be well. But if it twists and shuffles and equivocates and apologizes and dodges—now *this,* now *that*—as it has done so sadly hitherto, I shall give up all hope of the nation, and try to resign myself to the disgrace and humiliation of a divided land and a ruined people. It will only be God's just judgment upon a disobedient and stiff-necked generation, that deserved no better. But I have better hopes. Am inclined to believe that the uncertain attitude of the President hitherto has been because of a conscience ill at ease; and that, having at last 'dared to do right,' he will now walk steadfastly forward. A good man acting *against* his conscience, is always undecided; acting *with* his conscience, he may go on his way unmoved, and 'the gates of hell shall not prevail against him!' "

" HEADQUARTERS PATTERSON'S BRIGADE,
SICKLES' DIVISION,
NEAR ALEXANDRIA, VA.
Oct. 12, 1862.

"DEAR FRIENDS: Your package of official papers has arrived safely. * * * I cannot say the same, however, of your *Advocates*. Have received but one, since I left home, *viz.,* that of September 25, and that came about a week ago. I laid it aside to read to-day, and, I must say, have enjoyed it

---

[1] South Mountain, Antietam, etc.

greatly. It is a most excellent number, full of thoughtful and well-written articles, and have read it through as a great treat. I started for church this morning; but at division headquarters met with orders that compelled me to return; so that about my only Sabbath has been the *Advocate* and my pocket Testament (Oliver Cromwell's).

"It is a cold, raw, rainy, disagreeable day. The rain began yesterday; and with slight intermission has continued ever since. It is a regular fall storm; and here in tents is anything but pleasant. Have had a log fire built in front of my quarters; and so long as my face is turned to it, do pretty well. But, to tell the truth, I rather envy you your cozy living room, with its warm carpet and cheerful grate. However, this is a part of 'soldiering,' and am content. Fortunately, am feeling very well, and so get on.

"Have not much news to tell you. We are still where we were last Sunday, and with no immediate prospect of moving; though under 'marching orders' for the last three days. The fact is, we don't care much about marching orders any more. We have marched and fought so much, that it is about all one with us, whether we move, fight, or stay.

"I wish you to remember, that all my accounts with the United States were settled at the Treasury Department, down to the first of April, 1862, a week or so ago. Their accounts and mine *exactly agreed*." * * *

"CAMP NEAR ALEXANDRIA, VA.
Oct. 16, 1862.

"DEAR FATHER: Another change to me, a *promotion;* and yet I hardly know whether to be glad or sorry. Yesterday afternoon was relieved of brigade duties, and ordered to report to General Sickles, as division quartermaster. * * * My rank and pay continue the same, but the duties are lighter, and the position one notch higher.

"To-day I moved over to division headquarters, bag and baggage, and now write you from there. We are pleasantly situated on the lawn of a fine Secesh residence near Alexandria, in the shelter of a nice grove of trees. Have just returned from tea. The other officers of the staff are mostly strangers; but they have received me cordially. General Sickles himself is a fine talker, and a man of very considerable ability. It is a promotion from my old position, as brigade quartermaster, to a new one, as division quartermaster. It will probably result in my receiving the rank of *Major*, that is, *provided* General Sickles is made Major General, as he probably will be. So I will be 'Major,' after all!"

"HEADQUARTERS SICKLES' DIVISION.
Oct. 20, 1862.

"DEAR FRIENDS: I write you again to-night, not because I feel like it; but because it is Sunday night, and I know you will expect a letter.

"Had a letter from Henry to-day, dated October 17. Wrote you on the same day, I believe, announcing my promotion to division quartermaster. Have found the position pleasant, and the associations more agreeable than I anticipated. General Sickles is certainly a man of very great ability, intellectually and socially, and a better soldier than I have thought. * * *

"Am well, but tired; and so, good night!"

"HEADQUARTERS SICKLES' DIVISION.
Oct. 27, 1862.

"DEAR FRIENDS: * * * We have had a furious storm here for the last twenty-four hours, that has prostrated tents and played havoc generally. It has rained and blown 'great guns;' and, though the rain has ceased, the wind still continues. Fortunately, last week I secured a small stove, and its genial heat for the last twenty-four hours has amply compensated me for my outlay already. It is no bigger than 'a piece of chalk;' but it heats my tent very nicely."

"HEADQUARTERS SICKLES' DIVISION,
MANASSAS JUNCTION, VA.
Nov. 9, 1862.

"DEAR FRIENDS: Have only time to-night to address you the briefest line. It has been a cold, dismal, dreary Sabbath; every hour of which I have spent in endeavoring to organize and systematize the public business at this post. The quartermaster's department here at Manassas had come to a deadlock. The track was blocked with trains, and all was infinite confusion. Late last night an order came from corps headquarters, for me to take immediate charge, and clear the track at all hazards. I went to work early this morning, with a force of one hundred men, and all day long, till dark, have been frightfully busy. And there seems no end to it. Trains have to be unloaded, the track cleared, buildings erected, stores issued; and all is infinite confusion.

"At the same time am worrying along with the necessary duties of division headquarters, and hardly know where or how to turn myself. So much care and responsibility is suddenly thrust upon my shoulders, that I should quite despair, did I not know that all days have their end and all work is at last over."

"HEADQUARTERS SICKLES' DIVISION,
MANASSAS JUNCTION, VA.
Nov. 18, 1862.

"DEAR FATHER: Was not able to write on Sunday, and so write to-night, Tuesday. Wrote you on the previous Sabbath. As then, so ever since have been overwhelmed with business. Was never so occupied and oppressed in my life, as I have been since we arrived here, and hope I never shall be again. Thank heaven, it is nearly over. To-morrow we expect to leave here, for Fredericksburg, on our way to Richmond; and that will end my troubles, as depot quartermaster.

"Have not been out of sight of headquarters, since we have been here. Had thought to get enough time to ride down to the Bull Run battlefield, some six miles from here; but have failed, and so shall leave without seeing it. So I had thought to visit Dr. Osmun and the Hornbakers, and some other Jerseymen up at Brentsville; but my time has all been occupied, and it has been impossible. One of the Hornbakers, originally from near Brass Castle, Warren County, N. J., was here the other day, brought in by our pickets, as Secesh. We had him in the guardhouse one night, and the next morning, learning he was a Jerseyman, I went to see him, and had him released. He said he knew you; that you had called to see him, when you were out here before the war; and pressed me warmly to come and see him. I promised, but have been unable to fulfill it. We march by Brentsville, and I shall try to see some of the Jerseymen about there, as we move along.

"The army is making a great movement here, which I trust may be successful. Instead of going on to Gordonsville, after the retreating Rebels, it has swung boldly off to the left, and is marching rapidly on Fredericksburg. We do not know the program certainly; but we surmise, that it is intended to move rapidly on Richmond, by way of Fredericksburg, which is shorter than Gordonsville. If Burnside has a mite of genius, I believe we shall reach there.[1] Hooker commands the grand central division; and his old division is ordered to report to him for service and orders. This pleases everybody; but means *fight,* and

---

[1] He had succeeded McClellan shortly before.

I think this division has already had enough of that commodity.

"My accounts for October were all made up and dispatched to Washington yesterday.

"We have recovered Joe Abbott's body, and send it home to-day.[1] How glad his friends will be! Cousin Will Rusling at last is second lieutenant, and George Sandt, quartermaster. Justice, though sometimes slow, is always sure! Chaplain S—— has also recovered his son's body and sent it home."[2]

WASHINGTON, D. C.<br>Nov. 25, 1862.

"DEAR FRIENDS: Wrote you last from Manassas, just as we were about leaving it. At the last moment General Sickles changed his plan; and instead of marching by Brentsville, and so to Dumfries and Fredericksburg, marched us back to Bull Run, and thence to Centreville and Fairfax. We left Manassas early last Thursday morning. It had rained severely for the previous twenty-four hours, and the general feared the streams by way of Brentsville were so swollen that it would be dangerous to ford them. So I lost my last opportunity of seeing our Jersey friends there.

"It was a long time Thursday morning before we got finally started. Our train was about three miles long, and it seemed as if it never would get by. At last, however, we were fairly off; and then the rain recommenced. O, how it did pour! It seemed for an hour or two, as if the 'windows of heaven' really were open, and the 'floods' descending. Yet through it all we trudged along; and, by dint of hard marching (and much swearing), reached Fairfax Court House—some fifteen or sixteen miles—by

---

[1] Captain E, 7th N. J., of Trenton, N. J., killed at second Bull Run.
[2] See p. 275.

dark. The rain still continued; but we bivouacked by the roadside and made the best of it. The general and his staff were invited to supper by General Sigel, who had his headquarters at Fairfax Court House; for which we were duly grateful. Sigel is a little Dutchman. But he is all life, fire, and enthusiasm. He is one of our best German generals, and God bless him for the good hot supper he gave us, after that wet day's march!

"We all tumbled down for the night, on the floor, in one large room; and had such sleep as only tired soldiers enjoy.

"Next morning we moved again at seven o'clock. Long before breakfast I was in the saddle, and galloped miles up and down the road, to get the column in motion. When all were off, I returned to Fairfax and had a hasty breakfast, as I could snatch it. It proved to be a wretched day. The storm, instead of abating, had greatly increased; and to the rain of the day before was now added a sweeping wind that chilled you through. How the poor fellows on foot stood it, I do not know. Even on a horse, I was cold and wet and hungry, and as nearly 'disgusted' with campaigning as it is right to be. Never, in all my army experience, have I known two such frightful days as those. There was nothing in the Peninsula to equal them. Never want to see two such days again.

"The second day's march took us due south from Fairfax Court House, to the Station, and thence to the Occoquan—a distance of about ten miles. We made it easily by the middle of the afternoon; though the roads were horrible.

"Then came a tragic night, as the fit close of two such awful days. General Patterson (my old brigade commander) had been ill and acting strangely all the evening, and along about 2 A. M. suddenly his pistol went off, accidentally or otherwise, and poor Patterson was no more.

Another gallant spirit snuffed out! Good soldier, brave heart, generous soul, hail and farewell! * * * It was a tragic affair. It cast a deep gloom over the whole division, and everybody felt it like a personal sorrow. He was a very capable officer, and will be missed sadly. He was a special friend of General McClellan, and greatly regretted McClellan's removal.

"I left the division yesterday afternoon, and drove into Alexandria, and here for supplies. Have a large amount of business to look after. The division moves to-morrow for Falmouth, and shall probably rejoin it by way of Acquia Creek." * * *

"HEADQUARTERS SICKLES' DIVISION,
CAMP NEAR FALMOUTH, VA.
Dec. 4, 1862.

"DEAR FRIENDS: It is Thursday night. Am breaking my rule of writing you every Sunday, but doing the best I can.

"Arrived here yesterday, having left Alexandria yesterday morning. Came down to Acquia Creek on the boat, and thence rode twelve miles. We are encamped about two miles from Falmouth, which is a rickety, tumble-down Virginia village, and directly across the river lies Fredericksburg. Our forces line this side of the river; and the Rebels, the other. Both are strongly posted, and each seems waiting for the other to demonstrate. The country on this side is literally packed with troops. How many are on the other, I do not know. Everything is quiet; and God only knows what is going to be done. I don't think we will attempt a crossing here. There is talk of our crossing below here; but shall not be surprised if we embark and go elsewhere. Am quite disheartened with the appearance of things; and wholly disgusted with the stupidity and imbecility I see all around me. * * *

"I ought not to write thus, I suppose. But my heart is sick and brain weary with incessant work, that amounts to nothing in the end.

"This has been a busy day here. The division was reviewed by General Hooker, and the display was fine. Hooker looked well; and will fight, if they give him a chance. I suppose we shall have one more blunder, and then at last they will put *'Old Joe'* in the right place."

"HEADQUARTERS SICKLES' DIVISION,<br>
CAMP NEAR FALMOUTH, VA.<br>
Dec. 7, 1862.

"DEAR FRIENDS: It is Sunday afternoon, about sundown, and as I have a moment's leisure, I embrace it to write you. It has been a dismal Sabbath here. Forty-eight hours ago, we had a snowstorm that gave us three inches or more of that chilly material. Yesterday the sun was out, and we had a thaw; but last night it shut down clear and cold, and to-day again it is severe. The troops must suffer very much. They are all in small, thin 'shelter tents,' and many are quite destitute of shoes and clothing. Our own division is suffering in this last respect. The clothing, etc., which I ordered in Washington, has scarcely any of it arrived yet; and our troops need it badly. Have two officers and a squad of men, at Acquia Creek, to forward it by railroad, as soon as it arrives there from Washington; but it has been already delayed so long that we are very impatient.

"To-day I rode up to General Hooker's headquarters. He was very well, and glad to see me. Spent an hour there very agreeably, and then rode home in time for a late dinner. Dinner consisted of tough beefsteak, fried potatoes, hard-tack, and a cup of coffee. However, this is small compared with our other privations. It is very cold, and we have a hard time to keep warm. Think I have suffered more from the cold, in the last twenty-four hours, than any time last winter. Yet I cannot complain. I have a little stove in my tent, and am warm and comfortable, compared with what others endure. When you sit around your cozy fire, think of the gallant men, shivering here in flimsy tents; and remember to love well a country for which they are willing to endure so much.

"Of course, the rumor of my resignation in August last, is fabrication. Instead thereof, have constantly been on duty here with the division; and since then have been promoted from brigade to division quartermaster. It is not impossible, however, that I *may* soon resign. Am not entirely pleased with matters here, and am compelled to do more than my strength is equal to. But 'sufficient unto the day is the evil thereof.' * * *

"There is nothing whatever doing here. Was over to Falmouth on Friday, and had a sight of the Rebel pickets and earthworks. The river is about as wide as the Delaware, at Belvidere or thereabouts, and quite shallow. I suppose I could ford it with my horse almost anywhere. Fredericksburg, just on the other side, is a dilapidated old town, of some one thousand two hundred or two thousand population. I could see the Rebel pickets. Indeed, they were only a stone's throw across the Rappahannock. Three of them were grouped together, at the crossing, under some logs and boards, and looked desolate enough. Farther up and down the river were others, completing their chain of pickets; and just opposite, on this side, were ours. They talked across to each other, in a friendly way, and 'camp stories' allege that they exchange tobacco and coffee. We are told, that we will soon cross, either above or below the town, and make straight for Richmond. I doubt it. My own opinion is that we will soon go into winter quarters.

"And so passes another week. It may be, that ere another Sabbath we shall be off. In case we move, we may have a great battle near here; though I think the Rebels will rather fall back and meet us at the gates of Richmond."

"HEADQUARTERS SICKLES' DIVISION,
CAMP NEAR FALMOUTH, VA.
Dec. 14, 1862.

"DEAR FRIENDS: It is Sunday; and I write you, as I have an hour or two to spare, while awaiting orders. It has been a great week here. On Tuesday went to Alexandria and Washington, in search of supplies that had been ordered, but which had never reached us. Returned on Thursday morning, to find our people shelling Fredericksburg. It appears that on Tuesday night the whole army received orders to be ready for a movement at daylight on Wednesday. Camps were broken up, and the troops were massed at two points, in ravines and woods, near Falmouth and three miles or so lower down.

"At 5 A. M., Thursday, the engineers advanced to the river at Fredericksburg, and began to throw a pontoon bridge across. The Rebel pickets cracked away, and then retreated. The bridge was three fourths completed, when the Rebel sharpshooters opened from windows and behind the houses of Fredericksburg. The pontooniers fell by scores; but still the bridge went on, until at last were only a stone's throw across the Rappahannock. a single piece of Rebel artillery opened, and the bridge was shot to fragments. This exasperated Sumner, and he ordered Fredericksburg to be shelled. Our batteries immediately advanced, and for several hours they rained a perfect storm of shot and shell upon the devoted town. One of the batteries attached to our division fired fifteen hundred rounds before the day was over. Soon the town was on fire in several places, and houses were tumbling in all directions.

"Late in the afternoon, it occurred to somebody to send a regiment or two across in boats below the town, to flank the Rebel sharpshooters, and take them in the rear. The movement was soon executed, and ended in the capture of the entire force posted there. Night closed upon a hard day's skirmish, and the result was our possession of the town, and two bridges in position for crossing. All that night the troops poured across the river, and were massed in and around Fredericksburg. Meanwhile, farther down, some three miles, Franklin had succeeded in throwing three bridges over, and had crossed the most of his grand division with little opposition.[1]

"It is now ten o'clock, Sunday morning. So far the morning has been spent with shelling the woods. The Rebels have scarcely replied. I do not know exactly what we have accomplished; but it is reported Sumner on our right has turned the Rebel left, and thus opened communications with Sigel and Slocum, who are marching down from Winchester and Manassas. It has been a furious and desperate fight thus far. The spectacle yesterday was sublime and imposing, exceeding all that I ever read or thought of warfare; and will hereafter be painted in brilliant colors by the pen of the historian."

"HEADQUARTERS SICKLES' DIVISION,
CAMP NEAR FALMOUTH, VA.
Dec. 21, 1862.

"DEAR FRIENDS: I wrote you last from down at Franklin's Bridge, near the river, last Sunday. I then thought that we would win a victory, however dearly fought; but it seems that fate, or something else, was against us, and we had, instead, a repulse. We were not defeated. We were not driven back. We only failed to carry their impregnable works; and failing in that, un-

---
[1] For rest of this letter substantially, see chap. iv, pp. 47, 48.

molested, we fell back to the Rappahannock, and recrossed in safety.

"Of course, we feel bad about it. Our loss was very heavy, and the army is quite disheartened. Our sufferings have been intense. The weather is very cold and winterish. The ground is hard frozen up; and our poor fellows have nothing but flimsy 'shelter tents,' under which to lie and shiver. Talk about Valley Forge, and the huts Washington and his army had there! Why, they were infinitely better off than we are. They were but a small army, in the midst of a rich, fertile country, and could easily subsist. Their huts were warm and comfortable. Wood was near and abundant. But we are a vast army, of prodigious numbers, in the midst of a hostile people, and in a country laid waste and barren by the marches and countermarches of contending armies. We can buy nothing here. Everything literally has to be brought to us from abroad. The wood all about us is being rapidly consumed, and in another month we shall freeze as well as starve. If this intensely cold weather continues, the Potomac will be frozen up and we shall suffer extremely.

"Am not disheartened, but I face things as they are. This army has no general; or he would put it at once into winter quarters, and leave it there till spring. For my own part, am comfortable enough. But pity the common soldier. You people at home don't begin to know what he has to suffer and endure. And the line officers also. * * *

"Wishing you all a Merry Christmas and a Happy New Year, I remain, Yours affectionately."

## Men and Things I Saw in Civil War Days

"HEADQUARTERS SICKLES' DIVISION,
CAMP NEAR FALMOUTH, VA.
Dec. 28, 1862.

"DEAR FRIENDS: I expected to spend this Sabbath in Washington, but it is ordered otherwise. My intention was to get off yesterday and to return on Tuesday; but my application for leave of absence has been delayed, at some of the superior headquarters, and I am still here. I suppose your Christmas box is there. If so, I presume it will keep. I shall probably get it, either by going or sending for it, some time the present week.

"Everything is very dull and very quiet here. There is no doubt, I think, that we shall remain here, until spring. We may move a little up or down or back from the river, in order to take up more eligible quarters; but we shall do nothing in the military line, until spring again opens.

"I am very well, and the weather to-day delicious. Seldom have I seen such a lovely day in December. For several days past, the sky has been overcast and gloomy; but to-day the clouds have disappeared, and the sky smiles like a happy child.

"General Sickles and part of his staff went up to Washington yesterday. We expect them back to-day or to-morrow. I suspect he is working for his *Major Generalship*, and doubtless he will get it. He is one of those industrious, indefatigable, unconquerable men, that never leave a stone unturned when their mind is once 'set;' and such men usually accomplish whatever they undertake.

"I suppose you all read everything about the fight here. If so, do not omit the published testimony taken by the Committee of Congress. Read Hooker's especially. It shows that *he* had the clearest head of any of them. If Burnside had let him cross at Hartwood, when he was marching down from Warrenton (as he requested permission to do), we would now be pounding at the gates of Richmond, instead of huddling here. Mark my words: Hooker will yet have command. And we will yet see the end of this business. I believe in God; I believe in right and truth and justice, as *His* greatest attributes; and therefore, I believe, that however dark the present, our flag will yet float triumphant over every foot of American soil."

"HEADQUARTERS SICKLES' DIVISION,
CAMP NEAR FALMOUTH, VA.
Jan. 11, 1863.

"DEAR FATHER: * * * Another week has passed away. We moved camp on Thursday, about a mile farther to the southeast. The division is nicely quartered in the woods, about a quarter of a mile to the rear of us; already, the men have built huts and shanties, and look quite comfortable. Headquarters is pitched on the lawn in front of a fine old mansion, called the Fitzhugh House. This house is the old family mansion of an exceedingly large estate here, and is probably a hundred years old. The family fled last summer, and the negroes long since 'skedaddled!' The general occupies a part of the house; but the rest of us are in tents, and are as comfortable as we could expect to be under canvas, in the middle of January. I have a board floor, a piece of carpet, a small cast-iron stove; and am much more luxurious in my surroundings than most others.

"If I could only drop down among you for an hour, I think I would be satisfied. However, this war will be over some time, and then I shall appreciate the privileges of civilized life all the more."

"HEADQUARTERS SICKLES' DIVISION,
CAMP NEAR FALMOUTH, VA.
Jan. 18, 1863.

"DEAR FRIENDS: Am very busy and have only time to write a hasty line. On Thursday, we received orders to be ready to move on Friday; on Friday we received other orders to be ready to go, sure, on Sunday, at 1 P. M. But this morning, we had others again, postponing the movement until to-morrow at the same hour. It is either a sham or else a strange lack of brains; I scarcely know which. If it was really intended to make another demonstration, we should either have gone at once or else have no orders sent us until they were ready to go. Nevertheless, we have to make the same preparation as if we were really off. Have had everything ready in my department, since Friday noon; and now, like Micawber, am calmly waiting for 'something to turn up.'

"It is said, that we are to go up the river ten miles or so, and there cross. Well, this is more sensible, than butting one's head against the Heights of Fredericksburg; and I hope it may prove successful. But I am fully persuaded, that a winter campaign here will be fruitless of results, and will be attended by a frightful amount of disease and suffering."[1]

"OFFICE ASSISTANT QUARTERMASTER,
HEADQUARTERS SICKLES' DIVISION,
Feb. 11, 1863.

"DEAR FRIENDS: It is Wednesday, instead of Sunday, but I write you now, instead of then, because on that day I lacked the leisure.

"Arrived safe in Washington. * * * Saturday and Sunday I spent in the vain attempt to get a boat large

---

[1] Burnside's "Mud March" about this time. The above preliminary to it, I think. See p. 50.

enough for my spring wagon, ambulances, and horses; but on Monday I got off about 10 A. M. We went along pretty well, until just below Mount Vernon, when the machinery broke. We patched it up with a wooden peg; and so slowly steamed down to Acquia Creek. Got there at dark. Lay aboard the boat all night; early yesterday morning got ashore, and started for camp, about twelve miles off. We had met with so many delays and mishaps already, that I told my men we would probably be upset or mire down, or suffer some other such calamity.

"Sure enough, we had not got two miles from Acquia, when *snap* went the tongue of my spring wagon; and I was compelled to leave it by the roadside. The roads proved to be awful. Two miles farther on, one of the ambulance horses mired down to his belly, and we found it impossible to get him out. Presently a six-mule team came along. I *seized* upon the four lead mules, and putting them to the end of the tongue dragged out the ambulance, horses and all. We started again, and proceeded perhaps four miles farther, I walking most of the time; when we came to a clay hill, where both ambulances came hopelessly to a halt.

"Thereupon I bade them an affectionate farewell, and footed it through the mud up to camp! From there, I sent back fresh four-horse teams to each vehicle, and these succeeded in bringing them up to camp by dark. I thanked the Lord heartily when I regained my tent, and as for 'Bob'[1]—well, he had a sweet time in cleaning a cartload of mud ('sacred soil'), more or less, from my boots and clothing!

> "A soldier's life is always gay,
> So why be melancholy, boys,
> So why be melancholy?"

"Have found things here in rather a chaotic state.

---

[1] My colored servant.

General Sickles and four of his staff are in New York, and a General Berry, of Birney's division, is in command. General Birney is at corps headquarters, acting for Sickles in his absence. I suppose General Sickles will be here in a day or two; and then, I suppose, things will be straightened out.

"Am well and in good spirits. The roads are in a fearful condition, and it is still raining; the 'bottom' disappeared long ago, and I expect we shall have to 'bridge' and 'corduroy' everywhere.

"General Hooker is in command at last, and giving great satisfaction; and I predict success for him as army commander."

" HEADQUARTERS 2D DIVISION, 3D CORPS.
Feb. 16, 1863.

"DEAR FRIENDS: Wrote you Wednesday night. General Sickles has returned; but things are still in chaos here, and probably will remain so, for a week or two. But they will come out all right. *My* two rows of buttons and 'silver leaf' shoulder straps will surely come; and then I will be satisfied for this war.

"General Berry, who commands the division now, is a very pleasant gentleman.[1] I have Cousin Wlil here at headquarters, as *division* ambulance officer, which makes him feel good; as well as being a just promotion.

"Have been very busy. The weather is bad, and the roads still execrable. Saw General Hooker this morning."

" OFFICE ASSISTANT QUARTERMASTER,
HEADQUARTERS 2D DIVISION, 3D CORPS.
Feb. 22, 1863.

"DEAR FATHER: It has been a hard week here. The first part of the week, it snowed, and then rained contin-

---

[1] General Sickles had been made corps commander.

uously for three days. Friday it cleared off, and was a lovely day. Yesterday morning was as balmy as May; in the afternoon it clouded over, and grew cold; and last night it snowed furiously. This morning there was a foot of snow everywhere. It has snowed ever since; and as I write, 2 P. M., the storm still continues. Woke up this morning, with my blanket covered with snow that had drifted in under my tent, and altogether felt rather blue. Concluded, however, I might as well be jolly as anything else; and so am getting on somehow.

"It is a gay 'Washington's Birthday' here. We would have had a great time, had it not stormed so savagely. His 'Farewell Address' was to have been read, at the heads of regiments, and salutes fired at noon. The salutes were duly fired; the hoarse voice of the cannon roaring in all directions. But the reading of the 'Address' will have to be postponed until another year."

"OFFICE ASSISTANT QUARTERMASTER,
HEADQUARTERS 2D DIVISION, 3D CORPS.
March 13, 1863.

"DEAR FRIENDS: It is well-nigh two weeks since I wrote you, and I suppose I have no good excuse for not writing, when I ought to. The facts are, however, that last Sunday I was in Washington, and was so busy that I thought I would postpone writing, until I reached camp. Expected to leave there Tuesday morning; but was taken sick Monday night, and did not get away till Wednesday morning. That night, I lay aboard a box car, at Acquia, and could not sleep for the cold.

"Reached here yesterday morning about eight o'clock, and at 11 A. M. had to accompany the general and staff to a wedding that took place in the Seventh New Jersey. It was a 'big' affair. General Hooker, two other major generals, half a dozen brigadiers, and about a thousand other officers (more or less) were present. We got home about dark; cold and utterly worn out." \* \* \*

"OFFICE ASSISTANT QUARTERMASTER,
HEADQUARTERS 2D DIVISION, 3D CORPS.
March 21, 1863.

"DEAR BROTHER: Your last received to-day. \* \* \* As a rule, there are no Sundays in the army; and chaplains are at a discount. I love Christ, and try to serve him in my way; but my time is chiefly taken up with the absorbing cares and anxieties of army life. We are getting ready for the spring campaign here, making many changes, and really inaugurating some great reforms. But it requires labor and thought and anxiety, and a vast expenditure of body and brain. To-day, Sabbath as it is, I have been in the saddle most of the day, *ex necessitate*, wading and plunging through a sea of mud; and for the week to come shall have my heart and hands full. My *Lieutenant Coloneley* has not yet come; but it *will*, and that will compensate for much I now have to undergo.

"Am here to fight for your safety and your liberties; and see to it, that you duly appreciate them. If you turn Copperhead, or forget the flag that has so long flapped defiance to the enemies of mankind, may your right hands forget their cunning, and your tongues cleave to the roofs of your mouths! Fight! Never give in! Crush the Rebellion! That is the doctrine of patriotism, and of Christianity! And may God nerve our hearts and strengthen our arms and stiffen our backbones, to hold manfully out to the end! Your Jersey *Peace* Legislature has disgraced the State to all eternity."

"OFFICE ASSISTANT QUARTERMASTER,
HEADQUARTERS 2D DIVISION, 3D CORPS.
April 5, 1863.

"DEAR FRIENDS: It is a cold, snowy, and blustery day again. It had become delightful weather, and we were expecting soon to be on the move again. But yesterday the wind rose and blew a gale all day; and last night it set in to snow, and has snowed ever since. I was really afraid to undress and go to bed last night. The wind swept through camp, a perfect hurricane; and it seemed every moment as if the tents would come clattering down about our heads. But this morning the wind has moderated, and I presume the storm will soon be over.

"The storm has been the cause of a grievous disappointment to us. The President was coming down, with half of his Cabinet, to review our corps, and we should have had a 'big' time. However, I suppose, when the storm is past, and the ground once more dries, 'Father Abraham' will come anyhow.

"There has something gone wrong down here; though what it exactly is, I cannot say. A week ago, there is no doubt, we were just on the eve of a movement here; but on Wednesday or Thursday the program was changed, and now, I think, we are good for at least two weeks more here."

"HEADQUARTERS 2D DIVISION, 3D CORPS.
April 12, 1863.

"DEAR BROTHER: I write you again to-day, as usual. I got two good *Advocates*, etc., the other day; glad to receive all. The *Advocate* is a sterling Union sheet and I prize it highly. Am proud of it, as a periodical; and I honor your New Jersey Methodists for the unqualified manner in which they have 'spoken out' on the great question of the times. It is not so bad to be known as a Methodist, when the Church takes such high and patriotic ground, even in a Copperhead State.

"We are on the eve of a great movement here. The cavalry of the whole army move to-morrow, on some secret expedition; and before this reaches you, we may all be off. In expectation of it, I ran up to Washington last week, and deposited all my official papers at the Metropolitan there. They close up all my accounts to April 1, 1863; and will be subject to the order of my friends, should anything happen to me. Look out for great results. This army is in splendid trim, and under Hooker will fight mightily.

"I congratulate you on the reaction North; and pray God it may go on, until not a reptile is left to hiss at the old flag."

"HEADQUARTERS BERRY'S DIVISION, 3D CORPS.
April 19, 1863.

"DEAR FATHER: Another week has passed, and we are still here. Orders were issued, and we surely would have been off last Thursday morning; but Wednesday it set in to rain, Thursday it poured, and we have had no fit weather to move in since, until to-day. To-day it has been glorious. The sun has been even hot, and the air warm and balmy. The trees are budding out, the grass is springing all around us, and we shall soon have summer in earnest.

"Last year at this time, the army was before Yorktown, and I was in hospital at Fortress Monroe. It has been a great year; one of great events and great changes. Am thankful to heaven that I am still alive; and am inclined to believe, after all I have passed through, that I shall yet come out safe and sound. * * *

"Was at General Hooker's this morning, with General

Berry and General Mott; and afterward rode with General Mott down to the First Jersey Brigade. * * * General Hooker has gone down to Acquia to meet the President, Stanton, and Halleck. There is evidently something in the wind; we shall not lie idle many days more."

"HEADQUARTERS 2D DIVISION, 3D CORPS.
April 28, 1863.

"DEAR FRIENDS: The army has moved. A portion has already crossed the Rappahannock, and is moving on the enemy's left flank. The rest, among which is the Third Corps, go to-night. The trains move to-morrow. God give us a great and substantial victory.

"I cannot go without dropping you this line, especially as I did not write on Sunday. Will write you again, as soon as the fight is over.

"Governor Parker and Quartermaster General Perine were here, and reviewed us on Sunday. It was a fine day; and the review was magnificent. * * *

"Everything now is bustle and preparation; and I must close."

"HEADQUARTERS 2D DIVISION, 3D CORPS,
CAMP NEAR FALMOUTH, VA.
May 3, 1863.

"DEAR FRIENDS: It has been a sad day here. General Berry was killed this morning, at the head of our division. General Mott was again wounded; and every colonel in his brigade, except one, is either killed or wounded. The carnage, on both sides, has been awful. O what a Sunday!

"I suppose you have full accounts by the papers, ere this. We have Fredericksburg, and the formidable heights, for which we fought last winter; but our success on the right is yet uncertain. We hope and believe that to-morrow will wind up a week's fighting with a great and overwhelming victory.

"Have not time to write more. Write now merely to say I am unhurt and well. For which, *laus Deo!*"

"OFFICE OF CHIEF QUARTERMASTER,
HEADQUARTERS 3D ARMY CORPS,
BOSCOBEL, VA.
May 10, 1863.

"DEAR FATHER AND FRIENDS: I rejoice that I am able to write you once again. We have had a great and fierce time here; one of the most terrible battles on record. Unfortunately, we have not accomplished all we wished; but we gave the Rebels an awful drubbing, and then 'hauled off for repairs.' Everything was against us. It rained repeatedly; and the movement was delayed, until the Rebs knew all our plans and had brought up all their forces. Yet we made a brilliant fight. We have not done as I could have wished. Our brave fighting was in vain, and to-day we are back in our old camps. But the spirit of the troops is still unbroken; and there is every indication of a speedy movement again toward Richmond.

"I still believe in General Hooker. At any rate I cannot forsake him, because he has failed *once*. He never failed before; and McClellan always failed. Stoneman, under Hooker's orders and working out the plan of Hooker's brain, has done magnificently; and I have no doubt you all rejoice over his brilliant achievements. I stand by 'Joe' still. His fighting was magnificent. He himself was on the very front line. He was standing on the porch of a house at Chancellorsville, leaning against a pillar; when a shell came, struck the pillar, split it in two, and one-half knocked him senseless. I was talking to

Hooker myself an hour before, at the same place; and he was all right then. After that things went awry. No head anywhere.

"The army all did well, except the Eleventh Corps. That broke and ran, discreditably. *'I fights mit Sigel'* is played out. Tell S—— that his Dutchmen can't begin to stand up against the fury and rush of Americans, even if they are Rebels!

"When the Eleventh Corps broke, Hooker instantly sent for the Third, and ordered to the front his own old division. What a shout went up, as it filed along where he sat on his white horse! The Rebels were in full pursuit of the Dutchmen; and as the old division went by to the front, Hooker's only remark was: 'Receive them on your bayonets, boys! Receive 'em on your bayonets!'

"And they did! The old division went in, with a rush and a cheer, and rolled the tide of battle back; with the capture of no less than fifteen stands of Rebel colors. The battle ceased at midnight; to be renewed early next morning, when the gallant Berry fell. He was crossing the road, to rally a regiment, when a musket ball struck him in the shoulder and passed down through his heart. His body was recovered and sent back to the train; where I had a coffin made, and draping it with the garrison flag that flew at headquarters, forwarded it to his home in Maine. He was a brave man, a gallant soldier, and a true friend. About the same time, General Mott was wounded in the hand.

"I cannot recount all the losses. My old Jersey brigade performed prodigies of valor, and lost nearly a third of its entire number. May God give a sweet rest to their gallant souls!

"Have taken a severe cold, and am otherwise 'used up.' Campaign too much for me. Suffering with my throat, as I used to at home sometimes; but worse now. Am able to perform office duty; but if the corps moves, shall get leave of absence, and go to Washington or home.

"As you see, by the heading of this letter, I am now on duty at headquarters Third Army Corps. On the seventh, the corps quartermaster was relieved, for various misconduct, etc., during Chancellorsville campaign, and I was ordered here as chief quartermaster of the corps. General Sickles has behaved very handsomely. He has *already* asked the War Department for my appointment as corps quartermaster, with the rank and pay of lieutenant colonel, and to be assigned as such to this army corps. His request will undoubtedly be complied with within thirty days, and then—'How are *you,* Lieutenant Colonel!' So, you see, *patience* is a good thing! '*Time* at last, sets *all* things even!'

"Naturally I feel elated. Have risen from the lowest step in the department, regimental quartermaster, up through all the intermediate grades to the one next the highest—Chief Quartermaster of the Army. Here I am content to stop. Never expect to go any higher, in this war. Am duly thankful to the higher powers! Rejoice with me!" * * *

"OFFICE OF CHIEF QUARTERMASTER,
HEADQUARTERS, 3D ARMY CORPS,
BOSCOBEL, VA.
May 17, 1863.

"DEAR FRIENDS: Am glad to be able to write you that my *throat* is better. It is still sore and annoying; but then I am able to be about and ride, and that will soon restore me.

"Have not time to write much, and so, with this, will say good-by!"

"OFFICE OF CHIEF QUARTERMASTER,
HEADQUARTERS 3D ARMY CORPS,
BOSCOBEL, VA.
May 24, 1863.

"DEAR FRIENDS: It has been a very warm, but a very pleasant and agreeable Sabbath; which I have enjoyed very much. The weather here has become quite warm; but we have planted shade trees and constructed arbors, until we are quite comfortable. Have had no rain for a week or two; so that the country has become very dry. But, with this exception, we are getting on quite as well as we could expect. This is not war; it is simply *camp life;* which I rather enjoy, than otherwise.

"We are doing nothing whatever here, and I doubt if we shall for a month or so to come. We have lost very heavily; by battle, by disease, by discharge of two years' and nine months' regiments; so that we have really but comparatively a small army left. I doubt if we shall move much, before the 'conscripts' reach us.

"Grant's splendid campaign and the impending fall of Vicksburg, however, may change all this. If Grant has really had the great success he claims, then Rosecrans will be set free to move on East Tennessee and Northern Georgia and Alabama. This will compel the evacuation of Richmond, and a concentration of the Rebs in the 'Cotton' States, and then we shall probably get to Richmond at last; unless Rosecrans beats us there!

"My throat still troublesome, and unless it improves, shall come home."[1] * * *

---

[1] Soon afterward went home on "leave," and remained until June 10 or 12.

"METROPOLITAN HOTEL,
WASHINGTON, D. C.
June 15, 1863.

"DEAR FRIENDS: I am still here. Was taken ill while coming on from Philadelphia. Thursday was better, and thought I would proceed to the army on Saturday; but Friday was worse again, and my surgeon now thinks I will not get away before the close of this week.

"I hear from the corps every day nearly. They marched from Falmouth to Bealeton Station, on the Orange and Alexandria Railroad. Thence they are falling back on Centreville. Hooker's whole army is on the march for Centreville and Washington. I suppose you are greatly excited again up North. Pennsylvania has good cause to be; but the Rebs won't stay there long. Don't be disheartened. Maintain your faith, and stand by the flag!"

"WASHINGTON, D. C.
July 5, 1863. Sunday evening.

"DEAR FRIENDS: I am still here; but expect to leave to-morrow. Am pretty strong again; and so anxious to rejoin, that I must go.

"They have had a great fight at Gettysburg. Our corps has suffered again prodigiously. Yet, thank God! it seems to have been a 'good fight;' and will produce great results for the good cause.

"A great number of my old friends have been killed or wounded. Poor General Sickles is here. He left the corps Friday morning—having been wounded on Thursday evening—and arrived here this morning. A round shot or shell struck his right leg, just below the knee, shattering it badly; and his leg was amputated just above the knee that night. Next morning they started with him for the nearest railroad, some twenty miles off. They had to carry him on a stretcher, on their shoulders, the whole distance. On the way, the Rebel cavalry was reported near; and they turned off and stopped twelve hours at a retired farmhouse. And what do you think? This Pennsylvania patriot, not ten miles from the battle-field, within the sound of the Rebel guns, actually charged the general and his carriers for what they *ate* and *drank* that night!

"They reached the railroad safely, however, and then came on here. His door has been crowded all day; but only a few admitted to see him. The President called this afternoon, while I was there, and remained some time, discussing the battle, etc. He has great confidence in Sickles, and feels his loss just now very much. The general, however, is in good spirits. He thinks he will get well; and says, as soon as his leg heals, he will 'give the Rebs another *lick*.' He is not a man to despond. He says the army has won a great victory, and made the most splendid fight of the war. Am reluctant to leave him, but my duty calls me to the corps. Three of his staff are with him."

"OFFICE OF CHIEF QUARTERMASTER,
HEADQUARTERS 3D ARMY CORPS,
FREDERICK, MD.
July 8, 1863.

"DEAR FRIENDS: Arrived here yesterday from Washington, and at once assumed command of the train; which I found encamped on the borders of the town. We move again at one o'clock this afternoon, and shall reach Middletown, some ten miles, to-night. The corps is now on the march from Emmittsburg, and will join us at Middletown.

"The news here is all good. We have won a great and important victory. We shall give Lee battle again at Antietam or Williamsport, within forty-eight hours; and, if he escapes, will chase him through Virginia."

"OFFICE OF CHIEF QUARTERMASTER,
WAGON-PARK 3D ARMY CORPS.
July 12, 1863.

"DEAR FRIENDS: I write again to say, I am getting along very well. * * *

"Our wagon-train, with all the other trains of the army, is parked at the foot of South mountain, in the Middletown Valley. The country here is most enchanting. The soil is underlaid with limestone; of which material the fences, houses, and barns are mostly constructed. The crops of grass, wheat, rye, and corn, now growing, are very superior. The country is exactly like Cumberland Valley, Pa., and Warren County, N. J., and I am constantly reminded of my former homes in those localities.

"The people are mostly loyal, and generally very kind. They are all wrong on the 'Nigger' question; but, as their slaves are mostly gone, they are pretty much for the Union. They receive us very cordially; and we can get an excellent meal almost any time. Yesterday I spent at the front; and in returning at nightfall, stopped at a farmer's. He gave me excellent entertainment for the night, and a 'God-speed' this morning.

"Our troops are far in front, at least twelve miles from here. They were expecting to fight this afternoon. The two armies are directly in front of each other, and a collision will not long be delayed. The troops are in fine spirits. Gettysburg and Vicksburg, together, have wonderfully improved the tone of the army. Yet a great many officers are absent, and others are daily leaving. The fact is, the incessant marching and fighting of the last month have pretty much used up everybody; except those of the strongest constitution."

"HEADQUARTERS ARMY OF THE POTOMAC,
July 31, 1863.

"DEAR FRIENDS: I write a brief line to say, that I arrived at Warrenton last night, and this morning was ordered on duty here as special inspector of the Army of the Potomac. This places me on General Meade's staff at headquarters of army, and is a very pleasant position. * * *

"Half of the army lies here. The remainder near Warrenton Junction, some eight miles from here. Army headquarters move to-morrow at 8 A. M. to Germantown, some twelve miles. This means, we are going to Fredericksburg or about there, I think. * * *

"Address me, at Headquarters, Army of Potomac."

"HEADQUARTERS ARMY OF THE POTOMAC,
Nov. 8, 1863.

"DEAR FATHER: We move at nine o'clock this morning, toward the Rappahannock. Have not time to write much. * * *

"Am well, and will write again in a day or two."[1]

CINCINNATI, OHIO.
Nov. 13, 1863. Sunday evening.

"DEAR BROTHER: * * * No doubt you are surprised to hear of my being here. I, however, am glad of the change. My life at army headquarters was not altogether agreeable; and I had no prospect of a change, until General Sickles should again take the field. *When that would be, was exceedingly uncertain.* When at Centreville, he rejoined for that purpose, as you saw, no doubt, by the papers; but General Meade politely said he did not think him well enough for active service, and so sent him back to Washington.

"From this circumstance, as well as others, I was per-

---

[1] Letters for August, September, and October lost or mislaid. Very sorry.

suaded that General Sickles would never again command the Third Corps while Meade commanded the Army of the Potomac. * * * Sickles expects to be assigned to the Department of Washington, and I think he will; but I judge it will be two or three months before he gets there. His *leg* is still unhealed, and his health delicate; all that the papers say to the contrary.

"Meanwhile, I am here on my way to General Thomas. Was ordered by the Secretary of War to Nashville, Tenn., and as yet am uncertain whether I shall stop there, or proceed on to Chattanooga. Am content to do either. Shall see the country and make new friends; and, so long as I am in the service, am quite as well off in one portion of the army as another.

"My health is good and spirits excellent. Will write you more fully when I get to Nashville." * * *

" OFFICE CHIEF QUARTERMASTER
MILITARY RAILROADS,
DEPARTMENT OF THE CUMBERLAND,
NASHVILLE, TENN.
Nov. 21, 1863.

"DEAR FRIENDS: At last I am here and fairly settled. My orders from the War Department, were to proceed to Nashville, and report for duty to General Thomas or his chief quartermaster here. After a day or two's consideration, have been put on duty here as Chief Quartermaster of Military Railroads, Department of the Cumberland. Have general charge of receiving and forwarding all freight and passengers from here to the army at Chattanooga and about there.

"It is a heavy business; but I think I can manage it. Have plenty of help, of all kinds; some dozen or so of clerks, and about a thousand employees. Want some good experienced railroad men, and shall at once send

North for them. Have a fine freight house and depot, and a large three-story brick building for myself and offices.

"Colonel Donaldson, the chief quartermaster, is a very intelligent gentleman; and I have no doubt we will get along well. He has treated me with great kindness so far; and has manifested exceeding confidence in assigning me to so important a position. * * *

"What is to come of these various changes, I scarcely know; though I hope for the best. But for the present, I prefer to be with the army here. The main fight is going to be here. Here all interest centers. Here the troops are massed. A large number of the best staff officers in the East have been ordered here; and I suppose I was sent with the rest. Shall at least do my duty; and trust to that good Providence, whose watchful eye is over all his works."

"OFFICE CHIEF QUARTERMASTER
MILITARY RAILROADS,
DEPARTMENT OF THE CUMBERLAND,
NASHVILLE, TENN.
Nov. 29, 1863.

"DEAR FRIENDS: Have been so busy for the past week, that I have hardly had time to think of anything. The rush and pressure of business have been so great, that some days I worked from 5 A. M. to 11 P. M. I had some idea of the magnitude of the work, inasmuch as all the supplies for the great army in front have to pass through my hands; but I scarcely supposed that the business could be so illy arranged and disorganized. I got things into better shape and 'rushed' more cars to the front. But it was too much for me. I felt it was going to break me down again; and so requested to be relieved. Colonel Donaldson granted my request, and ordered me on duty at his office as his Chief Assistant; whither I go to-morrow.

"This morning it is cold and Decemberish here. We had a light fall of snow last night; and to-day it is not thawing anywhere, except in the sun. The climate is exceedingly variable. Last week it was delightful one day, and the next it blew up with rain and sleet. * * *

"We have great good news from the army in front,[1] as you have doubtless seen by the papers, ere this reaches you. Five thousand prisoners and forty pieces of cannon! Our brave lads have done nobly. Hooker has again vindicated himself;[2] and I believe will live to silence all his detractors." * * *

> "CHIEF QUARTERMASTER'S OFFICE,
> NASHVILLE, TENN.
> Dec. 13, 1863.

"DEAR FRIENDS: * * * We are very busy here, and work hard. No one can conceive of the immense labor of supplying the vast army in front. Our office opens at 8 A. M., and there is a constant stream of work until 8 P. M. Colonel Donaldson, myself, and seven clerks are kept perpetually at work. We have a great army in front, and are very proud of it. It accomplishes wonders. There is no see-sawing, backing, and filling—marching and countermarching—as in the Army of the Potomac; but a grand and steady advance, that carries all before it. What magnificent fighting that was at Chattanooga! The storming of Lookout Mountain and the assault of Missionary Ridge are among the greatest achievements of history; and Hooker, Sherman, Thomas, and Grant will live forever in the memory of mankind.

"Congress opens well. God be praised for such a

---

[1] Battle of Chattanooga.     [2] At Lookout Mountain.

speaker as Colfax. And Lincoln, too, is true to himself. No flinching, no faltering there! Abe may be a little slow; but in the end he always turns up true. The slave shall be 'henceforth and forever free!' That is the language of his 'Proclamation,' and he stands grandly by it. 'Praise and thanks for an honest man!'" * * *

"CHIEF QUARTERMASTER'S OFFICE,
NASHVILLE, TENN.
Dec. 20, 1863.

"DEAR BROTHER HENRY: Your last received to-day. The weather here, just now, is quite winterish. For a time, when I first came, it was delightful. But for several days past it has been so cold, that ice has formed every night in my water pitcher. I like such weather, however, at this season of the year. It tones up one's system, and makes a man feel brisk and lively.

"You say father wishes me to remain here. Has he thought the matter fully over? I am not yet decided as to what is best, and am often sorry I was not allowed to go on to Hooker.[1] There is much to be said on both sides. On the one side, is personal comfort. I am nicely situated, in a Secesh mansion, with Colonel Donaldson; who, with a kindness unlooked for, has shared his quarters with me. We have a comfortable office, and he entrusts me with great confidence and consideration. We go to the office at 8 A. M., to dinner at 3 P. M., and leave the office at 6 P. M. or soon after as practicable. This gives me the evenings mostly to myself. Thus, as Chief Assistant Quartermaster, I suppose I ought to be content for a man of my years; but am not.

"On the other hand, life at the front, with Hooker,

---

[1] In November was ordered to report to Hooker as his Chief Quartermaster. But the order was suppressed by Donaldson, who wanted me at Nashville; and I knew nothing of it until weeks afterward.

would be exceedingly rough; but it holds out the prospect of honor and promotion. I should instantly decide for Hooker; but his own position, as yet, is so uncertain, that it is unsafe to commit one's self to his fortunes. His command is only two corps; and it is not yet settled whether he will stay here or return East. * * *

"It is strange how one's acquaintances turn up. I never supposed for a moment, that anybody would know me here; and yet scarcely a day passes, that somebody does not come into the office that has 'heard Captain Rusling was in Nashville, and wants to see him.' Only yesterday, old Dr. John H. Phillips, of Pennington, N. J., came in. It seems he was appointed a surgeon some months ago, and shortly after was assigned to duty at Nashville; where he has been ever since. He has his family with him, and has charge of one of the hospitals here. Guess there is no getting out of the world—at least no getting anywhere where somebody will not know you!

"*Moral.*—Be careful how you conduct yourself, when you drop down into a new place, or among strange company!!

"I think of you all at home very often, and not unfrequently wish myself there. Especially on Sundays. * * *

"In conclusion, a Merry Christmas and a Happy New Year, and may Heaven grant you many of them!

"CHIEF QUARTERMASTER'S OFFICE,
NASHVILLE, TENN.
Dec. 28, 1863.

"DEAR FRIENDS: Have only time to write a line, to say that I am still alive and kicking.' Our chief clerk is away, to be gone a week, and I am compelled to do his duty, and mine as well." * * *

"CHIEF QUARTERMASTER'S OFFICE,
    NASHVILLE, TENN.
        Jan. 3, 1864.

"DEAR FRIENDS: Christmas and New Year's are both over, and the year has once more settled down to its wonted gravity and solemnity. We have not seen much Christmas here. We had a good dinner, and closed the office for a part of the day; but the general operations of the department went forward quite as usual. Take the week altogether, however, there has been less work than ordinarily; and I cannot say I have not enjoyed it. Am getting pretty well acquainted with officers here; and have become so familiar with the department, that much of what was disagreeable has become pleasant.

"We have old winter here, just now, quite as severely as you have at home. To-day it has been snowing all day, and the air is as wintry as any you have at Trenton. As I write, sleighs are passing the office, and the bells are jingling merrily. The cold weather has frozen up the railroad and telegraph, and we have no news from the North. I suppose you are having cold weather too. God help the poor!

"I am writing to you in the midst of an office full of people. Two officers are by my side, and I talk with them while writing to you. This may make my letter seem disjointed; but it is the best I can do.

"Just now, have some prospects of returning East again soon, and shall not be sorry." * * *

"CHIEF QUARTERMASTER'S OFFICE,
    NASHVILLE, TENN.
        Jan. 11, 1864.

"DEAR FRIENDS: We have had a cold and dreary week here. Snow, ice, and shivering generally. I am a confirmed disbeliever in the 'Sunny South.' If the past week is a fair specimen, then the 'Sunny South' is a myth, a humbug, a nonentity; and I shall never more believe in it.

"Such weather is especially detestable in this latitude. The houses are all mere shells, with great cracks at the doors and windows; and it is next to impossible to keep warm in cold weather. And then, besides, there are no stoves; nothing but open fireplaces and grates. The grates did very well for a while, and the cheery fire of the blazing bituminous coal was agreeable enough. But when the pinching cold of last week came, they 'played out.' I searched the town, and could only find two stoves for sale all told. These I seized upon; one for the office and the other for myself. Since then have made out very well.

"It has been a busy week; but have felt remarkably well, and things have gone through with a rush. Have enjoyed the work. It is a pleasurable duty to work hard, when one's body and mind are both in full play; and I have felt about like, I suppose, a spirited nag feels when he champs the bit and 'devours the ground with fierceness and rage.'" * * *

"CHIEF QUARTERMASTER'S OFFICE,
NASHVILLE, TENN.
Jan. 17, 1864.

"DEAR FRIENDS: We have had a great sensation and a real pleasure here. No less a person than Bishop Simpson arrived here two days ago, in company with one of the Book Agents in Cincinnati, on his way to East Tennessee. They came to look after Methodism in this benighted region; and to see what they could do toward reorganizing and reestablishing its institution. They stumbled into our office, with an order from General Grant, in quest of transportation to Knoxville. A blow in the face would scarcely have astonished me more than seeing the good Bishop standing by my side with his order.

"I wrote out the order for his transportation by railroad and steamboat, and then asked him if he didn't recognize me. He said he thought he did; and when I mentioned my name, and that I had taken tea with him at Bordentown during the New Jersey Conference there, in 1861, he at once remembered me. It was a pleasing incident. I went around to see him that evening; and this morning heard him preach in the State capitol. It was cold and disagreeable there, and a rainy, disagreeable morning without; but the Bishop preached with his usual power and eloquence, and I enjoyed it greatly. * * *

"I expect to be very busy the coming week. Colonel Donaldson is going to the front to-morrow, to inspect the condition of the railroad and the quartermaster depots, and I shall have charge of the department for the week. But I suppose I shall get through. At least, shall try."

"CHIEF QUARTERMASTER'S OFFICE,
NASHVILLE, TENN.
Jan. 24, 1864.

"DEAR FATHER: At last, we are having Southern weather here. Heretofore, since I have been here, the weather has been execrable, as a rule. But to-day the air is as warm and balmy as your days in May and June.

"Have not heard from home for now two weeks. I suppose the cold weather, which froze up the railroads, interfered with the mails, and that this warm weather will bring us all right again.

"Am not very well to-day. Troubled with malaria again. Affairs here not satisfactory. Everything depends on the railroad from here to Chattanooga; and it is a frail dependence. By our utmost exertions, we can only make about fifty cars a day to the front, and to supply the army well takes over a hundred.

"We work hard; but get embarrassed, and I fret and worry. I can never be happy unless entirely succeeding, and entire success is impossible here. True, I have no direct responsibility—Donaldson being chief; but it is a matter of pride with me, that all should go well.

"The country knows but little of the condition of affairs here, or they would be alarmed for this army. Half rations of food and one-quarter rations of forage are not much better than the Rebs have, if as good. But I trust in God, and hope all will yet be well. At least, no shortcoming on my part shall be said."

"CHIEF QUARTERMASTER'S OFFICE,
NASHVILLE, TENN.
Jan. 31, 1864.

"DEAR FRIENDS: * * * I regret to say, my box is still 'among the missing.' It has now been about a month on its journey, and I have pretty much given it up. * * * Still I hope not to lose it. * * *

"I think seriously of resigning in the spring. Will it do? How is business in Trenton; especially among the lawyers? I think something of settling here in Nashville. There are fine openings for young men here in Tennessee; and I know some loyal people here who would like me to remain for good."

"CHIEF QUARTERMASTER'S OFFICE,
NASHVILLE, TENN.
Feb. 14, 1864.

"DEAR FRIENDS: I am ashamed to confess, it is now two weeks since I wrote you. Last Sunday, I put it off, as I scarcely had time; and so from day to day it has run over, until now Sunday has come again, without my giving you the scratch of a pen. Such a thing, I believe, has not occurred before, since August, 1861, and I do not mean it shall again very often.

"Last week had a memorable day here. Had an early breakfast, and then rode out with Captain Irvin, one of our assistant quartermasters, to the 'Hermitage,' Andrew Jackson's old place, some ten or twelve miles from here. The morning was fine, the road good, and the ride superb. I have never seen a finer country than that through which we traveled. It is almost as level as the country from Trenton to Crosswicks; the turnpike even a better one; and the soil vastly superior. What a magnificent country this must have been before the war! The farms bore evidence of a high state of cultivation; and many of the mansions were really palatial in their dimensions and style.

"The 'Hermitage' itself is a bad imitation of Mount Vernon; and is going sadly to decay. The front yard is a fine grove of cedars. The house is about like the one you live in, though more pretentious in style. The garden is about the size of yours; with the tomb of Jackson and his wife in one corner. This tomb is surmounted by an urn, which is almost toppled over; and the plastering on the roof of the little sort of temple, which covers the grave of the great man, is almost all fallen off. The most interesting part of the premises is the parlor, in which hang several excellent portraits of the old hero, and there the spirit of the old Roman still seems to walk abroad. 'By the Eternal!' I thought, if he had ruled instead of James Buchanan, in 1860-61, we should never have had this wretched, sickening war that now desolates the land!

"I enjoyed the ride very much. I succeeded in cutting two good hickory canes; one of which I will send father by express, as soon as I can get it dressed up a little. By the way, I gave orders to a gang of men we have at work out there, felling timber for saw-logs, etc., when they got through, to clean up the 'Hermitage' property and put the tomb in good repair. The estate is now the property of the State of Tennessee; but, if she does fail to care for him, the 'Northern Vandals' will not fail to regard the old hero's bones!" * * *

"CHIEF QUARTERMASTER'S OFFICE,
NASHVILLE, TENN.
Feb. 21, 1864.

"DEAR FATHER: Another week has rolled by. We have had a cold snap again, and in common with many others, have caught cold. However, am better again this morning. The weather has moderated; and we are having as pleasant a Sunday morning as you usually enjoy the last of April or the first of May.

"I have nothing especially new to write. My last letter was so long, that I can afford to write a short one now. I have not been entirely idle this winter. In the midst of cares, have found time to write an article on 'The War,' which will appear in the *Quarterly Review*, for April. The other day I had another offer from General Hooker, to take the field as his Chief Quartermaster. Was strongly tempted to go. But after thinking the matter fully over, and consulting my friends here, decided *not* to go; unless appropriate rank was given me before leaving here. I replied to that effect, and am content to wait the chances. * * *

"My 'box' came at last, all right." * * *

"CHIEF QUARTERMASTER'S OFFICE,
NASHVILLE, TENN.
March 21, 1864.

"DEAR FRIENDS: I spent a very pleasant Sabbath yesterday. At 11 A. M., deserted the office, and went over to the Presbyterian Church; where I heard a good loyal Methodist sermon from a Calvinistic preacher of the uncommon name of Jones! He labored hard to show that 'spiritual things can be discerned only by the spiritually minded,' and made out a pretty good case for those who believe that human reason has nothing to do with matters of religion. I heard him with a good deal of interest, however, and think his sermon decidedly the best I have heard in Nashville, after Bishop Simpson's. * * *

"In the afternoon, had a fine gallop out by the camp of the Fifteenth U. S. Colored Troops; a regiment that reports to us for duty in the quartermaster department, as laborers. I took Major Patterson, from Freehold, of the Thirty-fifth New Jersey, formerly speaker of the House, out with me. The 'contrabands' are a splendid body of troops, and the major was delighted. He is just fresh from New Jersey, and never saw a colored regiment before. He is a pretty good war man now, and will ultimately turn out an Abolitionist; as all other sensible men. O, I am so glad that I had the sagacity, so long ago as 1856, to see the shadow of coming events; and to come out then boldly on the side of Freedom! A man is an owl who has continued pro-slavery all these days." * * *

"SENIOR AND SUPERVISING QUARTERMASTER'S OFFICE,
DEPARTMENT OF THE CUMBERLAND,
NASHVILLE, TENN.
April 1, 1864.

"DEAR BROTHER: Yours of the twenty-second is just received. As I have a leisure moment, in the midst of office business, I embrace it to answer at once.

"First, in reply to your question about my *horses*. I have to say I turned two of them over to the quartermaster department in Washington, and procured two others from the department here, in pursuance of existing orders. The other I left in the army to be sold, as he was lame at the time, and is only now getting well enough to be offered for sale. He had the 'heel-grease' badly, and came near dying. * * *

"Second, as to what I *am doing* here. I am serving with Colonel Donaldson, the senior and supervising quartermaster of the Department of the Cumberland, as his Chief Assistant; in other words, as the assistant chief quartermaster of the department. It is the highest position I have ever held; but, under the peculiar organization of the quartermaster department, gives no increase of rank, because United States law does not provide for it. * * *

"As to the work of our office, it is overwhelming. We have over a dozen quartermasters on duty here at Nashville. We employ over twelve thousand laborers, mechanics, and clerks. Our disbursements alone amount to over five million dollars per month. We run over six hundred miles of railroad, providing rolling stock, employees, and everything. We supply over a hundred thousand men, scattered from Knoxville to Chattanooga, and thence to Memphis. This is the biggest army depot to-day on the face of the earth. We have an office with seven clerks and five detectives; and thus run the whole machine. Of course, we work hard, but it is nice work. We have vast control and patronage and power, and this is pleasant to the human heart and intellect. Promotion of some sort will come at last, or else all history is false, and I am resolved to hang on and take my chances." * * *

"Senior and Supervising Quartermaster's Office,
Nashville, Tenn.
May 1, 1864.

"Dear Friends: I am well, but very busy. Extraordinarily well, indeed, for me. * * *

"Sherman is in the midst of a great movement, with all his disposable forces; and probably before you get this, there will have been fought one of the greatest and most desperate battles of the war. We all have implicit confidence in such a magnificent soldier, and bid him Godspeed!"

"Senior and Supervising Quartermaster's Office,
Nashville, Tenn.
May 8, 1864.

"Dear Friends: I am well. Hastily,
"J. F. R."

"Senior and Supervising Quartermaster's Office,
Department of the Cumberland,
Nashville, Tenn.
May 14, 1864.

"My Dear Friends: Have spent a very pleasant and delightful week here. With the commencement of operations at the front, our business has dropped off, and that has given us time for leisure. On Friday, I took a ride with a party of several others out into the country. It was a most charming day—

"'Sweet day, so cool, so calm, so bright,
The bridal of the earth and sky,'

as good George Herbert wrote—and I enjoyed it exceedingly. We went about six miles out, to the residence of General Harding, a noted rebel here in the time of Secesh. Now he has taken the amnesty oath, and calls himself a loyal United States citizen. He has a small farm of about three thousand acres, of the most superb land I ever beheld. It is naturally a limestone soil, with heavy black loam several feet thick all over it. Originally a large part of his land was a dense canebrake, but this was long since cleared off, and the land devoted to grain and grazing. The herbage of timothy, clover, and bluegrass is one dense mass; the finest for grazing I ever saw. About five hundred acres are appropriated to a magnificent park, where deer and goats run at large, almost as free as in their native wilds.

"Before the war, Harding was the greatest stock raiser in Tennessee. He raised fancy stock of all kinds. His horses especially were noted for their beauty, speed, and endurance. Our Union soldiers made sad havoc with his property, at first; he having been foolish enough to 'skedaddle' on our approach to Nashville. The remnants are still there, however, and his horses would do your eyes good to look upon. He has one horse, a dappled gray stallion, the handsomest creature I ever saw. He values him at the small figure of eighteen thousand dollars (!); and I presume he would bring it. He has several fine yearlings and two-year-old colts, that he values at four and six hundred dollars each.

"It is a grand old place he has. His father and grandfather lived there before him. You approach the place by the turnpike, between old-fashioned, Warren County, New Jersey, limestone wall fences, made to stand for generations. Good thing for Harding! If they had been rail or board or paling, the soldiers would have burnt them up long ago! But they can't burn stones! Turning in at the gate, you cross a fine, broad, clear stream of water, half as large and quite as clear as the Pequest, that runs through the entire estate. Then you wind your way up a gentle slope, among original old forest trees, to the house—a great, large, sprawling, spread-all-around, half old, and half new affair, that would accommodate a village, more or less, without much trouble.

"We were received very courteously and treated hospitably to refreshments, and then shown all about. It was a bad thing for quiet men. It woke all of one's bad ambitions, and made one half forget that slavery was such a curse after all. But, as a good Providence would have it, we had scarcely passed out into the main road on our way home, when, issuing from a field of Harding's, came three stout-looking, middle-aged colored women, dressed almost *a la Bloomer*, in dirty rags, and with long hoes over their shoulders.

"This was the other side of the picture. It was a fit *finale* and commentary on what had gone before, and revealed at last the skeleton, which we were inclined to forget. It brought to mind the fact, that Harding rolled in luxury by stealing the wages of others, and by driving to his fields women, whom heaven intended for other work. His ease and wealth repose on blood and crime; and the slaveholder is welcome to both. We came home thankful that our hands and consciences were at least clean of innocent blood, if we were not so well off in this world's goods; and so went content to sleep."

"SENIOR AND SUPERVISING QUARTERMASTER'S OFFICE,
DEPARTMENT OF THE CUMBERLAND,
NASHVILLE, TENN.
June 5, 1864.

"DEAR FRIENDS: Am well. Have nothing new to report. Everybody is anxiously awaiting the result of operations under Grant and Sherman. We are all hopeful, and even confident. I pray God to stand by the flag, and give success to our armies! O, the suffering and the agony of the nation! How long! O Lord! how long!"

"SENIOR AND SUPERVISING QUARTERMASTER'S OFFICE,
DEPARTMENT OF THE CUMBERLAND,
NASHVILLE, TENN.
June 12, 1864.

"DEAR FRIENDS: I have nothing especially to write about; and yet write because I think you will expect a letter. Don't you think, seriously speaking, that there is really some virtue in such conduct? For now these three years, have been writing you regularly every Sabbath, when not actually on the march or engaged in battle; and I think that is pretty good. * * *

"We are continuing to have the most delightful weather here. This country is a perfect paradise. O, how I do enjoy it! Am in the best of health, and have never yet been in any land, that I liked so well. Tennessee is bound to be a great State again. The work of reorganization goes slowly on. With all her troubles, she is yet to-day more loyal than Kentucky; and I predict a great future for her. The National Republican Convention has recently done a just thing for her great and patriotic statesman, Andrew Johnson. I know him well. He takes his nomination as a matter of course, and will undoubtedly be elected by an overwhelming majority.

"I think the American people were never wiser than when they renominated Abraham Lincoln. It is the bitterest pill that could have been tendered to the South. It is a safe rule always to do that which your enemies won't like. And its significance abroad will be most encouraging. It will show foreign nations, that a Democratic Republic can yet be steady enough in the midst of civil commotions to do the fit thing at the right time; and that we will always sustain and uphold our rulers when they do right.

"The platform is splendid. Maximilian had better take care. We shall upset him, as sure as fate, just as soon as the Rebellion is over. Slavery is gone up. The only thing left is to amend the Constitution, so as to legally abolish it, now and forever! And it will be done, sure, next winter. Glory, hallelujah!"

"SENIOR AND SUPERVISING QUARTERMASTER'S OFFICE,
DEPARTMENT OF THE CUMBERLAND,
NASHVILLE, TENN.
July 11, 1864.

"DEAR FRIENDS: I did not write you last week, because Mr. B—— was going home and was to call and see you. I knew he could tell you more and could answer more inquiries than I could in the compass of a letter; and therefore, I concluded to let the living tongue perform the service of the dead pen.

"Our Fourth of July passed off very well. Our town was far more patriotic than I supposed it would be; and the display of bunting was respectable. I made a holiday of it, as far as possible; discharging the most of our force at 8 A. M.; and spent the time as well as could be expected, so far away from home and in the midst of strangers. I send you one of our papers, as a specimen of Nashville patriotism; and think Trenton will find it hard to beat. * * *

"In addition to the books I wrote for, I want you to send me my volume of Plutarch. I want you also to send me monthly as early as you can purchase them, Harper's Monthly and the Atlantic Monthly Magazines." * * *

'SENIOR AND SUPERVISING QUARTERMASTER'S
OFFICE,
DEPARTMENT OF THE CUMBERLAND,
NASHVILLE, TENN.
July 21, 1864.

"DEAR FRIENDS: I am getting bad. It is positively Thursday, and yet I have not written my usual Sunday letter home. If I had not a pretty good reason for my delay, I suppose my conscience would cry aloud. * * *

"Last week, I went with a party of officers and ladies to visit the great Mammoth Cave, in Kentucky, about one hundred miles north of here, on the Louisville Road. We reached the cave about 9 A. M. Had a good breakfast, and at 10 A. M. entered the cave. There were twenty-five of us in all, and we had a good time. The cave is actually one of the greatest wonders in the world. We went in nine miles. When three miles in, we came to a subterranean river, forty feet wide and thirty-five feet deep, and sailed along this for half a mile. Then we came to a long, narrow winding way, about eight feet high, six feet wide, and two miles long. After this, we came to a long hall, sixty feet wide, forty feet high, and two and a half miles long. The roof of this was one mass of crystals that gleamed and sparkled in our lamplights, like a million diamonds. I collected a large number, and will send them home shortly.

"But I cannot tell you all now. I propose to write an account of our trip, and will send you a copy. It was one of the most delightful trips of my life. We spent two days in the cave, exploring it in all directions; and got back here about as 'played out' a set of people as you ever saw. Yet I would not have missed the trip for anything. It was my first absence from Nashville in nearly eight months, and I enjoyed it hugely." * * *

## Some Army Letters

"SENIOR AND SUPERVISING QUARTERMASTER'S OFFICE,
DEPARTMENT OF THE CUMBERLAND,
NASHVILLE, TENN.
July 21, 1864.

"MY DEAR FRIENDS: * * * I think it not improbable that I shall get home in August or September, for a brief visit, if nothing more. But I do not care to leave, so long as we have so much to do. We are very busy. We have to supply all the vast armies operating in Tennessee and down below, and you may be sure we have our hands full. We have nearly a score of officers and about sixteen thousand employees to assist; and the work done from week to week is truly astonishing.

"The books you sent me arrived all safely. Also, the clothes. For both of which, many thanks! You omitted to send me my copy of Burns. It is bound in red muslin and ought to be in my library. If so, please send it by express." * * *

"SENIOR AND SUPERVISING QUARTERMASTER'S OFFICE,
DEPARTMENT OF THE CUMBERLAND
NASHVILLE, TENN.
Aug. 7, 1864.

"DEAR FRIENDS: I had a letter from Henry a day or two ago, in which he says, among other things, that the reason why he did not send my copy of Burns was, that he could not find it. I am sure it is somewhere about, and I should like very much to have it here. * * * I am about commencing a course of study. My business is over after 6 P. M., as a rule; and I don't care to waste the time by loafing around in idleness and vice, as too many others do.

"Thank God! I have a love for books; and with good

books can always make my own society, and enjoy myself as I please. * * * I have no thought or care for many things others enjoy, and so fall back upon my old and constant and never-failing source of pleasure and profit—books. Thank God for books! They are the best and highest gifts of heaven to man (after woman); and to every thoughtful mind a really good book is

"'A thing of beauty and a joy forever!'

"We have no great news here. Sherman is still thundering at the gates of Atlanta; and we earnestly hope will soon enter in. If he does, he will be set down as one of the greatest captains of the age. His march from Chattanooga to Atlanta is one of the most famous, so far, in history. God grant that it may end in a magnificent success! He is a thorough soldier, every inch of him; and I applaud him to the skies.

"I fear he has made a mistake in losing Hooker; yet he knew Hooker better than I did; and therefore, I cannot blame him.[1] Hooker stood out well here, and is really a magnificent soldier. * * * Here is a tear to his *bravery*, anyhow!"

"SENIOR AND SUPERVISING QUARTERMASTER'S OFFICE,
DEPARTMENT OF THE CUMBERLAND,
NASHVILLE, TENN.
Aug. 22, 1864.

"DEAR FRIENDS: I did not write yesterday, because too busily engaged; and so take advantage of an early hour this morning, before business sets in, to write you now. Nor did I write you last Sunday, for reasons which you will find below.

"Last Wednesday week, August 10, at 2:30 A. M., I

---
[1] General Hooker had just resigned and gone North.

left here on a special train in company with Colonel D. C. McCallum, from Washington, D. C., general manager of United States Military Railroads, for the purpose of making a general inspection of railroads and quartermaster supplies from Nashville to Atlanta. Got to Chattanooga same night. Next day made an inspection of our depot there, and late in the afternoon ascended Lookout Mountain. This is a bold, outjutting mountain, that jumps up square from the level plateau of the Tennessee River to a distance of fully seventeen hundred feet; and the top stands naked and defiant against the sky. From the extreme 'Lookout' point, a great naked rock, a hundred feet square down its side, where it looks out over the valley, the scene is magnificent and grand.

"Chattanooga, in a level basin, five miles long by three wide, nestles at your feet. It is a little dilapidated town; swarming now with quartermaster storehouses, mules, and troops. By its side, seeming like a thread or band of silver, the Tennessee winds most crookedly along from the north. Off to the east, you look clear across no less than five distinct ranges of mountains, away a hundred miles to a faint line of blue, that they say is a ridge of great height in North Carolina. By your side you see the abandoned batteries, from which the Rebs were so ingloriously driven by the gallant Hooker. Just beyond the town looms up Missionary Ridge, that our boys stormed and carried so magnificently last winter.

"Hereafter, it will be just the world's wonder, how we managed to hold Chattanooga at all, much less repulse and defeat the Rebs. It is worth a voyage across the Atlantic and a trip across the Continent, just to see what the Republic did here, when beset by copperheads in the rear, and Rebels in the front.

"Altogether, I reckon, I rather enjoyed the sight; especially when, just at sunset, a thundershower went sailing over the mountains to the east, its outlines visible at each side, while in the middle the rain poured. As we gazed upon the singular sight, the clear sky shining blue all around it, suddenly as it reached the right angle for the sunrays, across the valley from Lookout to the shower, there sprang into view a grand and gorgeous rainbow. It couldn't be seen at all from the valley below; but to us sitting on Lookout Rock, seventeen hundred feet above the river, it was a sight never to be forgotten. It was long after dark, when we reached the foot of the mountain, and we were tired enough you may be sure; but I felt amply compensated for my fatigue by what I saw.

"Next morning at a quarter past two, we left for Atlanta. Crossed the Chattahoochee, and ran up to within half a mile of our works same evening. That night I went over to General Thomas' headquarters about a mile away. Was with him until near midnight, talking about our supplies, etc.; and then he sent me back in an ambulance. Next morning early ambulances were sent over to us from General Thomas'; and we all went over to General Sherman's headquarters, some four miles to the right. We spent the day there, consulting and arranging about army matters generally, of no particular interest to you civilians.

"I know Sherman well (saw much of him in Nashville last winter); and he showed us every courtesy and civility."[1]

"SENIOR AND SUPERVISING QUARTERMASTER'S OFFICE,
DEPARTMENT OF THE CUMBERLAND,
NASHVILLE, TENN.
Aug. 28, 1864.

"DEAR HENRY: I am in receipt of your letter of a few days since. * * * In the matter of *substitutes,* tell every-

---
[1] For rest of this letter substantially, see chap. viii, pp. 114-117.

body that I am not inclined to save, and will not lift my finger to save a single Jersey copperhead from the draft. The country has had three years of my life; now let it have some of theirs. If they are thoroughgoing copperheads, they are only fit 'food for powder,' anyhow.

"This has been a most delightful week. The weather has been cool and delicious; and the climate, generally, the most enjoyable in the world. They say here, that this weather is going to last far into the fall, or early winter, and I reckon it will. Altogether, I like Tennessee very much; and have half lost my love for Jersey, since she became so disloyal." * * *

"SENIOR AND SUPERVISING QUARTERMASTER'S OFFICE,
DEPARTMENT OF THE CUMBERLAND,
NASHVILLE, TENN.
Sept. 2, 1864.

"DEAR FRIENDS: All well here. The best of news from Sherman. Thank God! Atlanta has fallen; and victory at Atlanta means success everywhere! The star of the Republic is once more in the ascendant; and the friends of Freedom should take heart and rejoice! Am very well, and jubilant with joy. Our flags are out, our bells are ringing; and from Capitol Hill a hundred guns are thundering on the air the great Union victory!

"Next you will hear of the fall of Richmond. It is as sure as logic, and as inevitable as fate. I feel it 'in my *bones*.' The Rebs may flourish like a green bay tree 'for a time;' but in the end, you will look for them, and not *one* of them will be found! Good-by to McClellan and the copperheads! November will extinguish them forever."

"SENIOR AND SUPERVISING QUARTERMASTER'S
OFFICE,
DEPARTMENT OF THE CUMBERLAND,
NASHVILLE, TENN.
Sept. 11, 1864.

"DEAR FRIENDS: Am very well. The copy of Burns arrived safe. Will write more in a day or two."

"SENIOR AND SUPERVISING QUARTERMASTER'S
OFFICE,
DEPARTMENT OF THE CUMBERLAND,
NASHVILLE, TENN.
Sept. 12, 1864.

"DEAR HENRY: I have yours of September 1. It went astray to Chattanooga. * * *

"My account of the Mammoth Cave is in the press. Will send you a copy as soon as it is out.

"I had a letter from G—— some time ago about 'substitutes,' etc., and answered forthwith. I don't suppose he was pleased with my reply. The substance of it was, that the Secretary of War prohibited me from engaging in the business; that I would not do it anyhow; that I was in favor of drafting copperheads instead; that I had served three years, and now wanted to see some of the *stay-at-homes* take my place! General Sherman's admirable letter knocked the whole 'Southern colored substitute' business in the head, and I was immensely glad of it." * * *

"SENIOR AND SUPERVISING QUARTERMASTER'S
OFFICE,
DEPARTMENT OF THE CUMBERLAND,
NASHVILLE, TENN.
Oct. 2, 1864.

"DEAR FRIENDS: We are in the midst of considerable excitement here; and yet I must find time to drop you a line. The Rebs under Forrest, for a week past, have been raiding our railroads, and they are threatening Nashville. I opine it will not amount to a great deal; yet our people are pretty thoroughly scared, and we are making extra efforts to give the rascals a proper reception. We have stripped our teams and stables of all available horses and mules; and this afternoon we shall mount cavalry, infantry, and everything else, and push them straight upon the audacious riders. Troops are moving up, however, from Atlanta and Chattanooga to head them off; and I suspect, ere you get this, the danger will be chiefly over.

"For my part am not the least bit alarmed. We have seven thousand men, belonging to our department here, under arms; and are not afraid to venture out against Forrest with even these. It would be a sort of militia fighting; but at least two thirds of them are old soldiers, and they would back up the rest.

"The nights are getting quite cold; while it is very warm in the middle of the day. The result is that many are complaining of sickness. I have had two clerks flat on their backs for a week past, and two more that scarcely keep about. Not well myself, but have too much to do to get entirely down." * * *

"SENIOR AND SUPERVISING QUARTERMASTER'S OFFICE,
DEPARTMENT OF THE CUMBERLAND,
NASHVILLE, TENN.
Nov. 1, 1864.

"DEAR FRIENDS: Am quite unwell, but just as busy as a man can be! Things are pretty well 'mixed' here. Hood and Forrest are on a great raid North; and Sherman on an equally great raid South. Both movements look desperate, but we shall see, what we shall see. I have the most implicit faith in Sherman's generalship and sagacity."

"SENIOR AND SUPERVISING QUARTERMASTER'S OFFICE, NASHVILLE, TENN. Nov. 12, 1864.

"DEAR BROTHER: Yours of the sixth received. Am greatly gratified with the election, as you may well suppose.

"Am glad your Lincoln and Johnson demonstration passed off so successfully. Had hoped you would be able to carry the State; but see by the returns you did not. Well, never mind. You at least *deserved* success, and that is something. You reduced the Democratic majority handsomely, and gained one Congressman; and so deserve the thanks of the Nation. It is all right, anyhow, as it is. Lincoln is elected again, and the war and freedom are vindicated. It is the heaviest 'lick' the Rebs have received in four years, worth half a dozen ordinary victories; and the world at large will so regard it.

"I suppose you folks at home are somewhat muddled about our military affairs here. Never mind. We keep our own counsel. The next you hear of Hood, he will be on a two-forty race for southern Georgia or Alabama, with Thomas in pursuit; while Sherman will turn up at Savannah or Charleston before you know it. I am not at liberty to say more now, even to you; but rest assured in the conviction that we have more troops than the Rebs have; and that Sherman is more than an overmatch for Hood and Beauregard, both put together. I know Sherman, and he is decidedly the most able and brilliant commander the war has produced on either side, as yet."

## Some Army Letters

"SENIOR AND SUPERVISING QUARTERMASTER'S OFFICE,
DEPARTMENT OF THE CUMBERLAND,
NASHVILLE, TENN.
Nov. 16, 1864.

"DEAR HENRY: Am pretty well, and very busy. Donaldson has gone east, to Washington, etc.; and I am serving as Chief Quartermaster in his absence."

"SENIOR AND SUPERVISING QUARTERMASTER'S OFFICE,
DEPARTMENT OF THE CUMBERLAND,
NASHVILLE, TENN.
Nov. 24, 1864.

"DEAR FRIENDS: * * * General[1] Donaldson is away East, on leave, and I am doing all the work of the office. Very busy, of course.

"To-day is Thanksgiving Day, and we have a little more leisure. Not that we are entirely free from work, but I have shut up most of the offices and shops, and discharged all my own clerks, save one. For myself, I have been here most of the day; and now, at 3 P. M., am just closing up to go home to dinner.

"I suppose you are having a very pleasant and happy time. Have gone to church in the morning. Have come home to turkey and cranberries, perhaps some one with you; and are enjoying yourselves with 'the feast of reason and the flow of soul.' That means, pumpkin pie and Jersey coffee!

"Well, that is a good way to be thankful; and I am thankful, too. Am thankful in a national way, for victory in the field and triumphs at the polls. Thankful, in a State way, for your having cut down your copperhead majority from fifteen thousand to four thousand, and

---
[1] He had recently been promoted Brigadier-General by brevet, most deservedly.

gained one good Congressman. Thankful, in a personal way, for all the good I have had and the blessings I have enjoyed. I am not certain, that I am thankful for other things—disappointments, griefs, sorrows—though I suppose I ought to be; for God is wisest, best, truest, and by his very nature must 'do all things well,' for those who love and serve him. This is just how I feel.

"Don't know that it is exactly right, or exactly wrong. But suppose I would be more human and civilized and refined and better, if I was only home with you all and away from this ceaseless fret and worry and stretch of mind. Fact is, sometimes I feel pretty well worn out, and disgusted. A great department, with its endless wants, presses on us here ceaselessly and constantly. A hundred thousand men to supply. Five hundred miles of territory to supply them over; fifty thousand mules and twenty-five thousand horses. And here at Nashville alone, over fifteen thousand men to work and control.

"You may well think it a prodigious job. Heart and hands at all times full. No time for rest. No time for thought. Work, eat, sleep! Work, eat, sleep! And never 'get through.' This is the endless round from week to week, and from month to month. It is very wearing, and tells on a man. It has spoiled my handwriting, that was none too good before; and shall be very thankful if I come out safe at last. Nevertheless, after all, to-day, as I look back and consider, I am devoutly thankful to Almighty God for all that I do and all that I am. He has kept me and preserved me and guided me, and will yet uphold me by his power, now and forever!

"We have news to-day that Hood is moving, and he may give us some trouble; but I am not alarmed. We are strong here against all contingencies; and the Rebs will melt away in the end. Thomas is very strong and persistent; and we shall come out all right. Have no fears. You may have some squally news; but don't be alarmed. Trust in God, and keep your powder dry!"

"SENIOR AND SUPERVISING QUARTERMASTER'S OFFICE,
DEPARTMENT OF THE CUMBERLAND,
NASHVILLE, TENN.
Dec. 3, 1864.

"DEAR FRIENDS: We are all right here. Enemy within three miles; but we have plenty of men and everything else, and shall beat them to pieces if they dare attack our lines. Am very well, and very busy; and you must excuse for not writing more."

"SENIOR AND SUPERVISING QUARTERMASTER'S OFFICE,
DEPARTMENT OF THE CUMBERLAND,
NASHVILLE, TENN.
Dec. 11, 1864.

"DEAR FRIENDS: * * * I have forgotten now, in the hurry of affairs here, whether I wrote you last Sunday or not; but, at all events, I telegraphed you some time during the week, that 'I was well and all right.' Did you get it? As you know, General Donaldson has been away; and having full charge of everything here, have been exceedingly busy, and up till eleven and twelve o'clock at night, with scarcely an hour to call my own. It has so happened, however, that I have been very well and in splendid working condition; and, altogether, have rather enjoyed the press and crush of business, than otherwise. Now, however, Donaldson is back again, and 'all goes merry as a marriage bell.' * * *

"We are having great times here. No danger or anything of that sort; but Hood pens us in here; and we haven't much tried to prevent him, as yet. Our line of defense is a semi-circle, drawn around the city, from the

Cumberland around to the Cumberland again, with the enemy's line one half or three quarters of a mile distant.

"Our line is immensely strong, crowned with forts and bristling with cannon; and both ends of it covered by gunboats. The Rebs might as well butt their brains against the Rocky Mountains, as attempt to take it. Besides, our force is quite as numerous as theirs, if not more so; and if they don't 'skedaddle' soon, we shall have one of the 'biggest' fights you ever did see.

"Just now, both armies are doing their best to keep warm. For three days we have had bitterly cold, winter weather; diversified with rain, hail, sleet, and snow. The troops on both sides must have suffered terribly. As a consequence, the beautiful woods and groves that surrounded Nashville on all sides, and made it one of the most lovely towns I ever saw, are all going remorselessly *down* before the axes of the soldiers. We are getting in wood by the rail and river for the hospitals here; but the army beyond has to take care of itself.

"Just imagine an army of fifty thousand men in tents, stretching from the Delaware, around by the toll-gate on Crosswicks Pike, and around to the river again, say by Cadwallader's or the Asylum, in bitter winter weather, when ice forms everywhere and no thaw even at noon. Think how the poor fellows would shake and shiver; and then think how the trees would fly. Good-by, Linden Park! Good-by, Washington Grove! Good-by, State House Yard! The trees would go down everywhere, just as they are doing here; and it would take a century to replace them. Now imagine forty thousand or fifty thousand Rebs just beyond that line, a mile or so away; and you may form some idea of how we are off here. Of course, the Rebs must have wood too; and away it goes by the thousands of cord daily. If the Rebs coop us up here another fortnight, there won't be a tree left within five miles of Nashville. This is something awful, I know; but it is war, and war knows no law or humanities, nothing but necessities.

"Have no fears for us here. We are all right. We shall have a great battle in a day or two, as I think, and a great victory." * * *

"SENIOR AND SUPERVISING QUARTERMASTER'S OFFICE,
DEPARTMENT OF THE CUMBERLAND,
NASHVILLE, TENN.
Dec. 16, 1864.

"DEAR FRIENDS: I drop you a hasty line, merely to say I am well and things here are going well. The quartermaster department is in the trenches, some five thousand strong, holding the interior line of works from Battery 210 to Fort Morton. We have about six thousand troops cooperating with us. The rest are out in front, hotly engaging the enemy.

"We are fighting one of the greatest battles of the war, and of history. We massed our troops on the right yesterday at daylight, the gunboats covering our right flank; and soon after attacked vigorously. The Rebs resisted stoutly for a time; but ultimately we broke through their left wing, and then took them in flank. Step by step we rolled their line back on itself; and night ended with the loss of some twenty guns and two thousand prisoners on their side. This morning at daylight we advanced again, and found the Rebs had, during the night, abandoned their whole line of works. We pursued and brought them to bay some five miles off; and again attacked fiercely.

"As I write, the battle is still raging with great fury; but we have the best of reasons to suppose that night will close on a great victory. It is now 4 P. M. An hour ago, I returned from the front; and am now writing you this in my headquarters tent, near the trenches. We were up all night, and expect to remain up again to-night. But this matters not, provided we win the fight; as I think we are sure to do. Thank God! for his support thus far, and may he defend the right."

"SENIOR AND SUPERVISING QUARTERMASTER'S OFFICE,
DEPARTMENT OF THE CUMBERLAND,
NASHVILLE, TENN.
Dec. 18, 1864.

"DEAR FRIENDS: Am very well; but sadly tired out. Have been in the trenches and on the field of battle for three days and three nights, and can only say now that we have won a great and stunning victory that will carry joy to the loyal heart of the nation everywhere. You will already have seen everything in the papers.

"Praise and thanks for a man like Thomas!"

"SENIOR AND SUPERVISING QUARTERMASTER'S OFFICE,
NASHVILLE, TENN.
Dec. 26, 1864.

"DEAR FATHER AND FRIENDS: This is the day that you have set apart for Christmas, so A—— writes me. She asks me to come on and share it with you; but I can't, and so have done the next best thing, to wit, have written a telegram, and sent that instead. Hope you got it in time for dinner!

"I can't come home just now. It looks as if I was on the eve of promotion. * * * General Donaldson himself has both written and talked to Quartermaster General Meigs; and the rank, I am confident, is going to come. As the last effort in this direction, the Vice President-elect, Andrew Johnson, has written to the Secretary of War in my behalf.

## Some Army Letters

"I send you a copy of his letter for two reasons, first, that you may see that I have friends here; and second, as testimony to my standing in the army here. Andrew Johnson is not a man to say *yes*, when he means *no;* besides, he has now attained a position so exalted in the world, as second officer of the first nation on the earth, that his word will stand and be respected when the words of lesser men would be disregarded. * * *

"If I fall in this war, the testimony of Andy Johnson will survive, and our children's children will respect and honor it.[1]

"We have been and are very busy here. As you know already, we whipped Hood thoroughly on the hills about Nashville; and are now chasing him swiftly 'Away down South in Dixie's Land!' But when we got started, we found a world of work to do, in the way of rebuilding the railroads, reconstructing bridges, forwarding supplies, etc. Yesterday was Christmas, and I was scarcely out of my office, Sunday and holiday combined though it was, until late at night. To-day, we are busy again; but have deliberately run away from my office, and am now writing this in my private room. * * *

"In all respects I am pleasantly situated, and could hardly ask for more, if I had my just rank. That ought to come shortly now. * * * I live very comfortably with General Donaldson and family, in their Secesh quarters; and am treated kindly by all I care anything about. In other words, I am doing my duty, before God and Abraham Lincoln; and the country is taking care of me.

"How long I shall stay here, I cannot tell. There is some talk of being ordered to Savannah, but I guess it is only talk." * * *

---

[1] See Appendix, p. 392.

"SENIOR AND SUPERVISING QUARTERMASTER'S OFFICE,
DEPARTMENT OF THE CUMBERLAND,
NASHVILLE, TENN.
Jan. 1, 1865.

"DEAR FRIENDS: Tolerably well, and to you all I wish 'A Happy New Year!'"

"NASHVILLE, TENN.
Jan. 9, 1865.

"DEAR FRIENDS: I am still here, with no prospect of getting away for a fortnight yet. Business opens up and enlarges, as one gets fairly at it; and what I supposed a three weeks' job promises to extend to six! Such is life here!" * * *

"SENIOR AND SUPERVISING QUARTERMASTER'S OFFICE,
DEPARTMENT OF THE CUMBERLAND,
NASHVILLE, TENN.
Jan. 15, 1865.

"DEAR FRIENDS: I am very well, but too busy to write much. Have got 'Quartermaster Department on the brain,' and not fit for anything else just now."

"SENIOR AND SUPERVISING QUARTERMASTER'S OFFICE,
DEPARTMENT OF THE CUMBERLAND,
NASHVILLE, TENN.
Feb. 5, 1865.

"DEAR BROTHER: Sunday has come around again.

"Have received papers this week in considerable abundance from home, and have many thanks to somebody therefor; partly, I suppose, to you and partly to father. You are both very kind. * * *

"Things are all changed around and mixed up here. A large portion of our troops have gone East:[1] and a

---
[1] Schofield.

still larger portion gone down the Mississippi, I suppose to operate against Mobile. We haven't over thirty-five thousand men left just now. All this is *contraband;* but I say it to you here, so that you may be posted. The result, I apprehend, will be, that Donaldson and I will be ordered to Mobile or Savannah. * * * I am content."

"SENIOR AND SUPERVISING QUARTERMASTER'S OFFICE,
DEPARTMENT OF THE CUMBERLAND,
NASHVILLE, TENN.
Feb. 19, 1865.

"DEAR FRIENDS: Nothing new. Am very well, and in good spirits. Hope these lines will find you the same."

"SENIOR AND SUPERVISING QUARTERMASTER'S OFFICE,
DEPARTMENT OF THE CUMBERLAND,
NASHVILLE, TENN.
April 2, 1865.

"DEAR FRIENDS: It is Sunday again. I don't think I wrote you last Sunday; but if I didn't, I did a few days before, so it is just the same. Am sorry to say, I am not yet promoted; though I have definite information from Washington that the appointment has been ordered. If this is true, it will be along soon.

"Have been much engaged for the past month. General Donaldson has been away three weeks of the time, to Eastport, Knoxville, and Memphis on tours of inspection; and that has thrown all the work of the office on me. Too much for one man to do, though we keep eleven first-class clerks, and all busy. He got back Thursday last; but I am still weary, and considerably used up. * * *

"The spring campaign is opening, and we have our hands full. Have just finished moving into East Tennessee, by rail, forty thousand men, with their artillery, equipage, wagons, animals, all complete. It was no child's play. It was two hundred miles; and took us twenty days. I watched the thing by telegraph, night and day; and you may believe I was 'mighty' glad when the thing was all over, without a man hurt or a mule injured. It was a great tax on the brain, and I sleep better now it is done. I don't suppose we are going to have much fighting here; but if Lee wants to break through East Tennessee, and have a 'bout' with us, let him try it on!

"As you have seen by the papers, Wilson is off 'on the rampage' from Eastport. He left with a force of cavalry twelve thousand strong, for a general raid down through Mississippi and Alabama, to bring up at Mobile or perhaps Richmond, according to circumstances. What a bully time he will have! We are glad he is off; as he ate up a big pile of hay and grain every day, when here. Good luck to the bold riders, and God-speed them on their way!"

" SENIOR AND SUPERVISING QUARTERMASTER'S
OFFICE,
DEPARTMENT OF THE CUMBERLAND,
NASHVILLE, TENN.
April 12, 1865.

"DEAR FRIENDS: What grand good news we have had from all around! Not a reverse for a year! Petersburg captured, Richmond fallen, Lee surrendered! Why, it is almost too good to be true! We have been very jolly here. Nothing but cannon flying, flags firing, and people hurrahing! I have made a mistake there, about the '*flying* and *firing*,' but you know what I mean, so where's the difference?

"Am very busy, and must stop. Hurrah for the Union! Hurrah! and hurrah!"

## Some Army Letters

"SENIOR AND SUPERVISING QUARTERMASTER'S OFFICE,
DEPARTMENT OF THE CUMBERLAND,
NASHVILLE, TENN.
April 23, 1865.

"DEAR FRIENDS AT HOME: Am tolerably well to-day, and in much better spirits than last Sunday. The dull weight and pressure of the assassination[1] has worn off; and the natural spring of the American mind is bringing us all back again to the right tone and ring.

"We had a considerable time here last Wednesday. I sent you a paper giving details. There was one very striking incident. One morning early there were found scattered all over the town, posted on the corners, and lying in every doorway, little handbills, of which I send you a copy.[2] It has the most suprising effect. The most pestilent and virulent Rebels hung out flags and draped their houses in mourning. Before 9 A. M. the whole town was shrouded in blackness; and to-day there is not 'a shanty here, no matter how small, but has some piece of bunting or crape about it. 'Secesh' understands pretty well what 'Soldiers In Earnest' mean in this latitude, when the President lies murdered. If we should once *start*, we would clean this village out in less than no time; and Tennessee would know Nashville no more forever.

"What do you think of Andy Johnson by this time? Don't you think, as President, he has acquitted himself with dignity and ability, so far? You may depend upon it, he is a true and faithful American; and woe be to the

---

[1] President Lincoln's.
[2] OUR COUNTRY MOURNS.

A great and good man, the Chief Magistrate of our beloved country, has been assassinated by a fiend of this hellish rebellion.
Those who do not desire to be regarded as in sympathy with this most foul crime, are respectfully requested to show to the contrary by nine o'clock on Monday morning. Let our national emblem, appropriately draped, betoken the nation's grief, not only from the dwellings and business places of friends, but from those of its enemies also.
Treason is death ; for we swear that persistent traitors shall be extirpated.
SOLDIERS WHO ARE IN EARNEST.

traitors he lays his heavy hand on! He knows the rebellion all through. For hasn't he borne and suffered its multitudinous insults and indignities?"

> "SENIOR AND SUPERVISING QUARTERMASTER'S
> OFFICE,
> DEPARTMENT OF THE CUMBERLAND,
> NASHVILLE, TENN.
> May 5, 1865.

"DEAR FATHER AND FRIENDS: It is done. The long agony is over, and to-day I am *Colonel*, to date from April 29. No 'lieutenant colonelcy;' but *full Colonel* and *Inspector* of the quartermaster department, with headquarters at Washington. I hasten to tell you of the good news. * * *

"But I have other good news. I have also just been detailed by the Secretary of War, as member of board to examine all quartermasters south of the Ohio; and also, member of board to assemble in Washington, to revise the 'Rules and Regulations of the Army,' and prepare a 'Manual of Instructions to Quartermasters.' These are both very flattering appointments; the latter especially. All the rest of the board are regulars."

> "OFFICE INSPECTOR QUARTERMASTER
> DEPARTMENT,
> NASHVILLE, TENN.
> May 14, 1865.

"DEAR FRIENDS: I have only time to-night to say that I leave here in the morning for Chattanooga and Knoxville, on a tour of inspection. Am ordered by the quartermaster general to make an immediate inspection of all depots and posts in this department; and when that is completed, to report in Washington. It will take me probably a month; after which you may expect to see me in Jersey.

"Good-by, till I get back to Nashville."

## Some Army Letters

"OFFICE INSPECTOR QUARTERMASTER
DEPARTMENT,
NASHVILLE, TENN.
May 25, 1865.

"DEAR FRIENDS: I am here again, having got back from Chattanooga and Knoxville on Monday last, May 22. I ought to have written you then; but was busy and fagged out, and so did not.

"Things are very quiet here now. The Rebels are surrendering and coming in by hundreds, every day. They are the most completely whipped and 'subjugated' set of men you ever did see. They will make more loyal and better citizens every way than the majority of your Northern copperheads."

"OFFICE INSPECTOR QUARTERMASTER
DEPARTMENT,
NASHVILLE, TENN.
June 10, 1865.

"DEAR FRIENDS: Am afraid I forgot to write you last Sunday, as is my wont; and it is now Saturday. I have a good excuse, however; have been exceedingly busy, and have worked hard; so as to get away from here as soon as possible. I still think I shall get home by the Fourth of July; though I can't promise anything. Army life is very uncertain; and men must do, not as they want to, but must 'obey orders!'"

"OFFICE INSPECTOR QUARTERMASTER
DEPARTMENT,
NASHVILLE, TENN.
June 18, 1865.

"DEAR FRIENDS: Am glad to say, I am very well again, and standing the terrific heat of this climate quite as well as could be expected. We have had a fearful week here; but this afternoon God has sent us a thundershower, dissipating and purifying everything; and this evening, as I write, the air is again pure and balmy.

"I have just concluded my long report on the Department of the Cumberland, covering two hundred pages of writing, besides as many more of tables, etc.; and feel greatly relieved. It is in the hands of my clerks for copying, and will get off to Washington by Tuesday or Wednesday. Shall probably get orders by telegraph from Washington in a day or two; and will write you more fully then, as to my future movements."

"OFFICE INSPECTOR QUARTERMASTER DEPARTMENT,
NASHVILLE, TENN.
June 25, 1865.

"DEAR FRIENDS: I regret to find myself still here, though in daily expectation of leaving. My business is all closed up, and I have telegraphed to Washington for orders; but as yet am without any. Shall probably hear to-day or to-morrow; and will write you further.

"Since Tuesday have spent an idle week of it. It has been the laziest time I have had in two years; and doesn't agree with me. I would rather work than loaf any time; and have worked so steadily for two years past that it seems my second nature now."

"OFFICE INSPECTOR QUARTERMASTER DEPARTMENT,
NASHVILLE, TENN.
July 2, 1865.

"DEAR FRIENDS: Am just in receipt of orders to go to Chicago, Ill., and investigate certain alleged frauds there. Shall be off to-morrow, and reach there probably Wednesday.

"Can't tell how long I shall be at Chicago; but probably a week or two. Should like to hear from you there; as I have not heard from home for a week or two. Please address as usual, 'care of Chief Quartermaster, Chicago, Ill.' Will write you from there.

"Am well and in good spirits; and in a great hurry. Must get off quick."

> "OFFICE INSPECTOR QUARTERMASTER
> DEPARTMENT,
> CHICAGO, ILL.
> July 6, 1865.

"DEAR FRIENDS: Am here, safe; and from present appearances, shall be detained here for a fortnight to come. Had a hot and disagreeable ride here, from Nashville; but here there is a cool and delightful breeze.

"Am pleasantly located at the Tremont House, and receive many attentions. Only I want to get home, and must get home soon.". * * *

> "OFFICE INSPECTOR QUARTERMASTER
> DEPARTMENT,
> CHICAGO, ILL.
> July 16, 1865.

"DEAR BROTHER: Yours of the 11th is received. * * * Chicago has changed greatly since I was here six years ago. I hardly recognize it now, it has altered so. It is undoubtedly the greatest place out of New York; and if I ever go West to locate, shall pitch my shanty here.

"I have seen a good deal here. Have been introduced to the members of the Board of Trade, and treated handsomely. Have met many of their bankers and business men. Have been driven out to Camp Douglas and Hyde Park. Have been shown the Tunnels. And, on the whole, think there is more brain and nerve about Chicagoans, than any equal number of men I have ever met."

"OFFICE INSPECTOR QUARTERMASTER
DEPARTMENT,
CHICAGO, ILL.
July 23, 1865.

"DEAR FRIENDS: *At last,* I have the long-looked-for order to *come East.* Am ordered to report in person at Washington, as soon as I get through with my business here. * * *

"I expect to leave here, say, by Wednesday; and that ought to bring me to Washington by Friday. In that case, shall get home Saturday, or early in the following week. Should I be detained in Washington, will write or telegraph from there."

"UNITED STATES HOTEL, HARRISBURG, PA.
July 31, 1865. Monday morning.

"DEAR FRIENDS: Instead of being with you this morning, as I expected to, I am here at Harrisburg, on my way to Washington. Left Chicago Saturday at 5 P. M. (having been detained there), and arrived here at 3 A. M. today. Have to wait here, until 7.45 A. M. In the interval, have had two or three hours' sleep and taken breakfast, and now seize on a few minutes to drop you this.

"I expect to reach Washington this afternoon; and hope I shall not be detained there more than a day or two. At all events, expect me home by the close of the week. If anything turns up at Washington, to prevent this, will write or telegraph. My horses and most of my 'traps' are still at Nashville; but have ordered them to Washington, and will bring them home soon."

Immediately after this, I was granted a leave of absence and hastened home. This leave was afterward extended to November. Reporting for duty again, about November 18, I was ordered West and South on a tour of inspection, with a view to reduction of troops and war expenses. This took me to Chattanooga, Nashville, Louisville, Cairo, Memphis, Vicksburg, New Orleans, Mobile, Atlanta, Savannah, and Charleston; and occupied me busily until July, 1866.

Then I was ordered overland to the Pacific Coast and back *via* the Isthmus, on like duty; and did not reach Washington again until July, 1867.

I wrote similar letters home during both of these years, but they were not well preserved; and, besides, the substance of them the latter year (consisting of my overland observations and experiences) was published in a volume entitled, *Across America, or the Great West and the Pacific Coast*, in 1874, and it would be superfluous to reprint them here. Moreover, July, 1865, practically closed the war, and so naturally ends *Men and Things I Saw in Civil War Days*.

For the above inspection duty, I received the brevet of Brigadier General United States Volunteers, to date from February 16, 1866; "for faithful and meritorious services during the war." I was honorably mustered out September 17, 1867; being the *last* of six like Inspectors quartermaster department, two regulars and four volunteers.

# APPENDIX

See page 18.

From the issue of *The Christian Advocate* (New York), for February 27, 1896:

"In the year 1885 General James F. Rusling publicly related an account of an interview with President Lincoln at the sick bed of General Sickles. He had narrated this event to us at his table a number of years before, and we urged him to publish it; which, though he related it publicly in 1885, did not appear in print until October, 1891. It elicited some controversy, but the general informed us that General Sickles would undoubtedly remember it. We expressed the hope to him that in the series of war articles which he had contracted to furnish to *The Christian Advocate* he would give it in full. This promise he fulfilled; for the first of that admirable series appeared in *The Christian Advocate* of August 25, 1892, and the subject was "Abraham Lincoln." This is the account as given by General Rusling:" [Here follows the substance of pages 9 to 18, as given in said *Advocate* article.]

"Some time afterward, supposing that as soon as General Rusling died, unbelievers, after their manner, would deny the whole story, we wrote to General Sickles and received from him a response under date of March 2, 1894, inclosing a copy of a note he had written to D. A. Long, D.D., of Yellow Springs, Ohio:

"'HOUSE OF REPRESENTATIVES, U. S.
WASHINGTON, D. C., March 2, 1894.

"'J. M. Buckley, D.D.

"'DEAR SIR: Replying to your letter of the 24th ultimo, I have the pleasure to inclose a copy of a note sent to the Rev. D. A. Long to-day, replying to an inquiry identical with your own. I have been addressed so often on this subject that I am thinking seriously of having a reply stereotyped.

"'The Rev. Mr. Long asked permission to print my reply to his inquiry, to which I made no objection.

"'Sincerely yours, D. E. SICKLES.'

# Men and Things I Saw in Civil War Days

" 'March 2, 1894.
" 'The Rev. D. A. Long, D.D., LL.D., Yellow Springs, Ohio.

" 'DEAR SIR: Replying to your letter of the twenty-second ultimo, inclosing a newspaper cutting containing General Rusling's narrative of a conversation between President Lincoln and myself, when he visited me in Washington, soon after the battle of Gettysburg, early in July, 1863, I can only say, after the lapse of so many years, that I recall the general purport of what was said without undertaking to verify expressions or words used.

" 'General Rusling is a truthful, intelligent, and trustworthy gentleman; and I have no doubt that he has conscientiously given a faithful report of what took place according to his recollection. If I was sure that General Rusling made a memorandum of the conversation at the time it took place, I would indorse his statement unhesitatingly; but if written recently, and from recollection only, the narrative must be taken with some reservation as to phraseology at least.

" 'My own impression is that President Lincoln expressed a devout confidence and trust in the success of the Union arms at Gettysburg, prayerfully inspired; and that he described his convictions in earnest and touching language, characteristic of him in grave moments.          Sincerely yours, '     D. E. SICKLES.'

"This we sent immediately to General Rusling.
"From General Rusling we received the following reply:

" 'TRENTON, N. J., March 10, 1894.
" 'J. M. Buckley, D.D.

" 'DEAR SIR: In reply to yours of the eighth, I would say the conversation with President Lincoln and General Sickles took place July 5, 1863, precisely as narrated by me, but of course I do not pretend to give the exact phraseology. Doubtless it did not impress General Sickles as much as me, because he was an intimate of President Lincoln's, and often saw and talked with him, and also because he was then greatly suffering from his amputation; whereas it was my first full interview with President Lincoln, and naturally I studied him closely and all he said. Of course, I took no notes in his presence; but I wrote a letter to my father the same day. He preserved the letter, and it is now in my possession. I repeated the conversation to others immediately afterwards; and have since told it hundreds of times in private conversation, but never publicly until 1885. I think you urged me to write it out and give it to the public; but I am not positive. If you did not, many others did.

" 'In the fall of 1885, after the death of General Grant, there were memorial services held at Ocean Grove, at which Dr. Stokes, Gen-

## Appendix

eral Fisk, and myself made addresses; and in my address I gave the facts. The address was printed and I have a copy of it. In the summer of 1891, while at Ocean Grove, I had a conversation relative to it with Willis Fletcher Johnson, associate editor of the *New York Tribune*, and he urged me to send it to the *Tribune*. Accordingly I wrote it out roughly at Ocean Grove, one leisure day there; and after coming home in September or October, 1891, I rewrote it carefully and sent a copy to General Sickles for his consideration, requesting him to alter or amend as he thought best from his own best recollection of the facts. He returned it to me without altering a word, and said that while he could not recall the specific words, he still remembered the interview and some general idea of the conversation, and had no doubt my report was entirely correct.

" 'In October, 1891, I had occasion to make an address before the Young Men's Christian Association here, and as a part of my remarks read the whole paper, and submitted Mr. Lincoln to the young men as an example of a great Christian statesman. That same evening I happened to meet the editor of the *State Gazette* here, and he asked me about my address, and I told him the substance of it; including the Lincoln conversation, and the next morning he had a half column report in the *Gazette* concerning it, which presently went the rounds of the newspapers; and it now appears in Coffin's *Life of Abraham Lincoln*. In November, 1891, I sent it to Mr. Johnson, aforesaid, of the *New York Tribune*, and it appeared in full in the *Tribune* for November 29, 1891. I gave all the facts and circumstances and language there *ipsissima verba*, as nearly as I could possibly recollect; and that is as reliable as it is possible for the human mind to make anything. I gave his exact words to the best of my recollection; and I firmly believe *they were his exact words in the main, and wholly his in substance*. I had not any cause to do otherwise. I was moved only by a desire to fix what seemed to be an historic conversation that might be deemed of value in the future, and first and last I wrote the article *three* times before finally dispatching it to the *Tribune*, testing my recollection in every possible way. Afterward I condensed the statement and embodied it in my article on "Abraham Lincoln," which you printed in your *Christian Advocate* August 25, 1892.

" 'I have omitted to state that in April, 1892, I had a personal conversation with General Sickles about the matter at Jersey City during a reunion of the Second New Jersey Brigade there, and went over the conversation item by item; and while he could not, of course, remember the exact phraseology, yet he again said he well remembered the interview and conversation generally, and had no doubt of the correctness of my report.

" 'Very truly your friend,      JAMES F. RUSLING.'

## Men and Things I Saw in Civil War Days

"To our knowledge General Sickles, having refreshed his memory, recently on several occasions told the story himself in public, in particular at the annual dinner of the Loyal Legion of Washington, on February 12, 1895. It was reported in *The Press* of Philadelphia for February 23 by the regular correspondent. At the request of some of the general's comrades the story was given to *The Press* correspondent for publication, as follows:

"'I am getting to be a pretty old man, but before I die I want to tell of a meeting I had with President Lincoln shortly after the battle of Gettysburg. I desire to add it as a contribution to the memory of that grand man and as a refutation of the attempts to prove that Mr. Lincoln was not a firm believer in the Deity. I was brought to Washington badly wounded after the fight at Gettysburg. I was taken to rooms on F street, where Mr. Lincoln called on me very shortly after he learned of my arrival. I appreciated his visit very much, and it was one of the many evidences of his kind heart and sympathetic nature. After he had talked to me a few minutes in his kind, gentle way, I said to him:

"'"Mr. President, what of the future? Will we eventually put down the rebellion and restore the Union?"

"'"Well, general," he said, "until recently I sometimes had serious doubts, but I have them no longer. A few days ago I felt as if I could not do more than I had done, and that the brave men in the army had struggled long and patriotically; but success seemed as far away as in the beginning of the war. We had had our defeats as well as our victories, and the future looked gloomy. With this feeling weighing me down, I went to my closet, and on my knees I prayed to God for the success of our arms. I told Him from the depths of my soul how I had done all I could and all that human agency seemed capable of. I asked him if it was his will to grant a speedy and successful termination of the war. I prayed thus for hours; and, general, the answer came.

"'"When I arose from my knees all doubt had fled. I have from that hour had no fear of the result. We have won at Gettysburg. We have not yet had a word from Vicksburg; but, general, be prepared for great good news when it comes. All is right at Vicksburg."

"'When Mr. Lincoln was about to leave he took my hand and said very tenderly: "General, you will get well." I replied: "I don't know about that; the doctors give me but little hope." In strong, earnest tones he replied: "I am a prophet to-day general, and I say that you will get well, and that we will have glorious news from Vicksburg."

"'Several of my staff officers were present at this interview, but

## Appendix

only one of them, General Rusling, of New Jersey, is still living. I relate this incident now because I want you all to know how the great and good Lincoln put his faith in God, the Ruler of the universe.'

"We have known General Rusling since his youth, spent some years at the same preparatory school with him, and few among our acquaintances have a verbal memory of such extraordinary retentiveness."

Here is something more, of the same purport, from a conversation with President Lincoln in 1863, by Mr. Noah Brooks, afterwards editor of the *Daily Advertiser*, Newark, N. J.:

"I should be the veriest shallow and conceited blockhead upon the footstool, if, in my discharge of the duties that are put upon me in this place, I should hope to get along without the wisdom that comes from God, and not from man."—*Washington in Lincoln's Time*, page 222.

See page 30.

Curiously, since writing the foregoing, I have discovered an allusion to some such order in his "Official Report of the Peninsula Campaign" (*War Records*, Vol. XI, Part 1, page 60); and also in his *Own Story*, page 423. So, also in *War Records*, Vol. XI, Part 3, page 272, appears the following, also just discovered:

"HEADQUARTERS ARMY OF THE POTOMAC.
June 28, 1862.

"It is a matter of vital importance that all the transportation of the army should, in the movement now taking place, be employed exclusively for the carrying of ammunition and subsistence. All tents and all articles not indispensable to the safety or maintenance of the troops must be abandoned and destroyed. A reasonable supply of hospital stores will be taken, and all the intrenching tools in the possession of the troops. All unnecessary officers' baggage will be left behind; the sick and wounded that are not able to walk must necessarily be left. Every provision for their comfort must be made. Subsistence must be left and medical stores for their use in liberal quantities. Medical officers will be left in charge of the sick and wounded, and a sufficient number of attendants to supply the requisite care. They should be furnished with papers stating their character. It is enjoined upon commanders to lose no time in loading their wagons as required.

## Men and Things I Saw in Civil War Days

"The commanding general relies upon the cheerfulness and patience with which the sacrifice demanded of officers and men for the short season only, it is hoped, will be borne.

"By command of
"MAJOR GENERAL McCLELLAN.
"S. WILLIAMS, Assistant Adjutant General."

This does not seem to be the same order, but may be. At all events, it is scary and stampeding enough. But my recollection is, the order I read was briefer and more as I have given it.

See page 33.

"I told you, as I have already told him (the President), that McClellan could not be depended on to co-operate with me, and that I was sure he would fail me."—Pope to Halleck. *War Records,* Vol. XII, Part 3, page 818.

"I send you the last order from General Pope. * * * Wagons are rolling along rapidly to the rear, as if a mighty power was propelling them. * * * I hear they (Pope's army) are much demoralized and need some good troops to give them heart; and I think, head. We are working now to get behind Bull Run, and I presume will be there in a few days, if strategy don't use us up. The strategy is magnificent, and tactics in the inverse proportion. * * * I believe the enemy have a contempt for this Army of Virginia. I wish myself away from it, with all our old Army of the Potomac; and so do our companions. * * * If you can get me away, please do so."—Porter to Burnside, August 27. *War Records,* Vol. XII, Part 3, page 700.

"You will hear from us soon by way of Alexandria."—Porter to Halleck, August 28. *Ibid.,* page 717.

"I hope Mac is at work and we will soon get ordered out of this. It would seem from proper statements of the enemy, that he was wandering around loose; but I expect they know what they are doing, which is more than any one here or anywhere knows."—Porter to Halleck, August 29. *Ibid.,* page 731.

"When you contrast the policy I urge in my letter to the President [his presumptuous letter of July 7, 1862] with that of Congress and of *Mr. Pope,* you can readily agree with me, that there can be little confidence between the government and myself."—August 2. McClellan's *Own Story,* page 461.

"I will issue to-morrow an order giving my comments on *Mr. John Pope.* I will strike square in the teeth of all *his infamous*

# Appendix

*orders*, and give *directly the reverse* instructions to my army."—August 8. *Ibid.*, page 463.

"I presume Pope is having *his hands quite full* to-day; is probably being hard pressed by Jackson. I cannot help him." * * *—August 11. *Ibid.*, page 466.

"Just received a telegram from Halleck, stating Pope and Burnside are very *hard pressed;* urging me to push forward reinforcements and to *come myself as soon as I possibly can.* Shall put headquarters on board a vessel *to-morrow* morning, and *probably* go myself *to-morrow afternoon.*"—Yorktown, August 21. *Ibid.*, page 470.

In point of fact, he did not get off until August 23, 9.30 P. M., although he should have gone instantly, August 21, as a good soldier "obeying orders."

"I am clear, that one of two courses should be adopted: First, to concentrate all our available forces to open communication with Pope. Second, to *leave Pope to get out of his scrape*, and at once use all our means to make the capital perfectly safe."—McClellan to Lincoln and Halleck, August 29, 2.45 P. M. *Ibid.*, page 515.

As if he wanted to desert and abandon Pope to capture or destruction! To which he received the significant reply:

"I think your first alternative, to wit, to concentrate all our available forces to open communication with Pope, is the right one. * * * A. Lincoln."—August 29, 4.10 P. M. *Ibid.*, page 515.

See page 34.

"HEADQUARTERS ARMY OF THE POTOMAC,
SAVAGE'S STATION.
June 28, 1862, 12:20 A. M.

"The Hon. E. M. STANTON, Secretary of War: I now know the full history of the day. * * * Our men did all that men could do, but they were overwhelmed by *vastly superior* numbers. * * * Had I twenty thousand or even ten thousand fresh troops to use to-morrow, I could take Richmond; but I have not a man in reserve, and shall be glad to cover my retreat[1] and save the material and *personnel* of the army. * * * I have lost this battle because my force was too *small.*

"I again repeat, I am not responsible for this. * * * You must

---

[1] He did not call it " strategic change of base " here!

## Men and Things I Saw in Civil War Days

send me very large reinforcements, and send them at once. * * * I only wish to say to the President, that I think he is wrong in regarding me as ungenerous, when I said my force was too weak. * * * The Government must and cannot hold me responsible for the result. * * * The Government has not sustained this army. * * * If I save this army now, I tell you plainly that I owe no thanks to you or to any other persons in Washington.

"You have done your best to sacrifice this army.
"G. B. McCLELLAN."

The foregoing is from McClellan's *Own Story*, pages 424-5.

Of the same purport is his telegram of June 25, to Secretary Stanton:

"I incline to think Jackson (Stonewall) will attack my right and rear. The rebel force is stated at two hundred thousand, including Jackson and Beauregard. * * * I regret my great inferiority of numbers; but feel I am in no way responsible for it, as I have not failed to represent repeatedly the necessity of reinforcements. I will do all a general can do (with this army), and if it is destroyed by overwhelming numbers, can at least die with it and share its fate."— McClellan's *Own Story*, page 393.

Here is Mr. Lincoln's pathetic reply, June 26 (*War Records*, Vol. XI, Part 3, page 259):

"Your despatch of yesterday, suggesting the probability of your being overwhelmed by two hundred thousand, and talking of where the responsibility belongs, pains me very much. I give you all I can, and act on the presumption that you will do the best you can with what you have; while you continue ungenerously, as I think, to assume that I could give you more if I would. I have omitted and shall omit no opportunity to send you reinforcements whenever I possibly can. A. LINCOLN."

Here also is Mr. Stanton's grave and dignified reply, not to the foregoing telegrams, indeed, but to the whole McClellan complaint (*War Records*, Vol. XIX, Part 2, pages 725-8):

"[Private and confidential.]
WASHINGTON, May 18, 1862.
"The Rev. Heman Dyer.

"MY DEAR FRIEND: Yours of the sixteenth is welcomed as an evidence of the continued regard of one whose esteem I have always been anxious to possess. I have been very well aware of the calumnies busily circulated against me in New York and elsewhere,

## Appendix

respecting my relations to General McClellan; but am compelled, from public considerations, to withhold the proofs that would stamp the falsehood of the accusations and the base motives of the accusers, who belong to two classes: First, plunderers, who have been driven from the department, where they were gorging millions; second, scheming politicians, whose designs are endangered by an earnest, resolute, uncompromising prosecution of this war, as a war against rebels and traitors.

"A brief statement of facts, an official record, which I can make to you confidentially, will be sufficient to satisfy yourself that your confidence in me has not been misplaced.

"When I entered the Cabinet I was, and for months had been, the sincere and devoted friend of General McClellan; and to support him, and, so far as I might, aid and assist him in bringing the war to a close, was a chief inducement for me to sacrifice my personal happiness to a sense of public duty. I had studied him earnestly, with an anxious desire to discover the military and patriotic virtue that might save the country; and if in any degree disappointed, I hoped on, and waited for time to develop.

"I went into the Cabinet about the twentieth of January. On the twenty-seventh the President made his 'War Order, No. 1,' requiring the Army of the Potomac to *move*. It is not necessary, or perhaps proper, to state all the causes that led to that order; but it is enough to know that the Government was on the verge of bankruptcy, and, at the rate of expenditure, the armies must move or the Government perish. The twenty-second of February was the day fixed for the movement, and when it arrived there was no more sign of movement on the Potomac than there had been for three months before. Many, very many, earnest conversations I had held with General McClellan, to impress him with the absolute necessity of active operations, or that the Government would fail because of foreign intervention and enormous debt.

"Between the twenty-second of February and the eighth of March, the President had again interfered; and a movement on Winchester and to clear the blockade of the Potomac was promised, commenced, and abandoned. The circumstances cannot at present be revealed.

"On the sixth of March, the President again interfered, ordered the Army of the Potomac to be organized into army corps, and that operations should commence immediately.

"Two lines of operations were open. First, moving directly on the enemy by Manassas, and forcing him back on Richmond, beating and destroying him by superior force; and all the time keeping the capital secure by being between it and the enemy. This was the plan favored by the President. The second plan was to transfer the troops by water to some point on the Lower Chesapeake, and thence advance on Richmond. This was General McClellan's plan. The President reluctantly yielded his own views, although they were supported by some of the best military men in the country, and consented that the general should pursue his own plan. But, by a written order, he imposed the special condition that the army should not be moved without leaving a sufficient force in and around Washington to make the capital perfectly secure against all danger; and that the force required should be determined by the judgment of all the commanders of the army corps.

"In order to enable General McClellan to devote his whole energy to the movement of his own army (which was quite enough to tax the ability of the ablest commander in the world), he was relieved from the charge of the other military departments; it being supposed that their respective commanders were competent to direct the operations in their own departments. To enable General McClellan to transport his force, every means and power of the Government were placed at his disposal and unsparingly used.

"When a large part of his force had been transferred to Fortress Monroe, and the whole of it about to go in a few days, information was given to me by various persons that there was great reason to fear that no adequate force had been left to defend the capital in case of a sudden attack; that the enemy might detach a large force, and seize it at a time when it would be impossible for General McClellan to render any assistance. Serious alarm was expressed by many persons, and many warnings given me, which I could not neglect. I ordered a report of the force left to defend Washington. It was reported by the commander to be less than twenty thousand raw recruits, with not a single organized brigade! A dash, like that made a short time before at Winchester, would at any time take the capital of the nation. The report of the force left to defend Washington, and the order of the President, were referred to Major General Hitchcock and Adjutant General Thomas to report: First, whether the President's orders had been complied with; second, whether the force left to defend the city was sufficient.

"They reported in the negative on both points. These reports were submitted to the President, who also consulted General Totten, General Taylor, General Meigs, and General Ripley. They agreed in opinion that the capital was not safe.

"The President then, by written order, directed me to retain one of the army corps for the defense of Washington, either Sumner's or McDowell's. As part of Sumner's corps had already embarked, I directed McDowell to remain with his command, and the reasons were approved by the President.

## Appendix

"Down to this period there had never been a shadow of difference between General McClellan and myself. It is true that I thought his plan of operations objectionable, as the most expensive, the most hazardous, and the most protracted that could have been chosen; but I was not a military man, and, while he was in command, I would not interfere with his plan, and gave him every aid to execute it. But when the case assumed the form it had done by his disregard of the President's order, and by leaving the capital exposed to seizure by the enemy, I was bound to act; even if I had not been required by the specific written order of the President. Will any man question that such was my duty?

"When this order was communicated to General McClellan, it of course provoked his wrath, and the wrath of his friends was directed upon me, because I was the agent of its execution. *If the force had gone forward, as he had designed, I believe that Washington would this day be in the hands of the rebels.* Down to this point, moreover, there was never the slightest difference between the President and myself. But the entreaties of General McClellan induced the President to modify his order to the extent that Franklin's division (being part of McDowell's corps that had been retained) was detached and sent forward by boat to McClellan. This was against my judgment, because I thought the whole force of McDowell should be kept together and sent forward by land on the shortest route to Richmond, thus aiding McClellan, but at the same time covering and protecting Washington by keeping between it and the enemy. In this opinion Major General Hitchcock, General Meigs, and Adjutant General Thomas agreed. But the President was so anxious that General McClellan should have no cause of complaint, that he ordered the force to be sent by water, although that route was then threatened by the Merrimac. I yielded my opinion to the President's order; but between him and me there has never been the slightest shadow since I entered the Cabinet. And, excepting the retention of the force under McDowell by the President's order, for the reasons mentioned, General McClellan has never made a request or expressed a wish that has not been promptly complied with, if in the power of the Government. To me, personally, he has repeatedly expressed his confidence and his thanks in the dispatches sent me.

"Now, one word as to political motives. What motive can I have to thwart General McClellan? I am not now, never have been, and never will be a candidate for any office. I hold my present post at the request of a President who knew me personally, but to whom I had not spoken from the fourth of March, 1861, until the day he handed me my commission. I knew that everything I cherished and held dear would be sacrificed by accepting office. But I thought I might help to save the country, and for that I was willing to perish. If I wanted to be a politician or a candidate for any office, would I stand between the Treasury and the robbers that are howling around me? Would I provoke and stand against the whole newspaper gang in this country, of every part, who, to sell news, would imperil a battle? *I was never taken for a fool, but there could be no greater madness than for a man to encounter what I do for anything else than motives that overleap time and look forward to eternity. I believe that God Almighty founded this Government, and for my acts in the effort to maintain it I expect to stand before Him in judgment.*

"You will pardon this long explanation, which has been made to no one else. It is due to you, who was my friend when I was a poor boy at school, and had no claim upon your confidence and kindness. It cannot be made public for obvious reasons. General McClellan is at the head of our chief army; *he must have every confidence and support;* and I am willing that the whole world should revile me rather than *diminish one grain of the strength needed to conquer the rebels.* In a struggle like this, justice or credit to individuals is but dust in the balance. Desiring no office nor honor, and anxious only for the peace and quiet of my home, I suffer no inconvenience beyond that which arises from the trouble and anxiety suffered by worthy friends like yourself, who are naturally disturbed by the clamors and calumny of those whose interest or feeling is hostile to me.

"The official records will, at the proper time, fully prove—

"1—That *I have employed the whole power of the Government unsparingly to support General McClellan's operations in preference to every other general.*

"2—That I have not interfered with or thwarted them in any particular.

"3—That the force retained from his expedition was not needed and could not have been employed by him; that it was retained by express orders of the President, upon military investigation, and upon the best military advice in the country; that its retention was required to save the capital from the danger to which it was exposed by a disregard of the President's positive order of the sixth of March.

"4—That between the President and myself there has never been any, the slightest, shadow of difference upon any point; save the detachment of Franklin's force, and that was a point of no significance, but in which I was sustained by Generals Hitchcock, Meigs, Thomas, and Ripley; while the President yielded only to an anxious desire to avoid complaint, declaring at the same time his belief that the force was not needed by General McClellan.

## Appendix

"You will, of course, regard this explanation as being in the strictest confidence, designed only for your information upon matters wherein you express concern for me. The confidence of yourself, and men like you, is more than a full equivalent for all the railing that has been or can be expressed against me; and in the magnitude of the cause all merely individual questions are swallowed up.

"I shall always rejoice to hear from you, and am, as ever,

"Truly yours, EDWIN M. STANTON."

This sums up the whole business, and reads like a mastiff answering a poodle or a whiffet.

Read also the following choice extracts from McClellan's *Own Story:*

"Don't worry about the wretches [in Washington]. * * * I am sure I will win in the end, in spite of all their rascality. * * * History will present a sad record of these traitors, who are willing to sacrifice the country and its army."—McClellan's *Own Story,* page 310.

"I do not know what paltry trick the Administration will play next."—July 10, 1862. *Ibid.,* page 446.

"I have no faith in the Administration."—July 13, 1862. *Ibid.,* page 447.

"So you like my letter to the President? [his extraordinary letter of July 7, 1862, in which he presumed to dictate to Mr. Lincoln how he should carry on the war, without abolishing slavery or hurting the rebels much, etc.] You do not feel one bit more bitterly towards those people than I do. I do not say much about it, but I fear they [the Administration] have done all that cowardice and folly can do to ruin our poor country."—July 17, 1862. *Ibid.,* page 449.

"If our dear Government will show some faint indication of brains or courage, we can finish the work in a short time."—July 18, 1862. *Ibid.,* page 450.

"I owe no gratitude to any one but my own soldiers here; none to the Government or to the country. * * * They are my debtors, not I theirs."—*Ibid.,* pages 450-51.

"Marcy and I have just been discussing people in Washington, and conclude that they are 'a mighty trifling set.' * * * I begin to believe that they wish this army to be destroyed."—July 31, 1862. *Ibid.,* page 460.

## Men and Things I Saw in Civil War Days

And then, after wasting a month at Harrison's Landing, and doing nothing there as usual, when Mr. Lincoln in sheer despair ordered him back to Alexandria, he wrote (in disobedience of said orders):

"I hope to be ready to-morrow afternoon to move *forward in the direction of Richmond.* I will try to catch or thrash Longstreet [much *he* would have thrashed Longstreet!]; and then, if the chance offers, follow him to Richmond, while they are *lamming* away at Pope. It is in some respects a desperate step, but * * * I would rather even be defeated than retreat without an effort to relieve Washington. * * * If I fail, why, well and good, I will fall back. * * * I half apprehend they will be too quick for me in Washington, and relieve me before I have the chance of making the dash. * * * I am satisfied that the *dolts in Washington* are bent on my destruction, if it is possible for them to accomplish it."—August 10, 1862. *Ibid.,* page 465.

Of course, he never did it! Catch "Little Mac" doing any such aggressive thing! But here was proposed "disobedience of orders," and *how could he record it deliberately,* nearly a quarter of a century afterwards?

It is true, part of the above are from his private letters to Mrs. McClellan. But they show his *animus* in 1862, and what language for a Major General commanding our chief Union army!

General Lew Wallace (author of *Ben Hur*) in a recent speech (February 12, 1898) accuses McClellan of an intention to surrender to Lee; but his only evidence seems to be in a gloomy remark of President Lincoln, in July, 1862, after our arrival at James River, when he said to Wallace one day in Washington: "I must go to Harrison's Landing *to keep McClellan from surrendering the army.*" I give this for what it is worth; but it seems to be only a fear or suspicion of Mr. Lincoln's at the utmost.

See page 74.

Said Mr. Lincoln, in a characteristic letter to General Halleck, urging action by the Army of the Potomac:

"General Meade estimates the enemy in front of him at not less than forty thousand. Suppose, stretching as far back as Richmond and including everything, his whole force is sixty thousand; General Meade, as shown by his returns, has with him and between him and Washington * * * over ninety thousand. Neither can bring the whole

# Appendix

into battle, but each can bring as large a percentage as the other. For a battle, then General Meade has three men to General Lee's two. * * * If the enemy's sixty thousand are sufficient to keep our ninety thousand away from Richmond; why, by the same rule, may not forty thousand of ours keep their sixty thousand away from Washington, leaving us fifty thousand to put to some other use? * * * With no object, certainly, to mislead myself, I can perceive no fault in this statement, unless we admit *we are not the equal of the enemy, man for man.*"—*War Records*, Vol. XXIX, Part 2, page 207.

See page 55.

I think the letters of General Lee, relating to General Kearny, his sword, horse, etc., so touching and striking, and so honorable to both, that I append them here (*War Records*, Vol. XII, Part 3, page 807):

"HEADQUARTERS ARMY OF NORTHERN VIRGINIA,
September 2, 1862.

"Major General John Pope, United States Army.

"SIR: The body of General Philip Kearny was brought from the field last night, and he was reported dead. I send it forward under a flag of truce, thinking the possession of his remains may be a consolation to his family.

"I am, sir, respectfully, your obedient servant,

"R. E. LEE, General."

From the *War Records*, Vol. XIX, Part 2, page 645:

"HEADQUARTERS ARMY OF NORTHERN VIRGINIA,
CAMP NEAR WINCHESTER, VA.
October 4, 1862. Received October 7, 1862.

"The Hon. George W. Randolph,
"Secretary of War, Richmond, Va.

"SIR: Mrs. Phil Kearny has applied for the sword and horse of Major General Phil Kearny, which were captured at the time that officer was killed, near Chantilly. The horse and saddle have been turned over to the quartermaster of the army, and the sword to the chief of ordnance. I would send them at once, as an evidence of the sympathy felt for her bereavement, and as a testimony of the appreciation of a gallant soldier; but I have looked upon such articles as public property, and that I had no right to dispose of them, except for the benefit of the service. In this case, however, I should like to depart from this rule, provided it is not considered improper by the department; and I therefore refer the matter for your decision. An early reply is requested.

"I am, sir, very respectfully, your obedient servant,
"R. E. LEE, General."

(Indorsement.)
"October 8, 1862.

"The return of the horse and sword is authorized.
"G. W. RANDOLPH."

From the *War Records,* Vol. XIX, Part 2, page 381:

"HEADQUARTERS ARMY OF NORTHERN VIRGINIA,
October 4, 1862.

"Major General George B. McClellan,
"Commanding Army of the Potomac.

"GENERAL: I have the honor to inclose a letter to Mrs. Philip Kearny, and at the same time commit to your care the sword, horse, and saddle of Major General Kearny; which fell into our hands at the time of his death. Mrs. Kearny expressed a great desire to obtain the sword and horse of her husband, and I beg leave to hope that it may be convenient to you to forward them to her.

"The horse has accompanied the march of the army since its capture, and may have suffered from the journey. The bridle was either lost at the time of the capture or has not been recovered.

"I am, most respectfully, your obedient servant,
R. E. LEE, General Commanding."

From the *War Records,* Vol. XIX, Part 2, page 384:

"HEADQUARTERS ARMY OF THE POTOMAC,
October 5, 1862.

"General R. E. Lee,
"Commanding Army of Northern Virginia.

"GENERAL: I have the honor to acknowledge the receipt of your letter of the fourth instant, inclosing a letter to Mrs. Philip Kearny; and, at the same time, committing to my care the sword, horse, and saddle of Major General Kearny, to the end that, in accordance with the expressed wish of Mrs. Kearny, they may be placed in her keeping. The articles have been received and, with the letter, will be forwarded to Mrs. Kearny by the earliest opportunity. I beg you to accept my thanks for your courteous and humane attention to the request of the widow of this lamented officer. I shall be happy to

## Appendix

reciprocate the courtesy when circumstances shall place it in my power to do so.

"Very respectfully, your obedient servant,

"GEORGE B. MCCLELLAN, Major General Commanding."

The last sentence in General McClellan's letter seems unfortunate. But, of course, he meant it all right.

### See page 105.

Here is another estimate of Thomas, that accords with mine, and is well worth reading:

"Man was never born more true. He was essentially cast in a large mould, in mind and body; so modest that he shrank from command, for which he is peculiarly fitted; with courage of the stamp that ignores self; possessing steadfastness in greater measure than audacity, he yet lacked none of that ability which can deal heavy blows; while no antagonist was ever able to shake his foothold. Honesty in thought, word, and deed, was constitutional with him. A thorough military training, added to a passionate love of his profession and great natural powers, made him the peer of any soldier. Uniformly successful in all he undertook, from Mill Spring to Nashville, he has left a memorable name and an untarnished reputation. He perhaps falls as little short of the model soldier, as any man produced by this country."—Dodge's *Civil War*, page 301.

### See page 104.

Prior to the battle both Halleck and Grant had complained of Thomas. But now congratulations and compliments rained in upon him from all quarters, as follows (*War Records*, Vol. XLV, Part 2, pages 195, 210, 230, and 471):

"WAR DEPARTMENT, WASHINGTON,
December 15, 1864, 12 midnight.

"Major General Thomas,

"Nashville:

"I rejoice in tendering to you and the gallant officers and soldiers of your command the thanks of this Department for the brilliant achievements of this day; and hope that it is the harbinger of a decisive victory, that will crown you and your army with honor and do much toward closing the war. We shall give you a hundred guns in the morning.

"EDWIN M. STANTON, Secretary of War."

# Men and Things I Saw in Civil War Days

"WASHINGTON, D. C.,
December 15, 1864, 11:45 P. M.

"Major General Thomas,
"Nashville, Tenn.:

"Your dispatch of this evening just received. I congratulate you and the army under your command for to-day's operations, and feel a conviction that to-morrow will add more fruits to your victory.

"U. S. GRANT, Lieutenant General."

"WASHINGTON, D. C.,
December 16, 1864. Sent 11:25 A. M.

"Major General Thomas,
"Nashville, Tenn.:

"Please accept for yourself, officers, and men the nation's thanks for your good work of yesterday. You made a magnificent beginning. A grand consummation is within your easy reach. Do not let it slip. A. LINCOLN."

"HEADQUARTERS ARMY OF THE POTOMAC,
December 17, 1864, 6:30 P. M. Sent 6:40 P. M.

"Hon. E. M. Stanton:

"I congratulate the President, yourself, and the country on the glorious victory achieved by Major General Thomas and the troops under his command. I have directed a salute of one hundred guns to be fired to-morrow at sunrise in honor of this brilliant triumph.

"GEORGE G. MEADE, Major General Commanding."

"HEADQUARTERS ARMY OF THE SHENANDOAH,
December 17, 1864. Received on the eighteenth.

"Major General G. H. Thomas:

"The Army of the Shenandoah, through me, send their hearty congratulations to yourself and army for the brilliant victory at Nashville on the fifteenth and sixteenth instant. We have given you two hundred guns and much cheering.

"P. H. SHERIDAN, Major General Commanding."

"CLARKSVILLE,
December 17, 1864.

"Major General G. H. Thomas:

"I have the honor to acknowledge receiving, and to thank you for the early telegraphic copy of, your admirable official report to the President of your great and glorious victory over the enemy of our country and of mankind on the fifteenth and sixteenth instant. I am

## Appendix

deeply impressed with the belief that our whole country will now or hereafter appreciate the generalship, statesmanship, and patriotism of your campaign, resulting in the signal defeat of General Hood's army, in which centered the strength and hopes of half the rebellion; with little loss, under great difficulties, and with probably political consequences and more important than have followed previous achievements of the war. Permit me on this occasion to express my humble admiration of your distinguished public services, which evince all the high qualities of virtue, patriotism, and ability, characteristic of our first great countryman.

"Respectfully and faithfully yours,

"S. P. LEE, Acting Rear Admiral,
"Commanding Mississippi Squadron."

"NASHVILLE,
January 1, 1865.

"Major General George H. Thomas:

"The effect of the great victory over Hood's army at Nashville is being seen and felt in every part of the State; its withering influence upon rebels is more decided than anything which has transpired since the beginning of the rebellion. * * * It is not necessary for me to say that you have a nation's gratitude for what you have done in preserving the Government of the United States; but my prayer is that all your future efforts in the preservation of the Union may be, as the past has been, crowned with success and unfading honor.

"ANDREW JOHNSON, Military Governor of Tennessee."

See page 104.

Notwithstanding all Thomas had done, and was still doing, in spite of wind and weather, to smite Hood and destroy his army, Halleck (who had never done anything in the field himself) sent him this ungracious and uncalled-for telegram (*War Records*, Vol. XLV, Part 2, page 295):

"WASHINGTON,
December 21, 1864, 12 M. (Via Nashville, Tenn.)

"Major General Thomas:

"Permit me, general, to urge the vast importance of a hot pursuit of Hood's army. Every possible sacrifice should be made, and your men for a few days will submit to any hardship and privation to accomplish the great result. If you can capture or destroy Hood's army, Sherman can entirely crush out the rebel military force in all the Southern States. He begins a new campaign about the first of January, which will have the most important results, if Hood's army can now be used up. A most vigorous pursuit on your part is, therefore, of vital importance to Sherman's plans. No sacrifice must be spared to attain so important an object.

"H. W. HALLECK, Major General and Chief of Staff."

To which Thomas promptly made this crushing reply (*Ibid.*, pages 295, 296):

"HEADQUARTERS DEPARTMENT OF THE CUMBERLAND,
IN THE FIELD, December 21, 1864.

"Major General H. W. Halleck,
"Washington, D. C.:

"Your dispatch of 12 M. this day is received. General Hood's army is being pursued as rapidly and as vigorously as it is possible for one army to pursue another. We cannot control the elements, and, you must remember, that to resist Hood's advance into Tennessee I had to reorganize and almost thoroughly equip the force now under my command. I fought the battles of the fifteenth and sixteenth instant with the troops but partially equipped; and, notwithstanding the inclemency of the weather and the partial equipment, have been enabled to drive the enemy beyond Duck River; crossing two streams with my troops, and driving the enemy from position to position, without the aid of pontoons, and with but little transportation to bring up supplies of provisions and ammunition. I am doing all in my power to crush Hood's army, and, if it be possible, will destroy it; but pursuing an enemy through an exhausted country, over mud roads, completely sogged with heavy rains, is no child's play, and cannot be accomplished as quickly as thought of.

"I hope, in urging me to push the enemy, the Department remembers that General Sherman took with him the complete organizations of the military division of the Mississippi, well equipped in every respect as regards ammunition, supplies, and transportation; leaving me only two corps, partially stripped of their transportation, to accommodate the force taken with him, to oppose the advance into Tennessee of that army which had resisted the advance of the army of the military division of the Mississippi on Atlanta, from the commencement of the campaign until its close, and which is now, in addition, aided by Forrest's cavalry. Although my progress may appear slow, I feel assured that Hood's army can be driven from Tennessee, and eventually driven to the wall, by the force under my command; but too much must not be expected of troops which have to be reorganized, especially when they have the task of destroying

## Appendix

a force in a winter campaign which was able to make an obstinate resistance to twice its number in spring and summer. In conclusion, I can safely state that this army is willing to submit to any sacrifice to oust Hood's army, or to strike any other blow which would contribute to the destruction of the rebellion.

"GEORGE H. THOMAS, Major General."

Halleck had blundered, as usual; and now Stanton and Grant took a hand, as follows (*Ibid.*, page 307):

"WAR DEPARTMENT, WASHINGTON.
December 22, 1864, 9 P. M.

"Major General Thomas,
"In the Field:

"I have seen to-day General Halleck's dispatch of yesterday and your reply. It is proper for me to assure you that this Department has the most unbounded confidence in your skill, vigor, and determination to employ to the best advantage all the means in your power to pursue and destroy the enemy. No Department could be inspired with more profound admiration and thankfulness for the great deeds you have already performed, or more confiding faith that human effort could accomplish no more than will be done by you and the gallant officers and soldiers of your command.

"EDWIN M. STANTON, Secretary of War."

"CITY POINT, VA.
December 22, 1864.

"Major General Thomas,
"Nashville, Tenn.:

"You have the congratulations of the public for the energy with which you are pushing Hood. I hope you will succeed in reaching his pontoon bridge at Tuscumbia before he gets there. Should you do it, it looks to me that Hood is cut off. If you succeed in destroying Hood's army, there will be but one army left to the so-called Confederacy capable of doing us harm. I will take care of that and try to draw the sting from it, so that in the spring we shall have easy sailing. You now have a big opportunity, which I know you are availing yourself of. Let us push and do all we can before the enemy can derive benefit either from the raising of negro troops or the concentration of white troops now in the field.

"U. S. GRANT, Lieutenant General."

Here is Thomas's grateful acknowledgment (*Ibid.*, page 319):

"COLUMBIA, TENN.,
December 23, 1864, 8 P. M.   Received 1 A. M.
on the twenty-fifth.

"Hon. E. M. Stanton,
"Secretary of War, Washington, D. C.:

"Your two dispatches of 9 P. M., twenty-second instant are received. I am profoundly thankful for the hearty expression of your confidence in my determination and desire to do all in my power to destroy the enemy and put down the rebellion; and, in the name of this army, I thank you for the complimentary notice you have taken of all connected with it for the deeds of valor they have performed. * * *

"GEORGE H. THOMAS,
"Major General United States Volunteers Commanding."

But here was something more to the purpose (*Ibid.*, pages 318, 328, and 329):

"CITY POINT, Va.,
December 23, 1864, 6 P. M.

"Hon. E. M. Stanton,
"Secretary of War:

"I think it would be appropriate now to confer on General Thomas the vacant major generalcy in the regular Army. He seems to be pushing Hood with energy; and I doubt not but he will completely destroy that army.

"U. S. GRANT, Lieutenant General."

"WAR DEPARTMENT, WASHINGTON,
December 24, 1864, 3:18 P. M.   (Via Nashville, Tenn.)

"Major General George H. Thomas,
"Headquarters Department of the Cumberland:

"With great pleasure I inform you that for your skill, courage, and conduct in the recent brilliant military operations under your command, the President has directed your nomination to be sent to the Senate as a major general in the United States Army, to fill the only vacancy existing in that grade. No official duty has been performed by me with more satisfaction, and no commander has more justly earned promotion by devoted, disinterested, and valuable service to his country.

"EDWIN M. STANTON, Secretary of War."

# Appendix

And here is Thomas's manly answer (*Ibid.*, page 342):

"HEADQUARTERS DEPARTMENT OF THE CUMBERLAND,
MCKANE'S CHURCH, PULASKI ROAD,
December 25, 1864, 8 A. M. (Received 6 P. M.)

"The Hon. Edwin M. Stanton,
"Secretary of War, Washington, D. C.:

"I am profoundly sensible of your kind expressions in your telegram of December 24, informing me that the President had directed my name to be sent to the Senate for confirmation as major general, United States Army, and I beg to assure the President and yourself that your appreciation of my services is of more value to me than the commission itself.

"GEORGE H. THOMAS,
"Major General United States Volunteers Commanding."

And here was something more (*War Records*, Vol. XLV, Part 1, page 51):

"PUBLIC RESOLUTION, No. 24.—Joint Resolution of thanks to Major General George H. Thomas and to the army under his command:

"Be it resolved by the Senate and House of Representatives of the United States of America in Congress assembled, That the thanks of Congress are due, and are hereby tendered, to Major General George H. Thomas and the officers and soldiers under his command for their skill and dauntless courage, by which the rebel army under General Hood was signally defeated and driven from the State of Tennessee.

"Approved March 3, 1865."

Afterwards he learned of the Logan incident (to relieve him at Nashville, etc.); and here is how he felt about it, and justly so (*War Records*, Vol. XLV, Part 2, page 561):

"CHIEF QUARTERMASTER'S OFFICE,
"DEPARTMENT OF THE CUMBERLAND, NASHVILLE, TENN.,
January 10, 1865.

"Major-General M. C. Meigs,
"Quartermaster-General, Washington.

"DEAR GENERAL: * * * Thomas left yesterday for Eastport, where he is concentrating. I saw him on board, and he opened his heart to me. He feels very sore at the rumored intentions to relieve him

## Men and Things I Saw in Civil War Days

(by Logan), and the major generalcy does not cicatrize the wound. You know Thomas is morbidly sensitive, and it cut him to the heart to think that it was contemplated to remove him. He does not blame the Secretary, for he said Mr. Stanton was a fair and just man. * * *

"Very truly yours,
"J. L. DONALDSON, Chief Quartermaster."

He did not then know that Schofield (his subordinate) had also been ordered to relieve him, nor did he learn of this until years afterward; and then it broke his heart, or seemed to. For soon afterward he was found dead, in his quarters at San Francisco, with his records and order-books around him, writing a vindication of his Nashville campaign.

Here is his congratulatory order to his army, at the close of the campaign. This chapter would not be complete without it (*War Records*, Vol. XLV, Part I, pages 50, 51):

"*General Orders,*
"No. 169.

"HEADQUARTERS DEPARTMENT OF THE CUMBERLAND,
PULASKI, TENN.,
December 29, 1864.

"SOLDIERS: The major general commanding announces to you that the rear guard of the flying and dispirited enemy was driven across the Tennessee River on the night of the twenty-seventh instant. The impassable state of the roads and consequent impossibility to supply the army compels a closing of the campaign for the present.

"Although short, it has been brilliant in its achievements and unsurpassed in its results by any other of this war, and is one of which all who participated therein may be justly proud. That veteran rebel army which, though driven from position to position, opposed a stubborn resistance to much superior numbers during the whole of the Atlanta campaign; taking advantage of the absence of the largest portion of the army which had been opposed to it in Georgia, invaded Tennessee, buoyant with hope, expecting Nashville, Murfreesborough, and the whole of Tennessee and Kentucky to fall into its power an easy prey, and scarcely fixing a limit to its conquests; after having received the most terrible check at Franklin, on the thirtieth of November, that any army has received during this war, and later met with a signal repulse from the brave garrison of Murfreesborough in its attempt to capture that place; was finally attacked at

## Appendix

Nashville, and, although your forces were inferior to it in numbers, it was hurled back from the coveted prize upon which it had only been permitted to look from a distance; and finally sent flying, dismayed and disordered, whence it came; impelled by the instinct of self-preservation, and thinking only how it could relieve itself for short intervals from your persistent and harassing pursuits by burning the bridges over swollen streams as it passed them; until finally it had placed the broad waters of the Tennessee River between you and its shattered, diminished, and discomfited columns; leaving its artillery and battle-flags in your victorious hands, lasting trophies of your noble daring and lasting mementoes of the enemy's disgrace and defeat.

"You have diminished the forces of the rebel army, since it crossed the Tennessee River to invade the State, at the least estimate, fifteen thousand men; among whom were killed, wounded, or captured eighteen general officers.

"Your captures from the enemy, as far as reported, amount to sixty-eight pieces of artillery, ten thousand prisoners, as many stand of small arms, several thousand of which have been gathered in, and the remainder strew the route of the enemy's retreat, and between thirty and forty flags; besides compelling him to destroy much ammunition and abandon many wagons; and, unless he is mad, he must forever relinquish all hope of bringing Tennessee again within the lines of the accursed rebellion. * * *

"By command of Major General Thomas,
"WILLIAM D. WHIPPLE, Assistant Adjutant General."

Here is Mr. Lincoln's comment on Hood, and one of his best stories:

"Out in Illinois, in my country, there was a certain rough, rude, and bullying man, who had a bulldog, which was as rough, rude, and bullying as his master. Dog and man were the terror of the neighborhood. Nobody dared to touch either for fear of the other. But a crafty neighbor laid a plan to dispose of the dog. Seeing Slocum plodding along the road one day, his dog a little ahead, this neighbor took from his pocket a chunk of meat, in which he had concealed a big charge of powder, to which he had fastened a Deadwood slow-match. This he lighted, and then threw all into the road. The dog gave one gulp at it, and the whole thing disappeared down his throat. He trotted on a few steps, when there was a sort of smothered roar, and the dog blew up in fragments—a forequarter lodging in a neighboring tree, a hindquarter on the roof of a cabin, his head in one place, his tail in another, and the rest scattered along the dusty road.

Slocum came up and 'viewed the remains.' Then, more in sorrow than in anger, he said: 'Bill was a good dog; but, as a dog, I reckon his usefulness is over!'

"Hood's army was a good army," the President added, with a twinkle of his eye. "We have been very much afraid of it. But, as an army, I reckon, its usefulness is gone!"—Brooke's *Washington in Lincoln's Time*, page 293.

See page 108.

The whole letter is so patriotic and characteristic, that I quote it here entire (from Sherman's *Memoirs*, Vol. I, page 155):

"LOUISIANA STATE SEMINARY OF LEARNING
AND MILITARY ACADEMY,
January 18, 1861.

"Governor Thomas O. Moore, Baton Rouge, Louisiana.

"SIR: As I occupy a quasi-military position under the laws of the State, I deem it proper to acquaint you that I accepted such position when Louisiana was a State in the Union, and when the motto of this seminary was inserted in marble over the main door, 'By the liberality of the General Government of the United States. The Union—esto perpetua.'

"Recent events foreshadow a great change and it becomes all men to choose. If Louisiana withdraw from the Federal Union, I prefer to maintain my allegiance to the Constitution, as long as a fragment of it survives; and my longer stay here would be wrong, in every sense of the word.

"In that event, I beg you will send or appoint some authorized agent to take charge of the arms and munitions of war belonging to the State, or advise me what disposition to make of them.

"And, furthermore, as president of the board of supervisors, I beg you to take immediate steps to relieve me as superintendent, the moment the State determines to secede; for on no earthly account will I do any act or think any thought hostile to or in defiance of the old Government of the United States.

"With great respect, your obedient servant,

"W. T. SHERMAN, Superintendent."

See page 118.

What Congress then thought of him is well expressed in the following joint resolution (*Ibid.*, Vol. II, page 229):

# Appendix

"Joint resolution tendering the thanks of the people and of Congress to Major General William T. Sherman, and the officers and soldiers of his command, for their gallant conduct in their late brilliant movement through Georgia:

"*Be it resolved, by the Senate and House of Representatives of the United States of America, in Congress assembled,* That the thanks of the people and of the Congress of the United States are due and are hereby tendered to Major General William T. Sherman, and through him to the officers and men under his command, for their gallantry and good conduct in their late campaign from Chattanooga to Atlanta, and the triumphal march thence through Georgia to Savannah, terminating in the capture and occupation of that city; and that the President cause a copy of this joint resolution to be engrossed and forwarded to Major General Sherman.

"Approved January 10, 1865."

See page 129.

In answer to some criticism of General Sheridan, because absent from his command, when attacked at Cedar Creek; I would say, I have carefully weighed all I have found on both sides, and believe the facts fully exonerate him.

On October 13 he received a telegram from Secretary Stanton, requesting him to come to Washington, as he "proposed to visit General Grant and wanted to see him [Sheridan] first." He got ready to go; but the enemy being reported on the offensive, he delayed starting until satisfied they were too distant or too feeble to do much; and October 16 rode through Manassas Gap to the terminus of the railroad from Washington. Here he received another order from General Halleck to "come to Washington;" and taking the cars with his staff and horses arrived at Washington next morning "about eight o'clock." Soon afterward he reported to Mr. Stanton at the War Department, and the first thing he did was to request "a special train to be ready at twelve o'clock" to take him back to Martinsburg, with his staff and horses. Then he held a consultation with Stanton and Halleck, as to the facts and matters of his military department, comparing views, etc., that they had not been able otherwise to exchange. Promptly "at twelve o'clock" he left Washington for Winchester and Cedar Creek, *via* Martinsburg. He arrived at Martinsburg about dark; and found his escort of three hundred cavalry ready, which he had ordered while at Cedar Creek.

Early next morning, October 18, he mounted and started for Winchester, but did not reach there till between 3 and 4 P. M., though the distance is only twenty-eight miles, because of having two engineer officers with him from Washington, who were unaccustomed to horseback riding and could go no faster. Immediately, however, he despatched a courier to the front for a report of affairs there; and then took one of his new engineers to a height overlooking Winchester, "in order that he might overlook the country, and make up his mind as to the utility of fortifying there." By the time they had completed their survey "it was dark," and his courier returned from Cedar Creek "bringing word that everything was all right." So, about 10 P. M., he went to bed, "greatly relieved and expecting to regain headquarters at [his] leisure next day."

Early on the 19th, about 6 A. M., a picket officer came to his room (Sheridan being yet in bed) and reported artillery firing in the direction of Cedar Creek, "not sustained, but irregular and fitful." Sheridan concluded, this was only a reconnoissance that had been ordered; but grew restless and soon got up and dressed himself. A little later, the officer came back and reported, that the firing still continued, but he did not think it a battle." However, Sheridan requested "breakfast to be hurried and ordered the horses saddled," and about 8.30 A. M. was in the saddle and *en route* to the front.

Soon he grew anxious, the cannonading continuing; and presently as he rode forward there burst upon his view "the appalling spectacle of a panic-stricken army—hundreds of slightly wounded men, throngs of others unhurt but utterly demoralized, and baggage-wagons by the score, all pressing to the rear in hopeless confusion; telling only too plainly that a disaster had occurred at the front." Then putting spurs to Rienzi, he galloped to the front, rallying the stragglers and taking many back with him, and by 10:30 A. M. was at Cedar Creek, and in due time wrested victory from defeat.

Clearly he was not in error in going to Washington, and deserves great credit for his expedition, prudence, and heroism. It is true, it is claimed for General Wright, that he would have whipped Early all the same. But then, he might not. We only know, that he was surprised. And that Sheridan got there on time, and did the business handsomely. See Sheridan's *Memoirs*, Vol. II, pages 60 to 90.

# Appendix

See page 134.

It seems to me, this chapter on "Sheridan" would not be complete without Thomas Buchanan Read's "Sheridan's Ride;" and so I quote it here entire. It may not be precisely accurate; but it photographs and voices the whole "situation" so well, both horse and man, that it deserves to live forever in American song and story:

### SHERIDAN'S RIDE.

" Up from the south, at break of day,
Bringing to Winchester fresh dismay,
The affrighted air with a shudder bore,
Like a herald in haste to the chieftain's door,
The terrible grumble and rumble and roar,
Telling the battle was on once more,
   And Sheridan twenty miles away.

"And wider still those billows of war
Thundered along the horizon's bar;
And louder yet into Winchester rolled
The roar of that red sea uncontrolled,
Making the blood of the listener cold,
As he thought of the stake in that fiery fray,
   And Sheridan twenty miles away.

" But there is a road from Winchester town,
A good broad highway leading down;
And there, through the flush of the morning light,
A steed as black as the steeds of night
Was seen to pass, as with eagle flight;
As if he knew the terrible need,
He stretched away with his utmost speed;
Hills rose and fell; but his heart was gay,
   With Sheridan fifteen miles away.

" Still sprang from those swift hoofs, thundering south,
The dust, like smoke from the cannon's mouth,
Or the trail of a comet, sweeping faster and faster
Foreboding to traitors the doom of disaster.
The heart of the steed and the heart of the master
Were beating like prisoners assaulting their walls,
Impatient to be where the battlefield calls;
Every nerve of the charger was strained to full play,
   With Sheridan only ten miles away.

"Under his spurning feet, the road,
Like an arrowy Alpine river flowed;
And the landscape sped away behind,

Like an ocean flying before the wind;
And the steed, like a bark fed with furnace ire,
Swept on, with his wild eye full of fire.
But lo! he is nearing his heart's desire;
He is snuffing the smoke of the roaring fray,
　　With Sheridan only five miles away.

'The first that the general saw were the groups
Of stragglers, and then the retreating troops;
What was done? what to do?—a glance told him both;
Then striking his spurs, with a terrible oath,
He dashed down the line, 'mid a storm of huzzas,
And the wave of retreat checked its course there, because
The sight of the master compelled it to pause.
With foam and with dust the black charger was gray;
By the flash of his eye and the red nostril's play,
He seemed to the whole great army to say:
'I have brought you Sheridan all the way
From Winchester down to save the day!'

Hurrah! hurrah for Sheridan!
Hurrah! hurrah for horse and man!
And when their statues are placed on high,
Under the dome of the Union sky—
The American soldiers' Temple of Fame—
There with the glorious general's name
Be it said in letters both bold and bright:
　'Here is the steed that saved the day,
By carrying Sheridan into the fight,
　　From Winchester, twenty miles away!'"

　　　　　See page 140.

His enemies and detractors said he was "drunk," of course. But here is the exact fact:

"During this visit I reviewed Banks's Army, a short distance above Carrollton. The horse I rode was vicious and but little used; and on my return to New Orleans ran away, and shying at a locomotive on the street fell, probably on me. I was rendered insensible; and when I regained consciousness, I found myself in a hotel near by, with several doctors attending me. My leg was swollen from the knee to the thigh, and the swelling almost to the point of bursting extended along the body up to the arm-pit. The pain was almost beyond endurance. I lay at the hotel something over a week, without being able to turn myself in bed. I had a steamer stop at

## Appendix

the nearest point possible, and was carried to it on a litter. I was then taken to Vicksburg, where I remained unable to move for some time afterward."—Grant's *Memoirs*, Vol. I, pages 581-2.

See page 144.

In reply to the charge of Grant's unscientific fighting and heavy losses, 1864-5, I beg to say, it is true he lost heavily; but he lost less in beating Lee and taking Richmond, than McClellan and other commanders did in failing to do so. The aggregate losses of McClellan, from April 5, 1862, to August 8, 1862, during his Peninsula Campaign, from Yorktown back to Yorktown again (accomplishing nothing—*returning to the same spot from which he started*), exclusive of his sick, were twenty-four thousand four hundred and forty-eight.[1] So, the aggregate losses of McDowell, McClellan, Burnside, Hooker, and Meade, from Bull Run, July 21, 1861, to Brandy Station or Culpeper, May 4, 1864, with Lee still "in full feather" and Richmond safe as ever, were one hundred and forty-three thousand nine hundred and twenty-five. The total losses of General Grant from the Rapidan, May 4, 1864, to Appomattox, April 9, 1865, were one hundred and twenty-four thousand three hundred and ninety, which is nineteen thousand five hundred and thirty-five less than the others. It is conceded, these figures are large; but then he "got there," and "finished the business."

See *McClure's Magazine*, May, 1898, page 34. The Hon. Charles A. Dana, ex-assistant secretary of war, had these figures compiled from records of War Department.

See page 158.

Here is the "Parole of General Robert E. Lee and staff," which will likely interest many readers of this volume (*War Records*, Vol. XLVI, Part 3, page 667):

"We, the undersigned prisoners of war belonging to the Army of Northern Virginia, having been this day surrendered by General Robert E. Lee, Confederate States Army, commanding said army, to Lieutenant-General U. S. Grant, commanding Armies of the United States, do hereby give our solemn parole of honor that we will not hereafter serve in the armies of the Confederate States, or in any military capacity whatever, against the United States of America, or

---
[1] See p. 38.

render aid to the enemies of the latter, until properly exchanged, in such manner as shall be mutually approved by the respective authorities.

"Done at Appomattox Court House, Virginia, this ninth day of April, 1865.

"R. E. LEE, General.
"W. H. TAYLOR, Lieutenant Colonel and Assistant Adjutant General.
"CHARLES S. VENABLE, Lieutenant Colonel and Assistant Adjutant General.
"CHARLES MARSHALL, Lieutenant Colonel and Assistant Adjutant General.
"H. E. PEYTON, Lieutenant Colonel, Adjutant and Inspector General.
"GILES B. COOKE, Major and Assistant Adjutant and Inspector General.
"H. E. YOUNG, Major, Assistant Adjutant General, and Judge Advocate General.

(Indorsement.)

"The within-named officers will not be disturbed by the United States authorities so long as they observe their parole and the laws in force where they may reside.

"GEORGE H. SHARPE, Assistant Provost Marshal General."

Here is General Lee's "Farewell Address" to his army, which seems most touching and pathetic in the light of these after years (*War Records*, Vol. XLVI, Part 3, page 744):

"GENERAL ORDERS,
  "No. 9.
                "HEADQUARTERS ARMY OF NORTHERN VIRGINIA,
                        April 10, 1865.

"After four years of arduous service, marked by unsurpassed courage and fortitude, the Army of Northern Virginia has been compelled to yield to overwhelming numbers and resources. I need not tell the brave survivors of so many hard-fought battles, who have remained steadfast to the last, that I have consented to the result from no distrust of them. But, feeling that valor and devotion could accomplish nothing that could compensate for the loss that may have attended the continuance.of the contest, I determined to avoid the

## Appendix

useless sacrifices of those whose past services have endeared them to their countrymen. By the terms of the agreement officers and men can return to their homes and remain until exchanged. You will take with you the satisfaction that proceeds from the consciousness of duty faithfully performed; and I earnestly pray that a merciful God will extend to you his blessing and protection. With an unceasing admiration of your constancy and devotion to your country, and a grateful remembrance of your kind and generous consideration for myself, I bid you all an affectionate farewell.

"R. E. LEE, General."

Here is Grant's general "pass" to Lee, after his surrender; and he took good care it was respected, even by President Johnson (*Ibid.*, page 686):

"APPOMATTOX COURT HOUSE, VA.,
April 10, 1865.

"All officers commanding posts, pickets or detachments will pass General R. E. Lee through their lines north or south on presentation of this pass. General Lee will be permitted to visit Richmond at any time, unless otherwise ordered by competent authority, and every facility for his doing so will be given by officers of the United States Army to whom this may be presented.

"U. S. GRANT, Lieutenant General."

See page 165.

Here is a valuable and suggestive letter from the *Evening Post*, of New York, that well supplements and illustrates Chapter XII:

### "THE COST OF THE WAR.

"It is interesting and important to inquire what war actually is. In one of its phases, the question has been broadly answered by Camille Flammarion, who a few years ago made an historic study of the ruin wrought by war, and out of his research evolved some striking facts and figures. 'How many men are destroyed by war in a century?' he asked, and responded:

" 'We know that during the unaccountable Franco-German war of 1871 250,000 men were slain on the two sides; that during the Crimean war of 1854-'55 785,000 were slain; that during the short Italian war of 1859 63,000 men fell on the field of battle or died in hospitals; that the game of chess between Prussia and Austria in 1866 deprived 46,000 individuals of life; that in the United States the strife between the North and South caused the death of 450,000 men in 1860-'64; we know also that the wars of the First Empire poured out the blood of 5,000,000, and that France has taken up arms twenty times since 1815. On adding the number of victims of war during the last century, a total of 19,840,900 is reached in the civilized countries of Europe and in the United States.

" 'Commencing with the Trojan war, the case has been the same in all ages of history. Certain remarkable battles, fought hand to hand with knife or club, have had the memorable honor of leaving as many as 200,000 men dead on the field; as examples we cite the defeat of the Cimbrians and the Teutons by Marius, and the last exploits of Attila. Eighteen to twenty million men are killed every century in Europe by the enlightened institution of war. If these men, averaging thirty years of age, should join hands, they would form a line 4,500 leagues long, crossing all Europe and Asia.

" 'A great amount of money is necessary in order to kill in proper manner, for each man slain costs about $7,000. The increasing and multiplying taxes of all nations are never sufficient to pay for the butchery of human troops. Every year Europe spends more than $1,200,000,000 in shedding her children's blood; and France spends $400,000 every day.'

"When it is considered that the onward movement of the world in civilization has been wholly along the line of industrial development, the withdrawal of this great mass of human effort and accumulated capital from the world's business is appalling in itself. But when we reflect that war is, after all, only a duel between nations, and that the duel between individuals, from which it is copied, is merely a survival of the old superstition concerning the efficacy of the ordeal by combat in punishing wrong and promoting justice, it seems incomprehensible that in this unsuperstitious age even a handful of educated and intelligent men would seek war deliberately as long as there is any possibility of avoiding it. The trouble with a war is not confined to the immediate havoc which it causes. Its after effects are in some respects worse than those directly in view, for it leaves the seeds of moral and economic disease in the blood of a nation.

"This must be familiar to all Americans old enough to have lived through the Civil War and witnessed the struggles of the nation to get back to its old moorings, even after peace has reigned for more than thirty years. But to the younger generation, who have not seen and taken part in these struggles, at each successive stage, this reasoning is not so comprehensible. A clearer view of the economic side of war may be presented to them by considering how much they are now paying out of their own pockets for the satisfaction their fathers and grandfathers felt in making war upon their own brethren

# Appendix

before the present generation was born. A glance over the appropriation acts for the fiscal year 1898 presents this matter in a striking light. For convenience of reference, the items may be placed in a table, as follows:

| SUBJECTS. | APPROPRIATIONS. |
|---|---:|
| War claim for gold seized by United States Government in rebel territory in 1865. | $16,987 00 |
| Certified claims for pay and bounty, about. | 9,000 00 |
| Court of Claims cases, general, relating to Civil War, about | 1,007,700 00 |
| Horse claims and quartermasters' accounts, about. | 800 00 |
| Repairing old auditors' rolls, about. | 20,000 00 |
| Records of the Rebellion, army. | 130,380 00 |
| Records of the Rebellion, navy. | 36,930 00 |
| Record and Pension Office, War Department, share for the Civil War, about. | 591,430 00 |
| Record and Pension Office, Ford's Theater disaster damages. | 34,750 00 |
| Pensions: | |
| For payments to veterans, their widows and children. | 140,000,180 00 |
| Salaries in Pension Office, Washington. | 2,086,759 45 |
| Salaries of special examiners. | 195,000 00 |
| Expense of investigating claims. | 450,000 00 |
| Fees of examining surgeons. | 700,167 75 |
| Salaries of agency clerks. | 430,000 00 |
| Salaries of pension agents. | 72,177 44 |
| Rents of agencies in other than public buildings, repairs, fuel, lights, and contingent expenses, about. | 75,000 00 |
| National cemeteries. | 100,000 00 |
| National cemeteries, superintendents' salaries. | 61,880 00 |
| National cemeteries, headstones. | 25,000 00 |
| Artificial limbs, or commutation therefor, for maimed veterans. | 183,171 73 |
| Commutation of rations to ex-prisoners of war and furloughed soldiers. | 4,177 25 |
| Soldiers' Homes: | |
| Dayton, Ohio. | 567,200 00 |
| Milwaukee, Wis. | 276,500 00 |
| Togus, Me. | 265,800 00 |
| Hampton, Va. | 350,000 00 |
| Leavenworth, Kan. | 295,100 00 |
| Santa Monica, Cal. | 219,611 37 |
| Marion, Ind. | 188,383 04 |
| Danville, Ill. | 150,000 00 |
| General and incidental expenses. | 260,422 59 |
| Aid to State and territorial homes. | 880,000 00 |
| National military parks: | |
| Chickamauga and Chattanooga. | 93,045 00 |
| Gettysburg. | 50,935 00 |
| Shiloh. | 60,000 00 |
| Road-making, site-marking, and other incidentals. | 34,225 00 |
| Estimate for Potomac Memorial Bridge. | 2,500 00 |
| Total. | $149,925,122 62 |

"In round numbers, $150,000,000. Yet this list is not complete, for it leaves out of account all permanent appropriations; a number of petty annual appropriations which individually seem inconsiderable, but would swell the aggregate by some thousands; and, finally, the proportional but inseparable shares of large general appropriations which some of the enumerated items ought to have added to them. This last category includes the court costs, the legal fees, etc., involved in defending the government against suits on war claims; the cost of housing several of the pension offices in government buildings, all of which goes into the account of the Treasury Department as custodian of these buildings; and the like.

"One additional item we cannot afford to pass over, because it is so easy of calculation and makes so large a part of the grand total. That is the bonded debt of the nation. In 1860 the national debt stood at an almost insignificant figure—less than $65,000,000. By 1866 it had risen to $2,773,236,173, in consequence of the Civil War and its economic aftermath. By heroic efforts and many sacrifices we have succeeded in cutting down the principal of the debt to a little more than $1,800,000,000, and its annual interest charge to $34,387,315; hence the proportion of interest alone which may now be set down as an annual burden imposed by the Civil War is $33,000,000. Posterity will have the principal to pay; so that, formidable as it appears, that need not enter into our present calculation. The interest charge, added to the total of direct annual appropriations already noted in our table, brings the grand total up to about $183,000,000.

"Here, then, we have the amount of money still squeezed out of the pockets of our own people in a single year—and not an extravagant year, either—as their contribution toward a war which was fought before a majority of our present taxpayers were born or had attained responsible age.

"No statistics can tell the whole story of war even on the side which reduces it all to dollars and cents. The charge upon our whole people for pensions is only a part of the total pension charge; for the states of Alabama, Arkansas, Florida, Georgia, Louisiana, Maryland, Mississippi, Missouri, North Carolina, South Carolina, Tennessee, Texas, and Virginia are supporting their own pensioners who fought in the Confederate army, and as a State tax the money for each pension payroll or soldiers' home must come out of the pockets of the people of the State concerned. Again, in several of the States the people are still paying interest charges on money advanced to equip regiments, bounties to encourage enlistments, etc. Not a few Northern States are supporting soldiers' homes of their own, to which the federal government merely contributes a certain sum, as noted in our table; and to these must be added such direct and indirect expenditures as the erection of war monuments, by State appropriations, the remission of taxes to veterans, and the increase of

## Appendix

insanity and pauperism demanding relief from the State treasuries, and traceable to the losses and misery entailed by the Civil War.

"The necessary limits of space forbid deeper research into this subject. But though merely the surface has been upturned, has it not disclosed enough to raise the question, how much further the world might have advanced in civilization and comfort of living, if this great volume of money had been turned into the channels of industry and popular education, instead of being wasted on *the spilling of blood and the destruction of property ?* L."

The above gives graphically the cost of our Civil War on our own side mainly. But when one considers the Confederate side, it becomes almost incomputable. It is true, they did not lose so many men; but what did they not lose in railroads smashed, in fences and buildings burned, in crops and live-stock destroyed, in whole States ravaged, and especially in the wide swath of Sherman's march from Chattanooga to Atlanta, and from Atlanta to Savannah and Raleigh? It seems not too much to say, that the Rebellion cost the South at least five billions of dolllars, if not more, and cost the nation first and last (on both sides), at least a million of lives and ten billions of dollars.

See page 4 of Preface.

Here are extracts from a few letters, official reports, etc., that may interest somebody:

"HEADQUARTERS THIRD BRIGADE, SECOND DIVISION, THIRD CORPS,
April 13, 1863.

"I have known Captain James F. Rusling in the army since August, 1861, as regimental, brigade and division officer. He has always been efficient and prompt in attending to his duties, and I take great pleasure in recommending him for increased rank.

"G. MOTT, Brigadier General Volunteers."

"HEADQUARTERS SECOND DIVISION, THIRD CORPS,
April 20, 1863.

"Captain Rusling has served at these headquarters for the past six months—the last three months under my command. Intelligent, industrious, and devoted to duty, I consider him one of the best officers in the volunteer service, and take great pleasure in recommending him for promotion.

"H. G. BERRY, Major General."

# Men and Things I Saw in Civil War Days

"STATE OF TENNESSEE, EXECUTIVE DEPARTMENT,
NASHVILLE, Dec. 23, 1864.

"The Hon. E. M. Stanton,
"Secretary of War.

"DEAR SIR: I would respectfully ask your personal attention to the case of my friend, Captain[1] James F. Rusling, assistant quartermaster volunteers, Chief Assistant Quartermaster Department of the Cumberland, now before the quartermaster general, or in your own office, recommended for appointment as Chief Quartermaster of the depot here at Nashville, with the rank of Colonel. This depot, as you know, is now one of the largest in the Union, and has no chief quartermaster, as such; and Captain Rusling was recommended for the appointment by Brevet Brigadier General J. L. Donaldson, chief quartermaster Department of the Cumberland, now several weeks ago. Rusling has been General Donaldson's Chief Assistant here for now over twelve months, and has been before recommended for equivalent promotion, namely, as Inspector Quartermaster's Department, by Generals Hooker, Thomas, Donaldson, and others. He has been an earnest anti-slavery man since 1856; entered the army nearly four years ago; was made captain and assistant quartermaster volunteers in June, 1862—and I personally know him to be a man of character and ability—sober, steady, industrious; formerly a lawyer at Trenton, N. J.—and thus well fitted, as I believe, for the position indicated.

"In making this recommendation, I am of the opinion, that the interests of the public service will be advanced, and a worthy and deserving officer promoted, and it will, at the same time, fix an obligation on me, which will be duly appreciated.

"I have the honor to be,
"Very respectfully,
"Your obedient servant,

"ANDREW JOHNSON, Vice President-elect United States."

"HEADQUARTERS MILITARY DIVISION TENNESSEE,
NASHVILLE, TENN., July 1, 1866.

"Brevet Brigadier General James F. Rusling, Inspector, reported to me December 29, 1865. I at once assigned him to inspecting the Division wherever I thought a correcting hand was needed. The field was large, and the work diverse (embracing Kentucky, Ten-

---

[1] By United States law the rank of lieutenant colonel ceased when an officer ceased to serve at corps headquarters. Hence was *captain* again from July 1863, though higher in place and duties.

## Appendix

nessee, Mississippi, Alabama, and Georgia), requiring some nerve to do it effectually and impartially. General Rusling performed it to my entire satisfaction, reducing and cutting off without fear, favor, or affection; and this is the highest praise I can accord anyone. I commend him to your favorable notice as one who has done much to aid in reducing expenses in this division.

"J. L. DONALDSON, Brevet Major General United States Army."

"WASHINGTON, D. C.,
July 9, 1868.

"You fearlessly exposed errors and abuses, and always rendered very valuable service to the department. I gladly bear testimony to the zealous fidelity with which you entered upon and performed most responsible duties.

"M. C. MEIGS, Brevet Major General United States Army."

"WATERTOWN, N. Y.,
July 24, 1868.

"I have always regarded your war record as having been firmly and nobly established, wherever you served. Throughout the war your record for gallant conduct and meritorious services is unimpeachable. Many times have you placed me under personal obligations to you by your devoted services; and I have no doubt such is the fact with every commander with whom you have served. It is not necessary for me to say more.

"Your friend and servant,

"JOSEPH HOOKER, Major General United States Army."

"NEW YORK, July 26, 1868.

"In the campaigns of '62 and '63 you were on duty in the field with me, and your duties were all performed to my entire satisfaction. In every position you exhibited all the characteristic traits of an efficient officer, and in the movements intervening between Antietam and Fredericksburg, as well as Chancellorsville and Gettysburg campaigns especially, your vigilance, energy, zeal, and gallantry won honorable mention on frequent occasions. Afterward in '66 and '67, in your capacity as inspecting officer, your labors resulted in large reductions in the expenditures of the Government, and in salutary administrative reforms.

"Your friend and comrade.

"D. E. SICKLES, Brevet Major General United States Army."

## Men and Things I Saw in Civil War Days

"HEADQUARTERS DEPARTMENT OF THE CUMBERLAND,
LOUISVILLE, KY., July 11, 1868.

"General James F. Rusling reported for duty at Nashville, Tenn., in November, 1863, and continued with me until April, 1865. During all this time, and especiallly during the siege of Nashville and Hood's campaign, he proved himself an active and efficient officer.

"GEORGE H. THOMAS, Major General United States Army."

"HEADQUARTERS MILITARY DIVISION OF THE MISSOURI,
ST. LOUIS, July 30, 1868.

"General Rusling's reputation in the West was always good, and the indorsement of such a person as General George H. Thomas is sufficient for me to add my name.

"W. T. SHERMAN, Lieutenant General United States Army."

Extracts from reports of General Donaldson, senior and supervising quartermaster, Department of the Cumberland, 1864-5.

"I cannot conclude this report without calling your attention to the following-named officers on duty at this depot, to whom I feel largely indebted for the efficiency and success attending my operations: to Captain James F. Rusling, assistant quartermaster volunteers, on duty in my office as Chief Assistant Quartermaster, for faithfulness and energy, and for unwearied attention to the multifarious business necessarily centering here; thus leaving my own mind free for the more general operations of the department."—*War Records*, Vol. LII, Part 1, supplement, page 623.

"Captain James F. Rusling, assistant quartermaster volunteers, was my Chief Assistant Quartermaster from December 1, 1863, to April 29, 1865, when he received his appointment as Inspector Quartermaster Department. During the Atlanta campaign and afterward he was of great assistance to me in the work of supplying the army; and I witnessed his well-earned promotion with pleasure."—*War Records*, Vol. LII, Part 1, supplement, page 688.

Extracts from report of Secretary of War, etc., 1866-7:

"The officers who have been on inspection duty have accomplished a great amount of work during the year, pointing out the places and mode of effecting great economies. Inspections by Brevet Brigadier General James F. Rusling have been particularly extensive, thorough,

## Appendix

and useful. His various inspections in the States included in the Military Division of the Tennessee (1865-6) resulted in great reductions of material and personnel, and in great consequent economies. General Rusling is now engaged upon a minute inspection of the Posts on the route to San Francisco, and in those of the Military Division of the Pacific, and his reports give clear and precise information of the operations, necessities, and defects of the service in those remote districts, which is especially valuable."—Page 62, Senate edition.

Again:

"General Rusling has faithfully performed his arduous duties. His appointment, as Inspector, was fitly made. In his tour to the Pacific coast, he is giving a full, faithful, and valuable report of his operations, which will be of great value to the Department. He has fairly earned the brevet of Brigadier General United States Volunteers lately conferred upon him by the War Department."—Page 338.

"The actual reductions in the expenses of the government, resulting from inspections made by officers of this department, cannot be closely estimated. Brevet Brigadier General James F. Rusling, however, has embodied in his annual report a tabular statement, showing that at the depots and posts inspected by him, from about June 30, 1865, to July 31, 1866, the current expenses prior to his inspections aggregated $1,508,160.42 per month—the number of employees being twenty-one thousand five hundred and sixty-three; that he made recommendations involving a reduction of the expenditures to $512,806, and the employees to nine thousand and nine; that these reductions were for the most part carried out, involving a saving to the department of nearly one million dollars per month."—Page 340.

See page 165.

In our recent war with Spain our casualties from May 1, 1898, to February 28, 1899, were only as follows: Killed, 329; died of wounds, 125; died of disease, 5,277; total, 5,731.

# INDEX

## A

"A soldier's life is always gay," 167
Abolitionists, 321
Abbott, Capt. Joseph, 284
"Across America," 353
Accounts with U. S., 280, 284
Acquia Creek, 65, 231, 232
Albany, 166
Alabama, 305, 336
Alleghanies, 135
Allen, Gen. Robert, a great Quartermaster, 174; sufficient unto himself, 174; many great commanders Quartermasters previously, 174; Chief Quartermaster Military Division Mississippi, 174; at West Point, 174; in Mexico, 174; on Pacific Coast, 175; before the war, 177, 178; at Corinth, 178; his personal traits, 178; at St. Louis, 175, 176, 179; during Vicksburg campaign, 179, 181; at Louisville, 182, 183; with Sherman, 184; his report on Nashville, 184; his great work at Louisville, 185, 186; his vast disbursements, 187; his immense supplies, 188; approximate estimate of his services, 188; a soldier and a gentleman, 189
Alexander, 120, 145, 155
Alexandria, 32, 33, 44, 55, 70, 191, 197-199, 201-203, 221
Ambulances, 166
American Republic indivisible on line of Slavery, 17, 152; the raw recruit of the Nations, 161; its great men and great destiny, 161; God speed it, 161
American Revolution, 80
American Senate, 20
Among strangers beware, 314
An army a city on legs, 165; like a snake, 166
Anacostia, 224
Annandale, 32
Anderson, Gen., 151
Andersonville, horrors of, 150, 162
Angel of the Third Corps, 190; Woman in the war, 190; Soldier's Children's Home, 190; Mother Bickerdyke, 190; Miss Gilson, 190; her "outfit," 191; in camp, 191; at the White House, Va., 191; on James River, 192; at Potomac Creek, 193; our Florence Nightingale, 193; at Falmouth, 193; in South Carolina, 194
Antæus, 70
Antietam, 18; a drawn battle, 34, 41, 44, 55, 61, 63, 125; Lee worsted there, 150, 154
Antislavery utterances, 223
Antwerp, Siege of, 153
Appomattox, 18; Lee's surrender there, 132; the bells of, 144; the end of all things, 145, 153, 157
Appendix, 355
Apples, 214
Arkansas, 179
Army, what it is, 165, 166
Army Chaplains, 217
Army Corps, Organization by, 57
Army Inspections, some idea of, 393-395
Army Letters, 3, 195; from Washington, 195, 202, 204-206, 209, 215; from Alexandria, 197, 199, 201; from Charlotte Hall, 203; from Lower Potomac, 207, 208, 211, 212, 214, 216, 219, 221, 222, 224, 227, 236; James River, 237; Fortress Monroe, 238, 241; Yorktown, 242; Williamsburg, 244; West Point, 248; New Kent Court House, 249; Twenty-one miles from Richmond, 251; Bottom Bridge, 253; Savage Station, 255; Fair Oaks, 257, 260, 261; Harrison's Landing, 263; Washington, D. C., 267; Alexandria, 269; Fort Lyon, 273; near Alexandria, 274-280; Manassas Junction, 282; Washington, D. C., 284; Falmouth, 286-301; Boscobel, 302-305; Washington, D. C., 306; Frederick, 307; Headquarters Army of Potomac, 309; Cincinnati, 309; Nashville, 310-350; Chicago, 351; Harrisburg, 352
Army nurses, 190, 191
Army record of author, 4
Army roads, 214, 216, 217, 221, 249, 250, 255, 295
Army of the Cumberland, 80, 181
Army of the Mississippi, 189
Army of Northern Virginia, 143, 153

Army of the Potomac, 17, 24, 30, 36, 43, 44, 52, 53; losses at Fair Oaks, 259; on Peninsula, 37–40; under Grant, 153; generally, 385; at Fredericksburg, 56; condition after Fredericksburg, 56, 57, 59, 61, 68, 72; trains of, 74, 79, 164, 186, 189, 190
Arnold, Benedict, 23
Assassination of Lincoln, 17, 347
Asylum at Washington, Hooker there, 63
Atlanta Campaign, 59, 60, 83; capture of Atlanta, 84, 142, 144, 154, 170, 183, 186
Austerlitz, 24

## B

Badeau's *Life of Grant*, 4, 163
Baggage-destroying order of McClellan at Fair Oaks, 29, 359
Baker, Gen. E. D., 23; his death, 25
Balaclava, 68
Ball's Bluff, 25
Baltimore Cross Roads, 253
Banks, Gen. N. B., 223
Barracks, 177
Barry, Gen. W. F., 112
Barstoe, Capt. Samuel, his death in hospital, 241
Basis of Volume, 3
"Battle above the Clouds," Hooker's, 59
Battlefield at Fair Oaks, 259
Battle, front and rear of, 171
Battles in Civil War, 164
Battle of Nashville, 341
Bayard, Chevalier de, 54
Bayard, Gen. Geo. D., killed at Fredericksburg, 46
Be careful among strangers, 314
Bealton, 306
Beauregard, Gen. P. T., 81, 336, 362
Beef on hoof, 160
Bells of Appomattox, 144
Belvidere, 288
Ben Hur, 368
Berry, Gen. H. G., 296; fell at Chancellorsville, 301; recommends the author for promotion, 391
Bickerdyke, Mother, 190
Big Bethel, 22, 24
Big Black, Grant and Sherman at, 140
Birney, Gen., 296
Bishop Simpson at Nashville, 316
Board of Survey, 213
"Bob," 295
Books good things, 329
Bordentown, 317
Boscobel, 302, 304, 305
Boston, 185, 188, 191
"Botany Bay," 78
Bottom Bridge, 253
Bragg, Gen. Braxton, 5; at Stone River, 82;

at Chickamauga and Chattanooga, 82, 83, 141, 181
Brandy Station, 78
Brass Castle, N. J., 283
Brave contraband, 257
Brave men, 171
Breckinridge, J. C., as Vice President, 20
Brentsville, 75, 76
Bridgeport, 59
Brigade Bakeries, 57
Brigade Quartermaster, 203, 220
Bristoe, 30, 54; Generals Hill and Warren there, 76, 272
Brooks, Noah, on Lincoln, 359
Buchanan, James, as President, 8, 18, 20
Buckley, Rev. J. M., 355, 356; commendation of author, 355, 359
Budd's Ferry, 206
Buell, Gen. D. C., 223
Buena Vista, 164
Buford, Gen. John, at Gettysburg, 68
Building stables, 205
Bull Run, 24, 44; Hooker and Kearny at, 54, 74, 150, 228
Bunker Hill, 164
Burns, Robert, 329
Burnside, Gen. A. E., 41; ordered to relieve McClellan, 43; at Roanoke and Antietam, 44; in command of Army of the Potomac, 44; marches on Fredericksburg, 44; his pontoon train, 44; a bad march, 45; personal appearance, 45; battle of Fredericksburg, 45; his Mud March, 50; lacked confidence in himself, 50; in East Tennessee, 51; unfit to command Army, 56, 57, 132, 136, 142, 151, 152; the Blunderer, 155, 223, 232, 283, 292
Busy at Nashville, 316, 322, 338
Butler, Gen. B. F., 79
"By the Eternal," 319
"By the Left Flank, Forward!" 144, 153

## C

Cæsar, 120, 145, 163
Cairo, 17, 176, 177, 180, 181, 353
California, 175
Cameron, Hon. S., 18
Campaigning and soldiering, 159; Who wouldn't be a soldier? 159; discomforts and hardships, 159; "policing," 160; rations and fuel, 160; foraging, 160; drill and march, and march and drill, 160; shelter tents, 161; hard march, 161; corduroy roads, 161; digging trenches, 161; sentry duty, 162; getting "plugged," 162; malaria, 163; the battlefield, 163; losses in battle, 164, 165; what an army is, 165; different departments, 166; commander in chief controls

# Index

all, 167; army disabilities, 167; pensions, 168; victory pays for all, 169; Sherman on, 169, 173
Campbell, Judge, 86
Camp Detestable, 222
Camp life, around Washington and on Lower Potomac, 202, 206, 212, 214, 221; before Yorktown, 243; at night, 250; at Fair Oaks, 259, 260; in general, 280, 281, 287, 291, 293, 299
Capitol Hill, 195
Carlyle and his "job of work," 144
Carolinas, 60, 118, 154, 163
Carr, Gen. J. B., 64, 273, 275, 276
Carson, Kit, 119; his personal appearance, 121; Sherman's opinion of him, 122
Carthage, 179
Casey, Gen. S., 203
Casey's Division, 255, 258
Catlett's Station, 74
Cavalier, 139
Cedar Creek, 128, 129, 144
Cemetery Hill, 69
Center grand division, 55
Centreville, 25, 32, 33, 73-77, 273, 306, 309
*Century Magazine*, 61
Cerro Gordo, 175
Chain Bridge, 272
Chalmers, Gen., at Nashville, 94
Chancellorsville, Battle of, 57, 58, 60, 61, 67, 151, 193, 194, 301, 302
Chandler, Hon. Z., 18
Changing uniforms, 265
Chantilly, Kearny's death at, 34, 54, 273
Chaplains, 217
"Charge of the Light Brigade," 68
Charleston, 336, 353
Charleston Harbor, 20, 204
Charley, 198, 205
Charlotte Hall, 203
Chattahoochie, 60, 114, 332
Chattanooga, 18, 51, 59; battle of, 83, 135, 140, 312; Grant *en route* there, and there, 140-142; Sherman there, 150; Grant's orders there, 150, 157, 181-183, 186, 310, 317, 331, 348, 349, 353
Chelsea, 191, 194
Chicago, 350; a great place, 351, 352
Chickamauga, 22, 59; battle of, 82, 124, 140, 182; "Rock of," 90
Chickahominy, 27; malaria and misery there, 27, 28, 259, 260
Chickasaw Bluffs, 179
Chief Assistant Quartermaster, 322
China, 50
Chivalry, 200; of Gen. Lee, 55, 369, 370
*Christian Advocate*, 3, 200, 218, 279; a good Union paper, 299, 355

Christmas present wanted, 208; Christmas box received, 211, 291, 292; Christmas dinner, 315, 342
Cincinnati, 60, 180, 309, 316
City of Mexico, 175
Clarksville, 222
Climate of Tennessee, 333, 349
Cloud's Mills, 271
Cockpit Point, Va., 11, 52, 224, 226, 235
Coffin's *Life of Lincoln*, 357
Cold Harbor, 143
Colfax, Hon. S., 313
Colorado, 119
Columbus, 166
Commanding generals should be at front, 173
Commissary Department, 166
Confederate brigadiers gentlemen, 101
Confederate camp, 227; hospital train after Gettysburg, 69; losses in Civil War, 165; prison fare, 268, 269; tribute to Yankees, 18
Confederacy, cost of, 387, 391
Congress thanks Thomas for Nashville, 377; and Sherman for Atlanta and Savannah, 381
Conqueror at Gettysburg, Meade as, 67
Connecticut, 183
Contrabands, 200, 222, 270
Cook, Col. J., 197
Cooke, Major G. B., 386
Copperheads, 300, 332
Corduroy roads, 161, 216
Corinth, 123, 150, 178, 249, 259
Corps badges by Kearny and Hooker, 57
Corps, cavalry, 25
Corps, first, 55; second, 76; third, 4, 12, 29, 35, 52, 304; fourth, 85, 92; fifth, —; sixth, —; ninth, 43; eleventh, 57, 59—at Chancellorsville, 303; twelfth, 59; sixteenth, 92; twentieth, 59; twenty-third, 85, 92, 187
Corrals, 177
Cost of the War, 387, 391
Cotton States, 305
Couch, Gen., 58
Council of war at Williamsport, 70, 270
Court-martial, 263
Crimea, 193
Criticism cheap and easy, 145
Crittenden, Gen., 82
Crittenden, Thos. J., 18
Cromwell, Oliver, 18, 120, 136, 156, 169, 280
Crosswicks, 319
Croxton, Gen., at Nashville, 94, 98
Cruft, Gen., at Nashville, 93
Culpeper to Centreville and return, 73, 74
Cumberland Department, 350
Cumberland Gap, 135
Cumberland River, 86, 176, 179, 183, 185, 195
Cumberland Valley, 308

## D

*Daily Advertiser*, Newark, N. J., 359
Dakota, 184
Dalton, 114, 116
Dana, Hon. C. A., compares losses of Grant, McClellan, Burnside, etc., 385
Danville, 153
Dantzic, Siege of, 153
Davis, Jefferson, 81, 119, 175, 251
"Dead March in Saul," 162
Death in camp, 208, 218
Death in hospital, 241
Delaware, home of the whipping post, 80, 288
"*Delenda est Carthago*," 179
Department of the Cumberland, 17, 195, 310, 322
Departments, Quartermaster, 166; Commissary, 166; Medical, 166; Pay, 166; Ordnance, 166
Destroying tents and baggage at Fair Oaks, 29, 359
Detestable camp and weather, 222, 223
Diana, 191
Digging, 162
Dinwiddie Court House, Sheridan there, 131
Disbursements by Gen. Rob't Allen, 187
Disembarking horses at Ship Point, 242
Disease in war, 165, 218
Divine service in Alexandria, 277
"Dixie's Land," 100, 167, 197, 226, 343
Dodge, Gen. T. A., his estimate of Gen. Thomas, 371
Donaldson, Gen. J. L., at Nashville, 93; talk with Grant, 137; in general, 186, 189, 311-313, 317, 318, 322, 337, 339, 342, 343, 345
Donelson, Fort, 222
Don't want to be buried down South, 204
Douglas, Stephen A., 9, 10
Down the Potomac, 235, 236
Drill and march, 160
Dumfries, 284
Duties of commissary, 262; quartermaster, 262
Dyer, Rev. Heman, letter of Stanton to, 362

## E

Early, Gen. Jubal, in Shenandoah Valley, 127, 130
East Tennessee, 187, 305, 316, 345
Eastern Staff officers ordered West, 311
Easton, Gen., 189
Eastport, 181, 345
Edwards, Rev. Wm., 206
Effinger, Rev. John R., 204
Election of 1864, 336
Eleventh Corps, 57, 59
Ellsworth, Col., 199, 202
Emmittsburg, 307

Engineer Corps, 67
England and *Trent* affair, 210
Europe, 186
*Evening Post*, 381
Ewell, Gen., 46
Excelsior Brigade, 63
Expedition to Cockpit Point, 225-230
Exposures and hardships of soldiers, 159-163

## F

Fabius, Our American, 80
Falling Water, 72,
Falmouth worse than Valley Forge, 43, 45, 46, 66, 161, 193, 286, 288, 306
Fair Oaks, Battle of, 27, 255-258; campaigning there, 27, 28; destroying tents and baggage there, 29; Hooker and McClellan there, 35, 38; captured horse there, 47; Hooker's Division at, 53; Lee there, 150, 191; losses there, 259
Fairfax Court House, 33, 45, 54, 75, 161, 270, 271, 273, 284, 285
Fairfax Station, 75-77
Farewell address of Lee to his army, 286
Farragut, 140
"Father Abraham," 299
Fifteenth Amendment, President Johnson in favor of, 22
Fifteenth U. S. C. T., 321
Fifth Regiment, N. J. Vols., 10, 24, 63, 196, 206, 211, 213, 225
Fifty-sixth Pennsylvania, 236
"Fight it out on this line if it takes all summer," 143
"Fighting Joe," 48, 52, 54, 276
First Corps, Falmouth, 55
First Massachusetts, 230
First Maine Cavalry, 234
First Jersey Brigade, 301
First shot at Secesh and slavery, 209
Fisher's Hill, 128
Fisher, Surg. J. C., 196, 243
Fisk, Gen. Clinton B., 356
Fitzhugh House, 273
Five Forks, Sheridan at, 132, 145, 153
Flag of truce, 251
Foote, Admiral, 221
Foraging, 160
Forrest, Gen. N. B., at Nashville, 89, 99; slave driver turned soldier, 133; his raid on Nashville, 334, 335
Fort Corcoran, 276; Donelson, Grant's victory there, 138, 142, 154, 176, 182, 222; Ellsworth, 276; Gårland, 120; Henry, 176, 222; Lyon, 273—fine view from, 276, 278; Magruder, 26; Morton, 341; Sumter, firing on, 10, 20; Ward, 276; Washington, 276; Wool, 242; Worth, 276, 278

# Index

Fortress Monroe, 79, 176, 192, 231-233, 236, 268, 271, 300
Forward March, 172, 189
Fourth Corps, 85, 92
Fourth of July at Nashville, 327, 349
Franklin, Gen. W. B., his indifference to Pope, 32, 38; his inaction at Fredericksburg, 44, 46, 50; as commander, 56; at Second Bull Run, 150
Franklin, Battle of, 86
Franklin's Bridge, 290
Franklin's Division, 54
Frederick, Md., 307
Frederick the Great, 15; his favorite maxim, 61
Fredericksburg, Battle of, 11, 14, 45, 47; losses there, 49, 50; a slaughter-house, 51, 55, 67, 71, 77; Lee there, 150, 151, 161, 228, 231, 283, 284, 289; battle of, 290, 294, 301, 309
Freese, Capt. J. R., 245
Freestone Point, 207
Freehold, 321
Fremont, Gen. J. C., 175, 176
French Princes at Fair Oaks, 35
Front the place for commanders, 173
Front of battle, 171
Fuel for army, 163, 340
Fugitive slaves, 61, 62

## G

Galena, Grant at, 138
Gallant contrabands, 257
Georgia, 118, 142, 163, 182, 186, 305, 336
Germantown, 309
Getting "plugged," 162
Gettysburg, Mr. Lincoln prays for victory there, 12, 15, 17; in general, 58, 67, 69, 125, 139, 142, 151, 154, 181, 194; battle of, 306, 308, 358
Gilson, Helen L., 190, 194
Glad they were soldiers, 169
Glendale, 28
God bless the flag! 169
"God's country," 137
God's war, 15, 261
Good news from everywhere, 205; from Washington, 257
Good quartermasters, 189
Gordonville, 232, 283
Grand Review at Washington, 60, 119
Granger, Gen. Gordon, slow for Knoxville, 110
Grant, Gen. U. S., 3, 16, 125; Mr. Lincoln's faith in him at Vicksburg, 16; in general, 22, 23, 51, 57, 59, 78, 79; *en route* to Chattanooga, 82; his victory there, 83; his opinion of Sherman, 119, 120; on Sheridan, 126, 127; visits Sheridan, 128; Sheridan comes back, 130; council of war at City Point, 131; orders Sheridan to attack Lee, 131; his "Mud March," 132; at Chattanooga, Knoxville, and Lexington, 135; at Nashville after Chattanooga, 135; personal appearance and traits, 135, 136; knew how to decide, 137; his interview with Gen. Donaldson, 137; wife comes to Nashville, 137; goes to church on Sunday, 137; career before war, 138; seeks service under McClellan, but fails, 138; ignored by War Department, 138; gets Illinois regiment at last, 138; at Forts Henry and Donelson, 138; "Unconditional Surrender Grant," 138; "United States Grant," 138; at Pittsburg Landing, 138, 139; at Vicksburg, 139, 140; at New Orleans, 140; *en route* to Chattanooga, 141; his telegram to Thomas from Louisville, 141; at Chattanooga, 141, 142; relief of Knoxville, 142; at Nashville again, 142; appointed Lieutenant General, 142; with Army of Potomac, 142; his strength and Lee's, 142, 143; Wilderness Campaign, 143; at Spottsylvania and Cold Harbor, 143; "By the Left Flank, Forward!" 144; disgusts Lee and dismays him, 143, 144; his heavy losses, 144; before Petersburg, 144-146; uses Sheridan, 144, 145; compels Lee's surrender, 145; Confederates surrender, 145; his four great victories, 145; President Lincoln's opinion, 145; Sherman's opinion, 146, 150; at Pittsburg Landing, 146; at Chattanooga, 150; his courage and prescience, 146-150; as an organizer and drillmaster, 150; as commander, 151; as Methodist, 151-155; ended Lee in a campaign, 155; the true type of Northern democracy, 155; the consummate flower of American civilization, 155; the best representative of his age and time, 155; Lee not his superior nor equal, 155; Grant's supreme mission, 156; his magnanimity and clemency, 157, 158, in general, 163, 166, 167, 174, 179, 181, 182, 221, 305, 312, 316, 325; congratulations to Thomas on Nashville, 372; urges Thomas to push Hood after Nashville, 375; recommends Thomas for major-general in regular army, 376; his injury at New Orleans, 384; his losses in Virginia, 384, 385; his "pass" to Gen. Lee after his surrender, 387
Grapevine reports, 172
Gravelly Run, Grant at, 131
Great commanders previously quartermasters, 174
Greeley, Horace, 23
Grover, Gen., 275, 277

## H

Hale, Nathan, 169
Hall, Adjutant C. K., 243, 245
Hall Town, 128
Halleck, Gen. H. W., orders McClellan to attack Lee, 40; after Antietam, 42; after Gettysburg, 71, 123; on Sheridan, 129; permits Grant to move, 138, 140; at St. Louis, 176; at Corinth, 178; at Washington, 179, 268, 269, 301, 361; letter to, from Mr. Lincoln, 368; urges Thomas to use up Hood's Army, 373; Thomas's reply, 374
Hampton Roads, 237
Hancock, Gen. W. S., at Williamsburg, 26-62; at Fredericksburg, 47, 48, 55; at Gettysburg, 68
Handbills at Nashville, 347
Hankinson, Gen. Aaron, 261
Happy New Year, 291, 314, 344
Hard march, 45
Harding, Gen., 323; his plantation, horses, slaves, etc., 324, 325
Hardships and exposures, 45, 161, 210, 297, 308
Hardtack, 160
Harper's Ferry, 81, 214
Harrison's Landing, 26, 30-32, 38, 63, 192, 267, 277, 360
Hartwood, 292
Hazen, Gen., 81, 124
Hatch, Gen., at Nashville, 94, 98
Havelock, Gen. Sir Henry, on personal bravery, 107
Head of column, 172
Health in camp, 196, 206, 218
Heintzelman, Gen., 31; at Fair Oaks, 35; in general, 63, 232, 237
Helen L. Gilson, 191, 192
Helena, 179
Herbert, Geo., 323
"Hermitage," 319
Hickory canes from "The Hermitage," 319
Hill, Gen. A. P., 46; at Bristoe, 76
History looks at results only, 145
History of Civil War in America, 4
Hitchcock, Gen., 364-366
"Home, sweet home!" 214
Homestead Bill, 19
Horrors of war, 48, 161-168, 259
Hood, Gen., 84; his Nashville campaign, 84; his hopes, 84; defeat at Franklin, 86; siege of Nashville, 88; fighting strength, 88; misconception of Thomas, 90; crushing defeat, 94-96; first day at Nashville, 95; second day at Nashville, 99-102; his character, 103; in general, 117, 120, 151, 187, 335, 336, 338; at Nashville, 339, 342, 343, 373; Mr. Lincoln's comment on him after Nashville, 379

Hooker, Gen. Joseph, 52; his Division, 11; Fredericksburg review, 11; at Williamsburg, 26; at Fair Oaks, 27, 29; return to Yorktown and Alexandria, 31; his support of Pope, 32, 54; his reconnoissance at Fair Oaks, 35; at Fredericksburg, 48, 49; his personal appearance, 52; in Lower Maryland, 53; at Williamsburg and Fair Oaks, 53; in Seven Day's Battle, 53; loses Kearny, 54, 120; "Fighting Joe," 32, 48, 54, 155; as Division Commander, 53; as Corps Commander, 55; at Antietam, 55; relieves Burnside, 55; in command of Army of Potomac, 56; does good work there, 56, 57; invented Corps Badges, 57; reorganizes army, 57; at Chancellorsville, 57; his march to Pennsylvania, 58; Meade followed his plans at Gettysburg, 58; ordered West, 59; wanted author to accompany him, 59; at Lookout Mountain, 59; in Atlanta Campaign, 59; resigns command, 60; at Cincinnati, 60; a good soldier and great commander, 60, 61; against Slavery, 61, 62; anecdotes of him, 61, 66; his chivalry and courtesy, 63, 66; farewell to him, 66, 67; in general, 120, 136, 141, 150-152, 166, 206, 207, 220, 221, 226, 231, 234, 236; at Williamsburg, 244-246, 250; at Fair Oaks, 255, 258, 264; at Savage Station, 265, 272, 274; transferred to McDowell's Corps, 274; in general, 277, 279, 283, 287, 292, 293, 296, 297, 300, 301; at Chancellorsville, 302, 303, 312, 313, 320; resigns, 330; commends the author, 393
Hooker's Division, 52, 54, 55, 61, 161, 219; at Williamsburg, 244-247, 252, 274; at Chancellorsville, 303
Hornbakers, 283
Horses in camp, 196, 218, 321
Horse-sense, 178
Hospitals, 162, 166, 177, 241
Hotspurs, 191
Hunt, Gen., at Headquarters Army of the Potomac, 73
Howard, Gen. O. O., at Chancellorsville, 57; in command of Fourth Corps, 60; promoted over Hooker, 60; at Gettysburg, 68; at Williamsport, 72; in front of Atlanta, 114
Humphrey, Gen., at Gettysburg, 68; at Headquarters Army of the Potomac, 73
"Hurrah for the Union!" 346
Hygeia Hotel as a hospital, 238

## I

Illinois and Grant, 138
In the trenches, 162
Imboden, Gen., 69
Indiana Cavalry, 236

# Index

Indianapolis, Ind., 176
Indifference to danger, 260-263
Ingalls, Gen. Rufus, 73, 189
Inspections, Some idea of, 393-395
Intelligent contrabands, 75
Intemperance in army, 209
Interview with Lincoln and Sickles, 12-18, 355, 358
Intrenching, 162
Island No. 10, 179

## J.

Jackson, Andrew, 319; his residence and tomb, 319
Jackson, Stonewall, 28; at Fredericksburg, 46; at Chantilly, 54; his death at Chancellorsville, 58; in general, 133, 150, 151, 361, 362
James River, 28, 29, 53, 130, 143, 150, 152, 174, 187, 192, 233, 264, 266, 267; bathing in, 267, 368
Jefferson, Thomas, 80
Jersey Blues, 63, 207; Jersey Brigade at Williamsburg, 252; Jersey City, 357; Jersey turnpike, 220
Jerseymen living in Virginia, 283
"Job of work," A great, 144
"John Barleycorn," 276
"John Brown's body," etc., 223
Johnson, Andrew, 19; advocated Homestead Bill, 19; his Union speech in U. S. Senate, 1861, 19, 20; life threatened *en route* home, 21; Military Governor of Tennessee, 21; Vice President, 21; his political apostacy, 21-23; his character, 23; sought to arrest Lee, 157; at Nashville and Washington, 326, 347; his letter for author, 343
Johnson, Col. Adolphus J., 277
Johnson, Willis Fletcher, 357
Johnston, Gen. Joseph E., 4, 60, 81; his Atlanta Campaign, 111, 117; his surrender at Raleigh, 118, 120; as Quartermaster General, U. S. A., 178
Johnston, Capt. Thomas P., 243
Joint resolution of Congress thanking Thomas for Nashville, 377; Sherman for Atlanta and Savannah, 381
Julian the Apostate, 23

## K

Kearny, Gen. Philip, at Williamsburg, 26, 244-246, 255; at Fair Oaks, 27; his return to Yorktown and Alexandria, 31; his support of Pope, 32, 54; his death at Chantilly, 24, 54; his body, sword, etc., returned by Lee, 55; compared with Sheridan, 133; letters of Gen. Lee returning his body, sword, horse, etc., 369, 370; McClellan's reply, 370
Kearny's Division, 54

Kelly's Ford, 77
Kenesaw Mountain, 112
Kentucky Cavalry, 174
Kentucky, 177, 183, 221, 326
"King of France," etc., 40
Kilpatrick, Gen. Judson, at Williamsport, 72
Kingston, Ga., 184
Knoxville, 51, 135, 142, 316, 345, 348, 349

## L

Lalor, Lt. D. K., 245, 247
Landing horses at Ship Point, 242
Latin, Lee might air his, 40
Lee, Robert E., 30, 149; his contempt for McClellan, 31; at Antietam, 34, 41, 42; at Fredericksburg, 44, 46, 49; a Confederate game-cock, 51; returns Kearny's body, sword, etc., 55; at Gettysburg, 68, 69; at Williamsport, 69, 71; Culpeper to Centreville and return, 73, 74; baffles Meade, 77, 120; Sheridan's Raids, 126; Lee and Sheridan, 127; at Five Forks and Appomattox, 132; his surrender, 133, 142; his army at Petersburg robbed both the cradle and the grave, 144, 151; compared with Grant, 149; Lord Wolseley and others, 149; Lee failed to understand Secession, 149; was not loyal like Thomas, 149; in West Virginia, 150; at Fair Oaks, 150; in Seven Day's Battle, 150; at Malvern Hill, 150; compared with McClellan and Pope, 150; at Antietam, 150; at Fredericksburg, 151; at Chancellorsville, 151; at Gettysburg, 151; in Maryland and Pennsylvania, 152; in the Wilderness, 152; at Petersburg, 153; at Appomattox, 153; compared with Thomas and Sherman, 154; compared with Grant, 154; his antagonists, 155; analysis of Lee and Grant, 155; cannot rank with world's greatest commanders, 155, 156; his true place, 156; Grant surpassed him, 156; Lee's mission, 156; Grant's mission, 156; Grant in Lee's place, 156; Grant's magnanimity and clemency, 157; Lee in Grant's place, 157; he would have marched through Richmond, 157, 187; Grant's generosity, 157; our American triumvirate, 158; Lee a true type of Southern oligarchs, 155; a gentleman and patriot after his kind, 155; not Grant's superior or equal, 155, 251, 307; his surrender, 346; his letters returning body, sword, etc., of Gen. Kearny, 369, 370; McClellan's reply, 270; parole of self and staff, 385; farewell address to his army, 386; his pass from Grant after surrender, 387
Lee, Rear Admiral S. P., congratulations to Thomas on Nashville, 372

Left Grand Division, 56
Libby Prison, Horrors of, 150, 162
Life in hospital, 241
Life at Nashville, 329
Lincoln, Abraham, 9; "Honest Old Abe," 9, 14; his debate with Douglas, 9; at Trenton, N. J., 9; inauguration, 9; support by Douglas, 10; first call for troops, 10; camp visits, 10; Falmouth review, 11; on horseback, 12; with Gen. Sickles, after Gettysburg, 12, 355; prayers over Gettysburg and Vicksburg, 15, 16; religious faith, 17, 18, 355-358; his assassination, 17, 347; greatest figure of our Civil War, 18; at Harrison's Landing, 39; estimate of McClellan's losses on Peninsula, 39, 40; orders McClellan to attack Lee after Antietam, 42, 43; relieves McClellan, 43; relieves Burnside, 50, 55; his Proclamation of Emancipation, 56, 59, 67, 69, 81; rejoiced by Atlanta, 117, 120; congratulations to Sheridan, 129; with Grant at City Point, 131; his *sine qua non* of Virginia Campaign, 143; his opinion of Grant, 145, 152, 158; his story of an Illinois runaway, 163; in general, 178, 186, 261, 299, 301, 313, 326; his reëlection, 336, 343, 355-359, 362, 364, 366-368; his thanks to Thomas for Nashville, 372; his little story on Hood after Nashville, 379
Lincoln and Johnson, 336
"Little Mac," 26, 28, 31, 34, 41, 43, 150, 251
Little Napoleon, 37
Liverpool Point, 235
Logan, Gen. John A., ordered to Nashville, 102; halts at Louisville, 103; returns to Washington, 103; inferior to Thomas, 104; Thomas aggrieved by his appointment, 377
Long Bridge, 197
Long, Rev. D. A., 355, 356
Longstreet, Gen. James, at Fredericksburg, 46, 51; at Gettysburg, 69; in general, 133, 150, 154, 251
Lookout Mountain, battle of, 59, 182, 312, 331, 332; visit to, 331
Lookout Rock, 332
Losses of Confederates at Fredericksburg, 49; at Gettysburg, 69; at Nashville, 95, 101; in Nashville Campaign, 103; at Donelson, 157; at Vicksburg, 157; at Appomattox, 157
Losses in battle, 163, 165; in Franco-German War, 164; in Crimean War, 164; in Mexican War, 164; in Revolutionary War, 164; in Civil War, 164; in Spanish War, 165; in Fair Oaks, 259; in Fredericksburg, 49, 56
"Lost Cause" ground to powder, 156
Louisiana, 163, 380

Louisville, 182, 185, 187, 353
Louisville Railroad, 328
Lower Chesapeake, 364
Lower Potomac, 207
Loyal Legion, 358
Lucifer, 22

## M

MacCallum, Gen. D. C., escapes from Wheeler, 115, 116, 331
Magenta, 252
Magruder, Gen., 251
Mahone, Gen. Wm., 151
"Make a spoon or spoil a horn," 16, 157
Malvern Hill, 28; Lee there, 153, 154
Mammoth Cave, 328, 334
Manassas Junction, 45, 54, 161, 269, 270, 272, 273, 282, 284, 290
"Manual of Arms," 160
Marathon, 68
March, a hard, 45, 161; to Alexandria, 197; into Maryland, 204, 205, 284
Marengo, 24
Marietta, 114
Marshall House, 198, 199, 202
Marshall, Lt. Col. Chas., 386
Marye's Hill, 47; assault on, 48, 49
Maryland, 11; Lee's invasion a mistake, 152, 225, 226, 232
Maryland slaves, 61, 219
Mason and Slidell affair, 210
Massachusetts, 188
Massachusetts, First Regiment, 226
Massachusetts soldiers on slavery, 62
Mattewoman Creek, 229
Mattewoman River, 224
Maximilian, 327
McClellan, Gen. Geo. B., 3, 4; in West Virginia, 24; in command of Army of Potomac, 24; his personal appearance, 25; at Yorktown, 26; at Williamsburg, 26, 27; at Fair Oaks, 27; at Seven Day's Battle, Malvern Hill, etc., 28; his baggage-destroying order, 29, 359; under shelter of gunboats at Harrison's Landing, 30; retreat to Yorktown, 31; did not support Pope heartily, 31, 33; drifted into command again, 34; his Antietam Campaign, 34; ordered to Trenton, N. J., 35; his personal courage, 35; popularity with army, 36; as a scholar, 36; as an organizer and commander, 36, 37; the Unready or Little Napoleon, 37, 155; as candidate for President, 37; as Governor, N. J., 37; his strength and losses on Peninsula, 38, 40; his delay after Antietam, 41-43; talk of making him dictator, 43; relieved and ordered to Trenton, N. J., 43, 44, 51, 56, 57; his Maryland slave order, 61; in general, 120, 127,

404

# Index

136, 138, 143, 150, 152, 163, 192, 215, 216, 223, 232, 233, 236; at Williamsburg, 246, 248, 250, 252; his orders to quartermasters, 257; at Fair Oaks, 258, 263, 302, 333; on Pope, 360, 361; on Lincoln and his Cabinet, 367; proposed disobedience of orders, 368; letter to Lee relating to Kearny, 370; his losses compared with Grant's, 284, 385
McCall, Gen., 38
*McClure's Magazine*, 385
McCook, Gen., 82
McCullough, Capt. William, 261
McDowell, Gen. Irwin, 31, 55, 74, 364, 365
McLaws, Gen., 151
McKinstry, Gen., 175
McPherson, Gen., Death of, 60, 120, 151
Meade, Gen. Geo. G., 11, 13, 14, 17, 67; at Fredericksburg, 46, 55, 58; in Mexico, 67; at Fredericksburg and Chancellorsville, 67; in command of Army of Potomac, 67; personal appearance, 67; at Gettysburg, 67, 69; personal traits, 72, 73; delay at Williamsport excusable, 71; 'campaign from Culpeper to Centreville and return, 73, 74; believed Fredericksburg was the true route to Richmond, 77; good-by to author, 75, 79; outwitted by Lee, 79; a great commander, 79, 120; interview with Sheridan, 126; in general, 133, 136, 142, 144, 150, 151; a good, safe commander, 155, 166, 309, 368; congratulations to Thomas on Nashville, 372
Medical Department, 166
Meigs, Gen. M. C., 180, 183, 342, 364-366; commends the author, 393
Memoirs of Grant, Sherman, Sheridan, etc., 3
Memphis, 179-181, 345, 346, 353
Meridian, 181
Meridian Hill, 202, 204
"Merrimac" in Hampton Roads, 239; her appearance, 240, 242
Merry Christmas, 314
Methodism in Tennessee, 316
Methodist Episcopal Church, 219; Grant's attendance there, 137; his Methodist birth and training, 151; an honor to said Church, 151
Mexico, 67, 80, 136, 138, 174, 175
Middletown, 307
Military railroading, 311
Mill Springs, 81
Miller, Brigadier Gen., at Nashville, 93
Mine Run, 77, 78
Minerva, 191
Missionary Ridge, 124, 182, 312, 331, 332
Mississippi, 16, 17, 139, 154, 163, 179, 181-183, 345, 346
Missouri, 182

Mobile, 118, 140, 142, 345, 353
Mobile and Ohio Railroad, 139
Money disbursed by Gen. Allen, 187
"Monitor," her appearance, 238, 240, 242
Montana, 182
Montgomery, Gen., 198-200, 203
Monument to Miss Gilson, 194
Moore, Gov. O., 380
Moore, Rev. S. T., 220
Morals of the army, 196
Mosby's Cavalry, 33
Moscow, 118
"Moses," 205, 241, 257
Moses from Sinai, 15; Andrew Johnson as, 22
"Mother Bickerdyke," 190
Mott, Gen. Gershom, at Williamsburg, 63, 64; in general, 197, 225, 228, 229, 243, 277, 301; at Chancellorsville, 302; recommends the author for promotion, 391
Mount Vernon, 201, 204, 222
Moving troops into East Tennessee, 345
Mud before Yorktown, 242
"Mud March," Burnside, 50, 55, 294
Munson's Hill, 199
Murat, Marshal, compared with Sheridan, 133
Murfreesboro, 81, 164, 179
Mustered out, 353

## N

Napoleon, 37, 118, 120, 136, 145, 155, 171
Nashville, 21, 22, 78; campaign and battle of, 84, 105; situation, 88; in general, 135, 142, 151, 154, 183, 185-187, 189, 222, 310; winter in, 313, 315; army work there, 322; a great depot, 322; patriotism of, 327, 328; siege of, 339, 342; battle of, 341
"Naugatuck," her appearance, 240, 241
Navajos, 121
Newbern, 232
New England, 191
New Hampshire, 188
New Jersey Brigade, Second, 52, 206, 207, 216, 231, 235, 238; at Yorktown, 243; at Williamsburg, 244, 245, 247, 252; at Fair Oaks, 255, 260; Seven Day's Battle, 264, 266; in general, 268, 280; at Manassas Junction, 282; at Falmouth, 286, 300; at Boscobel, 302, 304
New Jersey Conference, 317; Methodists, 299; Peace Legislature, 298
New Jersey, Fifth Regiment, 10, 24, 63, 196, 206, 211, 213, 225, 235, 245, 249; Sixth Regiment, 206, 230, 245, 249; Seventh Regiment, 206, 230, 245, 259; Eighth Regiment, 206, 249, 259, 277; Thirty-fifth Regiment, 321
New Kent Court House, 249
New Mexico, 182

New Orleans, 140, 164, 182, 249, 353
Newport News, 239
New York, 152, 188
*New York Tribune*, 357
"Nigger catchers," 62
Nightingale, Florence, 193
Ninth Corps, 43
Norfolk, 233, 239, 249
North Carolina, 331
Not sorry they were soldiers, 168
Number of battles in Civil War, 164; enlistments in, 165; Union killed and wounded in, 165; Confederate killed and wounded in, 165; in war with Spain, 165

O

"Obey orders," 49, 159, 166, 349
Occoquan, 285
Ocean Grove, 356, 357
Officers at Nashville, 186
Official report of Atlanta campaign, 186
Ohio, 183, 185
"Old Brains," 176
"On to Richmond," 28, 253, 257
Ooray, head chief of Utes, 122
Opequan, 128, 144
Orange and Alexandria Railroad, 306
Ordnance Department, 166
Osmond, Dr., 283
Overton Knobs, 98; the fighting there, 100

P

Pacific coast, 175
Panic at Fair Oaks, 256
Paris, Comte de, 4, 26; in error as to wagon trains, 77, 163
Parker, Gov. Joel, 301
Parole of Gen. Lee and staff, 385
*Parturiunt montes*, etc., 40
Patterson, Gen. Rob't, 81
Patterson, Gen. Frank, 245, 248, 251, 256, 275, 277; his death, 285
Patriotism at Nashville, 327
Patterson, Major A. H., 321
Pay Department, 166
Pay of soldiers, 168
Paymaster around, 206
Pea Ridge, 179
Peach Tree Creek, Battle of, 60, 112, 170
Peninsula, 27, 31, 37, 38, 44, 53, 54, 67, 74, 163, 191; in 1862 crowded with soldiers, 250
Pennington Seminary, 219
Pennsylvania, 59, 61; Lee's invasion of, a political blunder, 152, 306; patriots, 307; reserves, Meade with, 67
Pensacola, 213
Pensions, 168
Perrine, Quartermaster General, 301

Personal bravery, 171
Petersburg, 127; Grant there, 127, 128; Lee evacuates, 132, 133; Lee at, 144; doomed, 152, 153; Titanic wrestle of Grant and Lee there, 153, 154, 346
Peyton, Lt. Col. H. E., 386
Philadelphia, 152, 306
*Philadelphia Press*, 358
Phillips, Dr. John H., 314
Phillips' House at Falmouth, 48
Pickets at Fredericksburg, 288
Pickett, Gen., his charge at Gettysburg, 68, 69, 151
Pittsburg Landing, 81; Grant there, 138, 146, 178
Place of Lee in history, 158; of Grant, 158
Platæa, 68
Plutarch, 327
"Policing," 160
Politics a queer profession and sad business, 23
"Pony," 196, 272
Pope, Gen. John, 31, 32; his gallant fighting, 33; his defeat at second Bull Run, 34, 44, 54, 150; the Overbold, 152; in general, 155, 179, 360
Porter, Admiral, 139, 140
Porter, Gen. Fitz John, 33; failed Pope, 33; his court-martial, 33; restoration, 34; at second Bull Run, 150; at Savage Station, 265; on Pope, 360
Porter's Division, 54
Port Republic, 268
Port Tobacco, 230
Portsmouth, 188
Potomac, 25, 58, 70, 151
Preaching in Alexandria, 277
Preface, 3
Presbyterian Church, 321
Proclamation of Emancipation, effect on army, 56, 278, 279, 313
Promoted, 203, 257, 261, 280
Puritan against cavalier, 159

Q

Quaker guns at Centreville, 25
*Quarterly Review*, 320
Quartermaster Department, 166; the business department of the army, 174; its evolution in Civil War, 174
Quartermaster's duty, 262
Quartermaster General's report 1860, 177; report 1865, 178; report 1863, 180
Quartermasters, Good, essential to great commanders, 174; quartermasters afterward commanders, 174, 189
Quartermasters ill, 249
Quarters at Nashville, 313

# Index

## R

Rainbow from Lookout Mountain, 332
Raleigh, 118
Randolph, Hon. Geo. W., 369
Rapidan, 70, 79, 143, 144, 152
Rappahannock River, 47, 49, 50, 58, 73, 74, 151, 288, 291, 301
Rappahannock Station, 74
Rations by Hooker, 57, 160
Ravages of war, 253
Rawlins, Gen. John A., talks with Sheridan and Grant, 132
Read, Thomas Buchanan, his "Sheridan's Ride," 129, 383
Rear of battle, 171
Rebellion, Cost of the, 39, 387
Rectortown, 43
"Red Patch" Division, 57
Regiment suffered most, 164
Repair shops, 177
Revere, Gen. J. W., 64
Reynolds, Gen. J. F., 29; fell at Gettysburg, 68
Richmond, 26, 27, 30, 31, 44, 53, 77, 130; Grant's campaign against, 143, 144; abandoned, 145; doomed, 153, 157; in general, 163, 191, 228, 232, 236, 249, 252, 255, 257, 259, 268, 283, 293, 305, 346, 361, 363, 368
Ride to Mount Vernon, 201
Right Grand Division, 55
Ripley, Gen., 364, 366
Rip-Raps, 242
Roads, Army, 214, 216, 217, 221, etc.
Roanoke Island, 44
Rob the cradle and the grave, 144
Rocky Mountains, 119, 135, 340
Rodgers, Capt., 30
Rosecrans, Gen. W. S., 22; in West Virginia, 24; at Stone River, 81; at Chickamauga, 82, 174, 127; against Lee in West Virginia, 150; in general, 179, 182, 305
Rucker, Gen. D. H., 189
Rum Point, 11, 52, 213, 218, 220, 225, 226, 229, 233, 235, 237
Rupert, 156
Rusling, Gen. J. F., prior to war, 4; army record, 4; with Lincoln at Trenton, 9; at Washington, D. C., 10; entering U. S. service, 10, 24; at Fredericksburg review, 11; interview with Lincoln and Sickles after Gettysburg, 12, 18, 355, 358; in Senate Chamber, March, 1861, 19; Wigfall against the Union, and Johnson's reply, 20, 21; Johnson as President in favor of Fifteenth Amendment, 22; did not apostatize with Johnson, 23; first promotion at Fair Oaks, 26; march to Centreville, 30, 31; not at Antietam, 42; from Manassas to Falmouth, 45; at Fredericksburg, 47, 48; at Rum Point, 52; at Chancellorsville, 57; promoted Lt. Col., 58; Hooker asks for him, 59; at Williamsburg, 63; with Hooker, 64-66; with Meade, 70, 71; at Williamsport, 72; at Headquarters Army of the Potomac, 72, 73; crossing the Rappahannock, etc., 74; at Brentsville, 75; orders from Meade, 75; at Bristoe, 76; at Centreville, 77; ordered West, 78; last interview with Meade, 78; at Nashville, 86, 87, 93, 99; at Overton Knobs, 100; talk with a Confederate brigadier, 101; dines Confederate brigadiers, 101; promoted full Colonel for Nashville, 105; at Atlanta, 112; visits Sherman before Atlanta, 112, 114; escapes Wheeler's Raid, 114, 117; with Sherman in Rocky Mountains, 119, 122; visits Kit Carson, 120, 122; with Miss Gilson at the White House and on James River, 191, 192; Army Letters, 195; at Washington and Alexandria, 195, 206; on Lower Potomac, 207; at Fortress Monroe, 237, 241; at Yorktown, 242; at Williamsburg, 244, 247; up the Peninsula, 248, 255; at Fair Oaks, 255, 260; promoted Capt. and A. Q. M., 257, 261; believes in war, 261; against Slavery, 261, 262; at Savage Station, 265; at White Oak Swamps, 265; in Seven Days' Battle, 266; at Malvern Hill, 267; home on "sick leave," 267; at Fairfax C. H., 273; at Fort Lyon, 276; at church in Alexandria, 277; at Fort Worth, 278; on Proclamation of Emancipation, 279; settles accounts with U. S. as Division Q. M., 280; on Gen. Sickles, 281; at Manassas Junction, 282, 283; at Centreville and Fairfax C. H., 285; at Occoquan, 285; on Gen. Patterson, 286; at Falmouth, 286-289; in winter quarters, 293; at Acquia Creek, 295; at an army wedding, 297; on army Sundays, 298; on Copperheads, 298; on *Christian Advocate*, 200; at Chancellorsville, 301, 303; promoted Lt. Col., 304; at Boscobel, 302, 305; on "sick leave," 305; not at Gettysburg, 306; at Washington, 306; interview with Lincoln and Sickles, 307; at Fredericksburg, 307; at Headquarters Army of the Potomac, 309; at Cincinnati, 309; at Nashville, 310; as Chief Q. M. Military Roads, 310; as Chief Assistant Q. M., 312, 313; on Bishop Simpson, 316; at "The Hermitage," 319; his work at Nashville, 322, 338; at Gen. Harding's, 323, 325; on Abraham Lincoln, 326; at Mammoth Cave, 328; at Chattanooga and Atlanta, 331, 332; on "substitutes," 332, 333; on Thanksgiving Day, 337; acting Chief Q. M. at Nashville, 339; at siege and bat-

407

tle of Nashville, 339, 342; commended by
Andrew Johnson, 343; his life at Nashville,
343; watches things by telegraph, 346; on
Lee's surrender, 346; on Lincoln's assassination, 347; promoted full Colonel, 348;
report on the Department of the Cumberland, 350; ordered to Chicago, 350; at Chicago, 351, 352; ordered East, 352; home
again, 352; inspections South and West,
352; promoted Brigadier General and mustered out, 353; commendations of Generals
Mott, Berry, Donaldson, Meigs, Hooker,
Thomas, Sherman, etc., 391, 395—by President Johnson and Secretary of War, 391,
394, 395
Rusling, Lt. W. J., 211; promoted, 223, 259;
as Division Ambulance Officer, 296
Russia and Russian bear, 210

S

Sailor's Creek, Sheridan there, 132, 145
Salisbury, 268, 269
San Francisco, 188
Sandt, Quartermaster Serg't, 243, 284
Sarragosa, siege of, 153
Savage Station, 28, 29, 255, 265
Savannah, 60, 113, 118, 142, 144, 154, 187, 336, 343, 348, 353
Schurz, Gen. C., at Chancellorsville, 57
Scipio, 179
Scofield, Gen., 85; at Franklin, 86; at Nashville, 87, 92, 93, 95, 96, 98, 99; in front of
Atlanta, 114; proposed appointment broke
Thomas's heart, 378
Scott, Gen. Winfield, 175
Sebastopol, Siege of, 153, 252
Secesh quarters, 200; trophies, 221; lady, 222
Secessia, 251
Secession a sophism, 149, 152; Thomas understood it, 152; its corner stone Slavery,
152
Second N. J. Brigade. See N. J. Brigade,
Second.
Sedan, siege of, 153
Sedgwick, Gen. John, at Fredericksburg, 58,
154
Seminary, Pennington, 219
Seminary Ridge, 69
Sentry duty, 162
Sermon in Alexandria, 277
Sermons in camp, 217
Seven Days' Battle, 28, 38, 53, 57, 60, 78;
Jackson and Longstreet there, 150; Lee
there, 153, 192
Seven Pines, 191
Seventh N. J., 230
Seward, W. H., 15, 18, 20, 23
Sewell, Capt. W. J., 201

Sewell's Point, 242
Sharp, Surgeon, 228
Sharpe, Gen. Geo. H., 386
Sharpsburg, 41
Shelling batteries on Lower Potomac, 207, 208
Shelling Cockpit Point, 224
Shellmire, Capt., 268
Shelter tents, 161
Shenandoah Valley, Sheridan there, 127, 130;
the Paradise of Virginia, 130; cleaned out
by Sheridan, 130; locks "back door" there,
144, 268
Sheridan, Gen. P. H., 3; in the Valley, 35, 51,
70, 120, 123; career before war, 123; first
duty in Civil War, 123; before Corinth, 123;
promoted Brigadier General, 123; at Stone
River, 124; at Chickamauga, 124; ordered
to Army of Potomac, 124; his personal appearance, 124, 125; as "Little Phil," 125;
his opinion of Jeb Stuart, 126; his raid
around Lee's right, 126; around Lee's
left, 126; in Shenandoah Valley, 127, 130;
smashes Early, 127, 129; at Winchester,
128; at Fisher's Hill, 129; at Cedar Creek,
129; congratulations from Lincoln and
Stanton, 129; cleans out the Valley,
130; raid around Richmond, 130; gets
back to Grant, 130; in council of war
with Grant and Sherman, 131; ordered to
attack Lee, 131; not "stuck in the mud,"
131; at Dinwiddie C. H., 131; with Grant
and Rawlins, 132; at Five Forks, 132; at
Sailor's Creek, 132; at Appomattox, 132;
Lee's surrender, 133; compared with others,
133; a great commander, 133; Grant's right
hand, 133; Grant's opinion, 134; Hurrah
for Sheridan! 134; his charger, 131; in
general, 141, 151, 153, 166, 167, 174, 175;
congratulations to Thomas on Nashville,
372; his absence from Cedar Creek justified,
381, 382
"Sheridan's Ride," 383
Sherman, Gen. W. T., 3, 20, 22, 51, 106; at
Atlanta, 35; not fair to Hooker, 60; his
opinion of Nashville, 104; his personal appearance, 106; his career prior to war, 107;
his loyalty to the Union, 108; in Kentucky,
108; at Pittsburg Landing, 108; at Vicksburg, 109; at Memphis, 109; his march
to Chattanooga, 109; leaves Knoxville,
110; report on Knoxville, 110; assigned
to the Military Division of the Mississippi, 110; his Atlanta Campaign, 111,
his strength, 111; at Kenesaw Mountain and Peach Tree Creek, 112; in front of
Atlanta, 113; his outfit when campaigning,
113; not disturbed by Wheeler's Raid, 117;
captures Atlanta, 117; his March to the Sea

408

# Index

and through the Carolinas, 117, 118; capture of Savannah, 118; consulted Census Reports, 118; compared with Napoleon, 118; Grant's opinion of his great march, 119; Stanton and the Grand Review, 119; in the Rocky Mountains, 119, 122; on Kit Carson, 122; in council at City Point with Grant and Sheridan, 131, 139; did not protest against Vicksburg, 139, 141; his opinion of Grant, 146, 150, 151, 166, 167; his ideas on war, battles, etc., 169, 173; in general, 174, 179, 181-184, 186, 187, 312; moves on Atlanta, 323, 325, 330, 332-336; his letter to Gov. Moore of Louisiana, 380

Sherman's March, 70, 117, 118
Sherman, John, 108
Shiloh, 81
Shipping Point, 207, 208, 224, 226, 230
Ship Point, 237, 238, 242
Sick soldiers, 27, 28, 162, 259
Sick quartermasters, 249
Sickles, Gen. D. E., his interview with President Lincoln after Gettysburg, 12; his wound at Gettysburg and splendid fighting there, 12, 13; at Gettysburg, 12, 14-16, 18, 68, 277, 306; wounded at Gettysburg, 306; arrival in Washington, 307; visited by Lincoln and Rusling, 307, 309, 310, 355-358; commends the author, 393
Siege, Lee never conducted a great one, 157; Grant did, and always won, 157
Siege of Nashville, 339, 342
Sigel, Gen. Franz, at Chancellorsville, 51, 57; in general, 285, 290
Simpson, Bishop, 206, 316
"Sick leave," 64, 65
Sixteenth Corps, 92
Sixth N. J., 230
Skedaddle, 28
Slaughterhouse at Fredericksburg, 51
Slave order by McClellan, 61; Massachusetts soldiers on, 62; Hooker's action on, 62
Slave pen at Alexandria, 199
Slavery hated, 223
Slavery in Virginia, 253, 254; in Tennessee, 325
Slaves at Falmouth, 193
Slocum, Gen., 290
Smith, Gen. A. J., at Nashville, 86, 87, 92-96, 98, 99
Smith, Gen. G., 251
"Smith's Guerrillas," 88
Snow in camp, 299
Soldier's Home, 13
Soldiers in action, 170
Soldiers indifferent to shot and shell, 260-263
Soldiers' pay, 168
Soldiering, 159
Soldiers' remittances home, 206

Sorties, 162
South Carolina, 20, 204
South Mountain, 308
Sovereign, Chaplain Thomas, 199; a brave old man, 275, 284
Southern Confederacy a hideous nightmare, 145; a political blunder, 145; assets at Appomattox, 145; a thing doomed, 152; a pirate ship, 149; its corner stone Slavery, 149; cost of, 387, 391
Spottsylvania, 143
Springfield, Ill., Grant at, 138; in general, 175-177, 179, 180, 182
Spring in Tennessee, 326
Stafford, army there, 11, 45, 48, 151
Stanton, E. M., 15, 17, 20, 22; after Antietam, 42, 59, 78, 81; on Meade, 79, 119; on Sheridan, 127; congratulations to Sheridan, 129, 140; refuses Allen to Sherman, 184, 301, 361; his reply to McClellanism, 362, 367; never taken for a fool, 366; believes God Almighty founded this Government, and expects to stand before Him in judgment, 366; supported McClellan with the whole power of the Government, 366; desires no office or honor, and is not a candidate for any, 365, 366; his thanks to Thomas on Nashville, 371; stands by Thomas, 275; makes Thomas Major General, U. S. A., 376; commends the author, 394, 395
"Star of the West," 20
Starr, Col. S. H., 201, 206, 220, 225, 235, 237, 238, 243; relieved of brigade, 247, 248
*State Gazette*, 357
Steedman, Gen., at Nashville, 89, 92, 93, 98, 99
Stephens, Alex. H., said Slavery was the corner stone of Southern Confederacy, 149
Stoneman, Gen. Geo., 302
Stone River, 81, 123, 164
Stuart, Gen. Jeb, at Williamsport, 72; Sheridan's opinion, 126; his death, 126; a Prince Rupert, 133
St. Louis, Grant at, 138, 175-177, 179, 180, 182
Stokes, Rev. E. H., 356
Storehouses, 177
"Substitutes," 332, 334
Sumner, Chas., 20, 23
Sumner, Gen. Ed., 27; as commander, 55, 246, 264, 272, 289
Sumter, 175
Sunday in the army, 195, 196, 198, 212, 216, 278, 298
"Sunny South," 315, 316
Surrender of Lee, 346
Supplies by Gen. Robt. Allen, 188, 189
Supporting battery, 172
Sunday raid and escape, 115
Swinton's Army of the Potomac, 4, 163

409

## T

"Tad Lincoln," 13
Takes a man's weight in lead to kill him in battle, 164
Taylor, Gen., 364
Taylor, Gen. Zachary, 174
Taylor, Lt. Col. W. H., 385
Tefft, Rev. Dr., 233
Tennessee, 19, 21, 51, 60, 78, 159, 163, 176, 177, 179, 182, 183, 185; climate of, 333
Tennessee River, 331
Tennyson, Alfred, his "Charge of the Light Brigade," 68; his Ode on the Duke of Wellington, 151
Tent life, 161, 202, 204, 206, 221, 299
Texas, 163
Thanksgiving Day, 1864, 337
Thiers, 163
Third Corps. See Corps, Third.
Thirty-fifth N. J., 321
Thomas, Gen. Geo. H., 80, 20, 22, 59, 78; his early life and personal appearance, 80; his Union wife, 80; his loyalty and fidelity, 81; at Harper's Ferry, 81; at Mill Springs, 81; at Pittsburg Landing, 81; in Atlanta Campaign, 83; Sherman's confidence in him, 84; his Nashville Campaign, 84; his troops at Nashville, 85; preparations for defense, 85; after Franklin, 86; interview with Scofield, Wood, and Smith, 87; his strength at Nashville, 88; Hood menaces his communications, 88; no real danger there, 89; he waits for Hood and tempts him, 90; the "Rock of Chickamauga," 90; his soldiers' "Old Pap Tom," 90; reasons of his delay, 91; Grant dissatisfied, and orders Logan to relieve him, 92; Thomas fights, and Logan arrives too late, 92; his plan of battle, 92, 93; his first day's battle, 93, 95; his second day's battle, 96, 101; the terrific fighting on both days, 99, 100; tribute of Confederate brigadier to Yankees, 100, 101; heavy Confederate losses at Nashville, 101; his pontoons went astray, 102; Union and Confederate losses in the campaign, 103; Lincoln, Grant, Stanton, Meade, and Sheridan congratulate Thomas, but Sherman *in laches*, 104; Congress gives him a vote of thanks, 104; promoted major general, U. S. A., 104; Thomas grieved by Grant's action, 104, 105; a great soldier and Christian gentleman, 105; in front of Atlanta, 114, 120, 124, 127; his telegram to Grant at Chattanooga, 141; in general, 149, 151, 166, 167, 187, 310, 312, 332, 336, 338, 342; his reply to Halleck about Hood, 374; grateful to Stanton and Lincoln, 376, 377; sore over Logan and Scofield, 377, 378; his congratulatory order to army after Nashville Campaign, 378; commends the author, 393
Thomas, Gen. Lorenzo, 80, 364–366
Thor, Grant the hammer of, 143
Thucydides, 163
"Tools to him who can use them," 51
Totten, Gen., 364
Trains of Army of the Potomac, 74; at Rappahannock Station, 74; at Brentsville, 79; at Savage Station, 265; Seven Days' Battle, 266
Trent affair, 210
Trenton, N. J., Lincoln there, 9, 19; McClellan there, 35, 44, 64, 195, 222, 245, 318, 319, 327
Trevillian, 126
Truax, Maj. W. S., 197
Tunstall's Station, 267
Twelfth Corps, 59
Twentieth Corps, 59
Twenty-third Corps, 85, 92, 187
Twiggs, Gen., 174, 175

## U

"Uncle Abe," 218, 220, 234, 271
Union, Lincoln's prayers did not harm it, 17; enlistments in Civil War, 165; losses in Civil War, 165, 385
Union men in Confederate prisons, 269
Union speech at Alexandria, 203
"Union's voyage o'er," 169
U. S. accounts, 280, 284
United States Ford, 151
Uprising of the North, 10
Utah, 182
Ute Indians, 119, 121, 122

## V

V——, Lieut., 64, 66
Valhalla of history, 156
Valley Forge, Falmouth worse than, 45, 291
Venable, Lieut. Col. C. S., 385
Vera Cruz, 175
Vicksburg, Mr. Lincoln prays for victory there, 12, 14, 16, 17, 135; Grant there, 139; it was Grant's plan, 139; Confederates surrender there, 140, 142; in general, 154, 163, 179, 180, 181, 305, 308, 353, 358
Virginia, 21, 59, 70, 80, 152, 307
Virginia Central Railroad, 126
Virginia roads, 50; Secessionist, 251, 252, 254; slave holder, 253, 254
Visit to Lookout Mountain, 331; to Mammoth Cave, 328
"Volunteers," 177
Von Moltke, 155, 157

# Index

## W

Wagon trains Army of the Potomac, 57, 74, 79, 265, 266
Wainwright, Capt., 200
Wallace, Gen. Lew, on McClellan, 368
War, Crimean, 164; Civil, 165; Franco-German, 164; Mexican, 164; Revolutionary, 165; with Spain, 165; cost of, 387, 391; records, 4; ravages of, 255; horrors of, 48, 161, 168, 259
War Department, Sherman at, 138; Grant at, 138
"War is hell," 167
Warren, Gen. G. K., at Gettysburg, 68; at Headquarters Army of Potomac, 73; at Bristoe, 76
Warren County, N. J., 308, 324
Warrenton, 43, 44, 54, 74, 77, 78, 292, 309
Warrenton Junction, 77, 78, 269, 272, 309
Washington's Birthday in army, 297
Washington, George, 10, 16, 18, 80, 120, 158, 193; his house at Mt. Vernon, 201, 291
Washington, D. C., Lincoln's inauguration there, 9, 10; in general, 11-13, 19, 21, 22, 24, 25, 31, 43, 44, 54, 59, 63, 65, 70, 71, 78, 127-130, 144, 176, 186, 188, 189, 191, 195, 196, 203, 204, 209, 215, 224, 230, 234, 236, 257, 272-274, 276, 278, 287, 292, 294, 297, 300, 307, 309, 337, 350, 352, 353, 364, 365, 368
Waterloo, 68
Webb, Major, 257
Webster, Daniel, 23
Webster, Gen. J. D., 104
Wedding in Seventh N. J., 297
Welles, Hon. G. J., 5
Wellington, 120, 136
Western cousin, 222
Western Territories, 19
West Point, 36, 52, 67, 80, 174, 189
West Point, Va., 187, 248
West Virginia, 24; Lee's campaign there, 150
What an army is, 165

Wheeler, Gen. J., 114; his raid, Marietta to Nashville, 114, 117, 133
"White Diamond" Division, 57
White House, 10, 22, 23, 59
White House, Va., 126, 150, 191, 260, 264
White Oak Swamp, 29, 264, 265
Wigfall, of Texas, 18; his speech in U. S. Senate, 20; reply of Andrew Johnson, 20
Wilderness Campaign, 70, 125, 127, 143; Lee in, 152, 153; Grant in, 152, 153
Wilkes, Lieut. Aaron, 245
William of Orange, 18
Williamsburg, 26, 27, 38; Hooker's Division at, 53; our losses there, 62; battle of, 244-248; losses at, 249; McClellan's injustice, 249, 252, 277
Williams, Gen. Seth, 66, 73
Williamsport, Lee and Meade at, 69, 72, 307
Wilson, Gen. J. H., at Nashville, 91, 94, 99, 346
Wilson's Cavalry, 85
Wilson, S. K., 19
Winchester, 128, 290, 363, 364
Winter in camp, 293, 297, 299, 340
Winter in Washington, 317
Wolf Run Shoals, 45
Wolseley, Gen. Lord, 149
Woman in the war, 190; Soldier's Children's Homes, 190
Wood, Gen. T. J., at Nashville, 87, 92-95
Wounds in War, 165
Wright, Gen., at Cedar Creek, 129
Wyoming, 182

## Y

York River, 238
Yorktown, 25; siege of, 26, 243, 259; return to, from Harrison's Landing, 31, 38; in general, 238, 239, 249, 252, 268, 271, 272, 300
Young, Major H. E., 386
Y. M. C. A., 357
"Young Napoleon" McClellanites, 24, 25, 35

www.ingramcontent.com/pod-product-compliance
Lightning Source LLC
Chambersburg PA
CBHW051727300426
44115CB00007B/502